Chicano School Failure
and Success

The Stanford Series on Education and Public Policy

General Editor: Professor Henry M. Levin, School of Education, Stanford University

The purpose of this series is to address major issues of educational policy as they affect and are affected by political, social and economic issues. It focuses on both the consequences of education for economic, political and social outcomes as well as the influences of the economics, political and social climate on education. It is particularly concerned with addressing major educational issues and challenges within this framework, and a special effort is made to evaluate the various educational alternatives on the policy agenda or to develop new ones that might address the educational challenges before us. All of the volumes are to be based upon original research and/or competent syntheses of the available research on a topic.

Chicano School Failure
and Success:
Research and Policy Agendas
for the 1990s

Edited by

Richard R. Valencia

 The Falmer Press

(A member of the Taylor & Francis Group)
London • New York • Philadelphia

UK   The Falmer Press, 4 John St, London WC1N 2ET
USA   The Falmer Press, Taylor & Francis Inc.,

© 1991 R.R. Valencia

First published 1991

Library of Congress Cataloguing-in-Publication Data
Chicano school failure and success: research and policy agendas for
   the 1990s / edited by Richard R. Valencia.
      p.   cm.
   Papers of a conference held at Stanford University, May 12, 1989.
   Includes bibliographical references and index.
   ISBN 1-85000-862-0: — ISBN 1-85000-863-9 (pbk.):
   1. Mexican American students.   I. Valencia, Richard R.
   LC2683.C47   1991
   373.1'2913089'68—dc20   90-46288
                                                CIP

British Library Cataloguing in Publication Data
Chicano school failure and success : research and policy agendas for
   the 1990s.
   1.   United States. Chicanos. Education
   I.   Valencia, Richard R.
   371.976872073

   ISBN 1-85000-862-0
        1-85000-863-9 pbk

Cover design by Caroline Archer
Set in 9.5/11 pt Bembo
by Graphicraft Typesetters Ltd, Hong Kong

Printed in Great Britain by Burgess Science Press, Basingstoke on paper which has a specified pH value on final paper manufacture of not less than 7.5 and is therefore 'acid free'.

Contents

v

Contents

Tables and Figures

Tables

Figures

Acknowledgments

Although the conceptual framework for this book was in my mind for some time, the actual solidification of the volume grew out of a conference, 'Chicano School Failure and Success: Research and Policy Agendas for the 1990s'. The conference was held on May 12, 1989 at Stanford University under my leadership while I was serving as a Visiting Professor in the School of Education as well in the Chicano Fellows Program/Undergraduate Studies on Mexican Society in the United States.

The Stanford University conference provided the basis for my colleagues and me to come together as an intellectual body to present our ideas in the form of delivered papers to an audience of scholars, school teachers, administrators, policy makers, community people, and graduate students. Eight of the eleven chapters in this book are based on papers that were presented at the 1989 conference.

This book would not have been possible without the support and contributions of many people. I am deeply indebted to the conference co-sponsors — the Stanford Center for Chicano Research (SCCR) and the Stanford University School of Education (SUSE). Special appreciation is extended to Armando Valdez (Associate Director) and Renato Rosaldo (Director) of the SCCR, who were very generous in their institutional support. As well, I thank Marshall Smith, Dean of the SUSE, who provided substantial financial support. Appreciation is also extended to the Board of Studies in Education at the University of California at Santa Cruz for its financial contribution. A special thanks goes to Hank Levin (General Editor of the Stanford Series on Education and Public Policy) who gave me editorial encouragement during the long process of publishing this volume.

To my colleagues who wrote the chapters for this volume — *muchísimas gracias*. Thanks also go to Angelina Brown at the University of Texas, Austin, for her excellent typing of my chapter drafts. Finally, sincere appreciation goes to my wonderful wife, Marta, who gave me moral and intellectual support during the long process of making this book a reality.

Richard R. Valencia
June, 1990

Preface

As we enter the 1990s, nationally the Chicano people number nearly 13 million people — approximately 63 per cent of the total Latino population of 20.1 million.[1] Notwithstanding a great deal of within-group variability, the large and rapidly growing Chicano population carries the dubious distinction of being the most undereducated of our nation's numerically large ethnic minority populations. There are indicators that such schooling problems and conditions are worsening.

This book is intended to examine — from various perspectives — the school failure and success of Chicano students. The deep roots and broad branches of Chicano school failure indicate that these poor schooling conditions and outcomes are profoundly influenced by institutional forces and structures that promote and maintain inequality. Of course, there is the alternative type of perspective that Chicanos are the makers of their own educational problems. According to this 'person-centered' explanation, the intellectual and motivational deficits of Chicano students are believed to be rooted in their inadequate familial socialization. It is unfortunate that the 'deficit' model — a theory rooted in racism, pseudoscience, and ignorance — held such high currency for so many decades. To some extent the dominance of deficit thinking in educational thought and practice has persisted for so long because, as Neisser (1986) notes, there has been '... an apparent lack of plausible alternatives' (p. ix).

In recent years, however, there have been gusts of air blowing fresh, invigorating scholarship into the study of the schooling problems of Chicano and other racial/ethnic minority students (e.g., Neisser, 1986; Trueba 1987, 1989). Although these new airways are far from being jet streams, movement can certainly be felt. The present volume joins these currents in an attempt to push along further a better understanding of what constitutes, maintains, and helps shape school failure among Chicano students. In addition, the various contributors of this book provide in varying degrees their own visions of research and policy needs that may help to realize Chicano school success.

By its very nature, school failure among Chicano students is a complex and multidimensional construct. Thus, to understand the factors and processes of such low academic achievement (and, as well, achievement enhancement) it is necessary to study the problems, research recommendations, and policy/reform implications through various windows and perspectives. As seen in the present volume, the contributors' research specializations range widely — cultural anthropology, bilingual education, educational history, special education, developmental psychology, educational testing, educational anthropology, and the political economy of education. Given the broad nature of the schooling problems experienced by Chicano students, it is necessary to throw out a wide scholarly net to capture the complexities of the issues and the resultant research and policy implications. I believe that in the future, understanding the plight and improvement of schooling for Chicanos will benefit greatly from having such interdisciplinary teams.

Richard R. Valencia

Note

1 The term 'Chicano' refers to Mexican-origin students born either in the United States or Mexico. 'Latino' refers to 'Hispanic'. See Valencia (chapter 1, this volume) for further demographic information on the numerical breakdown of the Latino population.

References

NEISSER, U. (Ed.) (1986) *The School Achievement of Minority Children: New Perspectives*, Hillsdale, NJ, Erlbaum.
TRUEBA, H.T. (Ed.) (1987) *Success or Failure: Learning and the Language Minority Student*, Cambridge, MA, Newbury House.
TRUEBA, H.T. (1989) *Raising Silent Voices: Educating the Linguistic Minorities for the 21st Century*, New York, Harper and Row.

This book is dedicated to the
memory of my mother, Veronica,
who taught me how to read and helped
put me on the path to knowledge.

— Richard R. Valencia

Part I
Current Realities of the Chicano Schooling Experience

Part I consists of three chapters and describes a number of major issues and harmful conditions that Chicano students, as a whole, routinely experience in the process of schooling. In chapter 1, 'The Plight of Chicano Students: An Overview of Schooling Conditions and Outcomes', Richard Valencia lays the foundation for a number of issues that follow. Discussion begins by the author providing a working definition of 'Chicano school failure'. The core of the chapter is an overview of eleven different schooling conditions and outcomes that describe the educational experience of many Chicano students. The chapter closes by discussing the changing demography of our nation's dramatic racial/ethnic shifts and transformations, how Chicanos fit into these current and future changes, and why the time for informed action and reform should be *now*.

Rubén Donato, Martha Menchaca, and Richard Valencia wrote chapter 2, 'Segregation, Desegregation and Integration of Chicano Students: Problems and Prospects'. In their coverage, the authors explore the linkages between segregation and Chicano school failure from both historical and current frames of reference. The ideolgical and structural bases of Chicano student segregation are examined in some detail. In addition, Donato *et al.* describe contemporary forms of resegregation, particularly language segregation. The authors also discuss a number of reform ideas that could potentially lead to integration. Chapter 3, written by Russel Rumberger, presents a comprehensive treatment of 'Chicano Dropouts: A Review of Research and Policy Issues'. Rumberger approaches the problem of Chicano dropouts by examining four facets: extent of the problem and incidence figures, correlates of dropping out, individual and social consequences, and some solutions to the Chicano dropout problem.

Chapter 1

The Plight of Chicano Students: An Overview of Schooling Conditions and Outcomes

Richard R. Valencia

There is a crisis in many of our nation's schools in which racial/ethnic minority students attend. We are not speaking of the charges of increasing mediocrity of schooling quality as described by a rash of 'excellence' reports in the 1980s (e.g., National Commission on Excellence in Education, 1983). Rather we are alluding to a considerably more grave problem — the massive school problems experienced by a large proportion of minority students enrolled in public kindergarten through twelfth grade (K-12) schools. With respect to Chicano students — the target group of this book — they are prime examples of pupils affected by the pernicious ideologies, institutional mechanisms, and outcomes of educational inequality.[1]

In this introductory chapter, three aspects of the Chicano schooling experience will be addressed. First, there will be an attempt to unpack the notion of 'Chicano school failure'. Second, I will provide a descriptive level of Chicano schooling problems by presenting an overview of numerous conditions and outcomes. Third, I will focus on the 'changing demography'; that is, I will describe the dramatic growth in the Chicano population and then discuss current and future implications of these demographic changes *vis-à-vis* the Chicano community and the schooling of its children.

Chicano School Failure

Although the notion of 'school failure' with respect to racial/ethnic minority students has been used and discussed by other scholars (e.g., Boykin, 1983; Erikson, 1987; Ginsburg, 1986), the term itself is in need of further theoretical development and refinement. Its heuristic value and potential in theory generation about the many schooling problems experienced by Chicano students appear to be vast. How might one conceptualize school failure, a construct, among Chicano students?[2] I offer this broad, working definition: school failure among Chicano students refers to their *persistently, pervasively, and disproportionately, low academic achievement.* Next, we turn to a brief discussion of each of the italicized terms.

Persistence

School failure among Chicanos is not a new situation. On the contrary, it is an old and stubborn condition. It refuses to relent. It continues even in the face of opposition. Imagine having a toothache that never goes away, and you can get a sense of the persistent nature of the poor academic performance of a substantial portion of the Chicano student population. In short, Chicano school failure is deeply rooted in history. When Chicanos did eventually gain wider access to public schooling at the turn of the twentieth century (Cameron, 1976), major schooling problems existed since the earliest period and such patterns continued unabated (Carter and Segura, 1979; Sanchez, 1966). For example, Drake (1927) compared the relative academic performance of Mexican (i.e., 'Chicano') and White seventh and eighth graders in Tucson, Arizona. Based on group-administered achievement tests, Chicano students performed considerably lower than their White peers. Reynolds (1933), in a comprehensive report more than fifty years ago (*The Education of Spanish-Speaking Children in Five Southwestern States*), quoted an Arizona study as follows: 'In general, the type of Mexican child taken into the Arizona school tends to be backward in rate of mental development, lags a year or two behind other pupils, shows a heavy failure percentage, and an early elimination from school' (p. 38). An example of such school failure was the finding that for every '... 100 Mexican children in grade 1 there are 7 in grade 8, while for 100 non-Mexican children in grade 1 there are 52 in grade 8' (p. 39). Another example of the persistent nature of Chicano school failure comes from Chapa's (1988) analysis of census data. In 1940, Chicanos in California (ages 25–64) completed an average of 7.5 years of schooling while Whites finished an average of 10.5 years — a gap of 3 years. Nearly forty years later (1979), the mean for Chicanos was 11.0 years and 13.4 for Whites — a gap of 2.4 years.

Pervasiveness

Chicano school failure is not confined to one single location. Wherever Chicano communities exist, school failure appears to be widespread among Chicano student enrollments. There are at least two evidential ways of looking at the pervasive character of this low academic achievement. First, one can analyze it from a geographical vantage point. Whether one views the academic performance data described in national (e.g., Coleman *et al.*, 1966), regional (e.g., US Commission on Civil Rights, 1972a), state (e.g., Brown and Haycock, 1985), or numerous local reports, the results are alarmingly consistent: Chicano students, on the whole, tend to exhibit low academic achievement. Second, one can study such data using a cross-sectional approach (i.e., comparing various grade levels at one point in time; for example, see Brown and Haycock, 1985). Again, Chicano academic performance — on the average — is characterized by poor achievement. In sum, the pandemic branches of Chicano school failure are clearly tied to their persistent roots.

Disproportionality

The modifying term, 'disproportionately', is an important qualifier in that Chicano school failure, which contains its explicit meaning of low achievement, also has a second denotation — comparative performance. In the context of examining the school achievement of Chicano students, their academic performance is compared to White students. Here, the common procedure is to use the aggregated performance (e.g., reading achievement as measured on a standardized test) of White grade-level peers as a referent and then to compare the aggregated performance of Chicano students to this standard. When this is done, the common result is one of *asymmetry*. That is, when the Chicano distribution of achievement test scores, represented as interval data, is juxtaposed to the curve of the White grouped scores, the Chicano distribution is typically skewed positively. Simply put, there is a disproportionately greater percentage of Chicano students — compared to their White peers — reading below the middle of the distribution. Conversely, compared to White students, there is a disproportionately lower percentage of Chicano students reading above the middle of the distribution.

In addition to examining the notion of disproportionality of achievement scores from a perspective of asymmetry, one can also look at *disparity*. For example, when a comparison is made between the percentage of Chicano secondary school dropouts to White dropouts (i.e., represented as dichotomous data — dropout/non-dropout), the common pattern shows disparity, where the Chicano rate of dropouts in secondary schools is higher than one would predict when compared to the percentage of Chicano students in the general secondary school population.

Before we leave the term, disproportionality, a caveat is in order. Although the difference between Chicano and White students in academic achievement is large, there is indeed variability in Chicano academic development and performance (see Laosa and Henderson, this volume, for a discussion of some predictors that help to explain such variability). Some Chicano students do read at or above grade level. Many Chicano students graduate from high school. In short, there are noticeable within-group differences, and thus the issue of disproportionality is not confined only to between-group (i.e., White/Chicano) differences. It is important to underscore, however, that given the current schooling outcomes experienced by Chicano students as measured by most achievement indicators — and despite the fact that some of these students will not have academic problems — the available evidence indicates that the low academic achievement is the norm for a substantial portion of the Chicano student population in the nation's public elementary and secondary schools.

Low Academic Achievement

Here, there is a need to provide a justification for the usage of 'low academic achievement'. First, we need to examine the term 'achievement'. Achievement (academic) is a concept, an '... abstraction formed from the observation of certain behavior of children ... associated with the "learning" of school tasks — reading words, doing arithmetic problems ... and so on' (Kerlinger, 1986,

p. 27). According to major reports and studies (e.g., California Superintendents' Council on Hispanic Affairs, 1985; US Commission on Civil Rights, 1972a), two of the most significant academic achievement indicators, particularly in the schooling of Chicano students, are (a) test performance in the content areas (especially reading) and (b) secondary school holding power (i.e., the '... school systems' effectiveness in its ability to hold its students until they have completed the full course of study', US Commission on Civil Rights, 1972a, p. 8).[3]

I have deliberately chosen the term 'low academic achievement' rather than the often used notion of 'underachievement'.[4] It is tempting to want to use the construct of underachievement as it connotes that the typical group performance of low test scores and high dropout rates are not truly reflective of what Chicano students are capable of achieving. Although there is likely a great deal of credence to the belief that, by and far, the depressed academic achievement of Chicanos does not mirror their potential, to try to interpret this discrepancy as 'under-achievement' presents several conceptual problems.

First, the converse notion of underachievement (that is, 'overachievement') appears to be '... a logical impossibility' (Anastasi, 1984, p. 131) because the term implies that a person is performing above his/her capacity. Second, the terms underachievement/overachievement are meaningless if not looked at from a measurement perspective. As a number of scholars have noted, the two terms tell us little more than the widely acknowledged fact that intelligence and achievement tests are far from being perfectly correlated (cf. Anastasi, 1984; Jensen, 1980). Third, the concept of underachievement is typically used in describing the special education category of learning disabilities (that is, a commonly accepted characteristic of learning disabilities is a marked discrepancy between measured intelligence and school achievement). The discrepancy index as such is particularly troubling in trying to describe the test behavior of normal Chicanos (i.e., non-special education students) in that it is fairly common for them to perform well within the normal range on intelligence tests but perform below the norm on achievement tests (see Valencia and Rankin, 1988). Given all the confusion and issues associated with the term underachievement, I have selected the term 'low academic achievement' — a more meaningful construct — for inclusion in my definition of Chicano school failure.[5] Now that we have dissected the notion of school failure and provided some semblance of its configuration, we move next to a description of conditions and outcomes that characterize current schooling of Chicanos.

Schooling Conditions and Outcomes: An Overview

Based on my knowledge of the Chicano schooling experience, there are at least eleven schooling generalizations that characterize conditions and outcomes for a sizable proportion of the Chicano public school population. The reader should keep in mind that the following descriptive overview contains broad-based general statements. That is, they are meant to capture what appears to be the norm for a good number of Chicano students, not every Chicano student.

Segregation

Chicano students are typically isolated from their White peers — and of course, vice-versa (White students have little contact with their Chicano peers). There is, however, an interesting new development to this condition of racial/ethnic isolation. As Menchaca and Valencia (1990) note, 'The segregation of school-age Latinos, of which two-thirds are Chicano, has increased to such an extent that they now have the dubious distinction of being the most highly segregated group of America's children' (p. 222; also see Orum, 1986). In 1968, 23 per cent of Latinos attended 90 to 100 per cent minority schools. By 1984, nearly 1 in 3 (31 per cent) of Latinos attended such ethnically segregated schools (Orfield, 1988). In short, the segregation of Chicano students has increased over the last twenty years. Given the sharp increase in the Chicano school-age population, Chicano/Mexicano migration and settlement patterns, the foot dragging of desegregation efforts, and other factors, it is very likely that the segregation of Chicano students will intensify in the years ahead.

The connection between school segregation and academic achievement of Chicano students has been widely documented (e.g., Espinosa and Ochoa, 1986; Haro, 1977; Orfield, 1988; Valencia, 1984). As the Chicano enrollment increases, achievement (as measured by standardized tests) decreases. These observed negative correlations are pervasive and strong in magnitude. For example, Valencia (1984) found a near perfect negative correlation between Chicano (and Black) school percentage and mean achievement scores in an analysis of eleven high schools in the Phoenix, Arizona Union School District. As the minority percentage of the high schools increased, test scores systematically decreased. Espinosa and Ochoa (1986) found a strong negative correlation between California Assessment Program test scores and Latino school concentration for a state-wide sample of third-graders.

It is clear that segregation has and continues to be a major institutional process in denying equal educational opportunities for Chicano students and thus has helped shape their school failure. Although one cannot imply causality from correlational data, it is safe to assume that segregation is implicated in creating barriers for Chicano students. Or as Orfield (1988) notes, such '... data does not, of course, show that the segregation causes the inequality, but it does show that Hispanic students tend to be concentrated in schools where the tone and the level of instruction are set by large proportions of poorly prepared students' (p. 29).

In recent publications, the unfolding of the history of the Chicano schooling experience has had school segregation as a prominent focus of attention (Alvarez, 1988; Gonzalez, 1985; Menchaca and Valencia, 1990; San Miguel, 1986, 1987). A major conclusion drawn by these scholars is that the segregation of Chicano students has operated throughout history as a key administrative practice leading to harmful schooling consequences (also see, Donato, Menchaca and Valencia, this volume). For example, Menchaca and Valencia (1990) discuss the issue in this manner:

> ... although contemporary school segregation of Chicano students is complexly related to social, economic, and population demographic factors over time, one should not ignore the historical blueprint of forced

segregative practices of the early 1900s. Although the knot between past and present school segregation cannot be snugly tied, there is ample evidence from California case studies that the segregative policies of the early 1900s have had long-term effects. Despite the variability among the communities of California, segregation of Chicano students today can generally be said to have been strongly influenced by Anglo-Saxon ideologies of the past. To the present day, the schools in the Chicano barrios continue to experience the deleterious impact of the 'separate but equal' policies passed by previous generations. (p. 243)

Language/Cultural Exclusion

The fact that Chicano students' language and culture are excluded from the school curriculum — which by the way is a longstanding historical practice — was brought to national limelight in the early 1970s by a report in the *Mexican American Education Study* (US Commission on Civil Rights, 1972b). It was reported that less than 7 per cent of the schools in the Southwestern US offered bilingual education. Furthermore, only 4 per cent and 7 per cent of the elementary and secondary schools, respectively, in the Southwest offered Chicano history.

Periodic reports since then have confirmed the existence of language and cultural exclusion. For example, Olsen (1988) reported there are over 600,000 limited-English proficient (LEP) students in California (about three-fourths of these are Latinos). Due in large part to the serious shortage of bilingual teachers (see Valencia and Aburto, this volume), less than 25 per cent of these LEP students are being served in bilingual classes staffed by qualified bilingual teachers. The other 75 per cent of LEP students are provided little, if any, instruction in their first language. Given the schooling benefits of having bilingual education for Chicano students (see Garcia, chapter 4, and Merino, chapter 5, this volume) as well as multicultural education (e.g., see Gonzalez, 1974), the inclusion of language/cultural components in instruction can certainly help turn the tide against school failure.

Two likely contributing factors that have helped shape the language/cultural exclusion issue are the limited multicultural education training and the apparent disinterest in such training during the preservice development of prospective teachers. With respect to the limited training concern, there is some evidence that teachers are inadequately prepared to teach multicultural education. A case in point is Olsen's (1988) finding that only 5 per cent of future teachers in California take any course in multicultural education. Regarding the issue of disinterest, Mahan and Boyle (1981) surveyed student teaching directors in twenty-five states. The authors reported that two-thirds of the respondents believed 60 to 100 per cent of students in teacher education training programs had no desire for preparatory experiences in multicultural education.

Academic Achievement

As we have previously discussed in our conceptualization of Chicano school failure, Chicano students — compared to White students — achieve at considerably lower levels on various group-based and individually administered standardized achievement tests (e.g., see Valencia and Rankin, 1988; see Valencia and Aburto, this volume, for a discussion of Chicano students' considerably poorer performance on minimum competency and school-based competency tests). The disproportionately lower performance of Chicanos on achievement tests is one of the most persistent and pervasive findings seen in the Chicano schooling literature. Clearly, the improvement of achievement test scores of Chicanos should be an educational priority during the 1990s. We should be very cautious, however, that the means to achieve such ends do not penalize Chicano students (see Valencia and Aburto, this volume) nor do they infringe on a Chicano's right to a democratic education (see Pearl, this volume).

On a related point there is evidence that test scores, in general, are increasing in the nation. We should be aware, though, of illusions that help to create a false sense of security for the Chicano community, as well as for policymakers (see Valencia and Aburto, Chapter 8 in this volume, note 22). As Gandara (1989) recently admonished:

> Nearly a quarter of America's children are on an educational path leading nowhere. While test scores appear to be on the rise all over the country, a closer look at the figures reveals that the least successful students are actually losing ground: The gap between their skills and performance and those of their peers is growing wider. These are the children of the poor, who coincidentally are also often ethnic minorities. (p. 38)

School Holding Power (Retention)

The fact that Chicano students, compared to their White peers, drop out of secondary school at considerably higher rates is one of the truly major tragedies of the Chicano schooling experience. Although it is difficult to obtain reliable data on dropout incidence data, there are estimates. Recent data indicate that about 1 in 2 Chicano students drop out of secondary schools (Rumberger, this volume).

The costs to the individual Chicano who leaves school before graduation go beyond the fact that there is now an abrupt severance to his/her intellectual growth. The stakes are very high for the Chicano dropout and for society. One researcher has estimated that in the Los Angeles Unified School District — a high density Chicano district — the loss in adjusted lifetime earnings for a male dropout is $187,000, in general; for a female dropout, the loss is about $122,000 (Catterall, 1985). Furthermore, in addition to the foregone income associated with dropping out, there are foregone tax receipts as well as the social costs to local governments of providing funding for welfare, health, and related services (Rumberger, this volume). In short, the dropout problem for Chicanos is extremely costly along 'quality of life' and social lines. Suffice it to say that there is widespread interest and activity in trying to cope with and solve the Chicano dropout problem (see Rumberger, this volume, for an overview of policies and programs).

On a final note about the dropout issue is the term itself. Orr (1987) comments in her book, *Keeping Students in School*:

> Although the implication of the term *dropout* is that the student has left school willfully and without good reason, there is overwhelming evidence that many so-called dropouts leave because of the treatment they receive at school or the failure of the school programs to meet their learning needs. In effect these students are forced out. (p. xii)

School Financing

Typically, the schools that Chicano students attend are underfinanced compared to the schools White students attend. For example, one study of the Los Angeles Unified School District demonstrated that large differences were evident in the amount of money spent in elementary schools along racial/ethnic lines. Fairchild (1984) found that as the percentage of Chicano and other Latino students increased among the various schools, per-pupil expenditures decreased. In contrast, as the proportion of White students increased, school financing increased.

It has been known for sometime that some states in the Southwest spend significantly less to educate Chicano students than their White counterparts. A case in point is Texas, the state with the second largest enrollment of Chicano students. The US Commission on Civil Rights (1972c) *Mexican American Education Study, Report Number 4 (Mexican American Education in Texas: A Function of Wealth)* linked financial inequities with schooling inequities in this manner:

> The Texas school finance system results in discrimination against Mexican American school children. Predominantly Mexican American districts are less wealthy in terms of property values than Anglo districts and the average income of Chicanos is below that of Anglos. These circumstances existing, the State of Texas has devised an educational finance system by which the amount spent on the schooling of students is a function of district and personal wealth. The end result is that the poor and those receiving inferior education continue to receive inferior education. (p. 28)

Shortly prior to the publication of the US Commission on Civil Rights (1972c) report on financial inequities in Texas, Demetrio Rodriguez and six other parents of the San Antonio Independent School District sued the district in 1968 charging that the Texas school finance system violated the US Constitution (*Rodriguez v. San Antonio Independent School District*, 1971). In one of the most critical legal cases in the history of Texas, and after twenty-one years of struggle, the Texas Supreme Court in a 9–0 decision declared on October 2, 1989 the state's public school system of financing to be unconstitutional (Graves, 1989a). The Court mandated state legislators to prepare a new, comprehensive funding plan by May 1990. As we enter the 1990s, the nation's eyes will be on Texas, closely observing its attempts to equalize the large funding discrepancies among the state's many districts and its efforts to bring an end to a pattern of education in Texas — one kind for the poor, one kind for the rich.[6]

Teacher-Student Interactions

There is longstanding evidence that Chicano students, as a whole, tend to be treated less favorably than White students by teachers. For example, Parsons (1965) found a great deal of racial/ethnic cleavage in a small farming community in California. Regarding schooling, Parsons observed that social relationships and interactions between students and students and teachers and students mirrored the larger social structure of the community — one of White dominance. Teachers routinely demonstrated preference for Whites over Chicanos by selecting the former students for leadership roles. Chicanos were also negatively stereotyped by teachers (e.g., perceived to be lazy, not bright).

In the most comprehensive study to date of teacher-student interactions involving Chicano students, the US Commission on Civil Rights (1973) *Mexican American Education Study, Report Number 5 (Teachers and Students: Differences in Teacher Interaction with Mexican American and Anglo Students)* found a great deal of differences in the quality and quantity of teacher-student interactions along lines of students' racial/ethnic background. Based on systematic observation and evaluation of behavior in over 400 classes in New Mexico, California, and Texas, the Commission staff found — among other results — that Chicano students, compared to Whites, received significantly less praise and encouragement from teachers. Furthermore, teachers were found to spend less time in asking questions of Chicanos, and they provided more noncriticizing talk to White pupils than to Chicanos. These and other findings of teacher-student disparities in interaction patterns led the US Civil Rights Commission to conclude:

> The basic finding of this report is that the schools of the Southwest are failing to involve Mexican American children as active participants in the classroom to the same extent as Anglo children.... The classroom is the setting in which a child's schooling takes place and the interaction between teacher and students is the heart of the educational process ... all elements of this interaction, taken together, create a climate of learning which directly affects educational opportunity. Consequently, the discovered disparities in teacher behavior toward Mexican Americans and Anglos are likely to hinder seriously the educational opportunities and achievement of Chicano pupils. These findings raise disturbing questions concerning the ability of our schools to meet the educational needs of all students adequately. (p. 43)

Although very little research of teacher-student interactions involving Chicano students has occurred since the time of the *Mexican American Education Study*, I believe it is safe to assume that some teachers in our nation's schools continue to respond more positively to White students than they do to Chicano students. As such, it is vital that our vision of schooling embraces philosophies and practices consonant with a democratic educational process in which useful knowledge, participation, rights, and equal encouragement are present (see Pearl, this volume).

Curriculum Differentiation

The sorting of students, based on perceived educability, into small groups or classes for instructional purposes has been an educational practice for many decades (Oakes, 1985). Chicano students are no exception to the practices of 'ability grouping' (elementary level) and 'tracking' (secondary level) (Oakes, 1985; US Commission on Civil Rights, 1974; Valencia and Aburto, this volume). Through such curriculum differentiation, Chicano students — compared to their White peers — are often exposed to greater amounts of 'low status knowledge' (e.g., non-challenging, rote-learning curriculum) and exposed to lesser amounts of 'high status knowledge' — that is, the knowledge that is deemed to be a prerequisite for college admissions (Oakes).

For Chicano students, the link between not having the necessary high status knowledge and not matriculating to college is tight. Orum (1986), for example, has reported that 75 per cent of Chicano and other Latino high school seniors have not completed a college preparatory program. Given the negative implications of curriculum differentiation for a sizable percentage of Chicano students, it is not surprising that a number of school reform efforts *vis-à-vis* Chicano pupils involve, in part, providing greater access of high status knowledge for them (e.g., Haycock and Navarro, 1988).

College Enrollment

Chicano students, compared to their White peers, have: (a) lower rates of college eligibility, (b) lower rates of enrollment to college (e.g., in the California State University and University of California systems), and (c) higher rates of attrition once enrolled in college (e.g., Brown and Haycock, 1985; Orum, 1986).

Recent research has documented a rather unfortunate situation: not only is there a very low college attendance rate of Chicanos, but it is *declining*. (Here we are defining college attendance rate as the percentage of Chicano and other Latino high school graduates who go on to college.) The Chicano and other Latino college attendance rate hit a peak of 36 per cent in 1976, dropped sharply to 30 per cent in 1980, and plummeted even further to 26 per cent in 1985 (Mingle, 1987). In short, from 1976 to 1985, the Latino college attendance rate dramatically declined 28 per cent. Orum (1986) adds this observation about the higher education issue:

> The popular perception that Hispanic participation in institutions of higher education has greatly increased is a myth. Despite the appearance of increased access to higher education through affirmative action programs, proportionately fewer Hispanics attended college in 1980 than in 1975. While the number of Hispanic students attending college between 1975 and 1980 remained steady, these students as a percentage of Hispanic high school graduates dropped markedly. This fact, coupled with the

soaring high school dropout rates, sends a clear message of the critical and continuing Hispanic under-representation in postsecondary education. (p. 37)

In sum, the low and declining proportion of Chicanos entering college represents another crisis within the larger crisis of Chicano schooling problems. In that college is the point of entry for prospective professional careers and leadership roles, it is imperative that institutions of higher education open their doors widely, as well as implement proactive measures during the collegiate experience to ensure Chicano school success.

Stress

Although the conceptual status of stress is somewhat problematic because of vague definitions and obscure mediating constructs (Wills and Langer, 1980), it remains an important area of study. Regarding school stress and anxiety, the available literature has documented higher amounts among students of lower socioeconomic status and/or racial/ethnic minority backgrounds (e.g., Coney and West, 1979; Hawkes and Koff, 1970). With respect to Chicano students, there is some evidence that they experience considerably high and harmful amounts of stress at the elementary school level (Gerard and Miller, 1975; Phillips, 1978) and college level (Munoz, 1986).

In the area of race relations, one particular 'environmental stressor' that has become a scholarly concern is race prejudice of Whites towards racial/ethnic minorities in the school setting. Theoretically, such '. . . stress is likely to adversely affect [minority] students' daily academic performance by reducing their willingness to persist at academic tasks and interfering with the cognitive processes involved in learning' (Goughis, 1986, p. 147).

In that the linkages between race prejudice, resultant stress, and the generally poor academic performance of Chicano students have not been empirically demonstrated, one can only speculate at this time about the parts and the whole of this socio-psychological process. For example, perhaps teacher prejudice against Chicano students can be looked at as an environmental stressor. A case in point is the study by Olsen (1988) who noted that more than a third of her total sample of 11 to 18-year-old California immigrant students (a very sizable percentage of whom were Mexican-origin) reported racial incidents of what they perceived to be caused by teacher prejudice (e.g., derogatory or stereotypic comments voiced in front of the class; cultural clashes; being punished or embarrassed for using their native language). In any event, and despite the absence of empirical studies documenting the existence between adverse stress and poor achievement, it is still important to move ahead in designing psychologically healthy learning environments for Chicano students.

Special Education

The system of special education with respect to Chicano students continues to have problems, particularly dealing with questionable or inappropriate assessment tools and practices, overrepresentation and underrepresentation of Chicanos in certain placements, the poor delivery of intervention services, and so on. Given these issues, and accompanied with the substantial increase in the Chicano school population, it will be important as we enter the 1990s to reform the special education system. Rueda (this volume) offers a critique of the existing system and presents a reconceptualization of how special education can be improved to address the academic development of those Chicano students who perform markedly below the norms (also, see Valencia and Aburto, this volume, for an overview of the abuses of educational testing and a discussion of how testing might be improved to promote Chicano school success).

Chicano Teaching Force

Finally, there is the subject — or perhaps we should say the dwindling numbers — of Chicano teachers. Recent studies show that the percentage of Chicano public school (K-12) teachers is extremely low and steadily declining (Valencia and Aburto, in press, a; Valencia and Aburto, this volume).

A major obstacle to Chicano teacher production is their high failure rate on teacher competency tests. In terms of a Latino student/Latino teacher national disparity analysis, Chicano and other Latino teachers are underrepresented by a huge 75 per cent (Valencia and Aburto, in press, a). The growing shortage of Chicano public school teachers is a concern for all in that it works against the need to have a multicultural teaching force at a time when our school system is becoming more and more culturally diverse. Chicano teachers are needed to serve as role models for Chicano students, to deliver bilingual education, and to help promote racial/ethnic understanding and respect among all students. As Valencia and Aburto note (this volume), for our country to dive into the twenty-first century without Chicano and other minority teachers is unpardonable. As such, we need to get on with the business of identifying and implementing strategies that will increase the percentage of Chicano teachers (see Valencia and Aburto, in press, b).

In summary, the general profile I just painted of schooling conditions and outcomes faced by many Chicano students is quite disturbing. The prognosis for a healthier and more equitable schooling experience for Chicanos attending school in the 1990s and beyond is not promising — unless reform begins *now*. That is, the transformation of Chicano school failure to Chicano school success involves the issue of timeliness. Given the tremendous current and future growth patterns in the Chicano population, now is the time for informed action — lest the grave problems Chicano students currently face will increase as concomitantly does their population. We turn next to this aspect of the 'changing demography' and its schooling implications for Chicanos.

The Changing Demography

More than a decade ago, the dramatic growth of the Chicano population captured the interest of demographers, and soon after, the media. The 'rediscovering' of the Chicano people was exemplified by lengthy news stories on Chicanos published in several national magazines. The articles ranged, for example, from the general ('Chicanos on the Move', *Newsweek*, January, 1979; 'Mexican Americans: A People on the Move', *National Geographic*, June, 1980) to the specific ('A Year With the Gangs of East Los Angeles', *Ms.*, July, 1978). A controversial movie (*Boulevard Nights*) that glorified Chicano gangs was viewed by millions of moviegoers nationally in 1979. In 1981, *Zoot Suit* — a powerful movie about oppression against Chicanos in the early 1940s — was released. In short, new attention was directed to the Chicano people. Some people predicted that the 80s would be the 'decade of the Hispanic'.

The 1980s: Rise of the Latino Population

In 1980, the national Latino population was 14.5 million and accounted for 6.4 per cent of the total US population of 228 million people (Miranda and Quiroz, 1989; Swibold, 1989).[7] During the 1980s Latinos increased nationally by 5.6 million, and by decade's end they numbered 20.1 million people — the highest estimate ever. From 1980 to late 1989, the total US population increased about 8.7 per cent (from 228 to 248 million). In contrast, the Latino population increased a huge 38.6 per cent (14.5 to 20.1 million) — growing during the 1980s at a rate *over four times faster* than the rest of the US population.

With respect to where Latinos are located in the US, California, Texas, New York, and Florida (in descending order), continue to account for almost 75 per cent of the total Latino population in late 1989 (Swibold, 1989). California is home to 34 per cent of all Latinos (6.8 million, mostly Mexican origin). Texas is number two with 21 per cent of the total Latino population (4.3 million, mostly Mexican origin). New York follows with 2 million Latinos (10 per cent of total, mostly Puerto Rican), and Florida contains 1.6 million (8 per cent, mostly Cuban). About 1.7 million Latinos (8 per cent of total, mostly Mexican origin) live in Arizona, Colorado, and New Mexico. New Jersey is the home to 640,000 Latino residents (3 per cent, mostly Puerto Rican), and finally, the remaining states contain 14 per cent of the total Latino population.

By all indications, the Chicano and other Latino population segments will continue to soar in size in the 1990s and well into the next century. For example, let us take the case of growth patterns in Los Angeles, California and Houston, Texas — the two cities with the largest Chicano populations (Staff, 1989).[8] In Los Angeles, the Chicano and other Latino population was 816,000 people (27.5 per cent of the total 2.97 million) in 1980. By the year 2000, Chicano and other Latinos will constitute 38.2 per cent of the total Los Angeles population (1.21 million of 3.16 million people). A similar pattern will be seen in Houston. In 1980, this city was the home for 281,000 Chicanos (and a very small percentage of other Latinos), comprising 17.6 per cent of the total population of 1.6 million. It is projected that by the year 2000, Chicanos (520,000) will account for 23.3 per cent of the total population of Houston (2.24 million).

Some population demographers have looked far into the future (US Bureau of the Census, 1986). In about seventy years from now, racial/ethnic shifts will occur nationally that will become highly significant markers in the history of the United States. In the year 2060, it is projected that the Latino population will number 54.2 million people and will surpass the Black population (projected to

Table 1.1: *Projections of California's school-age population by racial/ethnic background*

Year	White (%)	Latino (%)	Black (%)	Asian (%)	Other (%)
			Race/Ethnicity		
1971	71	16	9	4	na
1986	52	29	10	7	2
2000	45	35	8	11	2
2030	33	44	6	16	1

Source: Adapted from Population Reference Bureau (1985; years 1986, 2000, 2030) and
        Watson (1988; year 1971).
Note: na: not available.

be 53.7 million) to become the nation's largest racial/ethnic minority group. The Latino population in 2060 will account for 17.5 per cent of the total population of 309.7 million. (Currently, Latinos account for about 8.1 per cent of the total US population.)

   In sum, the demographic predictions of the late 1970s laid the foundation for what is occurring now and will continue well into the future. That is, the terms 'minority' and 'majority' are undergoing radical transformations with respect to numerical and social significance.

The Chicano/Latino School-Age Population: A Look to the Future

The unprecedented growth rate of the Chicano and other Latino school-age segments is a clear reflection of the rise in the general Chicano/Latino population. Here, we will discuss California as a case in point and then describe some patterns in the national scene. Demographers predicted in 1978 that by 1990 the combined racial/ethnic minority K-12 population in California (i.e., Chicano and other Latino, Black, American Indian, Native Alaskan, Asian, and Philipino) will be the new 'majority' and White students will be the new 'minority' (Foote, Espinosa, and Garcia, 1978) Well, that projection was slightly in error — the racial/ethnic shift occurred two years earlier than predicted. The combination of declining White birthrates, booming school enrollments of minority students, and unprecedented immigration from Latin America and Asia brought the racial/ethnic transition sooner than forecast (Watson, 1988).

   In short, the school enrollment shifts in the numerical status of 'majority' and 'minority' groups are no longer mere future projections. They are a current reality and will become more pronounced as racial/ethnic minority populations — particularly Latinos and Asians — continue to increase in large numbers. On the other hand, as the years go by, Whites will gradually comprise proportionately less and less of the school-age population. To illustrate this, we continue our discussion with the racial/ethnic shifts in California, as an example. The following points (numbers 1, 3, and 4) can be gleaned from Table 1.1.

   1 Approximately twenty years ago, 7 in every 10 California K-12 students were White, and about 3 in 10 were racial/ethnic minority background (Watson, 1988).

Table 1.2: National public school enrollment changes by race/ethnicity, autumn 1968–autumn 1986

| Year | Race/Ethnicity | | | | | |
| | White | | Latino | | Black | |
	% of total	millions of total	% of total	millions of total	% of total	millions of total
1968	80.0	34.70	4.6	2.00	14.5	6.28
1986	70.4	28.96	9.9	4.06	16.1	6.62
Change	−9.6	−5.74	+5.3	+2.06	+1.6	+0.34

Source: Adapted from Orfield (1988).

2 At the start of the 1988–89 school year, White students dipped under 50 per cent of the total K-12 public school enrollment — the first time since the beginning of public education in California about 140 years ago. The most obvious implication to be made from this significant transformation is that at the present time no single racial/ethnic group constitutes a numerically majority population (Watson).

3 In about forty years from now — in the year 2030 — we will likely see in California's public elementary and secondary schools a virtual reversal of what the school-age population resembled in 1971. That is, White students will comprise 1 in 3 students, and combined students of racial/ethnic 'minority' background will account for nearly 7 in 10 students (Population Reference Bureau, 1985).

4 In 2030, Chicano and other Latino students in the public schools of California will form the *single largest* group, comprising about 44 per cent of the total K-12 enrollment (Population Reference Bureau).

The tremendous school-age racial/ethnic shifts we presently are experiencing, and will continue to experience in California, are similar to changes occurring nationally. Orfield (1988), in a report titled 'The Growth and Concentration of Hispanic Enrollment and the Future of American Education', has underscored the enormous growth in the proportion of Chicano and other Latino public school students in the United States (as well as a decline in the percentage of White students).

As Table 1.2 shows, in 1968–69, the Latino public school enrollment accounted for 4.6 per cent (2.0 million) of the national total. By the 1986–87 school year, Latinos made up 9.9 per cent (4.1 million) of the total — that is, the Latino share of the total public school enrollment doubled in less than two decades. White students during this same period decreased 5.7 million, and the Black enrollment rose a modest .3 million students. Orfield (1988) translates these changes as such:

Eighteen years [1968–69] ago there were more than three times as many Blacks as Hispanics in the school population; now the Hispanic enrollment is approaching two-thirds of the Black numbers. There was one

Table 1.3: Projections of racial/ethnic youth populations: 1982–2020

	Race/Ethnicity							
	White		Latino		Black		Other	
Year	% of total	millions of total	% of total	millions of total	% of total	millions of total	% of total	millions of total
1982	73.0	45.9	9.3	5.9	14.7	9.3	2.9	1.8
2020	54.5	40.0	25.3	18.6	16.5	11.9	4.2	3.0
Change	−18.5	−5.9	+16.0	+12.7	+1.8	+2.6	+1.3	+1.2

Source: Adapted from Pallas, Natriello, and McDill (1988).
Note: 'Youth' refers to newborn to age 17 years.

Hispanic student for every seventeen White students eighteen years ago; in 1986–87 there was one for every seven Whites. (p. 6)

In short, during this eighteen-year period, Chicano and other school-age students increased in raw numbers 103 per cent, Whites actually dropped by 17 per cent, and Black students were up by only 5 per cent.

While the Chicano and other Latino public school enrollment is growing nationally, actually only a small number of states are the ones that are accounting for the growth. Orfield (1988) notes that eight states (which have about 40 per cent of the nation's total population) enrolled a total of 3.57 million Latino students in 1986. These eight states represent 88 per cent of the total Latino public school enrollment.[9] By far, California (with 1.38 million Latino students) and Texas (with 1.09 million Latino students) enroll the vast majority (i.e., nearly 7 in every 10 Latino students, overwhelmingly of Mexican origin) of the total 3.57 million Chicano and other Latino students in the eight identified states. In short, California and Texas — which have long educated most Chicano students — accounted for (and will continue to account for) the great majority of enrollment increases of Chicano students in the country.

In another recent national demographic report, Pallas, Natriello, and McDill (1988) examined long-term projections from 1982 to the year 2020. Using the newborn to age 17 years population as the target group, it is expected that the total US population of newborns to 17-year-olds will increase by 17 per cent over the thirty-eight year period. That is, estimates are that the number of children in this age group will rise from 63 million in 1982 to 73 million in 2020.

Merely studying the general growth rate, however, is not very revealing. When one disaggregates the overall growth of these 10 million children from 1982 to 2020 along racial/ethnic lines, clear patterns can be discerned.

Pallas *et al.* (1988) observed that the overall increase indicates two different forces. First, as seen in Table 1.3, the number of White youngsters is actually expected to decline 13 per cent, or 6 million over this period. Second, the number of Chicano and other Latino children, on the other hand, will more than triple — increasing from 6 million in 1982 (a time which they comprised 9 per cent of the national youth population) to 19 million in 2020 (when they will make up 25 per cent of the country's youth population). In short, the anticipated increase in the Latino youth population of nearly 13 million more than offsets the projected decline of 6 million in the White youth population. In fact, the remarkable increase in the Chicano and Latino youth population will account '... *for most of the overall [youth] population growth* [italics added] expected between 1982 and 2020' (Pallas *et al.*, p. 22).

In summary, in the decades ahead our nation will witness a profound transformation of the youth population. As Pallas *et al.* (1988) comment, almost 3 in 4 children in 1982 were White. In 2020, only about 1 in 2 will be White. In, 1982, only 1 in 10 children were Chicano and other Latino. By 2020, about 1 in 4 are expected to be Chicano and other Latino. Regarding long-term projections, it is predicted that in the year 2050 the Latino school-age population (5 years to 17 years of age) will number 9.02 million and will surpass Black youth (8.86 million) to become the nation's largest racial/ethnic minority school-age group (US Bureau of the Census, 1986). The following excerpt from Orfield (1988) captures the wider implication of Latino school-age growth patterns:

> Should these trends continue very long they will fundamentally change the social structure of American education. Hispanics will become the nation's largest minority group and the proportion of Whites will fall substantially. All signs show that these changes are continuing. (pp. 6–7)

The 1980s: 'Decade of the Hispanic?'

Accompanying the national attention that Chicanos and other Latinos received in the late 1970s and early 1980s was the often stated claim that the 1980s would be the 'decade of the Hispanic'. There were expectations within and outside the larger Latino community that Chicanos and other Latinos would benefit from their growing presence. Gains were anticipated along educational, economic, political, and general 'quality of life' aspects.

Contrary to the expected gains during the 'decade of the Hispanic', the 1980s left many Latinos — particularly Chicanos and Puerto Ricans — worse off. In a recent report by the National Council of La Raza, *The Decade of the Hispanic: A Sobering Economic Retrospective* (Miranda and Quiroz, 1989), seven trends were identified that characterized Latinos' economic situation during the 1980s. This retrospective identified the following:

1 Latinos benefited least from the economic recovery in that their incomes stagnated and high rates of poverty continued. For example, in 1979, 21.8 per cent of Latinos were poor; in 1988, the rate was 26.8 per cent.
2 Latinos had higher rates of children living in poverty in 1988 (37.9 per cent) compared to 1979 (28.0 per cent).
3 There was no economic improvement for Latina-maintained households.
4 Latino married-couple families experienced deepened hardships (e.g., poverty rates increased from 13.1 per cent in 1979 to 16.1 per cent in 1988).

5 There was a widening income disparity. For example, Latinos in 1988 were 14 per cent more likely to make under $10,000 a year than they were in 1979.

6 Although in some areas there were slight educational gains, Latinos overall continued to feel the full impact of the educational crisis. For example, in 1978, 12.5 per cent of Latino families with householders who completed four years of high school lived in poverty. In 1988, the figure climbed to 16 per cent. In short, Latinos continue to experience unequal benefits from education.

7 Although Latinas (year-round, full-time workers) showed a slight increase in annual earnings from 1979 ($13,795) to 1988 ($14,845), male Latino workers dropped in earnings from $20,626 to $17,851 from 1979 to 1988, respectively.

In sum, Miranda and Quiroz (1989) conclude that, 'By any standard, Hispanics lost ground economically during the 1980s' (p. 27). Among several immediate policy interventions, 'improving educational opportunities' was targeted by the National Council of La Raza.

The 1990s: A Time for Informed Action

The plight of Chicano students (as previously described in the overview of current schooling conditions and outcomes), the soon-to-be and remarkable transformation of the racial/ethnic makeup of American youth, and the gradual erosion of economic and educational gains of Chicanos all point to the immediate need for school reform. When the schoolbell rings throughout the barrios in the 1990s, hopefully it will call us all to action. There is little doubt that resources — both human and monetary — will be needed on an unprecedented scale to mount a serious offensive on the schooling problems faced by Chicano students. The path we travel in the 1990s to the door of the next century could be the most important trek in the educational experience of Chicano students. But, let us not be naive. Linking theory, research, and policy is no easy matter. As Orfield (1988) admonishes, Latino students '... are increasing very rapidly in the United States, so rapidly that both research and policy are running far behind the demographic changes' (p. 32). As such, it is the intent of the remaining chapters in this book to help push along the research, policy, and demographic connections by discussing some agendas for the 1990s and beyond. Now is the time for informed action, a time to begin a very serious commitment to transforming Chicano school failure to Chicano school success.

Regarding research, the various chapters will be attempting, in part, to draw from what we know and what we do not know in order to ask how the research community of the 1990s can move ahead *vis-à-vis* its efforts and Chicano schooling issues. Given the large finite universe of possible research concerns, which ones are more important to address? Why is it significant to address these unanswered research questions? In which ways can answers to these questions provide insights to the theoretical and practical sides of the Chicano schooling experiences? That is, resultant from such proposed research what might be some theoretical implications and practical applications? Can we frame research proposals in such ways that future researchers can feasibly tackle them? In short, what might some research agendas for the 1990s look like?

With respect to proposed policy agendas, the challenge before scholars is to assess the extent to which research has influenced and should influence educational policy and practice. Regarding Chicano students, there are numerous questions about policy one can ask. For example, what are the central policy considerations? How are these policy issues currently framed? Are there alternative ways to frame them? Is current policy based on solid research and scientific evidence, and how can such an evaluation prove useful in formulating research-driven policy agendas for the 1990s? What are the prevailing paradigms used to examine the issues? Is there a need for paradigm shifts? What drives specific interventions (if any) that seek to address the problem? What is the current level of attention focused on the problem? What specific resources are committed — or need to be committed — to the problem? With an eye to the 1990s, what might be some proposed policy agendas regarding the schooling problems faced by Chicano students?

In addition to the multitude of research and policy questions/statements regarding Chicano schooling issues that can be formulated, there is the subject of doing what is good *now* for the sake of what will be good for the *future*. Hayes-Bautista, Schink, and Chapa (1988) in a recent study of California's changing demography (*The Burden of Support: Young Latinos in an Aging Society*), point out that aging Whites will increasingly become dependent on young Latino workers. The aging of the 'Baby Boom Anglos' in California will result in a more than tripling of the 65-and-over population around 2030. The young, vastly undereducated Latino population will likewise triple in size. Therefore, the 'burden of support' for the elderly (e.g., health care; income support) will fall primarily on the shoulders of the Latino workers. Hayes-Bautista *et al.* argue that if the currently working-age generation in California invests in improving schooling for Latino youth, this will assist in providing a stronger economic foundation for its own security in the future. On a broader, national scope, Miranda and Quiroz (1989) draw similar conclusions:

> In the 1990s, reducing inequality between Hispanics and the rest of society will not be a moral preference, but an economic imperative. Hispanics will constitute about one-third of overall labor force growth between now and the end of the century, and a growing proportion of taxpayers supporting Social Security, Medicare and other transfer payment systems needed to support an aging society. An untrained and underemployed labor force will not only retard direct economic output, but increase demand for public assistance and diminish the tax base necessary for the support of essential government services. Improving the Hispanic community's economic standing — and the human capital characteristics of individual Hispanics — clearly services the economic interest of the nation. . . . Hispanics are a 'good bet' for future public policy investments. (p. 28)

In light of our discussion thus far on the plight of Chicano students, it would be most fitting to conclude by presenting a few lines form Henry Trueba's recent and fine book, *Raising Silent Voices: Educating the Linguistic Minorities for the 21st*

Century. In his concluding chapter, Trueba (1989) offers these sober-minded but encouraging words:

> The end of the twentieth century is rapidly approaching. The children who will crowd our schools are already among us. Minority children are rapidly becoming, or already have become, the majority in a number of cities and areas of this country.... Moral, humanitarian, and economic arguments can be made to motivate us to support minority education in our schools. The future of this country will be in good hands if we extend our support to minority children today. (pp. 185–6)

Notes

1 Here I am conceptualizing educational inequality as a form of oppression. Chesler (1976) in an essay on theories of racism — which by the way, can be generalized to the study of other forms of oppression — argues that there are three forms of evidence from which theorists can draw to contend the existence of oppression. These evidential bases are: (a) personal attitudes or cultural values — as seen in symbol systems and ideology; (b) institutional processes — as seen in mechanisms that lead to differential advantages and privileges; (c) effects or outcomes — as seen in differentials among groups.

2 Here, I follow the logic of Kerlinger (1986) who describes the distinctions between a concept and a construct. 'A *concept* expresses an abstraction formed by generalizations from particulars' (p. 26), and although a construct is a concept, a construct has an added meaning '... of having been deliberately and consciously invented or adopted for a special scientific purpose' (p. 27). Furthermore, as Kerlinger notes, constructs can be of the *constitutive* and *operational* type. A constitutive defintion defines a construct by using other constructs, and are particularly valuable in theory construction. An operational definition describes, with some precision, how a particular construct will be observed and measured. In the present analysis, our use of Chicano school failure is largely along constitutive lines, yet it can be refined in an operational sense.

3 The 'dropout rate', which is the converse of school holding power, is simply estimated by subtracting the school holding power (a percentage) from 100 per cent.

4 Underachievement refers to a discrepancy between measured aptitude (i.e., intelligence) and achievement (see for example, Kubiszyn and Borich, 1987). When one's obtained aptitude score is higher than one's obtained achievement score, a student is typically labeled as an 'underachiever'. Conversely, an 'overachiever' is a student whose aptitude score is lower than his/her obtained achievement score.

5 The problems attached to the term underachievement (as well as overachievement) are so grave that they have led Cronbach, a highly noted tests and measurement expert, to conclude: 'The terminology of over- and underachievement should be abandoned' (1984, p. 255).

6 In 1989 there were 1,060 school districts in Texas. Some districts spent as much as $19,600 per student, and others spent as little as $2,000 (Graves, 1989b). Poor school districts (defined as those with property tax wealth below the state average) abound in Texas. That is, 205 (81 per cent) of Texas' 254 countries contain poor school districts (Phillips, 1989). A disproportionately higher number of poor school districts, however, are located in South Texas, the region where Chicanos are mostly concentrated.

7 Of the total 20.1 million Latinos in the US in 1989, the largest segment by far is the Mexican-origin population (12.6 million, 62.7 per cent of the total). In descending

order, the other Latino populations are: Central and South American (2.5 million, 12.4 per cent), Puerto Rican (2.3 million, 11.4 per cent), Cuban (1.07 million, 5.3 per cent), and Spanish or other Latino (1.63 million, 8.1 per cent) (Miranda and Quiroz, 1989; Vickers, 1989).

    With respect to within-group growth rates, data comparison between 1982 to 1989 shows that Central and South Americans had the sharpest increase (67 per cent). The 'other Hispanic' increased by 31 per cent, followed by: Mexican origin (30 per cent), Puerto Rican (14 per cent), and Cuban (12 per cent) (Vickers, 1989).

8 This report (based on an article in *Ebony* magazine; see Staff, 1989) is also interesting in that it provides projections for cities that will have large percentages of Latino and Black populations. By the year 2000, it is predicted that Black and Latinos combined will constitute a clear majority in about one-third of the country's fifty largest cities. In the ten most populated cities in the nation — including the four largest (in descending order, New York, Los Angeles, Chicago, and Houston) — Blacks and Latinos will be the majority in six of these top ten cities. For example, in Los Angeles, in the year 2000, they will number about 53 per cent. In Chicago, 50 per cent. In New York, almost 50 per cent.

9 The eight states with their respective enrollments (in millions) in descending order are: California (1.38), Texas (1.09), New York (.39), Illinois (.16), Arizona (.16), Florida (.15), New Jersey (.13), and New Mexico (.13) (Orfield, 1988).

References

ALVAREZ, R., JR. (1988) 'National politics and local responses: The nation's first successful desegregation court case', in H.T. TRUEBA and C. DELGADO-GAITAN (Eds) *School and Society: Learning Content Through Culture*, New York, Praeger, pp. 37–52.

ANASTASI, A. (1984) 'Aptitude and achievement tests: The curious case of the indestructible strawperson', in B.S. PLAKE (Ed.) *Social and Technical Issues in Testing: Implications for Test Construction and Usage*, Hillsdale, NJ, Erlbaum, pp. 129–40.

BOYKIN, A.W. (1983) 'The academic performance of Afro-American children', in J. SPENCE (Ed.) *Achievement and Achievement Motives*, San Francisco, CA, W.H. Freeman, pp. 321–71.

BROWN, P.R. and HAYCOCK, K. (1985) *Excellence for Whom?* Oakland, CA, The Achievement Council.

CALIFORNIA SUPERINTENDENTS' COUNCIL ON HISPANIC AFFAIRS (1985) *Response to the First Term Report*, Sacramento, CA, State Department of Education.

CAMERON, J.W. (1976) 'The History of Public Education in Los Angeles, 1910–1930', unpublished doctoral dissertation, University of Southern California, Los Angeles.

CARTER, T.P. and SEGURA, R.D. (1979) *Mexican Americans in School: A Decade of Change*, New York, College Entrance Examination Board.

CATTERALL, J.S. (1985) *On the Social Costs of Dropping Out* (Report 86–SEPI-3), Stanford, CA, Stanford Education Policy Institute, Stanford University.

CHAPA, J. (1988) 'The question of Mexican American assimilation: Socioeconomic parity or underclass formation?', *Public Affairs Comment*, **35**, pp. 1–14.

CHESLER, M.A. (1976) 'Contemporary sociological theories of racism', in P.A. KATZ (Ed.) *Towards the Elimination of Racism*, New York, Pergamon Press, pp. 21–71.

COLEMAN, J.S., CAMPBELL, E.G., HOBSON, C.J., MCPARTLAND, J., MOOD, A., WEINFELD, F.D. and YORK, R.L. (1966) *Equality of Educational Opportunity*, Washington, DC, US Department of Health, Education, and Welfare, Office of Education.

CONEY, Y. and WEST, C.K. (1979) 'Academic pressures and the black adolescent', *Contemporary Educational Psychology*, **4**, pp. 318–33.

CRONBACH, L.J. (1984) *Essentials of Psychological Testing*, 4th ed., New York, Harper and Row.

DRAKE, R.H. (1927) 'A Comparative Study of the Mentality and Achievement of Mexican and White children', unpublished master's thesis, University of Southern California, Los Angeles.

ERIKSON, F. (1987) 'Transformation and school success: The politics and culture of educational thought', *Anthropology and Education Quarterly*, **18**, pp. 335–56.

ESPINOSA, R. and OCHOA, A. (1986) 'Concentration of California Hispanic students in schools with low achievement: A research note', *American Journal of Education*, **95**, pp. 77–95.

FAIRCHILD, H.H. (1984) 'School size, per-pupil expenditures, and academic achievement', *Review of Public Data Use*, **12**, pp. 221–9.

FOOTE, T.H., ESPINOSA, R.W. and GARCIA, J.O. (1978) *Ethnic Groups and Public Education in California*, San Diego State University, CA, The California School Finance Project and the California Association for Bilingual Education.

GANDARA, P. (1989) '"Those" children are ours: Moving toward community', *NEA Today*, **7**, pp. 38–43.

GERARD, H.B. and MILLER, N. (1975) *School Desegregation: A Long-Term Study*, New York, Plenum.

GINSBURG, H.P. (1986) 'The myth of the deprived child: New thoughts on poor children', in U. NEISSER (Ed.) *The School Achievement of Minority Children: New Perspectives*, Hillsdale, NJ, Erlbaum, pp. 169–89.

GONZALEZ, G.C. (1985) 'Segregation of Mexican children in a southern California city: The legacy of expansionism and the American Southwest', *The Western Historical Quarterly*, **16**, pp. 55–76.

GONZALEZ, J.M. (1974) 'A Developmental and Sociological Rationale for Culture-Based Curricula and Cultural Context Teaching in the Early Instruction of Mexican American Children', unpublished doctoral dissertation, University of Massachusetts.

GOUGHIS, R.A. (1986) 'The effects of prejudice and stress on the academic performance of black-Americans', in U. NEISSER (Ed.) *The School Achievement of Minority Children: New Perspectives*, Hillsdale, NJ, Erlbaum, pp. 145–67.

GRAVES, D. (1989a) 'School finance woes echo across nation', *Austin American Statesman*, October 7, pp. A1, A15.

GRAVES, D. (1989b) 'Court strikes down school finance plan: Justices set May 1 deadline for equitable system', *Austin American Statesman*, October 3, pp. A1, A6.

HARO, C.M. (1977) *Mexicano/Chicano Concerns and School Segregation in Los Angeles*, Los Angeles, CA, Chicano Studies Center Publications, University of California.

HAWKES, T.H. and KOFF, R.H. (1970) 'Differences in anxiety of private school and inner city public elementary school children', *Psychology in the Schools*, **7**, pp. 250–9.

HAYCOCK, K. and NAVARRO, M.S. (1988) *Unfinished Business: Fulfilling our Children's Promise*, Oakland, CA, The Achievement Council.

HAYES-BAUTISTA, D.E., SCHINK, W.O. and CHAPA, J. (1988) *The Burden of Support: Young Latinos in an Aging Society*, Stanford, CA, Stanford University Press.

JENSEN, A.R. (1980) *Bias in Mental Testing*, New York, The Free Press.

KERLINGER, F.D. (1986) *Foundations of Behavioral Research*, 3rd ed., New York, Holt, Rinehart and Winston.

KUBISZYN, T. and BORICH, G. (1987) *Educational Testing and Measurement: Classroom Application and Practice*, 2nd ed., Glenview, IL, Scott, Foresman.

MAHAN, J. and BOYLE, V. (1981) 'Multicultural teacher preparation: An attitudinal survey', *Educational Research Quarterly*, **6**, pp. 97–112.

MENCHACA, M. and VALENCIA, R.R. (1990) 'Anglo-Saxon ideologies and their impact on the segregation of Mexican students in California, the 1920s–1930s', *Anthropology and Education Quarterly*, **21**, pp. 222–49.

Mingle, J.R. (1987) *Focus on Minorities: Trends in Higher Education Participation and Success*, Denver, CO, A joint publication of the Education Commission of the States and the State Higher Education Executive Officers.

Miranda, L. and Quiroz, J.T. (1989) *The Decade of the Hispanic: A Sobering Economic Retrospective*, Washington, DC, National Council of La Raza.

Munoz, D.G. (1986) 'Identifying areas of stress for Chicano undergraduates', in M.A. Olivas (Ed.) *Latino College Students*, New York, Teachers College Press, pp. 131–56.

National Commission on Excellence in Education (1983) *A Nation at Risk: The Imperatives for Educational Reform*, Washington, DC, US Government Printing Office.

Oakes, J. (1985) *Keeping Track: How Schools Structure Inequality*, New Haven, CT, Yale University Press.

Olsen, L. (1988) *Crossing the Schoolhouse Border: Immigrant Students and the California Public Schools*, Boston, MA, California Tomorrow.

Orfield, G. (1988) 'The growth and concentration of Hispanic enrollment and the future of American education', paper presented at the National Council of La Raza Conference, Albuquerque, NM, July.

Orr, M.T. (1987) *Keeping Students in School*, San Francisco, CA, Jossey-Bass.

Orum, L.S. (1986) *The Education of Hispanics: Status and Implications*, Washington, DC, National Council of La Raza.

Pallas, A.M., Natriello, G. and McDill, E.L. (1988) 'Who falls behind: Defining the "at risk" population — current dimensions and future trends', paper presented at the meeting of the American Educational Research Association, New Orleans, LA, April.

Parsons, T.W. (1965) 'Ethnic Cleavage in a California School', unpublished doctoral dissertation, Stanford University.

Phillips, B.N. (1978) *School Stress and Anxiety: Theory, Research, and Intervention*, New York, Human Sciences Press.

Phillips, J. (1989) 'Districts agree: Schools are underfunded — rich and poor see huge infusion of money as only lasting solution', *Austin American Statesman*, October 3, p. A6.

Population Reference Bureau (1985) *Population and California's Future*, Washington, DC, Author.

Reynolds, A. (1933) *The Education of Spanish-Speaking Children in Five Southwestern States* (Bulletin 1933, No. 11) Washington, DC, Government Printing Office.

Rodriguez v. San Antonio Independent School District (1971) Civil action no. 68-175-5A (W.D.Tex.).

San Miguel, G., Jr. (1986) 'Status of the historiography of Chicano education: A preliminary analysis', *History of Education Quarterly*, **26**, pp. 523–36.

San Miguel, G., Jr. (1987) 'The status of historical research on Chicano education', *Review of Educational Research*, **57**, pp. 467–80.

Sanchez, G.I. (1966) 'History, culture, and education', in J. Samora (Ed.) *La Raza: Forgotten Americans*, Notre Dame, IN, University of Notre Dame Press, pp. 1–26.

Staff (1989) 'The biggest secret of race relations: The new White minority', *Ebony*, April, pp. 84, 86, 88.

Swibold, D. (1989) 'US Hispanic numbers rise 39% since 1980', *San Antonio Light*, October 12, pp. Al, A12.

Trueba, H.T. (1989) *Raising Silent Voices: Educating the Linguistic Minorities for the 21st Century*, New York, Harper and Row.

US Bureau of the Census (1986) *Projections of the Hispanic Population: 1983 to 2080* (Current Population Reports, Series P-25, No. 995) Washington, DC, US Government Printing Office.

US Commission on Civil Rights (1972a) *Mexican American Education Study, Report 2: The Unfinished Education: Outcomes for Minorities in the Five Southwestern States*, Washington, DC, Government Printing Office.

US COMMISSION ON CIVIL RIGHTS (1972b) *Mexican American Education Study, Report 3: The Excluded Student: Educational Practices Affecting Mexican Americans in the Southwest*, Washington, DC, Government Printing Office.

US COMMISSION ON CIVIL RIGHTS (1972c) *Mexican American Education Study, Report 4: Mexican American Education in Texas: A Function of Wealth*, Washington, DC, Government Printing Office.

US COMMISSION ON CIVIL RIGHTS (1973) *Mexican American Education Study, Report 5: Teachers and Students: Differences in Teacher Interaction with Mexican American and Anglo Students*, Washington, DC, Government Printing Office.

US COMMISSION ON CIVIL RIGHTS (1974) *Mexican American Education Study, Report 6: Toward Quality Education for Mexican Americans*, Washington, DC, Government Printing Office.

VALENCIA, R.R. (1984) *Understanding School Closures: Discriminatory Impact on Chicano and Black Students* (Policy Monograph Series, No. 1) Stanford, Stanford University, Stanford Center for Chicano Research.

VALENCIA, R.R. and ABURTO, S. (in press, a) 'Competency testing and Latino student access to the teaching profession: An overview of issues', in J. DENEEN, G.D. KELLER and R. MAGALLAN (Eds) *Assessment and Access: Hispanics in Higher Education*, Albany, NY, State University of New York Press.

VALENCIA, R.R. and ABURTO, S. (in press, b) 'Research directions and practical strategies in teacher testing and assessment: Implications for improving Latino access to teaching', in J. DENEEN, G.D. KELLER and R. MAGALLAN (Eds) *Assessment and Access: Hispanics in Higher Education*, Albany, NY, State University of New York Press.

VALENCIA, R.R. and RANKIN, R.J. (1988) 'Evidence of bias in predictive validity on the Kaufman Assessment Battery for Children in samples of Anglo and Mexican American children', *Psychology in the Schools*, **22**, pp. 257–63.

VICKERS, R.J. (1989) 'Hispanic population tops 20 million in US', *Austin American Statesman*, October 12, p. A12.

WATSON, A. (1988) 'Changing classes: State's minority students to make a majority next fall', *San Jose Mercury News*, May 15, pp. 1A, 12A.

WILLS, T.A. and LANGER, T.S. (1980) 'Socioeconomic status and stress', in I.L. KUTASH, L.B. SCHLESINGER, and Associates (Eds) *Handbook on Stress and Anxiety*, San Francisco, CA, Jossey-Bass, pp. 159–73.

Chapter 2

Segregation, Desegregation, and Integration of Chicano Students: Problems and Prospects

Rubén Donato, Martha Menchaca and Richard R. Valencia

Segregation has been, and continues to be, a schooling reality for a substantial proportion of the Chicano elementary and secondary school-age population. In that segregation practices and conditions are not conducive for optimal learning, it is not surprising that school segregation is inextricably linked to Chicano school failure. As noted by Valencia (chapter 1, this volume), the segregation of Chicano students constitutes a major obstacle in their schooling experience — that is, segregation can be considered a key institutional process in denying Chicanos equal educational opportunities.

In this chapter, we will examine the connections between segregation and Chicano school failure from both historical and contemporary vantage points. We begin by providing a descriptive overview of the current prevalence of Chicano segregation, as well as an empirical look at the adverse relation between school segregation and diminished academic achievement. Second, we provide an overview of the roots of Chicano school segregation. Our contention is that in order to understand the current problems and remedies associated with segregation, one needs to examine its ideological and structural foundations. In particular, we examine the relation between racism and the implementation, maintenance, and persistence of school segregation. In this historical section we also discuss, in brief, the efforts Chicano parents exerted to desegregate barrio schools in their pursuit for a better schooling for Chicano youth. Third, we describe the contemporary manifestations of segregation — with a special emphasis on language segregation as a form of resegregation. The chapter closes with a discussion of reform. Granted that school integration (and not merely desegregation) is a desirable goal, how might true integration (e.g., interethnic contact, equal status) be achieved by the Chicano community? How can we move towards integration and Chicano school success? In our discussion we weave in research and policy dimensions.

The Segregation of Chicanos: Prevalence and Adverse Effects

Prevalence of Segregation

The isolation of Chicano students in 'Mexican schools' or in high-density ethnic minority schools is a longstanding fact of the Chicano schooling experience. Historian Gilbert Gonzalez (1990) notes that Mexican children were denied admission to 'American' schools as early as 1892.[1] This case in point involved the school district in Corpus Christi, Texas, where a separate school was built just for the Mexican students. Within years the school enrolled 110 students, and by the late 1920s the same school had an enrollment of 1,320 Mexican children (Gonzalez). The segregation of Mexican students would continue to escalate in Texas and elsewhere, and as Gonzalez comments, by 1920 segregation was in full force as 85 per cent of school districts in the Southwest practiced the segregation of Mexican students in the form of either having 'Mexican schools' or 'Mexican rooms' (i.e., Mexican students were deliberately isolated in ethnically mixed schools).

With the increase in the Mexican-origin population and the barrioization of Chicano communities, school segregation from the 1920s to the 1970s became an entrenched condition for numerous Chicano students throughout the Southwest. In 1971, the landmark US Commission on Civil Rights *Mexican American Education Study (Report Number 1: Ethnic Isolation of Mexican Americans in the Public Schools of the Southwest)* made public what Chicano parents had known for many years: their children were relatively isolated from White children. Based on a well-designed and extensive data-gathering procedure, the Commission reported that nearly 1 in 2 Chicano students in the Southwest in 1968 attended elementary and secondary schools in which they comprised the predominant ethnic group (i.e., 50 to 100 per cent Chicano enrollment). It was also found that 1 in 5 Chicano students in 1968 attended schools in which they were the near total enrollment (80 to 100 per cent).

In the 1970s, school segregation actually declined nationally for Black students. Yet, for Chicano and other Latino students (particularly Puerto Ricans), segregation increased. This steady rise in school segregation has been to such a degree that Latino students (two-thirds of whom are Chicanos) now have the unfortunate characteristic of being the most segregated of America's student groups (Orum, 1986).[2] In 1980, 68.1 per cent of Latino students nationally were enrolled in schools with minority enrollments of 50 per cent or greater, and more than 25 per cent of Latinos attended schools in which minority density was 90 to 100 per cent (Orum).

More recent data (Orfield, 1988) confirms the intensification of Chicano and other Latino student segregation. Table 2.1 shows Latino public school segregation nationally by region from 1968 to 1984. Reported are data for (a) percentage of Latinos enrolled in predominantly White schools, and (b) percentage of Latino students in near total (i.e., 90 to 100 per cent) minority schools.

The data presented in Table 2.1 reveal distinct patterns: on a region-by-region basis, the percentage of Latino students attending predominantly White schools declined from 1968 to 1984. Conversely, the percentages of Latino students enrolled in near total minority schools increased in each of the four US regions. Using the national data in Table 2.1 as a fairly representative indicator of

Table 2.1:   Latino segregation by region, 1968–1984

Region	% of Latino students in predominantly White Schools		Change (%)	% of Latino students in 90–100% minority schools		Change (%)
	1968	1984		1968	1984	
West	58	32	−44.8	12	23	+91.7
South	30	25	−16.7	34	37	+8.8
Northeast	25	22	−12.0	44	47	+6.8
Midwest	68	46	−32.3	7	24	+242.9
US	45	29	−35.6	23	31	+34.8

Source: Adapted from Orfield (1988).

Latino segregation, we can see that the percentage of Latinos enrolled in White schools over the sixteen-year period dropped by 36 per cent, whereas the percentage of Latino students attending 90–100 per cent minority students jumped 35 per cent. In sum, taking all the available information together, there is clear and ample evidence that as a whole, Chicano and other Latinos students are becoming more and more isolated from their White peers — and vice versa.

Adverse Effects of Segregation

Historically, the context for learning in Chicano segregated schools has been extremely poor. There is no doubt that the separate schooling Chicano students experienced was inferior. Gonzalez (1990) describes these early conditions as such:

> Inadequate resources, poor equipment, and unfit building construction made Mexican schools vastly inferior to Anglo schools. In addition, school districts paid teachers at Mexican schools less than teachers at Anglo schools, and many times a promotion for a teacher at a Mexican school meant moving to the Anglo school. Quite often, however, teachers in Mexican schools were either beginners or had been 'banished' as incompetent. (p. 22)

There are a number of references that document the considerably poor conditions endured by Chicano students in segregated schools. For example, Menchaca and Valencia (1990) contrast the Mexican and Anglo schools built in the mid-1920s in Santa Paula, California. The Mexican school enrolled nearly 1,000 students in a schoolhouse with eight classrooms (grades kindergarten through eighth) and contained two bathrooms and one administrative office. On the other hand, the Anglo school enrolled less than 700 students and contained twenty-one classrooms, a cafeteria, a training shop, and several administrative offices. In short, the Mexican school — compared to the Anglo school — had a much higher student per classroom ratio and inferior facilities. Fifteen miles away from Santa Paula, in the coastal city of Oxnard, Chicano students fared no better in segregated schools. McCurdy (1975) in a *Los Angeles Times* article reported how several past school superintendents described the deplorable schooling conditions Chicano children experienced in the 1930s.[3]

One school was described as 'literally no more than a chicken coop. It had a dirt floor, single thickness walls, very run down, some stench from the toilet facility. Another school had a floor made from 'just black asphalt of the type you would see placed on street pavement', a former superintendent said. 'In the classroom, there was a single light bulb, not a large one . . . It may have been a 100-watt bulb, screwed into an outlet in the center of the ceiling', he said.

Suffice it to say that the inadequate educational conditions experienced by Chicano students in the past were detrimental to promoting an optimal learning environment. Although the current facilities in Chicano segregated schools may not be as deplorable as in the past, the legacy of inferiority continues. A major contributing factor to the maintenance of inferior conditions as manifested in resources in Chicano segregated schools is school financing inequity (see Valencia, chapter 1, this volume). As the funding discrepancy between rich and poor schools narrows, however, there is some optimism that learning opportunities will improve in Chicano segregated schools (e.g., Pinkerton, 1989).

Notwithstanding the extreme importance of attaining equity in school financing for Chicano schools, there remains the stubborn relation between school segregation of Chicanos and lowered academic achievement. For example, Jaeger (1987; cited in Orfield, 1988) examined the relation between test scores and percent Black and Latino high school students in metropolitan Los Angeles (1984–85 school year). The observed correlations were very strong: (−.90), mathematics (−.88), and writing (−.85). That is, as minority enrollment increased, achievement decreased. Jaeger reported that the correlations between school enrollment percentage of White students and achievement test scores were likewise of very high magnitudes, but of the opposite direction (i.e., as White enrollment in the high schools increased, test scores also increased). Finally, Jaeger disaggregated the data and found that when only the percentage of Latino students in the high schools was correlated with achievement, the relations were not as strong for the Black/Latino aggregate, but still quite substantial (range from −.53 to −.58).

Espinosa and Ochoa (1986) have also provided supporting evidence for the connection between Chicano segregation and diminished achievement in California — a state in which Chicano school segregation has also increased in the last twenty years. Using a large state-wide sample (4,268 public elementary schools and 791 public high schools), Espinosa and Ochoa correlated California Assessment Program (CAP) scores (average of math and reading achievement) with percent of Latino students in grades three, six and twelve. The relation between Latino concentration and CAP achievement was strongly defined (e.g., at grade twelve the observed r was −.49).

In another investigation, Valencia (1984) also found a substantial relation between minority concentration in schools and academic achievement. The setting for the study was the Phoenix Union High School District (PUHSD) No. 210. Valencia — as part of his work as an expert witness in a school closure trial in the PUHSD — calculated the correlation between the percentage of Black/Latino enrollment with mean stanines of the Comprehensive Tests of Basic Skills for grades nine through twelve in the District's eleven high schools. Table 2.2

Table 2.2:   *Rank order comparison between percentage of minority student body enrollment and academic achievement*

School %	Minority student enrollment %	Minority rank	Achievement rank (lowest)
Union	94.2	1	1
South	87.7	2	2
Hayden	75.0	3	3
North	64.4	4	4
East	56.7	5	5
West	25.7	6	7
Maryvale	19.5	7	8
Browne	18.0	8	6
Alhambra	13.2	9	9
Central	9.4	10	11
Camelback	7.8	11	10

Source: Valencia (1984).
Based on autumn, 1978 mean stanines of the Comprehensive Tests of Basic Skills for grades 9–12. ρ = .96 (significant <.01).

lists the ranking of the eleven schools by minority student enrollment accompanied by each school's respective rank (lowest to highest) on achievement.

The statistical analysis (Spearman rank-order correlation) computed by Valencia revealed that the association between Black/Latino percentage of the various high schools with their respective test scores was very strong (ρ = .96) — once again underscoring the ubiquitous connection between school segregation and low academic performance.

On a final note, there is evidence that the relation between school segregation and schooling problems is not confined to test score outcomes. For example, Orfield (1988) found that the correlation between graduation rate with the percentage of Black/Latino students in metroplitan Chicago high schools was a staggering –.83. Furthermore, a correlation of –.47 was observed between percent minority high school students and percent of students taking the college entrance examinations. Orfield also reported that the Black/Latino percentage of schools was very negatively associated (r = –.92) with average college admissions test scores. When the analyses were disaggregated by ethnicity, the correlations for Latino high school students were –.40 (percent Latino with graduation rate) and –.43 (percent Latino with college entrance scores). A clear and direct implication stemming from the findings of Orfield and others is that the school segregation of Chicanos is linked to their very limited matriculation to higher education. Orum (1986), for example, has identified poor high school preparation as a key obstacle in college access for Chicano and other Latino students. She reported that the Latino eligibility pool for entrance to college is substantially reduced, as 75 per cent of Latino high school graduates have not completed a college preparatory curriculum. Also, approximately 33 per cent of Latino high school graduates have very low grades ('D' or 'F' averages) in one or more vital academic subjects.

In conclusion, there is a great deal of historical and contemporary evidence that the school segregation of Chicano students in our nation's public elementary and secondary schools is connected to school failure, hence inequality. Various sources inform us that segregated Chicano schools tend to be schools characterized by low funding, high dropout rates, low achievement test scores, a disproportionately high percentage of low-income students, and few college preparatory courses. There is no doubt that the isolation of Chicano students in schools that suffer from inequities in facilities, resources, and curricula offerings is far from desirable. The desegregation of Chicano schools and the subsequent integration of Chicano and other 'minority' and 'majority' students in equitable learning contexts is a commendable goal. Later, we share our thoughts and ideas how such integration may be realized. But first, it is necessary to understand the historical roots of segregation. Our proposition is that in order to move towards the goal of desegregation and integration of Chicano students, one must have a sense of the events and forces that helped shape the educational isolation of Chicanos.

Racism and Chicano School Segregation in the Southwest: An Historical Perspective

Racism and the Structural Foundation of Segregation

There is ample evidence that the ideological foundations of school segregation date back to the nineteenth century racial belief that White groups should not socially interact with biologically inferior colored races (Konvitz 1946; Menchaca 1987; Menchaca and Valencia, 1990). During the nineteenth century, White supremacy ideologies helped to promote the belief that racial minority groups were inherently inferior and helped to provide the rationale to segregate the 'colored races' (Comas, 1961; Jackson, 1986). Racism was institutionalized within the academic, religious, and governmental spheres and it culminated in the passage of *de jure* segregation (Menchaca and Valencia). Within the academic sphere, historians were at the forefront in proselytizing a White superiority ideology and argued in favor of eugenics to ensure that the White races would remain pure (Feagin, 1989; Gossett, 1953, 1977). Historians also favored the social segregation of the colored races as being the most practical method of preventing racial intermingling. The religious sphere was also included in the racist ideologies of the era, in which some churches practiced segregation. The belief that the Anglo-Saxons were 'God's Chosen People' provided the rationale to support the view that God did not intend the races to mix because he had 'not created all the races equal'. Within the Protestant Church, White supremacist pastors interpreted the doctrine as God's plan to rid the world of the 'colored' races and thus make room for the superior White races. For example, the genocide of the American Indian was figuratively interpreted to be the result of God's predestined will to improve the racial makeup of the world (Gossett, 1953, 1977; Newcombe, 1985). In many congregations, racism was manifested in the total exclusion of racial minority groups. 'Colored people' were expected to attend services in their own churches, and in more tolerant congregations racial minorities were allowed to attend church but were expected to sit apart from the White congregation (Cadena, 1987; Glazer and Moynihan, 1963; Menchaca, 1987, 1989; Menchaca and Valencia, 1990).

White supremacist views also surfaced in the governmental sphere and culminated in the legislation of segregationist laws. The passage of 'separate but equal legislation' in the nineteenth century reflected the government's endorsement of the widespread racial ideologies of the period (Feagin, 1989; Hendrick, 1977; Wollenberg, 1978). At the federal level the passage of *Plessy v. Ferguson* in 1896 was a blatant example of the government's approval of the rationale that the colored races should not mix with Whites. Though *Plessy v. Ferguson* was passed with the specific intention of segregating Blacks, the case was used to justify all forms of social segregation. At the local level, city governments used the legislation to segregate other racial minority groups by arguing that the spirit of the law applied to all 'coloreds' (Hyman and Wiecek, 1982; Konvitz, 1946). Moreover, *Plessy v. Ferguson* represented a symbolic action on part of the federal legislators to enact an undisputable law that gave the states the right to practice segregation.

By the early 1900s, most states practiced some form of social segregation and had institutionalized school segregation as the main vehicle to maintain a segregated society (Feagin, 1989). The rationale being that if the children of the White and 'colored' races were socialized not to intermingle, the groups would not marry, and thus the purity of each race would be retained (Konvitz, 1946). Racial minorities questioned the extension of segregationist legislation to the educational domain and therefore took their plight to the Federal Supreme Court. In several Federal Supreme Court cases, however, the courts asserted the states' rights to segregate the 'colored races' and ruled against anti-segregationist practices. For example, in 1927 the Federal Supreme Court ruled in *Gung Lum v. Rice* that the separation of the colored races in the schools was within the discretion of the State and not in conflict with the fourteenth amendment (Konvitz, 1946). Over a decade later, the rule of separate but equal facilities in educational institutions was reasserted in the US Federal Supreme Court of 1938 in *Gaines v. Canada*. Although the federal courts did not legislate a mandate that 'all colored children must be segregated', they supported the states' rights to institute school segregation if desired by the legislators.

Paradoxically, although Chicanos were not specifically mentioned in the 'separate but equal legislation' there is ample evidence that they were often treated as 'colored' and were consequently segregated in most social spheres. Historically, the rationale used to socially segregate Mexicans was based on the racial perspective that Mexicans were 'Indian', or at best 'half-breed savages' who were not suited to interact with Whites (Menchaca and Valencia, 1990; Paredes, 1978; Surace, 1982). Although the ratification of the Treaty of Guadalupe Hidalgo had guaranteed Mexicans the political privileges enjoyed by Whites, state legislators in the latter half of the nineteenth century and early 1900s attempted to violate the agreement (Menchaca, 1990). Legislators sought to limit the Mexicans' political and social rights based on the rationale that Mexicans were Indians. They argued that because Indians by law were prohibited from voting, residing in White neighborhoods, and attending schools with White children, these laws also applied to Mexicans (Heizer and Amquist, 1971). For example, in California the state constitution prohibited 'Indian-looking Mexicans' from voting and only extended that privilege to 'White-looking Mexican' males (*California State Constitution of 1849*, article 11, section 1; Menchaca, 1990; Padilla, 1979). In the area of naturalization the federal government also attempted to deny Mexican immigrants their right to apply for citizenship on the basis that they were Indian

(Hull, 1985; Kansas, 1941; Konvitz, 1946; *People v. De La Guerra*, 1870; *Rodriquez v. Texas Circuit Court*, (1893. 81F:337–355).

Racial discrimination against the 'Indianism' of Mexicans was also manifested in the form of residential segregation. This exclusionary practice eventually provided the underlying structure for the school segregation of Mexican students, and thus it is important to examine the structural relation between residential and school segregation. By 1870, the residential segregation of the Mexican was firmly entrenched in the multiethnic structure of the Southwest and such housing patterns were viewed by Anglo-Americans to be the natural division between the inferior 'half-breed Mexican' and the 'superior' White race (Acuna, 1988; Camarillo, 1984a). Using nineteenth-century archival records, historian Alberto Camarillo attributes the early stages of Mexican residential segregation to Anglo-American racial prejudice. Camarillo states, 'The old Mexican pueblos were viewed by most Americans as "foreign", "backward", and undesirable locations in which to live' (p. 224). For example, in California the residential segregation of the Mexican began as early as 1850 and the process was completed by 1870. In San Francisco, San Jose, Santa Barbara, Los Angeles, San Diego, Santa Cruz, and Monterey, Anglo-American settlers restructured the old pueblos by constructing new subdivisions in the towns and prohibited Mexicans from moving into Anglo neighborhoods. Throughout California the residential segregation of the Mexican was enforced by the use of racial harassment and violence, and in many cities by the use of housing covenant restrictions prohibiting Mexicans from residing in the White zones (Hendrick, 1977).

Social historian David Montejano (1987) also reports that a similar process of residential segregation became widespread and provided the foundation for school segregation in Texas. Throughout the state, Mexicans were segregated in separate sections of the cities, and in many Anglo-American farm communities local *de jure* laws were used to prevent Mexicans from establishing residence. Residential segregation was planned by the ranchers and town developers and maintained through local laws and real estate policies. For example, in Weslaco, Texas, Mexicans were only allowed to buy property in designated areas near the Missouri Pacific Railroad tracks, and municipal ordinances required that Mexican neighborhoods and businesses only be established in those areas.

By the early 1900s the intensification of Mexican residential segregation became more complex in Texas, California, and other parts of the Southwest. Contributing factors were the industrial and urban development of the Southwest. It is very clear, however, that the growth of such residential segregation accompanied school segregation and was strongly linked to Anglo-American racial prejudice. Later, we will discuss the need for policy makers to explore strategies that might lead to residential integration — a major solution to eliminate school segregation.

The Rooting of Chicano School Segregation

The period of Mexican immigration to the United States in the 1920s delineates how racism continued to be the ideological force that pushed forward the growth of all forms of segregation, in particular residential and school segregation (Camarillo, 1984a, 1984b; Montejano, 1987). That is, when the size of the

Mexican population increased in the Southwest, the Anglo Americans responded by demanding residential and school segregation (Wollenberg, 1978). It also became common to segregate Mexicans in most public facilities including swimming pools, theaters, restaurants, and schools. In California, for example, when the Mexican-origin population tripled in the 1920s, from 121,000 to 368,000, the local school boards responded by instituting widespread school segregation (Wollenberg). In 1928, sixty-four schools in southern California responded to a government survey and reported that they had 90 to 100 per cent Mexican enrollments. Three years later, the state of California conducted a second survey and reported that 9 out of 10 school districts practiced school segregation in some form or another (Leis, 1931; cited in Gonzalez, 1985). Hendrick (1977) also reported in 1931, 85 per cent of California schools surveyed by the state government reported segregating Mexican students either in separate classrooms or in separate schools.

The school segregation of Mexican students was also widespread in Texas and coincided with a period of dramatic growth in the immigrant population (Montejano, 1987). As in California, segregated schools were a direct outgrowth of residential segregation, increasing Mexican immigration, and in particular racial discrimination. In the early 1900s, segregated schools were established by large-scale growers as a means of preventing the Mexican students from attending White schools. One of the first Mexican schools was established at the turn of the century in Central Texas (Seguin), and afterwards the process of separate Mexican schools became a common practice throughout the state (Rangel and Alcala, 1972). Moreover, in the late 1920s school segregation became more intense and it coincided with the growth of the Mexican immigrant population (Montejano). In the areas where the newcomers were concentrated, such as the lower Rio Grande Valley, the school segregation of Mexican students radically increased. Reconstructing the educational histories of local communities in the lower Rio Grande Valley, Montejano concluded that Mexican immigration and residential and school segregation were inextricably part of the same process:

> The towns of Edinburg, Harlingen, and San Benito segregated their Mexican school children through the fourth and fifth grades. And along the dense string of newcomer towns of Highway 83 — the 'longest mile' of McAllen, Mercedes, Mission, Pharr-San Juan, and Weslaco — Mexican school segregation was an unbroken policy. On the Gulf Coast plains, Raymondville, Kingsville, Robstown, Kenedy, and Taft were among the new towns where segregation was practiced. And in the Winter Garden area, Mexicans were segregated through the fifth grade in Crystal City, Carrizo Springs, Palm, Valley Wells, Asherton, and Frio Town. (p. 168)

By 1930, 90 per cent of the schools in Texas were racially segregated (Rangel and Alcala, 1972).

The rationales used to segregate Mexican students ranged from racial to social deficit justifications. Overall, these beliefs were ideological smokescreens used to prevent Chicano students from attending White schools. For example, in California during the 1920s and 1930s, government officials attempted to classify Mexican students as Indians in order to segregate them on the basis that they were 'colored'. On January 23, 1927, the Attorney General of California stated that Mexicans could be treated as Indians, thereby placing them under the mandate of *de jure* segregation (Hendrick, 1977). In 1930, the Califonia Attorney General once again issued an opinion on the racial background of the Mexican students. According to Attorney General Webb, Mexicans were Indians and therefore should not be treated as White. Webb stated, 'It is well known that the greater portion of the population of Mexico are Indians and were [sic] such Indians migrate to the United States, they are subject to the laws applicable generally to other Indians' (cited in Weinberg, 1977, p. 166). Webb's opinion was used by school boards to classify Mexicans as Indians and therefore attempted to segregate them on the basis that they were non-White. Finally, in 1935, the California legislature passed a law to segregate officially Mexican students on the basis that they were Indian. Without explicitly mentioning Mexicans, the 1935 school code prescribed that schools segregate Mexicans who descended from Indians. The California school code of 1935 stated:

> The governing board of the School district shall have power to establish separate schools for Indian children, excepting children of Indians who are the wards of the US government and children of all other Indians who are the descendents of the original American Indians of the US, and for children of Chinese, Japanese, or Mongolian parentage. (Cited in Hendrick, 1977, p. 57)

Although the school code did not mention Mexicans by name, it was explicit that the state's intention was to segregate dark-skinned Mexican students. Thus, Mexican children became the principal target of the discriminatory school code without being identified, and American Indians, though named directly, were released from legally mandated segregation.

Language was a second rationale used to segregate Mexican students. Allegedly, Mexican students were not permitted to attend classes with their Anglo American peers because they needed special instruction in English (Gonzalez, 1990; Menchaca and Valencia, 1990; San Miguel, 1986, 1987). The pedagogical rationale was that the limited- or non-English-speaking Mexican children would impede the academic progress of the Anglo children. The racial overtones of these practices were blatantly seen when Mexican American students, who did not speak Spanish, were also forced to attend the Mexican schools (Alvarez, 1986; Menchaca, 1987). The need to acculturate Mexican students in special Americanization classes was a third major excuse used to justify segregation. Mexican students were characterized as dirty, dull, unchristian, and lacking any social etiquette. Therefore, the educational belief was that Mexicans needed special classes where they would learn to emulate their Anglo American counterparts (Garcia, 1979; Gonzalez, 1990).

The results of IQ tests were also used, in part, to segregate Mexican students and provided the alleged scientific rationale. Lewis Terman, Professor of Education at Stanford University, presented many findings from racial studies of intelligence testing research supporting the view that Blacks, Indians, and Mexican Americans were intellectually inferior to Whites (Blum, 1978). In the case of Mexican Americans, William Sheldon of The University of Texas at Austin also used IQ tests such as the Cole-Vincent and Stanford-Binet tests to measure the mental ability of Mexican Americans in Texas (Wollenberg, 1974). Sheldon concluded that Mexican students, as measured by IQ tests, only had '85 per cent of the intelligence' of White students. Moreover, Thomas Garth of the University of Denver administered the National Intelligence Test to over 1,000 Mexican-origin students in Texas, New Mexico, and Colorado and discovered that the median IQ of those tested was 78.1 (the lowest of any study to that date). According to Garth, there was a connection between the Mexican children's heritage and their very low IQ, thus suggesting a racial interpretation (Wollenberg, 1974).

Using the research of the social scientists, school boards manipulated the IQ data to support their racist beliefs. Because it was common for Mexican students to score considerably lower than their White peers, school boards members used test results in part to separate the Mexican and Anglo students. It was rationalized that Anglo students must be instructed in separate schools in order to prevent them from getting behind. Mexican students, on the other hand, were identified to be slow learners needing special instruction in separate schools. Gonzalez (1974, 1990) also posits that IQ testing was an ideological foundation used to track minority students in the schools and to provide them with inferior education.

The Mexican community in the Southwest did not idly stand by while its children were being segregated in inferior facilities. The struggle for desegregation was initiated in Texas and California in the early 1930s. In Del Rio, Texas, Mexican parents successfully proved that the Independent School District had illegally segregated Mexican students on the basis of race (Rangel and Alcala, 1972). The court ruled in the case of *Del Rio Independent School District v. Salvatierra* (1930) that Mexicans were White and had been arbitrarily segregated because they were Mexican. The judgment, however, was overturned by the appellate court on the basis that the school board had the right to segregate Mexican students because of their 'language problems'.

In California, the Mexican parents of Lemon Grove were able to successfully overturn school segregation on March 13, 1931. *Alvarez v. Lemon Grove School District* represented one of the first successful desegregation cases of Mexican students in the United States. The court ruled in favor of the Mexican community on the basis that separate facilities for Mexican students were not conducive towards their Americanization and retarded the English language competency of the Spanish-speaking children.

In 1945, the era of *de jure* segregation finally came to an end for the Mexican community of the Southwest. The highly touted *Mendez v. Westminster* (1947) case ended *de jure* segregation in California and provided the legal foundation to end the school segregation of Mexican students throughout the Southwest. In *Mendez*, Judge McCormick concluded that the school board had segregated Mexicans on the basis of their 'Latinized' appearance and had gerrymandered the school district in order to ensure that Mexican students attend the Mexican schools. Judge McCormick concluded that this was an illegal action because there was no constitutional or congressional mandate that authorized school boards to segregate Mexican students. On the contrary, he stated that the fourteenth amendment and the ratification of the Treaty of Guadalupe Hidalgo had guaranteed Mexicans equal rights in the United States. Although the *Mendez* case helped to end *de jure* segregation, the school segregation of Mexican students remained widespread (Hendrick, 1977), and increased over the generations. Moreover, as Gonzalez (1990) notes when speaking of the *Mendez* case, 'Eventually, *de jure* segregation in schools ended throughout the Southwest, but not before an educational policy reinforcing socioeconomic inequality severely victimized generations of Mexican children' (p. 29).

Following the *Mendez* case, the *Delgado v. Bastrop Independent School District* (1948) in Texas was another example of the Chicanos' struggle for desegregation. The court ruled that placing Mexican students in separate schools was discriminatory and illegal. Paradoxically, although the court passed this ruling it also allowed school boards to segregate Mexican students within a school on the basis of their limited-English competency. Thus, this initated a new form of school segregation within desegregated school settings based on a language rationale (San Miguel, 1987).

In conclusion, the history of Chicano school segregation is a troubled one — filled with numerous events of forced isolation. History informs us that racism was a driving force in the relations between school segregation and Chicano school failure. But, Chicano communities did not idly stand by. *Salvatierra, Alvarez, Mendez, Delgado,* and others are testimony to the the Chicano's struggle for desegregated schools and equal educational opportunity. Notwithstanding these legal accomplishments, one can argue that to some degree these were empty victories: that is, although Chicanos won the battle against *de jure* segregation, their isolation in segregated schools continued. We now turn to an analysis of a modern form of school segregation in desegregated schools — resegregation.

Contemporary Issues in Chicano School Segregation: Resegregation

Thus far, we have examined the historical inequalities that structured Chicano segregated elementary and secondary public schools. With the end of *de jure* segregation of 'Mexican schools', the process of school desegregation in the Southwest began slowly. Furthermore, desegregation over the few decades touched only a small number of Chicano students and contained a number of pitfalls. In this section, we will examine these problems by analyzing the phenomenon of resegregation; that is, the process of Chicanos being segregated within desegregated settings. We discuss five aspects of current school desegregation and resegregation. First, we will briefly look at Chicano segregation as a silent problem; second, language segregation as an old problem but new issues brought forth; third, the relationship between bilingual education and desegregation; fourth, the bilingual teacher shortage and its impact on resegregation; and fifth, academic resegregation and its implication for the schooling of Chicanos.

Chicano School Segregation: A Silent Problem

In 1954 the Supreme Court decision in *Brown v. Board of Education* stated that public schools could not place students in separate facilities based on race, religion, or national origin. Racially segregated schools were 'inherently unequal' and practices fostering them were unconstitutional (*Brown*, 1954). The impact of *Brown* was so dramatic in the United States that many social scientists concurred that the case helped launch the modern civil rights movement. School desegregation, thus, became one of the leading and most controversial issues in American educational history (Welch and Light, 1987). During the 1960s and 1970s school desegregation received an enormous amount of public attention. Stories depicting communities in conflict over the school desegregation process became a common observance for anyone who kept up with the issue. Social scientists and political commentators wrote extensively about school desegregation. In the initial stages of the process, studies focused on the desegregation of schools in the deep South, but then as the movement gathered momentum, the focus shifted to eastern, mid-western, and western regions of the nation (Crain, 1968; Edwards and Wirt, 1967; Kirp, 1982; Rist, 1979). Given the scholarly and public attention that school desegregation received, most Americans immediately identified the school desegregation process exclusively as a Black/White issue. As Orfield, Monfort, and George (1987) have noted, 'School segregation has been widely understood as a problem for blacks. There is little public discussion of the fact, however, that black students are now less likely to attend schools with less than half whites than are Hispanics' (p. 24).

Although Chicanos were actively involved in several court cases for desegregated schooling throughout the Southwest during the pre-*Brown* era, they quickly became an invisible minority group and did not receive much attention in the desegregation process after the 1950s. The two most important cases in the post-*Brown* era concerning the desegregation of Chicano children were *Cisneros v. Corpus Christi Independent School District* in Texas (1970) and *Keyes v. School District Number One* in Denver, Colorado (1975). Brought on by Mexican Americans in the Corpus Christi area, the *Cisneros* case was extremely significant in their struggle for desegregated schools. This case demonstrated how Mexican Americans thought it was necessary to be identified as a separate class or an identifiable minority group in order to benefit from *Brown*. Because the court ruled that Mexican Americans were an identifiable ethnic minority group, they were found to be unconstitutionally segregated in Texas public schools. As San Miguel noted, Mexican Americans wanted to discard '... the "other white" legal strategy used ... during the 1940s and 1950s to eliminate segregation and substitute the equal protection argument used in black desegregation cases' (San Miguel, 1987, p. 178).

The *Keyes* case in Colorado was similar to the *Cisneros* case in the sense that it compelled the court to recognize '... how to treat Mexican American children in the desegregation process' (San Miguel, 1987, p. 180). Originally brought on by Blacks, the court was forced to make the decision whether to recognize Chicano students as 'White' and to integrate them with Blacks or view them as an identifiable minority group and mix them with White children. Once again, Chicano students were in fact recognized as an identifiable minority group and thus entitled to special services in desegregated settings in Colorado. Yet, despite the importance of *Cisneros* and *Keyes*, the educational isolation of most Chicano students continued — in both segregated and desegregated American public schools.

Language Segregation: Old Problem New Issues

Language segregation is not a new issue. American public schools have attempted to segregate Chicano children based on language for over six decades. The defendants in the *Del Rio v. Salvatierra* (1931), *Alvarez v. Lemon Grove* (1931), and the *Delgado v. Bastrop* (1948) cases all ventured, to some degree, to use the argument that the Chicano students' inability to speak English justified the use of separate classes. Two decades after the *Brown* decision, however, the Supreme Court case in the landmark *Lau v. Nichols* (1974) litigation brought forth new issues of equity that dramatically changed the course of schooling for Chicano students. The decision held that public schools had to provide an education that was comprehensible to limited-English-proficient (LEP) students. Because the English language was the *only* vehicle of instruction, LEP children were being denied access to a meaningful educational experience. The Supreme Court recognized that in order for LEP students to participate in the schooling process, they first had to understand the English language. This dilemma was an educational contradiction and thus made 'a mockery of public education' (*Lau*, 1974). Because LEP children, in general, could not benefit from an education that was conducted entirely in English, many Chicano LEP students were not able effectively to participate in the American educational system.

After *Brown* (1954), providing schooling in desegregated institutions was the law of the land. But, it was not until after the *Cisneros* (1970) and *Keyes* (1973) decisions that the 'ethnicity' of Chicano students was clarified. That is, they were no longer considered to be 'White' or 'other-White' in the desegregation process. They were now considered to be an 'identifiable minority group' and had to be integrated with White children. Twenty years after *Brown*, following the *Lau* (1974) decision, these same public schools found themselves in a position where they had to provide Chicano LEP children an education that considered their special language needs. These benchmark decisions placed Chicano LEP children in school settings where educators were mandated to address an additional host of background needs. Given the legal forces behind *Brown* and *Lau*, a new form of school segregation began to emerge in American public schools — that is, language segregation within desegregated schools, a new form of resegregation.

Amidst heated national discussions over school desegregation, some educators began to voice concerns about the education of Chicano LEP students (Feagin, 1989; US Commission on Civil Rights, 1972). The growth rate of LEP students, low academic achievement, and high dropout rates — coupled with increasing segregation and their low socioeconomic backgrounds — encouraged Congress to pass a number of educational programs in the late 1960s. As it was argued for Black children, poverty was perceived as a major culprit of Chicano school failure. The increasing number of Chicano children who could not communicate in English, however, caused educators and legislators to question that perception. The passage of Title Vll of the Elementary and Secondary Education Act (ESEA) in 1965, the Bilingual Education Act of 1968, and ESEA Title I remedial programs resulted in federal resources that were sought by politically and socially conscious minority groups (Solomone, 1986). Many programs were developed with federal funds in order to improve schooling for Chicano students, but the passage of these programs purporting to shift the

Chicano LEP student into the educational mainstream did not have much of an impact.

Although *Lau* did not prescribe specific remedies or pedagogical strategies for the limited-English proficient, this ruling paved the way for more equitable opportunities for Chicano LEP children in public schools. In California, for example, many educators became actively involved in, and supportive of, enhancing educational opportunities for Chicano LEP children. The California State Department of Education passed a bill (AB-1329) requiring bilingual education in its public schools two years after the *Lau* decision (California State Department of Education, AB-1329, 1976; AB-507, 1982). This passage motivated an interest in equity for LEP students and provoked many influential policy makers throughout the nation to respond to the educational needs of the limited-English proficient. Schools not only had to provide a 'comprehensible education' for Chicano LEP children, but it was also intended that they receive their education in ethnically and linguistically mixed classroom settings. Unfortunately, as we shall see next, this was not to be the case in many instances.

Bilingual Education and Linguistic Segregation

In the mid-1970s, researchers and policy makers began to examine the legal ramifications of policies stemming from the joint application of the Supreme Court's ruling in the *Lau* and *Brown* decisions. Almost immediately, some researchers pointed to a potential 'conflict' between bilingual education (although not mandated by *Lau*) and school desegregation (Cardenas, 1975; Carter and Segura, 1979). By the late 1970s, friction between bilingual education and desegregation began to attract more attention. Although educators were beginning to recognize that bilingual education and desegregation were both essential elements in the schooling process promoting educational equality for Chicano students, the issue was much more complicated than most had initially realized. For example, Zerkel (1977) argued that bilingual education and desegregation had different, if not opposite, meanings. Desegregation typically meant '... scattering Black students to provide instruction in "racially balanced" settings. Bilingual education, on the other hand, has usually meant the clustering of Spanish-speaking students so they could receive instruction through their native language' (p. 181). Even if bilingual education and desegregation were not completely conflicting remedies, Zerkel argued, '... they were not fully compatible' (p. 181). He further asserted that bilingual education and desegregation were at conflict because the two mandates competed with each other in school systems with limited resources.

Educators as well as the layperson were copious about the desegregation process. Mixing ethnic minority students, in order to reach racial/ethnic balance in schools, was not difficult to conceptualize. Integrating Chicano LEP students with their English-speaking counterparts, however, was more complex. For many policy makers responsible for school desegregation, it appeared that the language issue only complicated the process. One year after the landmark *Lau* case, Cardenas (1975) began to write about school systems throughout the Southwest that were beginning to pit the educational needs of Chicano LEP children (bilingual education of native language instruction programs) against the desegregation process. He found many Chicano LEP children to be in '... either segregated bilingual education or integration without bilingual education ...' (p. 20). It was not long before many educators throughout the nation took advantage of the 'either/or situation'. Many recalcitrant school systems circumvented the implementation of bilingual education programs by scattering LEP children throughout their districts; others used bilingual education as an opportunity to segregate Chicano LEP children, thus separating them from White children (Cardenas, 1975; Carter, 1970).

By the early 1980s, desegregation and bilingual education increasingly received more attention. Although some desegregation experts were impartial about bilingual education in general, astute researchers pointed out that successful plans should '... include in the desegregation plan provisions that preserve existing bilingual programs' (Stephan and Feagin, 1980, p. 323). By 1983, bilingual education and desegregation became a serious enough problem that the California State Department of Education (1983) sponsored the Desegregation and Bilingual Education Conference to address the issue. Speakers attended from the US Department of Education, the Office for Civil Rights, and the California State Department of Education; scholars, legal experts, and policy makers from various school districts throughout the state also attended. During the conference, participants seriously discussed issues and concerns over the friction between bilingual education and desegregation. Researchers, policy makers, and practitioners concurred that '... integration and bilingual education, [were] in effect, looking at two different but valid definitions of equality' (California State Department of Education, 1983, p. 7). Most presenters were optimistic that '... integrated education and bilingual education [were] partners in the social enterprise' (p. 15). Most everyone concluded that schools could provide quality education to the limited–English proficient in integrated classroom settings. Bilingual education and desegregation were thus perceived as two harmonious forces working together for the LEP student in California.

Some educators were optimistic that bilingual education and desegregation could work without being a risk. Most were cognizant that bilingual education should not be used as an excuse to linguistically segregate LEP children. At the same time, the desegregation process was not intended to dismantle bilingual programs. In reality, most school systems overlooked (or neglected) the needs of the limited-English proficient in the desegregation process (Arias and Bray, 1983). For example, many desegregation plans threatened bilingual education programs because they broke up racially/ethnically segregated schools and assigned students throughout school districts without considering their language needs. In districts where bilingual programs were already operative, there was a concern that desegregation planners would dismantle them. On this issue Roos (1978) argued:

> If all children in need of bilingual education programs were dispersed without consideration of that [language] need, it is unlikely in most communities that there would be sufficient numbers of children in any school or area to justify separate classes for comprehensive bilingual-bicultural instruction. (p. 135)

Cognizant that bilingual education could not be used as a method to justify language segregation, it was also argued that it was absolutely necessary to ensure that adequate numbers of LEP students be grouped together so these programs could be established (Roos, 1978).

In the late 1970s, Lau Centers were established throughout the nation with the mission to technically assist school systems, providing more equitable opportunities for LEP children (Roos, 1978). One of the objectives of Lau centers was to convince policy makers to think about the importance of language integration in bilingual classrooms. The controversial Boston case was one example in the early 1980s where bilingual education and desegregation were simultaneously analyzed (Roos). Legal experts argued that Boston's desegregation plan had: (a) ordered a specific number of LEP students to specific schools in order to attain linguistic integration in classrooms and (b) made certain that the proper delivery of curriculum and instruction in certain classrooms was provided. Roos stated:

> The court resolved the problem by initially concluding that three consecutive bilingual classes were the minimum necessary for an effective program of bilingual instruction, which would mean an enrollment of sixty LESA [limited-English speaking ability] students — twenty students for each grade level. Then the court determined how large the minority population in each school should be. (p. 136)

The Boston school system in its reconciliatory negotiations with the courts demonstrated how a large inner-city school system was able to assign LEP students to certain schools in order to ensure that bilingual programs were implemented in integrated classroom settings. Although not always carried out in practice, the court's motive was not only to assign students to schools according to race/ethnicity but that their language backgrounds were considered as well. In Boston as well as other school systems across the nation, it appeared that some educators and legal experts ultimately wanted to prevent resegregation — that is, language segregation within desegregated schools. On paper many schools appeared to be racially balanced, but beneath the facade of many 'desegregated schools' there was an increasing trend that many LEP children would be linguistically segregated.

Over the last few years, some social scientists have unfairly blamed the segregation of Chicano LEP children on bilingual education. Adversaries of bilingual education argue that '... for the sake of bilingual education, some thirty-five years after *Brown v. Board of Education*, we have resegregated the classroom along ethnic and linguistic lines' (Bikales, 1989). Evidence shows that Chicano LEP children are clearly experiencing an increasing segregation trend in public schools. We contend, however, that this cannot be attributed to bilingual education. A study conducted by Baratz (1985) found that in spite of the increasing numbers of segregated schools, '... 68 per cent of eighth-grade and 82 per cent of eleventh-grade language minority students received neither bilingual or English-as-a-second language instruction' (cited in Valdivieso, 1986, p. 191). To argue that bilingual education is the culprit for language segregation is inaccurate because evidence suggests that a substantial proportion of LEP students who are eligible are not (and have not been) enrolled in bilingual classroom settings. For example, Olsen (1988) found that 75 per cent of LEP students in California public schools received little, if any, instructional support in their native language. To blame bilingual education as the cause for language segregation only distorts a more complicated issue. That is, how does one go about meeting the challenge of linguistically integrating classrooms in a desegregated school setting?

In conclusion, most Chicano LEP students are segregated whether they are placed in bilingual or non-bilingual classes. But the linguistic segregation of Chicano LEP students in desegregated schools is becoming a new form of resegregation. One can argue that segregation based on language is just as harmful as segregation based on race or ethnicity. Unless language segregation in desegregated schools is taken more seriously, such resegregation is likely to intensify in the 1990s and beyond. The current and projected numbers of language minority students has brought forth an enormous amount of attention to Chicano, other Latino, and Asian students in our nation's public schools. For example, California's overall public school LEP enrollment more than doubled from 6.8 per cent in 1976 to 14.1 per cent in 1988–89 (California State Department of Education, CBEDS, 1976–1989). In Texas, LEP enrollments grew tenfold, from 0.9 per cent in 1982 to 9.0 in 1988 (Texas Education Agency, 1982–1988). These percentages, however, are but state averages and they do not reflect an accurate picture of the impact LEP children have at the local level. For example, in the 1988–89 academic year the Los Angeles Unified School District had a 31.0 per cent LEP enrollment; San Francisco Unified School District was at 28.7 per cent; San Diego Unified School District, 16.3 per cent; Denver Public Schools, 16.9 per cent; Houston Independent School District, 15.5 per cent; Albuquerque Unified School District, 42.6 per cent; and the Chicago Public School, 8.9 per cent (LAUSD; SFUSD; SDUSD; DPS; HISD; AUSD; and CPS District Surveys, 1988–89).

The percentage of LEP students at the national level are projected to increase at dramatic rates over the next three decades. Pallas, Natriello, and McDill (1988) estimated that there were slightly under 2 million LEP children in the United States in 1982. The number of LEP children is expected to triple, reaching 6 million by the year 2020. Pallas *et al.* underscore that more than two-thirds of the LEP population is located in three states, California, Texas, and New York. With respect to the Chicano student population, California and Texas combined contain a majority of the nation's LEP students (these two states have 70 per cent of the total national Chicano student population; see Valencia, chapter 1, this volume).

In sum, given the growing number of Chicano LEP students it is perplexing why little has been written about the issues of linguistic segregation in desegregated schools. For example, *A Nation at Risk* (National Commission on Excellence in Education, 1983) only briefly mentioned language minorities, and then only in terms of demographic trends, completely ignoring their unequivocal and protracted educational problems. National reports and reforms focusing on the improvement of education for the Chicano LEP student have not received much attention. There are, however, some educators who are voicing their concerns about the general linguistic isolation of Chicano LEP students. In addition, these educators are raising serious questions about an exacerbating factor — the small number of properly trained bilingual teachers to provide an appropriate education to Chicano LEP students in desegregated schools. We now turn to this issue.

The Bilingual Teacher Shortage and its Impact on Resegregation

Valencia and Aburto (in press), as well as Orum (1986), report that bilingual education has the largest percentage of teacher shortage of any field in education. The limited and dwindling supply of certified bilingual teachers is so severe that the situation has placed increased pressure on many school systems. Because some desegregated school systems are required to meet both *Brown* and *Lau* mandates, policy makers, school principals, and teachers are pedagogically torn between meeting the needs of Chicano LEP children in segregated bilingual classroom settings or ethnically mixing these students without providing the native langue instruction in mainstream classrooms. As such, bilingual education and desegregation have reached a numerical 'catch 22' in some large inner-city public school systems. For example, Donato and Garcia (in press) reported LEP enrollment increases in California desegregated school systems have been so dramatic that many Latino and Asian children are either (a) linguistically segregated in bilingual classrooms where many of them are receiving the appropriate curriculum and instruction, or (b) they are enrolled in mainstream classes, but the instruction is often incomprehensible to the student.

Given the shortage of certified bilingual teachers many Latino LEP students are clustered together in classrooms where the priority is to serve as many of them as possible in their native language. There is no doubt that these students experience very little contact with their English-speaking peers. But in those desegregated schools where linguistic/ethnic classroom integration is a priority, a large number of Latino LEP students assigned to mainstream classes do not receive an education that is comprehensible to them — thus violating the whole essence of the *Lau* decision.

The actual need for bilingual teachers is difficult to determine. Evidence suggests that the number of bilingual teachers needed throughout the nation depends largely on specific criteria used to identify LEP students. That is, the criteria used to identify LEP students varies by state (and by school systems within each state). Regardless of the method used, the need for more bilingual teachers is growing steadily. The number of bilingual teachers needed at the national level has grown from 120,000 in 1976 to a projection of 170,000 in the year 2000. This projection includes teachers of all languages, although Spanish-speakers comprise the highest percentage (72 per cent). The severity of the problem becomes clearer when these needs are broken down by state. California, for example, projected that its public schools would need another 12,000 bilingual teachers in 1990 and almost 17,000 more by the year 2000. Early projections, however, significantly underestimated the need according to a recent survey conducted by the state. The California State Department of Education (1987–88) now estimates that 23,000 bilingual teachers will be needed in 1990 and 29,000 by the year 2000. The state had severely underestimated its needs by approximately 11,000 teachers for 1990 and 12,000 for the year 2000. In Texas, the supply of bilingual teachers is similarly dismal and the demand is enormous. The 1980s witnessed a moderate growth (approximately 9,000) in the number of bilingual teachers; however, during the late 1980s through the early 1990s, that growth (an increase of roughly 12,000 teachers) will not be enough to compensate for the increasing number of LEP students (Macias, 1989).

Throughout the Southwest, many stubborn school systems are unwilling to adhere to bilingual education implementation/compliance. Some school systems do not report the precise number of LEP students. By underreporting the number of LEP students, the number of teachers needed is dramatically underestimated. The increasing number of LEP students and the small pool of qualified bilingual teachers cannot satisfy most school district needs. As a result, many districts have moved in the direction of developing their own alternative certification plans in order to meet their bilingual teacher shortages. Large school districts in Texas such as Dallas, Houston, and many school systems in the Rio Grande area are now training and certifying their own bilingual teachers. District alternative certification plans will be somewhat helpful in meeting the demand for bilingual teachers, but the final results are not yet available. In theory, if more bilingual teachers were available, integration would be more manageable (Olsen, 1988).

Resolution of the conflicts brought on by the *Brown* and *Lau* decisions has not received much attention in recent educational history. Although the issue has been raised by a small number of scholars over the past decade and a half, few answers are forthcoming. Furthermore, the influence of a rapidly growing number of Chicano LEP students in our public schools has been ignored to a large extent. Indeed, the new form of resegregation (language segregation in desegregated schools) will inevitably gain more attention as LEP students continue to increase. The growing number of Chicano LEP students and continuing shortage of bilingual teachers will intensify the pressure on policy makers as concerned parents, interest groups, and teachers press for immediate solutions. Depending on the philosophical positions of school systems, policy makers may choose bilingual education over integration or integration over bilingual education. In our judgment, Chicano LEP students should not be pawns in this contentious discourse. It is imperative that they receive their native language instruction in linguistically/ethnically integrated classrooms.

School systems functioning under voluntary or court-ordered desegregation, however, have had more experience with this issue posed by *Brown* and *Lau*. The growing numbers and the lack of coordination within individual school systems make it almost impossible to integrate the limited-English proficient. It is common throughout the nation that the physical mixing of students from different racially and ethnically diverse backgrounds continues to be the primary goal. We have no quarrel with this objective, but in the final analysis the language needs of most Chicano LEP students often take a back seat in the desegregation process.

If the number of certified bilingual teachers does not increase, Chicano LEP students in desegregated settings will either be segregated in bilingual classes or they will be ethnically/linguistically mixed without the proper native language instruction. What may ultimately happen — given the growing number of Chicano LEP students and the limited supply of bilingual teachers — is that policy makers will have a more difficult time meeting the goals of both *Lau* and *Brown*, thus making it more difficult to accommodate the curricular and pedagogical needs of Chicano LEP children in the truest sense of integrated educational experiences. Granted, providing an integrated bilingual educational environment for Chicano LEP students will be extremely challenging for educators in the 1990s and beyond. Yet, we are optimistic that appropriate reform can be achieved.

Academic Resegregation

Another form of resegregation in desegregated schools is referred to as 'academic' or 'intellectual' resegregation. This type of resegregation '... generally takes place when schools that have been racially desegregated go to a system of academic tracking or ability grouping' (Hughes, Gordon, and Hillman, 1980, p. 14) It is widely acknowledged that ethnic minority students, as a whole, achieve at lower levels than their White peers. Thus, under circumstances when minority and White students attend the desegregated setting, there is likely to be a stratified and hierarchical structure in the delivery of instruction. On the general issue of tracking, Brophy and Good (1974) note:

> The effects of student achievement differences on teachers are magnified when the school uses a tracking system ... students in the high tracks are likely to be from high SES homes, which usually means preferential treatment in the teacher assignments and resources allocations made by school administrators ... the tracking systems insures that the highest achieving children are likely to get the best education that the school system has to offer, while the low achievers are likely to get the worst. Over time this factor alone is liable to increase the differences between the two groups of children. (p. 85)

The contention of Brophy and Good (1974) and related empirical literature (e.g., Oakes, 1985; Rist, 1970; US Commission on Civil Rights, 1974) raise critical issues about the practices of homogeneous groups and resultant curriculum differentiation in shaping the denial of equal educational opportunity for minority students. There is a fairly strong consensus in the available scientific literature that ability grouping at the elementary level and tracking at the secondary level have adverse psychological and cognitive effects on students placed in 'low-achieving' groups. For example, Oakes in her study of tracking, reports that students in low tracks typically were denied access to 'high status' knowledge — i.e., the knowledge that is a prerequisite for college admissions and academic success.

Aside from the broad issue of ability grouping, and tracking, is there evidence that Chicano students experience academic resegregation in desegregated schools? Direct evidence is difficult to come by. There is some research, however, that provides indirect confirmation that academic resegregation occurs. For example, Valencia (1984) examined potential curriculum differentiation in a Phoenix high school that was likely to undergo considerable ethnic mixing in light of a school closure court case. The anticipated enrollment of Central High School — a 90 per cent White, high-achieving, high SES background school — was to increase in size by 57 per cent in the 1982–83 school year (a jump from 2,044 to 3,200 students). This dramatic 1,000 plus increase in enrollment would be predominantly Chicano and Black students from two high schools that were being proposed for closure (Phoenix Union, 94 per cent minority; East, 56 per cent minority).

In the Phoenix case, minority plaintiffs from the schools targeted for closure sued in order to keep their schools open. Valencia (1984) — an expert witness for the plaintiffs — predicted that academic resegregation would occur at Central High School, the host school. This hypothesis was given some credence based on Valencia's analysis of 1982–83 resegregation statistics in which preregistration course-by-course enrollments were listed by ethnicity. In court, Valencia testified that because of the very sharp differences in academic performance between the high-achieving Central High White students and the incoming, low-achieving Chicano and Black students, there would be serious academic resegregation at Central High. To provide some support for this claim of resegregation along lines of achievement, Valencia did a comprehensive analysis of the preregistration data and prepared exhibits for the court. His discussion of the resegregation findings as presented in trial testimony are:

> In a series of exhibits, tabular data were presented for Anglo vs. minority enrollment across grade (9–12), subject area (English, mathematics, science, and social studies), designation (Alpha, Gamma, and Beta), and curriculum type (remedial, basic, less advanced, advanced/college preparatory, and special). The major result of this analysis revealed that minority students were overrepresented in remedial courses, showed parity in enrollment in basic courses and were underrepresented in advanced/college preparatory courses. For example, in mathematics courses, 228 students were preregistered for remedial courses. Of these, 61 (26.6 per cent) were Anglo and 167 (73.4 per cent) were minorities. This meant that minorities were overrepresented by 73.1 per cent, compared to their overall student body presence of 42.4 per cent. For the 939 students enrolled in basic mathematics courses, 421 (44.8 per cent) were Anglo, and 518 (55.2 per cent) were minority, indicating a minority overrepresentation of 30.2 per cent. Finally, regarding the 1,047 students enrolled in advanced/college preparatory courses, 748 (71.4 per cent) were Anglo, while 299 (28.6 per cent) were minority, a minority underrepresentation of 67.5 per cent. This similar pattern was also observed for courses in English, science, and social studies. Therefore, in contrast to the defendants' claim that tracking or ability grouping by ethnicity would not be practiced at Central, it appeared that in fact a form of ethnic resegregation by ability was extremely likely to occur. Clearly, this 'dual' educational system at Central raised serious issues of equal educational opportunity. (pp. 86–7)

Although the Phoenix situation was not a desegregation case, *per se*, it had all the ingredients of one (e.g., the typical one-way transfer of minorities to a White host school; mixing of low-achieving minorities with high-achieving White students). Thus, one can draw inferences from this case to understand more fully the potentialities of academic segregation within a desegregated setting. As Valencia (1984) concluded, there was sufficient predictive evidence that Central High School would undergo considerable curricular stratification between White and Chicano/Black students. Such a separation — as in other instances of academic resegregation — would likely result in the raising of barriers to equal educational opportunity for minority students. The bottom line, as Valencia underscores, is '. . . that resegregation on intellectual grounds is just as invidious as segregation on racial grounds' (p. 94). The lesson we learn from academic resegregation is that desegregation planners and educators must work with commitment and vigor to avoid homogeneous grouping. Integration, in its truest sense, has as a cornerstone the goal of equity, in which all students in a desegregated school should have equal access to knowledge.

Towards Integration

Although there have been scattered attempts in recent decades to desegregate our nation's schools, very little has improved in the reduction of racial/ethnic isolation. As Orfield *et al.* (1987) comment, much of the standoff in desegregation struggles is related to opposition at the national level:

> Three of the four Administrations since 1968 were openly hostile to urban desegregation orders and the Carter Administration took few initiatives in the field. There have been no important policy initiatives supporting desegregation from any branch of government since 1971. (p. 1)

As seen in the case of Black student segregation, Chicano and other Latinos have also suffered from the lack of national leadership regarding school desegregation. Orfield *et al.* (1987) analyzed segregation/desegregation statistics for Latino students in the Southwest. The target locations were fifteen metropolitan areas (e.g., Los Angeles, Phoenix, Denver) with enrollments over 50,000 students and which contained more than 10 per cent Latino students. It was found (with some exceptions) that 'there was little evidence of any desegregation plans in the West powerful enough to substantially increase Hispanic integration' (p. 30).[4] That is, Orfield *et al.*, contend that none of the metropolitan areas (e.g., Los Angeles) experiencing increased Chicano school segregation had in effect desegregation plans. True, the intensification of Chicano segregation in the Southwest is partially due to a groundswell of immigration patterns and the very high Latino birthrate. Yet, little evidence was found of voluntary desegregation or mandatory, court-ordered desegregation plans.[5] In short, the segregation of Chicano students is easy to summarize '... it is clear that there is a very strong tendency in American society today for an increasing isolation of Hispanic children and there have been no policies that have been able to reverse that tendency' (p. 28).

In this closing section of the present chapter, we attempt to fill this gap by discussing a number of research/policy suggestions that perhaps can serve as starting points to help reverse the intensification of Chicano school segregation and to help promote integration. We offer discussions on the following ideas: (a) community case studies of historical segregation, (b) residential integration, (c) busing, (d) two-way bilingual education (e) multicultural education in teacher education programs, (f) proactive technical assistance in desegregation planning, and (g) a conceptualization of school integration.

Community Case Studies of Historical Segregation

To understand the origins and persistence of school segregation of Chicano students, an historical community case study approach can provide the methodological base to explore this phenomenon (Alvarez, 1988; Menchaca and Valencia,

1990). In particular, case studies may be useful in providing the background for the litigation of school segregation cases. In light of the very limited amount of current Chicano and other Latino-initiated desegregation litigation (see Orfield *et al.*, 1987), it is likely that such lawsuits may be forthcoming in the 1990s and beyond as Chicano segregation further increases. A bonanza in these cases would be testimony, for example, on the roots of *de jure* segregation at the particular school district level.

An approach to community case studies of historical segregation includes: a collection of oral histories, analysis of residential patterns, analysis of the dates and construction of schools, and a review of available school records. Oral histories can provide data indicating if people attended segregated schools. Studying residential patterns will suggest whether the barrioization of the Mexican community was voluntary or involuntary, or both. Collection of school records will provide a documented history of the school board's intentional or unintentional plans in overall school district development, and can also be used to verify or discredit the oral histories. And, most important of all, an analysis of the dates and location of the construction of schools can possibly provide data to discern if the 'Mexican' schools were constructed for the specific purpose of segregating Chicano students.

In sum, many research queries with resultant policy implications might arise from community case studies. For example, could the 'Mexican' schools have been located in zones where both Mexican and Anglo students may have attended, rather than constructing the Mexican schools in the interior of the barrios or the Anglo school in the Anglo residential zones? And, did the construction of new schools follow a historical pattern indicating that the size of the student population did not necessitate the construction of new 'Mexican' or 'White' schools? Was the Chicano community included in the decision-making process in the construction and location of schools? The answers to these and related questions may potentially advance our understanding of the history of segregation in Chicano communities, particularly in litigation involving desegregation.

Residential Integration

As we have discussed earlier, a contributing source of Chicano segregated schools has historically been attributed to residential segregation or ethnically isolated residential zones (Camarillo, 1984a; Montejano, 1987; Menchaca and Valencia, 1990). We agree with Gottlieb (1983) that '... school and housing segregation are so deeply intertwined that much greater attention needs to be given to the interrelationships ...' (p. 106). As Gottlieb argues, ideally the best solution for bringing an end to school segregation is to terminate housing segregation. Of course, this will not be an easy goal to obtain.

One approach to attack this problem is for policy makers to lobby assertively for residential integration. Although it will be difficult to integrate existing neighborhoods, it can be achieved through long-term urban and suburban planning. For example, in order to attract minority families, affordable housing (i.e., single-family homes) will need to be constructed near or in White middle-class neighborhoods.

Furthermore, in White neighborhoods that are ethnically isolated, but are located adjacent to Chicano neighborhoods, the construction of new schools in the border zones might lead to ethnic mixing in the local schools. That is, when a school is constructed in the border zone of two ethnically isolated neighborhoods, an ethnically mixed school community would be formed. Although the neighborhoods would not be integrated, the students of the ethnically isolated neighborhoods would attend the same school and this may lead to the formation of interethnic friendships. Possibly these friendships may encourage the students to cross the residential boundaries and this may lead to ethnic mixing on a social basis. Although this does not lead to residential integration, it at least contributes to the formation of interethnic community bonds.

In conclusion, we strongly support efforts to achieve residential integration. Given the sharp increase in the Chicano school-age population and the growing desire for many of these families to buy homes, segregated municipalities have grand opportunities to realize residential integration. As Gottlieb (1983) notes, for those cities who remain silent on this issue, they reinforce their reputations as being closed communities.

Busing

Since the landmark *Swann v. Charlotte-Mecklenburg* (1971) case, in which busing was upheld as an acceptable means for desegregating schools, the use of busing for such purposes has created enormous controversy (Coles, 1974; Mills, 1973, 1979; Pettigrew, 1975). Criticisms, typically from White parents, have ranged from charges that busing is dangerous to complaints that bus rides are much too long. Pettigrew contends that such opposition to busing reached such virulent levels in the 1970s that a national mania occurred.

There are an array of facts that make school busing for desegregation purposes a perplexing target (Pettigrew, 1975). First, busing as a perfunctory and major means of transporting students to schools was legally authorized throughout the nation in 1919. Millions of students travelling billions of miles have traditionally been bused to their respective schools each year. In contrast, busing for purposes of desegregation constitutes a miniscule percentage of students. Thus, the issue is not busing, *per se*. Rather, using buses for integration purposes has not been an 'acceptable' reason. In short, widespread busing for regular transportation of students to school is fine, but busing to achieve desegregation is typically deemed unacceptable. As a White mother from Richmond, Virginia candidly revealed, 'It's not the distance.... It's the niggers' (Pettigrew, 1975, p. 232). A second myth of school busing for desegregation purposes is that busing is dangerous with respect to potential accidents. Contrary to this belief, busing by far is one of the safest modes of transportation. School buses — compared to regular buses, automobiles, and even walking to school — are clearly safer (Pettigrew).

In sum, we suggest that as our society enters the 1990s, the desegregation of Chicano students could be realized through the use of busing. We do acknowledge that any mention of busing for desegregation purposes is likely to be met with fierce opposition — from some White parents, and to a lesser degree, some Chicano parents. Yet, such opposition needs to be challenged with logic and goodwill. There is no doubt that busing is the most efficient means of achieving desegregation. If busing is to be promoted for the reduction of Chicano and White student isolation, we contend that such plans incorporate certain principles. For example, Chicano students should not be forced to carry the exclusive burden of busing (i.e., one-way busing to White host schools). White students need to share in the adjustment problems associated with desegregation, including transportation. Second, the time and distances White and Chicano students travel to their host schools should not be excessive.

Taking all matters together, it is not surprising that resistance to busing for desegregation ends is filled with subtleties of racist overtones. After all, as we have discussed earlier, connections between racism and the history of Chicano segregation are well documented. As in the past, the present racial motives to keep Chicano and White students from attending school together are unacceptable. If opposition to busing continues (as it clearly is), our nation is very likely to see Pettigrew's (1975) foreboding prediction materialize: '. . . a future historian is likely to conclude that "busing" became in our time the polite, culturally sanctioned way to oppose the racial desegregation of the public schools' (p. 232).

Two-way Bilingual Education

The growing number of language minority students and the limited supply of certified bilingual education teachers will inevitably exacerbate language segregation in our nation's public schools. Ovando and Collier (1985) maintain, however, that 'two-way bilingual education' may be the only way to reduce the language segregation in desegregated schools. Two-way bilingual education is a model in which students of two different language backgrounds (i.e., Spanish- and English-speakers) are brought together in a bilingual class setting in order for both groups to become truly 'bilingual'. For example, the goal of a two-way bilingual education requires that English-speakers learn Spanish and Spanish-speakers learn English. But more important, '. . . two-way bilingual education can be seen as an effective method of teaching a second language to English-dominant students in the United States as well as providing an integrated class for language-minority students' (Ovando and Collier, 1985, pp. 40–1).

Two-way bilingual education appears to be the only model that places and sensitizes English-speakers in a second language learning environment; it also stresses linguistic integration in the classroom. There is no question that implementing two-way bilingual education programs will be difficult because of the continued resistance to bilingual education in general. The most challenging facet of two-way bilingual programs will be to convince English-speaking parents about the value of their children learning a second language. Related to the politics and academic achievement in two-way bilingual programs, Crawford (1989) asks: 'Could language-majority and language-minority children, learning side by side as assisting each other, become fluent bilinguals while making good progress in other subjects?' (p. 165). Crawford contends that if public schools follow the criteria for effective two-way bilingual education programs, than it can be accomplished. We propose that once English-speaking parents recognize the life-long value of bilingualism for their children, there will be more of a need to train additional bilingual teachers in the profession. Thus, both Chicano LEP and majority language students will benefit. In the final analysis, language integration as proposed in the two-way bilingual model should become more manageable.

Multicultural Education in Teacher Education

During the late 1960s and early 1970s, ethnic minorities became extremely vocal in public school politics. Minority groups contended that public schools were ethnocentric, monocultural, and undemocratic. They demanded 'multicultural education' at all levels in the schooling process. That is, they wanted educators to become more aware and sensitive to the cultural, linguistic, and learning style differences of minority students (Pai, 1990). A major step in the development of multicultural education in the United States was the 1972 publication by the American Association of Colleges for Teacher Education (AACTE) entitled: *No One Model American.* Cognizant that colleges and universities had a major responsibility in teacher training programs, AACTE (1972) stated that education for cultural pluralism included four parts:

> . . . (1) the teaching of values which support cultural diversity and individual uniqueness; (2) the encouragement of the qualitative expansion of existing ethnic cultures and their incorporation into the mainstream of American socio-economic and political life; (3) the support of explorations in alternative and emerging life styles; and (4) the encouragement of multiculturalism, multilingualism, and multidialectism. (Pai, 1990, p. 100)

Although AACTE recommended that multicultural education be a major part in teacher training programs, Pai (1990) noted that many recalcitrant colleges and universities felt that '. . . multicultural education components were unnecessary in their programs because their institutions either did not have minority students or were located in ethnically homogeneous areas' (p. 101). Despite the rapidly changing 'color' of our schools, colleges and universities continue to disregard the need for multicultural experiences in teacher training programs. Valencia and Aburto (in press) recently noted that only a very small number of prospective teachers take a multicultural education class. Moreover, most prospective teachers are unqualified to teach in ethnically mixed urban settings. Valencia and Aburto note that 'Perhaps the limited preservice training in multicultural education received by prospective teachers explains, in part, teacher prejudice against minority groups' (p. 16). Educators continue to view multicultural education as a separate component in the teacher training process and, unfortunately, misconstrue the need for prospective teachers to gain a multicultural understanding.

Looking at both the changing ethnic demography in our public schools and teacher education training programs from a desegregation context, we recommend that colleges and universities emphasize a true multicultural education curriculum that is incorporated throughout its programs. Prospective classroom teachers need to be prepared for the real world. That is, assuming that school desegregation will occur, future teachers need to be trained to teach in a multicultural setting. Furthermore, they should be given an opportunity to better understand their own cultural identity so that they can learn how their culture influences their perceptions of other ethnic groups. More important, they should also be able to recognize and accept that they have prejudices that might affect them in the desegregated classroom. By recognizing their own biases, preservice teachers can perhaps develop strategies to help them work more effectively in multicultural classroom settings in order to better understand Chicano students in desegregated classrooms and schools.

Proactive Technical Assistance in Desegregation Planning

Our intent here is to offer — in very general terms — a brief policy discussion of the need for desegregation planners to provide technical assistance to school districts that are faced with the challenge of desegregating high-density Chicano and White schools. By 'proactive' assistance, we mean guidance and advice from desegregation experts that are *actively sought* by school officials — either resultant of a voluntary desegregation plan, or a mandatory, court-ordered desegregation plan.

We are well aware of the literature indicating that voluntary desegregation plans sometimes do not work and, in general, are only partially successful in the reduction of racial/ethnic isolation (e.g., Hawley and Smylie, 1988; Orfield, 1978, 1988; Rossell and Hawley, 1983). Perhaps in such plans, the quality and quantity of voluntary planning could have been improved by a closer relationship of all agents involved. Of course, this improvement is based on the premise that all participants — which ideally would be minority and White parents, school officials, expert planners, and other community members — work in good faith and toward a common, shared and equitable vision.

How proactive technical assistance in desegregation of predominantly Chicano and White schools would occur is open for discussion. The federal government has allocated funds for Desegregation Assistance Centers (DACs) throughout the US in order to provide free assistance to school systems for the last few years. These centers have been very instrumental in providing technical assistance to many school systems in the desegregation process. Like many government agencies, however, they are underfunded and understaffed. For example, California currently has over 100 school systems under voluntary desegregation and about six large inner-city school systems under court-ordered desegregation. DACs are not capable of servicing all those school systems attempting to desegregate their schools. Should the federal government fund more DACs? If more money becomes available to fund more DACs, (given the fact that a DAC can only offer its services upon school district request) should they continue to operate the same way or should they become more assertive in shaping desegregation policy at the local level? These and other suggestions about desegregation assistance need to be addressed by school officials and policy makers so the desegregation of Chicano schools can be done more quickly and effectively.

Conceptualization of Integration

A common misconception is that school desegregation is synonymous with school integration. Frequently, one will see (particularly in the media and political circles) the two terms used interchangeably. On the contrary, although desegregation and integration are related, they have very different meanings. Desegregation is best looked at as a mechanical process involving the physical mixing of students of different racial/ethnic backgrounds in a particular school setting that was formerly segregated. A more formal definition of desegregation is 'the reassignment of students and staff by race or ethnic identity so that the racial identifiability of the individual school and classes within the school is removed' (Hughes *et al.*, 1980, p. 168). Such desegregation is the law of the land.

The concept of integration is related to the notion of desegregation in the sense that in order for the former to occur, one must first have the physical mixing of students of racially/ethnically diverse backgrounds. While desegregation involves a mandatory, court-ordered (or in some cases voluntary) mechanical process of a predetermined numerical mix of racially/ethnically diverse students, integration is a social process involving mutual acceptance. Thus, integration cannot be mandated. That is, people cannot be legally forced to care for and accept one another on an equal basis. As such, the notion of integration involves 'affirmative efforts that facilitate the elimination of racial and ethnic indifference and at the same time provide multiethnic atmosphere and mechanisms to encourage mutual respect, understanding, and acceptance' (Hughes *et al.*, 1980, p. 169).

Suffice to say that in light of the above conceptualization of school integration, the goal of achieving integration of Chicano and White (and perhaps other minority) students in desegregated schools is no easy task. On the broader research level, there is evidence that desegregation can and does work, but there are few indications of integration (Hughes *et al.*, 1980). It has become widely acknowledged that in order for integration to occur, there has to be a concerted effort by state and federal agencies, school officials, teachers, and the local community. As seen in other contexts of improving race/ethnic relations, concerned leaders and participants need to strive for attainable objectives and workable processes.

There is some evidence, however, that schools have been lax in working towards integration. Sagar and Schofield (1984; cited in Bennet, 1990) in a research study of how host schools respond to desegregation, identified four possible response patterns: (a) business–as–usual, (b) assimilation, (c) pluralistic coexistence, and (d) integrated pluralism. The business–as–usual response — as the terms implies — contains no proactive efforts by school officials. That is, the same curriculum, same standards, same teaching methods, and so on, that prevailed in the segregated setting continue under desegregation. The assimilationist response, as noted by Sagar and Schofield, is basically designed to make racial/ ethnic minority students more like White students. Under these circumstances, minority students who fail to assimilate become academic casualties — the dropout, the suspended student, and so forth. The third type of response — pluralistic coexistence — is based on separation in which 'students are allowed to maintain different styles and values, but within a school environment of separate turfs for different racial groups' (Bennett, 1990, p. 23). In short, the pluralistic coexistence response (as are the business–as–usual and assimilationist responses) results in resegregation.

The fourth and final response — integrated pluralism — is far different from the first three. Its major mark of distinction is that '... *integrated pluralism* actively seeks to avoid resegregation of students' (Bennett, 1990, p. 24). The host school attempts to achieve this by striving to attain the following:

[It] is pluralistic in the sense that it recognizes the diverse racial and ethnic groups in our society and does not denigrate them just because they deviate from the white middle class patterns of behavior. Integrated pluralism affirms the equal value of the school's various ethnic groups, encouraging their participation, not on majority-defined terms, but in an evolving system which reflects the contribution of all groups. However, integrated pluralism goes beyond mere support for the side-by-side coexistence of different group values and styles. It is integrationist in the sense that it affirms the educational value inherent in exposing all students to a diversity of perspectives and behavioral repertoires and the social value of structuring the school so that students from pre- viously isolated and even hostile groups can come to know each other under conditions conducive to the development of positive intergroup relations.... Integrated pluralism takes an activist stance in trying to foster interaction between different groups of students rather than accepting resegregation as either desirable or inevitable. (Sagar and Schofield, 1984, pp. 231–2)

In sum, how the host school responds to the process of desegregation is critical in determining whether or not all students receive a culturally pluralistic and equitable schooling experience. We urge host schools that are undergoing desegregation to become aware and avoid those institutional responses that are unacceptable and to strive for that goal which is acceptable — integrated plural- ism. By knowing the difference between desegregation and integration (and using that knowledge), school officials and desegregation planners — working closely with the community — can help provide the setting for improved racial/ ethnic relations as well as optimal academic development for Chicanos and other students.

But is this mere rhetoric, or can integration actually be realized? As Bennett (1990) underscores, there are at least three necessary conditions that underlie the practice of cultural (i.e., integrated) pluralism in the school. First, there are positive teacher expectations. Teachers in integrated schooling must have high and reasonable expectations for Chicano student success (also, see Valencia and Aburto, this volume). Second, in integrated schooling it is critical that there be a learning environment that supports and encourages positive interracial/ interethnic contact. Bennett notes that contact theorists are quite specific as to the nature of positive interaction (e.g., Chicanos and Whites share equal status; Chicanos and Whites be given opportunities for intergroup cooperation). Third, it is vital that Chicano and other students attending an integrated school be provided the opportunity to be exposed to a multicultural curriculum. What should such a curriculum contain and how might it be implemented? The vision of multicultural curriculum we find especially attractive is the one described by Bennett. She speaks of four core democratic values that underlie multicultural perspectives: '... (1) acceptance and appreciation of cultural diversity, (2) respect for human dignity and universal human rights, (3) responsibility to the world community, and (4) reverence for the earth' (p. 281). From these core values, Bennett notes that teachers can develop a number of multicultural curriculum goals (e.g., to combat racism; to build skills along lines of social action).

Conclusion

In closing, we wish to leave the reader with several summary points that capture the core of this chapter. First, as history informs us, it is abundantly clear that racism is a driving force behind school segregation and Chicano school failure. Therefore, if we are to desegregate and integrate Chicano students, it is critical that we confront overt and institutional racism in the larger society, in particular within the educational system. Desegregation and integration of our schools must be viewed as important stages in the long struggle to combat and dismantle racism in the nation. Although adults are often resistant to accepting and building a culturally diverse and equitable society, children and youth are considerably more open. If Chicano students and other students from ethnically diverse backgrounds are mixed in classrooms and involved in multicultural education, then interethnic communication can be enhanced and integrated pluralism is likely to be attained. Thus, school desegregation — as a first step — can be viewed as a tremendous potential leading to integration and to the promotion of and respect for cultural diversity.

Second, there is the issue of resegregation — especially among Chicano LEP students. Notwithstanding the significant advances made by Chicano parents in their desegregative legal battles, the reality is that Chicano students continue — to a large degree — to remain segregated within desegregated settings. This is a mounting concern that certainly requires the attention of school officials, researchers, and policy makers in the years ahead. We cannot forget the changing demography and the increasing number of LEP students in our public schools. Chicano LEP students must receive the native language instruction in 'linguistically integrated' settings. Anything less than this is unacceptable.

Third — and our final summary point — is concerned with the issue of pace. It has been over four decades since *Mendez* and over three decades since *Brown*. There has been a lot of deliberation, but very little speed in eliminating school segregation in our nation. As noted earlier, Chicano segregation is intensifying. Given the projection that over the next thirty years, the Chicano/Latino youth population will account for *nearly all* of the increase in the country's youth sector (see Valencia, chapter 1, this volume), it is sad to predict that the next generation of Chicano students will experience school segregation far more severely than the current generation. This issue alone should stir educators, politicians, and parents of the 1990s to quicken the pace of desegregating and integrating our schools. *Now* is the time for concerted action.

In this chapter, we have covered a number of issues and aspects concerning the segregation, desegregation, resegregation, and integration of Chicano students. Suffice it to say that the numerous concerns and suggestions discussed can — if seriously considered — provide researchers and policymakers of the 1990s with full agendas. There is no doubt in our minds that the ethnic isolation of Chicano pupils constitutes one of the major educational issues of the times. Hopefully, the issues covered in this chapter will spark a renewed interest among concerned individuals and agencies to push forward in pursuing Chicano school success.

Notes

1 In our discussion of historical segregation in this chapter we typically refer to Mexican-origin students as 'Mexican', as that was the term generally used in the earlier periods.
2 Orum (1986), however, does provide this qualifier about Black and Latino segregation differences:

> While the segregation of Black students declined between 1968 and 1980 in every region of the country except the Northeast, the segregation of Hispanic students increased nationwide. While Black students were more likely than Hispanic students to attend schools with minority enrollments of 90–100 per cent, Black enrollments in the nation's most segregated schools fell by 31.1 per cent between 1968 and 1980, while Hispanic attendance in those same schools rose during the same period by 5.7 per cent. (p. 19)

3 McCurdy's (1975) references are testimony given by former Oxnard Superintendents who testified in a desegregation trial in Oxnard in the mid-1970s.
4 An exception, for example, is Denver, Colorado, which is under a comprehensive desegregation order resultant from a 1973 Supreme Court decision (Orfield *et al.*, 1987).
5 One exception, however, is the San Jose, California, major urban case won by Chicano plaintiffs (Arias, 1987).

References

ACUNA, R. (1988) *Occupied America*, San Francisco, CA, Canfield Press.
ALBUQUERQUE UNIFIED SCHOOL DISTRICT (1988–89) *Racial/Ethnic Survey*, Albuquerque, NM, Office of Research and Development, Author.
ALVAREZ, R. (1986) 'The Lemon Grove incident: The nation's first successful desegregation court case', *Journal of San Diego History*, Spring, pp. 116–35.
ALVAREZ, R., JR. (1988) 'National politics and local responses: The nation's first successful desegregation court case', in H. TRUEBA and C. DELGADO-GAITAN (Eds) *School and Society: Learning Content Through Culture*, New York, Praeger, pp. 37–52.
ALVAREZ V. LEMON GROVE SCHOOL DISTRICT (1931) Superior court of the state of California, County of San Diego, Petition for Writ of Mandate No. 66625.
AMERICAN ASSOCIATION OF COLLEGES FOR TEACHER EDUCATION (1972) 'No one model American: A statement on multicultural education,' *The Journal of Teacher Education*, **24**, pp. 264–5.
ARIAS, B.M. (1987) *Bilingual Education and Desegregation in the San Jose Unified School District Elementary Schools*, a report submitted by the office of the compliance monitor.
ARIAS, B.M. and BRAY, J.L. (1983) *Equal Educational Opportunity and School Desegregation in Triethnic Districts* (Report submitted to NIE) LEC-83-14.
BENNETT, C.I. (1990) *Comprehensive Multicultural Education: Theory and Practice*, 2nd ed., Boston, MA, Allyn and Bacon.
BIKALES, G. (1989) 'Maximum feasible misunderstanding: Bilingual education in our schools', *IMPRIMIS*, **16**, October, pp. 1–6.
BLUM, J. (1978) *Pseudoscience and Mental Ability: The Origins and Fallacies of the IQ Controversy*, New York, Monthly Review Press.
BROPHY, J.E. and GOOD, T.L. (1974) *Teacher-Student Relationships: Causes and Consequences*, New York, Holt, Rinehart and Winston.
BROWN V. BOARD OF EDUCATION (1954) 347 US 483.

CADENA, G. (1987) 'Chicanos and the Catholic Church: Liberation Theology as a Form of Empowerment', unpublished doctoral dissertation, University of California, Riverside.

CALIFORNIA STATE CONSTITUTION OF 1849, Article 11, Section 1.

CALIFORNIA STATE DEPARTMENT OF EDUCATION (1976) Assembly Bill 1329.

CALIFORNIA STATE DEPARTMENT OF EDUCATION (1976 and 1988–89) CBEDS data collection.

CALIFORNIA STATE DEPARTMENT OF EDUCATION (1982) Assembly Bill 507.

CALIFORNIA STATE DEPARTMENT OF EDUCATION (1983) *Desegregation and Bilingual Education — Partners in Quality Education*, Sacramento, CA, Conference Proceedings, Author.

CALIFORNIA STATE DEPARTMENT OF EDUCATION, (1987–88) '*Estimate of bilingual teacher demand*' (Report No. 87-4C) State Summary, Sacramento, CA, Bilingual Office.

CAMARILLO, A. (1984a) *Chicanos in California: A History of Mexican Americans in California*, San Francisco, Boyd and Fraser.

CAMARILLO, A. (1984b) *Chicanos in a Changing Society*, Cambridge, MA, Harvard University Press.

CARDENAS, J. (1975) 'Bilingual education, desegregation and a third alternative', *Inequality in Education*, **14**, pp. 19–22.

CARTER, T. (1970) *Mexican Americans in Schools: A History of Educational Neglect*, New York, College Entrance Examination Board.

CARTER, T. and SEGURA, R. (1979) *Mexican Americans in Schools: A Decade of Change*, New York, College Entrance Examination Board.

CHICAGO PUBLIC SCHOOLS (1988–89) *Racial Ethnic Survey*, Chicago, The Bureau of Management Information, Author.

CISNEROS V. CORPUS CHRISTI INDEPENDENT SCHOOL DISTRICT (1970) 234 F. Supp. 599, S.D. Tex., appeal docket, No. 71-2397 (5th Cir., July 16, 1971).

COLES, R. (1974) *The Buses Roll*, New York, W.W. Norton.

COMAS, J. (1961) 'Racial myths', in UNITED NATIONS EDUCATIONAL, SCIENTIFIC AND CULTURAL ORGANIZATION (Eds) *Race and Science*, New York, Columbia University Press, pp. 13–35.

CRAIN, R. (1968) *The Politics of School Desegregation: Comparative Case Studies of Community Structure and Policy-making*, Chicago, IL, Aldine.

CRAWFORD, J. (1989) *Bilingual Education: History, Politics, Theory, and Practice*, Trenton, NJ, Crane.

DELGADO V. BASTROP INDEPENDENT SCHOOL DISTRICT (1948) No. 388 (W.D. Texas).

DEL RIO INDEPENDENT SCHOOL DISTRICT V. SALVATIERRA (1930) Tex. Civ. App., 4th Dt.

DEL RIO INDEPENDENT SCHOOL DISTRICT V. SALVATIERRA (1931) 33 S.W. 2d 790, Cert. denied, 284 US 580.

DENVER PUBLIC SCHOOLS (1988–89) *Racial/Ethnic Survey*, Denver, CO, Public Information and Services, Author.

DONATO, R. and GARCIA, H. (in press) 'Language Segregation in Desegregated Elementary Schools: A Question of Equity', manuscript submitted for publication.

EDWARDS, B.T. and WIRT, F.M. (1967) *School Desegregation in the North: The Challenge and the Experience*, San Francisco, CA, Chandler.

ESPINOSA, R. and OCHOA, A. (1986) 'Concentration of California Hispanic students in schools with low achievement: A research note', *American Journal of Education*, **95**, pp. 77–95.

FEAGIN, J. (1989) *Racial and Ethnic Relations*, 3rd ed., Englewood Cliffs, NJ, Prentice-Hall.

GAINES V. CANADA. (1938) 305 US 337.

GARCIA, M. (1979) 'Americanization and the Mexican immigrant, 1880–1930', *Canadian Ethnic Studies*, **6**, pp. 19–34.

GLAZER, N. and MOYNIHAN, D. (1963) *Beyond the Melting Pot: The Negroes, Puerto Ricans, and Irish of New York*, Cambridge, MA, Harvard University Press.

GONZALEZ, G.G. (1974) 'The System of Public Education and Its Function Within the Chicano Communities, 1910–1930', unpublished doctoral dissertation, University of California, Los Angeles.

GONZALEZ, G.G. (1985) 'Segregation of Mexican children in a southern California city: The legacy of expansion and the American Southwest', *The Western Historical Quarterly*, **16**, pp. 58–76.

GONZALEZ, G.G. (1990) *Chicano Education in the Era of Segregation*, Philadelphia, PA, The Balch Institute Press.

GOSSETT, T. (1953) 'The Idea of Anglo Superiority in American Thought, 1865–1915', unpublished doctoral dissertation, University of Minnesota.

GOSSETT, T. (1977) *Race: The History of an Idea in America*, Dallas, TX, SMU Press.

GOTTLIEB, H.N. (1983) 'The school effects of Chicago suburban housing segregation', *Integrated Education*, **21**, pp. 105–9.

GUNG LUM V. RICE (1927) 275 US 78.

HAWLEY, W. and SMYLIE, M.A. (1988) 'The contribution of school desegregation to academic achievement and racial integration', in P.A. KATZ and D.A. TAYLOR (Eds), *Eliminating Racism: Profiles in Controversies*, New York, Plenum, pp. 281–97.

HEIZER, R. and AMQUIST, A. (1971) *The Other Californians: Prejudice and Discrimination under Spain, Mexico, and the United States*, Berkeley, CA, University of California Press.

HENDRICK, I. (1977) *The Education of Non-Whites in California, 1848–1970*, San Francisco, CA, R & E Associates.

HOUSTON INDEPENDENT SCHOOL DISTRICT (1988–89) *Racial/Ethnic Survey*, Houston, TX, Research and Evaluation Department, Author.

HUGHES, L.W., GORDON, W.M. and HILLMAN, L.W. (1980) *Desegregating America's Schools*, New York, Longman.

HULL, E. (1985) *Without Justice for All: The Constitutional Rights of Aliens*, Westport, CT, Greenwood Press.

HYMAN, H.M. and WIECEK, W.M. (1982) *Equal Justice under Law: Constitutional Development, 1835–1875*, New York, Harper and Row.

JACKSON, A. (1986) 'Melville Herskovits and the search for Afro-American culture', in G. STOCKINGS (Ed.), *Malinowski, River, Benedict, and Others*, Madision, WI, University of Wisconsin Press, pp. 95–126.

JAEGER, C. (1987) *Minority and Low Income High Schools: Evidence of Educational Inequality in Metro Los Angeles* (Report No. 8), University of Chicago, Metropolitan Opportunity Project.

KANSAS, S. (1941) *US Immigration Exclusion and Deportation and Citizenship of the US of America*, New York, Mathew Bendercs.

KEYES V. SCHOOL DISTRICT NUMBER ONE (1975) 380 F. Supp. 673 (D. Colo. 1973), 531 F.2d 465 (10th Cir.).

KIRP, D. (1982) *Just Schools: The Idea of Racial Equality in American Education*, Berkeley, CA, University of California Press.

KONVITZ, M.R. (1946) *The Alien and the Asiatic in American Law*, New York, Cornell University Press.

LAU V. NICHOLS (1974) 414 US 563, 566.

LEIS, W. (1931) 'The Status of Education for Mexican Children in Four Border States', unpublished master's thesis, University of Southern California.

LOS ANGELES UNIFIED SCHOOL DISTRICT (1988–89) *Racial/Ethnic Survey*, Los Angeles, Research and Evaluation Department, Author.

MCCURDY, J. (1975) 'School board minutes play big role in Oxnard desegregation', *Los Angeles Times*, January 19.

MACIAS, R. (1989) *Bilingual Teacher Supply and Demand in the United States*, Los Angeles, University of Southern California Center for Multilingual and Multicultural Research.

MENCHACA, M. (1987) 'Chicano-Mexican Conflict and Cohesion in San Pablo, California', unpublished doctoral dissertation, Stanford University.

MENCHACA, M. (1989) 'Chicano-Mexican cultural assimilation and Anglo-Saxon cultural differences', *Hispanic Journal of Behavioral Sciences*, **11**, pp. 203–31.

MENCHACA, M. (1990) 'Chicano Panindianism: Appropriating a Mestizo Racial Identity', manuscript submitted for publication.

MENCHACA, M. and VALENCIA, R.R. (1990) 'Anglo-Saxon ideologies and their impact on the segregation of Mexican students in California, the 1920s–1930s', *Anthropology and Education Quarterly*, **21**, pp. 222–49.

MENDEZ V. WESTMINSTER (1947) 64 F. Supp. 544 (S.D. Cal 1946), Aff'd, 161 F. 2d 744 (9th Cir.).

MILLS, N. (Ed.) (1973) *The Great School Bus Controversy*, New York, Teachers College Press.

MILLS, N. (Ed.) (1979) *Busing USA*, New York, Teachers College Press.

MONTEJANO, D. (1987) *Anglos and Mexicans in the Making of Texas, 1836–1986*, Austin, TX, University of Texas Press.

NATIONAL COMMISSION ON EXCELLENCE IN EDUCATION (1983) *A Nation at Risk: The Imperatives for Educational Reform*, Washington, DC, US Government Printing Office.

NEWCOMBE, W. (1985) *The Indians of Texas*, Austin, TX, University of Texas Press.

NICHOLS, L.B. and BROWN, W.S. (1989) 'Recruiting minorities into the teaching profession: An educational imperative', *Educational Horizons*, Summer, pp. 145–8.

OAKES, J. (1985) *Keeping Track: How Schools Structure Inequality*, New Haven, CT, Yale University Press.

OLSEN, L. (1988) *Crossing the Schoolhouse Border: Immigrant Students and the California Public Schools*, Boston, MA, California Tomorrow.

ORFIELD, G. (1978) *Must We Bus? Segregated Schools and National Policy*, Washington, DC, Brookings Institution.

ORFIELD, G. (1988) 'The Growth and Concentration of Hispanic Enrollment and the Future of American Education', paper presented at the National Council of La Raza Conference, Albequerque, NM, July.

ORFIELD, G. (1988) 'School desegregation in the 1980s', *Equity and Choice*, **4**, pp. 25–8.

ORFIELD, G., MONTFORD, F. and GEORGE, R. (1987) *School Segregation in the 1980s: Trends in the States and Metropolitan Areas*, University of Chicago, National School Desegregation Project, report to the Joint Center for Political Studies.

ORUM, L.S. (1986) *The Education of Hispanics: Status and Implications*, Washington, DC, National Council of La Raza.

OVANDO, C. and COLLIER, V. (1985) *Bilingual and ESL Classrooms: Teaching in Multicultural Contexts*, New York, McGraw-Hill.

PADILLA, F. (1979) 'Early Chicano legal recognition: 1846–1897', *Journal of Popular Culture*, **13**, pp. 564–74.

PAI, Y. (1990) *Cultural Foundations of Education*, Columbus, OH, Merrill.

PALLAS, A.M., NATRIELLO, G. and McDILL, E.L. (1988) 'Who Falls Behind? Defining the "At Risk" Population — Current Dimensions and Future Trends', paper presented at the American Educational Research Association, New Orleans, LA, April.

PAREDES, A. (1978) 'The problem of identity in a changing culture: Popular conflict along the lower Rio Grande Border', in S. Ross (Ed.) *Views Across the Border: The United States and Mexico*, Albuquerque, NM, University of New Mexico Press, pp. 68–94.

PEOPLE V. DE LA GUERRA (1870) 40, Cal. 311 at 343.

PETTIGREW, T.F. (1975) 'The racial integration of the schools', in T.F. PETTIGREW (Ed.) *Racial Discrimination in the United States*, New York, Harper and Row, pp. 224–39.

PINKERTON, J. (1989) ' "The future is secure": Edgewood savors hard-fought victory', *Austin American Statesman*, October 3, pp. A1, A6.

PLESSY V. FERGUSON (1896) 163 US 551–552.

RANGEL, S.C. and ALCALA, C.M. (1972) 'Project report: De jure segregation of Chicanos in Texas schools', *Harvard Civil Rights-Civil Liberties Law Review*, **7**, pp. 307–91.

RIST, R. (1970) 'Student social class and teacher expectations: The self-fulfilling prophecy in ghetto education', *Harvard Educational Review*, **40**, pp. 411–51.

RIST, R.C. (1979) *Desegregated Schools: Appraisal of an American Experiment*, New York, Academic Press.

RODRIQUEZ V. TEXAS (1893) Circuit Court, 81F 333–355.

ROOS, P.D. (1978) 'Bilingual education: The Hispanic response to unequal educational opportunity', *Law and Contemporary Problems*, **42**, pp. 111–40.

ROSSEL, C.H. and HAWLEY, W.D. (Eds) (1983) *The Consequences of School Desegregation*, Philadelphia, PA, Temple University Press.

SAGAR, H.A. and SCHOFIELD, J.W. (1984) 'Integrating the desegregated school: Problems and possibilities', in D.E. BARTZ and M.L. MAEHR (Eds) *Advances in Motivation and Achievement: The Effects of School Desegregation on Motivation and Achievement*, **1**, Greenwich, CT, JAI Press, pp. 203–42.

SAN DIEGO UNIFIED SCHOOL DISTRICT (1988–89) *Racial Ethnic Survey*, San Diego, CA, Community Relations and Integration Services Division, Author.

SAN FRANCISCO UNIFIED SCHOOL DISTRICT (1988–89) *Racial/Ethnic Survey*, San Francisco, CA, Department of Planning, Research, and Information System, Author.

SAN MIGUEL, G. (1986) 'Status of the historiography of Chicano education: A preliminary analysis', *History of Education Quarterly*, **26**, pp. 523–36.

SAN MIGUEL, G. (1987) *Let Them All Take Heed: Mexican Americans and the Campaign for Educational Equality in Texas, 1910–1981*, Austin, TX, University of Texas Press.

SAN MIGUEL, G. (1987) 'The status of historical research on Chicano education', *Review of Educational Research*, **57**, pp. 467–80.

SOLOMONE, R. (1986) *Equal Education under Law*, New York, St. Martin's Press.

STEPHAN, W.G. and FEAGIN, J.R. (1980) *School Desegregation: Past, Present and Future*, New York, Plenum.

SURACE, S. (1982) 'Achievement discrimination and Mexican Americans', *Society for the Comparative Studies in Society and History*, **24**, pp. 315–39.

SWANN V. CHARLOTTE-MECKLENBURG BOARD OF EDUCATION (1971) 402 US 1.

TEXAS EDUCATION AGENCY (1988) *Special Programs: Planning and Implementation*, Austin, TX: Bilingual Education Department, Author.

US COMMISSION ON CIVIL RIGHTS (1971) *Mexican American Education Study, Report 1: Ethnic Isolation of Mexican Americans in the Public Schools of the Southwest*, Washington, DC, Government Printing Office.

US COMMISSION ON CIVIL RIGHTS (1972) *Mexican American Education Study, Report 3: The Excluded Student: Educational Practices Affecting Mexican Americans in the Southwest*, Washington, DC, Government Printing Office.

US COMMISSION ON CIVIL RIGHTS (1974) *Mexican American Education Study, Report 6: Toward Quality Education for Mexican Americans*, Washington, DC, Government Printing Office.

VALDIVIESO, R. (1986) 'Hispanics and schools: A new perspective', *Educational Horizons*, **64–65**, pp. 190–6.

VALENCIA, R.R. (1984) *Understanding School Closures: Discriminatory Impact on Chicano and Black Students*, (Policy Monograph Series, No. 1), Stanford, CA, Stanford University, Stanford Center for Chicano Research.

VALENCIA, R.R. and ABURTO, S. (in press) 'Competency testing and Latino student access to the teaching profession: An overview of issues', in J. DENEEN, G.D. KELLER, and R. MAGALLÁN (Eds) *Assessment and Access: Hispanics in Higher Education*, Albany, NY, State University of New York Press.

WEINBERG, M. (1977) *A Chance to Learn: The History of Race and Education in the United States*, Cambridge, MA, Cambridge University Press.

WELCH, F. and LIGHT, A. (1987) *New Evidence on School Desegregation*, Washington, DC, US Commission on Civil Rights (Clearing House Publication 92).

WILLIE, C.V. (1984) *School Desegregation Plans that Work*, Westport, CT, Greenwood Press.

WOLLENBERG, C. (1974) '*Mendez v. Westminster*: Race, nationality and segregation in California schools', *California Historical Society Quarterly*, **53**, pp. 317–22.

WOLLENBERG, C. (1978) *All Deliberate Speed: Segregation and Exclusion in California Schools, 1855–1975*, Berkeley, CA, University of California Press.

WYNER, N.B. (1989) 'Educating linguistic minorities: Public schools and the search for equity', *Educational Horizons*, Summer, pp. 172–6.

ZERKEL, P. (1977) 'Bilingual education and school desegregation: A case of uncoordinated remedies', *The Bilingual Review*, **4**, pp. 180–8.

Chapter 3

Chicano Dropouts: A Review of Research and Policy Issues

Russell Rumberger

One visible form of school failure is dropping out of high school. Dropping out of school has always been costly, both for the individual and for the larger society. By one recent estimate the economic costs alone amount to more than $200,000 for individuals over a lifetime and more than $200 billion for a one-year cohort of dropouts (Catterall, 1987). But interest in school dropouts among policymakers, educational practitioners, and researchers is even greater today than in any recent period. At least two additional factors can account for this recent interest. One is that demographic changes in the US population are increasing the number of persons who have higher risk of dropping out of school. These changes include the growth of minority populations, the poor, and youngsters living in single-parent households (Pallas, Natriello and McDill, 1989). The other factor is that a variety of recent policy reports suggest that the educational demands of work in the US will increase in the future, which could further erode employment opportunities for dropouts (e.g., US Departments of Labor, Education, and Commerce, 1988). Together these trends suggest that the number of dropouts in the US could be increasing at the very time that economic opportunities are decreasing, which could further exacerbate the already poor economic and social circumstances of dropouts.

Much of recent attention to the dropout problem has focused on the Hispanic population. One reason is that the proportion of dropouts in the Hispanic population is significantly higher than any other major ethnic group. For instance, in 1986 more than 25 per cent of all Hispanic youth aged 18 and 19 years old were dropouts, compared to 15 per cent of Blacks and 12 per cent of Whites (Table 3.1). Another reason for this attention is that the Hispanic population is expected to grow faster than any other major ethnic group. Between 1985 and 2020, the number of White youth aged 18–24 is expected to *decline* by 25 per cent, while the number of Hispanic youth will *increase* by 65 per cent (Rumberger, 1990, Table 14.2). Thus, based on current dropout rates, the total number of young dropouts could actually increase over the next thirty-five years.

These trends are not lost on employers, who are now among the most vocal proponents of educational reform (e.g., Committee for Economic Development, 1987). The growth of the Hispanic population and its potential impact on the future labor force is particularly pressing on regions and communities in the

Table 3.1: Number and proportion of dropouts in population by age, gender, race, ethnicity: 1986

| | Age Groups (years) | | | | | | |
	14–15	16–17	18–19	20–21	22–24	25+	Total
Number (in thousands)	176	455	872	1,089	1,726	37,049	41,367
White							
Males	66	215	370	470	741	14,292	16,113
Females	63	179	323	403	667	16,058	17,950
Black							
Males	17	26	74	95	139	2,610	3,089
Females	21	26	83	94	134	3,131	3,601
Hispanic origin							
Males	12	47	95	151	254	2,234	2,531
Females	13	53	69	114	182	2,418	2,668
Mexican origin							
Males	3	31	73	125	220	1,476	1,928
Females	12	49	57	92	120	1,457	1,787
% of Population	2.4	6.1	12.3	14.8	14.3	25.4	23.5
White							
Males	2.2	6.9	12.8	15.9	15.0	24.9	
Females	2.2	6.0	11.0	12.9	13.0	25.7	
Black							
Males	3.0	4.7	14.9	18.1	17.3	38.5	
Females	3.8	4.7	15.2	16.7	15.6	37.0	
Hispanic origin							
Males	3.7	14.4	26.8	34.9	38.2	50.8	
Females	3.7	14.7	24.1	30.9	35.1	52.2	
Mexican origin							
Males	1.5	14.3	31.7	44.6	46.6	56.1	
Females	5.0	20.3	35.3	37.5	36.2	57.2	

Sources: US Bureau of the Census (1988a) Table 37; (1988c) Table 1; (1988d) Table 1.
Note: Hispanic origin and Mexican origin may be of any race. For persons 16 to 24 years old, dropouts are defined as persons with less than 12 years of school and not currently enrolled in school; for persons 25 years old and over, dropouts are defined as persons with less than 12 years of schooling.

United States where Hispanics already represent a sizable proportion of the population. Even for the US as a whole, the Hispanic population, which currently represents less than 10 per cent of the US labor force, will comprise more than 25 per cent of the net labor force increase expected between 1986 and the year 2000 (Fullerton, 1987, Table 3.1).

While concern for various ethnic groups in the US is clearly warranted and gratifying, it is also becoming increasingly clear that substantial differences can exist within major ethnic groups. Such is the case with Hispanics. Hispanic generally refers to persons of Mexican, Puerto Rican, Cuban, Central or South American, or other Spanish culture or origin, regardless of race (Brown, Rosen, Hill and Olivas, 1980, p. 2). Along a variety of educational and economic indicators, the differences among Hispanic sub-groups are actually greater than differences between Hispanic and non-Hispanic populations. For instance, in 1988, differences in dropout rates between Cuban and Mexican, origin populations —

were greater than differences in dropout rates between Hispanic and non-Hispanic populations (US Bureau of the Census, 1988a, Table 1). Therefore, attention to sub-group differences is as warranted as attention to major ethnic group differences.

Mexican Americans or Chicanos represent two-thirds of the Hispanic population in the United States, by far the largest of the Hispanic sub-groups (US Bureau of the Census, 1988a, Table 1; also, see Valencia, chapter 1, this volume). Chicanos represent an even larger proportion of the Hispanic population in Texas and California (Orum, 1986, p. 7). Moreover, they generally have the lowest socioeconomic status and the lowest level of educational attainment of all the Hispanic sub-groups (US Bureau of the Census, 1988a). Thus the educational and economic circumstances of Chicanos warrant particular attention by researchers and policy makers. Of course, Chicanos themselves are a diverse group who differ in such ways as language use, immigration status, and their own ethnic identities (Matute-Bianchi, 1986).

The purpose of this chapter is to examine the current state of knowledge and research about the Chicano dropout problem. Four facets of the problem will be examined, based on a framework used to examine the overall dropout problem (Rumberger, 1987). The first facet addresses the extent of the dropout problem and trends in the incidence of dropping out. The second facet discusses the factors that predict or are possible causes of the dropout problem. The third facet examines the individual and social consequences to dropping out. The last facet discusses solutions to the Chicano dropout problem.

For each facet of the problem, I will first discuss the current state of research and knowledge about the facet in general and then I will discuss what is known about this facet of the problem with respect to the Chicano population. In the latter case, an attempt will be made to highlight where the nature of the Chicano dropout problem and proposed solutions are similar or dissimilar to that of other ethnic groups, particularly other Hispanic sub-groups and the non-Hispanic, White population. Understanding the extent and nature of these differences may be the key to effective social interventions. Such comparisons are not always possible, however, because existing research and data have not always identified and examined ethnic group or sub-group differences. Ethnic differences are further compounded by gender and socioeconomic differences (Grant and Sleeter, 1986).

The Incidence of the Problem

One reason the dropout problem has received considerable attention is because the incidence of dropping out among particular social groups — and in some educational settings — is considered to be too high and possibly getting worse. But exactly how bad is the dropout problem?

Defining and Measuring Dropouts

The answer depends on how one defines a dropout. Because there is no universal definition of a dropout, it is difficult to know from existing data exactly how extensive the dropout problem is in the US.

In general, a dropout is a person who is not currently enrolled in school and does not have a high school diploma or equivalent certificate. A close examination of this definition reveals a fundamental problem with the entire notion of dropping out. Dropout status, as well as enrollment status and graduation status from which it is determined, are bivariate conditions that reveal little about the varying rate of learning and knowledge that students acquire in school. We use the status of school enrollment and graduation as indications of learning and knowledge when, in fact, the former may reveal very little about the latter. Students who are enrolled in school may not be attending classes and hence learning anything, while students who graduate from school may have acquired very little useful knowledge. For example, a recent study found that more than a quarter of Chicago's recent high school graduates could read only at or below the eighth grade level (Designs for Change, 1985, Table 1).

In other words, we use dropping out as a visible and convenient measure of academic failure and graduation as a visible and convenient measure of academic success when neither reveal much about how much or how little knowledge a student has acquired. Thus, in some respects, too much attention is being placed on dropping out and graduating, when we should be more concerned with student engagement, learning, and knowledge.

Despite the inherent limitations what dropout status means, there will always be continued need and interest in measuring dropouts. Unfortunately, available data on dropouts are potentially inaccurate and incomparable because they are collected by different agencies, using different definitions, and different sources of data. The major source of data at the national level is provided by the US Census Bureau, which annually collects national information on the school enrollment and dropout status of the population from household interviews. Census data may understate the extent of dropping out because school enrollment information is often supplied by parents who may not know or accurately report the enrollment status of their children. However, the data are the most comprehensive available and have been collected for many years, which allows analyses of trends.

The Census computes the proportion of dropouts in the population in two different ways. For persons under the age of 35 years, dropouts are persons who are not enrolled in school at the time of the Census survey and not high school graduates; for persons 35 years of age and over, dropouts are persons who have completed less than twelve years of school or do not have a high school certificate. What do these data show?

The Extent of the Dropout Problem

In 1986 there were more than 41 million dropouts in the United States (see Table 3.1). The proportion of dropouts in the population varies by age, with the higher rates among the adult population and lower rates among the younger age groups. Among adults 25 years and over, 25 per cent were dropouts in 1986, compared to 12 per cent among 18- to 19-year-olds. In general, dropout rates are similar for males and females.

At virtually every age group, dropout rates are higher for Chicanos — roughly twice that of Whites and higher than any other ethnic or racial group except American Indians. Among adults, for example, dropout rates for Chicano males and females were 56 per cent and 57 per cent compared to rates of 50 per cent and 52 per cent for all Hispanics, respectively, and 25 per cent for both White males and females. Chicanos also have the highest dropout rates among all the Hispanic sub-groups identified in the Census. In 1988, for example, the dropout rate for Mexican-origin Hispanic adults was 55 per cent, compared to 49 per cent for Puerto Ricans, 40 per cent for Cubans and 37 per cent for Central and South Americans (US Bureau of the Census, 1988a, Table 1).

One other notable ethnic difference in dropout rates concerns when students leave school. Hispanic males are almost twice as likely to quit school before completing one year of high school as Hispanic females or Whites. Almost 50 per cent of all 14-to-24-year-old Hispanic males who left school between October 1984 and October 1985 did so before completing one year of high school (nine years of schooling), compared to 28 per cent for Hispanic females and White males (US Bureau of the Census, 1988b, Table 7).

Trends in Dropout Rates

Historically, dropout rates have improved dramatically in the US. In 1940, only 25 per cent of the adult population had completed four years of high school; by 1986, 75 per cent of the adult population had completed high school (US Bureau of the Census, 1988c, Table 19). In recent years, however, improvements have slowed. In the twelve-year period between 1974 and 1986, dropout rates among 18- and 19-year-olds declined from 17 per cent to 12 per cent, while among 25-to-29-year-olds, dropout rates declined from 16 per cent to 14 per cent (Table 3.2). The greater improvement in the younger cohort is attributable to the greater proportion of 18- and 19-year-olds still enrolled in school, which increased from 10 per cent to 13 per cent in this period (US Bureau of the Census, 1975, 1988d).

Only recent trends in Hispanic and Chicano dropout rates can be examined because the Census did not identify Hispanics until 1974 and Mexican-origin Hispanics until 1979. Among Hispanics 25 to 29 years of age, the proportion of male dropouts has remained unchanged at around 40 per cent between 1974 and 1986, while the proportion of female dropouts declined in this period from 50 per cent to 37 per cent. Similar trends occurred for Chicanos from 1980 and 1986, with rates improving for females, but not males. Dropout rates for White females also improved in this period, while dropout rates for White males did not. In contrast, dropout rates among Blacks in this age group improved for males and females.

Among 18- and 19-year-olds, there are more consistent patterns among racial and ethnic groups, with both male and female rates improving in this period. In this age group, Hispanics in general and Chicano males in particular have made dramatic improvements in their dropout rates. The dropout rate among Chicano males, for example, declined from 50 per cent to 32 per cent between 1980 and 1986 (Table 3.2). At least some of this improvement is attributable to an increase in the proportion of Chicano males still enrolled in school, which increased from 11 per cent in 1980 to 17 per cent in 1986 (US Bureau of the Census, 1985, Table 26, 1988d, Table 1).

Overall, Census data reveal general improvements in dropout rates national-

Table 3.2: Dropout rates by age group, sex, race, and ethnicity: 1974, 1980, 1986
(% of the population)

	1974	1980	1986
Total: 18–19-year-olds	16.6	15.7	12.3
White			
Males	17.4	16.1	12.8
Females	13.9	13.8	11.0
Black			
Males	26.9	22.7	14.6
Females	20.2	19.8	15.2
Hispanic origin			
Males	35.1	43.1	29.1
Females	25.1	34.6	24.1
Mexican origin			
Males	—	50.3	31.7
Females	—	39.3	35.3
Total: 25–29-year-olds	16.1	13.9	13.9
White			
Males	13.8	12.7	14.2
Females	15.9	12.7	12.4
Black			
Males	23.9	22.1	16.7
Females	28.5	22.9	19.4
Hispanic origin			
Males	41.9	40.1	40.3
Females	50.1	41.7	36.7
Mexican origin			
Males	—	46.4	46.7
Females	—	46.1	42.6

Sources: US Department of the Census (1975) Table 1; (1985) Table 1; (1988d) Table 1.
Note: Hispanic origin and Mexican origin may be of any race. Dropouts are defined as persons
of a given cohort who are not enrolled in school in October of the year in question and
have not received a high school diploma or an equivalent high school certificate.

ly, especially for Hispanic- and Mexican-origin populations. Yet, dropout rates for Hispanics and Chicanos still remain more than twice as high as the rates for Whites.

The Causes of the Problem

Much of the research on the dropout issue has focused on identifying the causes of the problem. This focus is part of the larger and more general effort to build models and identify the factors associated with student achievement. The major difference is that in dropout research the educational outcome of interest is dropout status, whereas in student achievement research educational achievement is most frequently measured by grades or test scores.

Attempts to fully understand the causes of dropping out are hampered by the same set of factors that confronts the study of student achievement more generally. First, there are a large variety of factors that predict or influence dropout behavior, ranging from family background to school characteristics. Second, these factors tend to be highly interrelated making it difficult to assess the influence of any one factor. Third, because dropping out is often viewed as a longer-term, cumulative process of disengagement, it requires a longitudinal perspective to more fully understand how this process takes place and the factors that affect it. Finally, as is the case with any human behavior, dropping out itself is a complex phenomenon. Not all dropouts are the same, just as not all high school graduates are the same. As they themselves report, dropouts leave school for different reasons (Rumberger, 1983, Table II).

The research literature on the causes of high school dropouts is based on a number of social science disciplines — including anthropology, psychology, and sociology — and employs a number of research techniques, ranging from ethnography to large-scale statistical studies. Each research tradition has strengths and weaknesses in improving our understanding of the dropout problem.

Ethnographic studies provide rich descriptions of the circumstances and experiences of students' academic and social lives. But such studies typically focus on only a few, select number of students, which restrict their ability to generalize to the larger, national population of students and dropouts. Large-scale statistical studies typically employ large, national surveys of students, such as the *High School and Beyond* survey of 58,000 high school sophomores and seniors throughout the US in 1980 (Peng, Fetters and Kolstad, 1981). Studies based on large, nationally representative surveys can provide results that can be generalized to the national population of dropouts, but they are restricted by the populations and variables that are surveyed.

For instance, the *High School and Beyond* (HSB) survey, which has been used by a number of recent studies on high school dropouts, was first conducted on a sample of high school sophomores and seniors in the Spring of 1980. Follow-up surveys in 1982, 1984, and 1986 have been used by a number of studies to examine the correlates of dropout behavior among the sophomore cohort. But the sophomore cohort may not be representative of all high school dropouts because many leave school before the end of the tenth grade. This is especially true for Hispanic dropouts, as noted above. Thus, national surveys are not immune to the problem of generalizability.

Another problem shared by most research on dropouts is that studies can only show associations or correlations between dropout behavior and a host of other factors, such as family background or school experiences. Strictly speaking, they can never prove cause and effect. Yet more sophisticated studies are able to more strongly suggest causal relationships by statistically controlling for a variety of spurious or intervening variables. Nonetheless, strict causality should not be inferred from even more sophisticated studies. In the discussion below, the term influence is used to denote association, but not causality.

While all research has limitations, the cumulative findings from all existing studies are able to provide a more complete picture of the many factors that influence dropout behavior. These influences can be grouped into four major categories: family background, schools, community, and personal characteristics. In reviewing the research literature in these four areas, I will address the following questions:

Table 3.3: *Selected demographic characteristics of children under 18 years and high school dropout rates by race and ethnicity*

	Total	White	Black	Hispanic
Demographic characteristics				
% living below poverty level, 1987	20.0	15.0	45.1	39.3
% with parents who have completed high school, 1987	79.1	80.8	69.4	45.1
% living with both parents, 1987	75.0	80.9	43.1	68.2
High school dropout rates*				
Total	14.4	13.0	17.2	19.1
Composite family SES		M/F	M/F	M/F
Lowest quartile	22.3	23.8/23.7	19.9/16.7	23.3/22.8
Highest quartile	7.0	8.5/3.9	18.0/8.1	10.0/11.5

Sources: US Bureau of the Census (1988) *Money Income and Poverty Status in the United States: 1987*, Current Population Reports No. P-60, No. 161 (Washington, DC, US Government Printing Office), Table 16; US Bureau of the Census (1988), *Marital Status and Living Arrangements: March 1987*, Current Population Reports No. P-20, No. 423 (Washington, DC: US Government Printing Office), Table 9; Barro and Kolstad (1987) Table 4.1.

* *Proportion of 1980 high school sophomores who dropped out of school.*

1 Which factors appear to influence dropout behavior?
2 Do these factors influence dropout behavior directly or indirectly, by influencing other antecedents of dropout behavior such as grades and promotion?
3 Do these factors influence dropout behavior similarly for Chicanos as for other ethnic groups, particularly non–Hispanic Whites?
4 To what extent do differences in these factors explain observed differences in dropout rates between Chicanos and other students?

Family Background

As is the case with other measures of student achievement, family background exerts a powerful influence on dropout behavior. The most widely studied aspect of family background is socioeconomic status (SES), which is typically a composite measure of a series of family demographic variables such as family income and parental education. For example, descriptive data from the sophomore cohort of the national *High School and Beyond* study, show that dropout rates are almost three times higher for students from low SES families than from high SES families (Table 3.3). These data also show that the general relationship between family SES and dropout behavior appears to be true for both Whites and Hispanics, but not for Blacks.

Much of the influence of family background on dropout behavior is indirect. That is, family background has been shown to be a powerful predictor of other measures of student performance — such as student grades, test scores, and retention — which, in turn, are strongly associated with dropping out. For example, high school sophomores in 1980 were twice as likely to drop out if they had been held back a grade, whereas students in the lowest quarter of ability were three to five times as likely to drop out as students in the highest quarter of ability (Barro and Kolstad, 1987, Table 6.1). These factors influence dropout behavior for Hispanics and Chicanos as well as Blacks and Whites, males as well as females, although the relative importance of these three factors appears to vary somewhat between gender, racial, and ethnic groups (Ekstrom, Goertz, Pollack and Rock, 1986; Fernandez, Paulsen and Hirano-Nakanishi, 1989; Rumberger, 1983; Velez, 1989).

Yet even controlling for these other measures of student achievement, most multivariate statistical studies still find a direct effect of family SES on dropout behavior, although in most studies the relationship only holds for Whites but not Hispanics and Chicanos (Ekstrom *et al.*, 1986; Fernandez *et al.*, 1989; Rumberger, 1983). This suggests that for Hispanics and Chicanos, SES influences dropout behavior indirectly, through its influence on other measures of student achievement.

Other aspects of family background also appear to influence dropout behavior, but like SES, they tend to have mostly a direct influence on the dropout behavior for Whites but not for Chicanos and Hispanics. One factor is family composition. In general, research suggests that students from single-parent households are more likely to drop out of school than students from families where both parents are present even controlling for other, intervening factors (Bachman, Green and Wirtanen, 1971; Ekstrom *et al.*, 1986; Fernandez *et al.*, 1989; Rumberger, 1983; Velez, 1989). But of the four studies that examined Hispanics or Chicanos separately from Whites, two found no effects for Hispanics or Chicanos (Fernandez *et al.*, 1989; Rumberger, 1983), while the other two did (Ekstrom *et al.*, 1986; Velez, 1989).

Family size also appears to influence dropout rates: students from larger families tend to have higher dropout rates than students from smaller families (Bachman *et al.*, 1971; Fernandez *et al.*, 1989; Rumberger, 1983). But again the direct influence of family size on dropout rates, after controlling for other factors, only holds for Whites in one study and for Hispanic females in another (Fernandez *et al.*, 1989; Rumberger, 1983).

Two other aspects of family background are of particular interest in understanding Hispanic and Chicano dropout behavior: immigration status and language proficiency. Most evidence suggests that both immigration status and language use influence dropout behavior only indirectly, through their effects on other measures of student achievement, such as grades and retention (Steinberg, Blinde and Chan, 1984). But at least two research studies found that more recent immigrants are more likely to drop out of school than other students, even controlling for other intervening variables (Rumberger, 1983; Velez, 1989).

Immigration status and language use are both associated with SES. More recent Mexican immigrants generally have lower SES than second and third generation Mexican Americans, and are more likely to be proficient in Spanish rather than English (Buriel and Cardoza, 1988). Family socioeconomic status has already been shown to influence dropout behavior, largely through its effects on student academic achievement. Research also reveals that lack of English proficiency is strongly associated with grade retention and academic performance among both Spanish-speaking students and other non-English-speaking students (Steinberg *et al.*, 1984).

Altogether, to what extent do differences in family background between Chicanos and other ethnic groups help explain observed differences in dropout rates among groups? First, Census data reveal widespread racial and ethnic differences in several aspects of family background. In 1987, for example, about 40 per cent of Black and Hispanic children were living in families with incomes below the poverty level, compared to 15 per cent for White children (see Table 3.3). And only 45 per cent of Hispanic parents had completed high school, compared to 69 per cent for Blacks and 81 per cent for Whites.

A couple of recent empirical studies of two different national survey data sets found that at least three-quarters of the differences in observed dropout rates between Whites and Hispanics and Whites and Mexican Americans can be attributable to differences in family background (Fernandez *et al.*, 1989; Rumberger, 1983). These findings suggest that much if not all of the high dropout rates for Hispanics and Chicanos could be eliminated by raising their SES status to that of Whites.

While large-scale statistical studies are able to demonstrate the importance of family background in influencing dropout behavior, generally they are unable to reveal exactly *how* this influence operates. This is because most large surveys usually ascertain *structural* characteristics of families — such as income, parental education, size, and composition — but little about family *processes* or mechanisms. Increasingly, research is now attempting to discover the various mechanisms through which families influence student achievement and dropout behavior (Coleman, 1988). This is where small-scale, ethnographic studies are particularly valuable because they can reveal the complex array of family mechanisms and their interrelationships (e.g., Trueba, Spindler and Spindler, 1990).

Existing research suggests that there are at least several different ways in which families influence the educational achievement of their children. Each of these influences could help explain why Hispanic and Chicano students are more likely to drop out than non-Hispanic, White students.

One important influence is parental *academic involvement*. Regardless of ethnic background, parents of high school graduates — compared to parents of dropouts — are more likely to be actively involved in their children's education through such activities as monitoring homework and attending school and teacher conferences (Delgado-Gaitan, 1988, 1990; Rumberger, Ghatak, Poulos, Ritter and Dornbusch, 1990). There are at least several possible explanations why some parents are more involved than other parents. In some cases, poor parents simply lack the time and resources to fully participate. In some cases, parents, especially recent immigrants, feel they lack the skill and knowledge to more fully participate and end up deferring responsibility to school officials (Delgado-Gaitan, 1988, 1990; Lareau, 1987). Yet schools are also to blame: a recent survey found that inner-city parents are more involved with their children's schools when the schools have strong programs to encourage parental involvement (Dauber and Epstein, 1989).

Another way that families influence student achievement is through proper *academic encouragement*. Research has shown that extrinsic rewards and punishments reduce internal motivation, which leads individuals to explain their own behavior as the product of outside forces (Lepper and Greene, 1978). In contrast, parents who offer encouragement, praise, and other positive responses leave their children ultimately responsible for their own behavior, which helps develop internal motivation and improves academic performance (Dornbusch, Elworth and Ritter, 1989). This process may also operate on dropout behavior since dropouts in all ethnic groups tend to demonstrate lower levels of internal control and lower educational aspirations than other students (e.g., Ekstrom *et al.*, 1986; Rumberger, 1983; Rumberger *et al.*, 1990). Yet there is no evidence that differences in the type or amount of academic support can explain higher Chicano dropout rates independent of SES.

A final way that families influence student achievement is by providing proper *social support*. Social support, in part, is shaped by parenting styles, which reflect parent-child interactions and decision-making which, in turn, can lead to differences in the amount of autonomy and psychosocial maturity in children. A parenting style that is too permissive can lead to excessive autonomy, more influence from peers, improper social attitudes and behaviors which, in turn, can hurt academic performance and increase the likelihood of dropping out (Dornbusch, Ritter, Leiderman, Roberts and Fraleigh, 1987; Rumberger *et al.*, 1990; Steinberg, Elman and Mounts, 1989). In contrast, students from families that stress joint decision-making are socially more mature, less influenced by their peers, have better social attitudes and behaviors and do better in school.

Some evidence suggests that Hispanic and Mexican American families are less likely than non-Hispanic White families to foster the type of independence that tends to improve academic performance. Dornbusch *et al.* (1987) found that Hispanic students were less likely than White students to come from families with the authoritative parenting styles that are associated with higher grades in school. Anderson and Evans (1976) found that Mexican American students were given less independence training and were granted less autonomy in decision-making in their families compared to Anglo-American students, which reduced their confidence to succeed in school and their school achievement. In both studies, however, Hispanic and Mexican American families had lower SES than Anglo families, suggesting that differences in social support are related to SES, not to ethnic or cultural differences in families.

Clearly more research is needed to better understand how SES, ethnicity, and other family characteristics shape these various family mechanisms as well as how these family mechanisms shape student achievement. But to more fully understand how families influence student achievement and dropout behavior, one must also examine the interaction between families and schools in order to understand why certain types of attitudes and behaviors fostered and supported in the family may or may not be useful in helping students succeed in school. This issue is also relevant to the discussion of schools.

Schools

Despite the powerful influence of family background, schools still make a difference. One recent study of the sixty-three Chicago public high schools found that the actual dropout rates were 50 per cent higher to 50 per cent lower than the rate expected given the composition of the students in the schools (Toles, Schulz and Rice, 1986, Table 1). Thus the types of schools that students attend can help to compensate for other disadvantages that students bring into school or simply compound them.

Of course the kinds of schools that students attend is influenced by their place of residence and social class. Many Hispanics and other minorities attend inner-city schools that generally are considered poor and have dropout rates as high as 50 per cent (Carnegie Foundation for the Advancement of Teaching, 1988; Hess and Lauber, 1986). In 1984, 27 per cent of all Hispanic students were enrolled in the twenty largest school districts in the United States where minorities represented 70 per cent of student enrollment (US Department of Education, 1987, Table 1:27). Hispanics are now even more likely than Blacks to attend minority concentration schools (see Donato, Menchaca and Valencia, this volume). Moreover, achievement levels in large and segregated schools, in general, are much lower than in other school settings and appear to be attributable, at least in part, to poorer school climate and more staff and student discipline problems (Bryk and Thum, 1989; Espinosa and Ochoa, 1986; Pittman and Haughwout, 1987)

Exactly *how* schools influence dropout behavior is less clear. Ethnographic studies show that dropouts report poor schooling conditions and experiences; schools either fail to engage some students or they actively try to push the difficult and problematic students out (Fine, 1986; Olsen and Edwards, 1982). Engagement can be on two levels: academic and social. Several studies suggest that students who are less socially engaged in school — have fewer friends and are less engaged in formal social activities — are more likely to drop out (Tidwell, 1988; Valverde, 1987; Velez, 1989). Research also shows that students who are less academically engaged — cut class, are absent, and have discipline problems in school — are also more likely to drop out (Ekstrom *et al.*, 1986; Velez, 1989). These relations hold for Hispanics as well as Whites.

As suggested earlier, to better understand how both schools and families influence achievement and dropout behavior, one must focus on the interaction between families and schools. This may be particularly important for understanding the achievement of Chicano children. For instance, research suggests that in the US lower social class children in general and Hispanic children in particular often face learning environments in school that foster poor academic performance and may be dysfunctional to the type of learning style and reward structure found in the home (Laosa, 1977; Ortiz, 1988; Trueba, 1989). In contrast, in Japan there appears to be a complementary and reinforcing relationship between the learning environments and reward structures found in Japanese families and schools (Holloway, 1988).

Community Influences

A third influence on dropout behavior is the community, or the environment outside of the school and the family. This environment includes other social institutions, such as churches or community organizations, the labor market, and peers. Research suggests that the community can exert a powerful influence on student achievement and dropout behavior. And there is at least some evidence to show that Hispanics may be more influenced to drop out by conditions in the community, notably work opportunities and peers.

With respect to labor market influences, males in general and Hispanic males in particular are more likely to report that they left school for economic reasons, including the desire or the need to work (Rumberger, 1983, Table II). In addition, there may be less economic incentives for Hispanic males to finish high school than other male students because the relative rewards for finishing school — earnings and employment rates — are lower for Hispanics than for either Blacks or Whites (see below).

Another community influence on dropout behavior is peers. Recent research reveals that peers exert a powerful influence on children, especially teenagers (Ianni, 1989). Although the influence of peers on dropout behavior has not been the subject of much study, ethnographic studies report that dropouts of all ethnic backgrounds are more likely to associate with other youth who drop out or have low educational aspirations (Delgado-Gaitan, 1986; Fine, 1986; Olsen and Edwards, 1982; Valverde, 1987). Survey studies also confirm that higher educational aspirations of peers are associated with lower dropout rates, even controlling for a host of other factors (Ekstrom *et al.*, 1986; Hanson and Ginsburg, 1988; Rumberger, 1983). Hispanic females especially may be more influenced by the educational aspirations of their friends than other students (Rumberger, 1983, Table IV). Finally, dropouts may be more susceptible to the influence of peers than other students because they are more likely to have difficulties at home or at school (Delgado-Gaitan, 1986; Steinberg and Silverberg, 1986).

Personal Characteristics

The final set of influences on dropout behavior includes a variety of personal characteristics, attitudes, and behaviors. A host of such factors — low educational aspirations, discipline problems, drug use, teenage pregnancy — are associated with increased rates of dropping out of school (Ekstrom *et al.*, 1986; Mensch and Kandel, 1988; Rumberger, 1983). Yet, in general, these characteristics do not explain higher dropout rates for Hispanics and Chicanos.

For example, higher educational aspirations are associated with lower dropout rates for all ethnic groups, including Chicanos (Buriel and Cardoza, 1988; Delgado-Gaitan, 1988; Rumberger, 1983). Yet, in general, Hispanics and Chicanos as well as their parents share the same high level of educational aspirations as non-Hispanic Whites (Delgado-Gaitan, 1988; Rumberger, 1983). Even Chicanos who differ in immigration status show virtually no differences in educational aspirations (Buriel and Cardoza, 1988). Similarly, although teenage pregnancy is associated with dropping out for all females, differences in the incidence of teenage pregnancy do not appear to explain the higher rate of dropping out among Chicano females (Rumberger, 1983).

To summarize, research suggests that a complex myriad of factors leads to dropping out of school. In general, these factors operate similarly on all ethnic groups. Thus it is the *incidence* of these factors that explains the higher dropout rates of Hispanic and Chicano students. The most visible and powerful single factor is SES. Hispanics and Chicanos are more likely to come from low SES families, families where children are more likely to drop out of school regardless of ethnicity. The mechanisms by which families influence dropout behavior are not well understood, but they include both direct effects on students' attitudes, behaviors, and performance in school as well as indirect effects on the types of schools that students attend.

Consequences of the Problem

Dropping out of high school has severe economic and social consequences for both the individual and society at large. The economic consequences are well known: dropouts, in general, have more difficulty getting a job and receive lower wages from the jobs they do get. But there are also a host of other social consequences to dropping out, ranging from increased crime and drug use to poorer health that have not been well documented but, nonetheless, can be considered costly (Rumberger, 1987). An important question in the current discussion is whether the economic and social consequences of dropping out of school are the same for Hispanics and Chicanos as for other ethnic groups.

Economic Consequences

The most often discussed consequence of dropping out of school is economic. Dropouts, in general, have higher rates of unemployment and lower earnings than high school graduates. For example, as shown in Table 3.4, youths who dropped out of high school during the 1984–85 school year had unemployment rates about 50 per cent higher than high school graduates who were not enrolled in college (36 per cent versus 25 per cent). In 1986, male high school dropouts had a median annual income that was 32 per cent lower than male high school graduates, while female dropouts had a median annual income that was 30 per cent lower than female high school graduates (see Table 3.4).

These differences persist over the entire working lifetime and thus can be sizeable. In 1985, the expected difference in lifetime earnings between a male high school graduate and a male high school dropout amounted to $212,00, while the difference for females amounted to $142,000 (Rumberger, 1990, Table 14.6).

In general, therefore, there appears to be a powerful economic incentive for students to finish high school. But is this economic incentive similar for Hispanics and Chicanos as for Whites and other groups? Recent data suggest that the answer may be no.

As shown in Table 3.4, unemployment rates in October 1985 for White youths who dropped out of high school during the 1984–85 school year was almost twice as high as high school graduates from the year before who were not enrolled in college. But for Hispanics, dropouts had an unemployment rate only slightly higher than high school graduates. And Black dropouts had unemployment rates than were actually lower than Black high school graduates! Of course these estimates are based on rather small samples and are therefore subject to error, but they do suggest that the employment benefits to completing high school may not be as great as commonly believed. Differences in earnings for Hispanic dropouts and graduates were more similar to differences for Blacks and Whites, although male Hispanics still received a lower economic payoff to completing high school than Whites.

Table 3.4:   Unemployment and income of high school graduates and dropouts by race/ethnicity and sex, 1985 and 1986

	Total	White	Black	Hispanic
Unemployment rate (%), October 1985 (1984–85 high school dropouts and graduates)				
Dropouts	35.6	35.2	43.5	45.2
Graduates not enrolled in college	24.6	18.1	55.1	40.8
Ratio Dropouts/Graduates	1.45	1.94	.79	1.11
Median Income ($), 1986 (Persons 25 years and older)				
Males				
Dropouts (1–3 years of high school)	13,401	14,000	11,318	12,253
Graduates	19,772	20,468	14,465	16,102
Ratio Dropouts/Graduates	.68	.68	.78	.76
Females				
Dropouts (1–3 years of high school)	5,831	5,938	5,190	5,855
Graduates	8,366	8,388	8,244	8,453
Ratio Dropouts/Graduates	.70	.71	.63	.69

*Sources: Sharon R. Cohany, 'What happened to the high school class of 1985?' Monthly Labor Review, **109** (October 1986) Table 1; US Bureau of the Census, (1988) Money Income of Households, Families, and Persons in the United States: 1986, Current Population Reports, Series P-60, No. 159, Washington, DC, US Government Printing Office, June, Table 35; US Bureau of the Census (1988a), Table 17.*
Note: Hispanic origin may be of any race.

Other data further support the notion that Hispanics receive a lower economic benefit to graduating from high school than Whites. In 1986, White high school dropouts were more than twice as likely as graduates to have no work experience during the year — 11.8 per cent versus 4.8 per cent — but for Hispanics there was little difference — 9.6 per cent versus 8.9 per cent (Markey, 1988, p. 41). Another study found that differences in wages between White high school graduates and dropouts were much higher than differences between Hispanic high school graduates and dropouts (Stern and Paik, 1989). Yet another study found that Hispanic high school graduates only earned 5 per cent more than Hispanic dropouts of similar ability levels, while the relative advantages for Whites and Blacks were 8 per cent and 30 per cent, respectively (Berlin and Sum, 1988, Table C-3). Finally, historical data suggest that the economic incentives to Hispanics to graduate from high school appear to have diminished over time (Rumberger, 1987, Table 4).

Social Consequences

The social consequences to dropping out of high school include the economic consequences discussed above, since society as a whole suffers from foregone earnings and taxes from individuals with inadequate schooling. But the social consequences of dropping out are even greater. In the only comprehensive study that has ever been done on the social consequences of dropouts, Levin (1972) identified seven social consequences of dropping out of high school (p. 10):

1 forgone national income;
2 forgone tax revenues for the support of government services;
3 increased demand for social services;
4 increased crime;
5 reduced political participation;
6 reduced intergenerational mobility;
7 poorer levels of health.

For each of these areas he examined the research literature on the relation between education and that particular social outcome. He then estimated the social costs associated with the first four outcomes. For a cohort of male dropouts 25–34 years of age in 1969, foregone income over a lifetime was estimated at $237 billion and foregone government tax receipts were estimated at $71 billion (Levin, 1972, p. IX). In addition, welfare expenditures attributable to dropouts were estimated at $3 billion per year and criminal expenditures were estimated at another $3 billion dollars (*ibid.*).

Recent research continues to support the conclusions that dropping out leads to a variety of adverse social consequences. For example, high school dropouts were twice as likely to live below the poverty level in 1986 than as high school graduates (Rumberger, 1990, Table 14.6). Young female dropouts are 50 per cent more likely to give birth to a child out of wedlock than young female graduates with similar backgrounds (Berlin and Sum, 1988, p. 41). Dropouts are more likely to engage in criminal behavior and get arrested than graduates (Berlin and Sum, 1988; Thornberry, Moore and Christenson, 1985). And dropouts are more likely to use both legal drugs (cigarettes and alcohol) and illegal drugs (marijuana and cocaine) than high school graduates (Mensch and Kandel, 1988). Although the incidence of these activities is rarely disaggregated by ethnicity in these studies, there is no reason to expect them to be any different for Hispanics and Chicanos than for other ethnic groups (for one study, see Bruno and Doscher, 1979). One recent study of Los Angeles, which has a high concentration of Hispanic students, estimated that the foregone income associated with one cohort of dropouts in 1986 was $3.2 billion and the social costs to local government of funding criminal services, welfare, and health attributable to dropouts were $488 million (Catterall, 1987, Table 4).

In summary, there are sizable economic and social consequences to dropping out of school for all ethnic groups. Yet there is at least some evidence to suggest that Hispanics and Chicanos may have less to gain economically from finishing high school than other students. If students respond to incentives or disincentives in the labor market, as some people suggest (Bishop, 1989), then as such evidence becomes evident to students it becomes harder for parents, teachers, and other persons to convince non-college-bound Hispanic and Chicano students to remain in school.

Solutions to the Problem

The problem of high school dropouts is more than an academic concern. There is widespread interest and activity both inside and outside of the education community in trying to solve the problem. Policy makers at the federal and state levels have enacted a variety of policies and programs to help solve the dropout problem (e.g., Council of Chief State School Officers, 1987). Foundations have funded programs to address the problem. And education and community organizations have developed and implemented a wide variety of dropout prevention and recovery programs (Orr, 1987; Rumberger, 1990). But are these efforts likely to solve the dropout problem in general, and the dropout problem among Hispanics and Chicanos in particular?

The answer depends on how one views the dropout problem. If one views the dropout problem as largely a problem of educational failure that affects a relatively small proportion of students, then *programmatic solutions* might be able to effectively solve the problem. In this case, one could be quite sanguine about 'solving' the dropout problem. If, however, one views the dropout problem as a larger, endemic social problem that affects the majority of students in some schools and districts, then solving the problem may require more *systemic solutions*. And because such changes are more sweeping and difficult to achieve, it is harder to be as sanguine about the prospects for success. A case can be made for each perspective.

Programmatic Solutions

Most of the effort to solve the dropout problem can be classified as programmatic solutions. Currently there are hundreds of local programs around the country that are designed to keep potential dropouts in school and help existing dropouts to get additional schooling or training. Unfortunately, there is little comprehensive information available at a national level about how much is being spent on dropout programs, how many students are being served, and whether these programs are successful.

The only recent effect to try to document dropout efforts nationally was conducted by the General Accounting Office (GAO) in the autumn of 1986. After reviewing literature and contacting a large number of national, state, and local agencies, the GAO compiled a list of more than 1,000 dropout programs (US GAO 1987, Appendix I). But a mail survey of those programs yielded useful information on a total of only 479 programs. Twenty-six of these programs primarily served Hispanics, so it is possible to compare these programs with the total sample of programs.

Survey information included descriptions of the major features of the dropout programs. Generally, dropout programs provide a wide array of services (Table 3.5). This array of services reflects the fact that programs are often designed to serve multiple objectives and to meet the various needs of their clients. These needs and objectives fall into several categories:

Basic skills training One of the fundamental needs that recovery programs serve is to provide basic skills training in such areas as language and mathematics,

Table 3.5: Services provided in all dropout programs and programs primarily serving Hispanics

	All Dropout Programs		Hispanic Programs*	
	% of Programs	% Served	% of Programs	% Served
Personal counseling	94	74	100	46
Basic education	91	84	92	87
Career counseling	76	67	85	46
Parental involvement encouraged	74	62	89	65
Assistance in obtaining social services	70	48	69	75
Job search assistance	69	41	77	43
Job skills training	62	45	65	43
Part-time employment placement	56	31	69	42
Pregnancy/parental counseling	54	31	50	60
GED preparation	46	28	39	10
Day care	23	18	23	32
English as a second language	14	16	50	11
Number of programs	479		26	

Source: US General Accounting Office (1987) Table 2.4.
* Programs serving at least 50 per cent Hispanic youth.

where many dropouts are highly deficient. For example, a recent survey of young Americans (21–25 years of age) found that only one quarter of all dropouts with 9–12 years of schooling could read at the level of an average eleventh grader and only one-half could read at the level of an average eighth grader (Kirsch and Jungeblut, 1986, Table 6). The GAO survey found that 91 per cent of all dropout programs provided basic education and that 84 per cent of program participants received basic education services (see Table 3.5). Similar proportions were reported in programs that primarily serviced Hispanics. A much larger proportion of Hispanic programs, however, offered services in English as a second language (50 per cent versus 14 per cent for all programs), although only a small percentage of program participants were served by such programs.

In addition, about one-half of all dropout programs surveyed provide preparation to take the General Educational Development (GED) Test, administered by the GED Testing Service of the American Council on Education (1986), which provides alternative means for students to obtain a high school equivalency certificate from their state. But only about one-quarter of all program participants are involved in GED preparation and only 10 per cent of participants in Hispanic programs are involved (see Table 3.5).

Job-oriented services Another need that dropout programs are designed to serve is for job-oriented services, which include vocational training, pre-employment skills training (e.g., interview techniques), and job-placement services. About two-thirds of the dropout programs surveyed by the GAO provided such services, with about half of all participants using them. Similar proportions were reported in Hispanic dropout programs.

Support services   A third and often critical component of dropout programs is support services. Investigations of the dropout problem have found that dropouts frequently leave school because of a variety of school problems, including pregnancy, drugs, family problems, or other personal problems (Olsen and Edwards, 1982; Rumberger, 1987). In order for many of them to successfully complete their schooling, these social problems need to be addressed. Thus most dropout programs in general and those primarily serving Hispanics provide an array of social services, ranging from career and personal counseling to day care (see Table 3.5).

Dropout programs not only serve students who are at risk of dropping out, but also students who have already left school. While there are no national data on exactly how many students are being served by either type of program, it is known that a sizeable number of dropouts eventually receive a high school diploma or equivalent certificate. A national survey of persons 21–25 years of age in 1985 found that almost 50 per cent of persons with less than twelve years of school had studied to take the GED exam, with about 40 per cent of those persons receiving one (Kirsch and Jungeblut, 1986, Figure 3). Thus, these data suggest about 20 per cent of all young dropouts eventually receive a high school diploma by passing the GED exam. Another study based on the *High School and Beyond* survey of high school sophomores in 1980 who later dropped out of school found that 45 per cent had received a high school diploma within six years, with one-third of those actually graduating from high school and two-thirds receiving an equivalent certificate by passing the GED exam (Kolstad and Kaufman, 1989, Table 1). Among Hispanic dropouts, only one-third eventually finished school, with almost 80 per cent of those passing the GED exam.

In order for programmatic solutions to the dropout problem to be successful, it is important to know which programs are the most effective and the most cost-effective. Unfortunately, such information is rarely available. The GAO survey of dropout programs generated only twenty rigorous evaluations of the 479 programs that responded to the survey (US GAO, 1987, p. 19). It appears that many more resources are being used to fund programs than to find out whether the programs are actually effective. This appears to be true with other education programs as well (Slavin, 1989). Such a view is short-sighted, however, because scarce public resources would be better used to fund and implement only the most successful programs.

Although information on program effectiveness is generally lacking, there is some information on the factors contributing to successful programs (where success is identified by program providers). The majority of respondents to the GAO survey of dropout prevention and recovery programs identified five factors that had the greatest impact on program effectiveness (US GAO, 1987, Table 2.3):

1   a caring and committed staff;
2   a non-threatening environment for learning;
3   a low student-teacher ratio;

4   individualized instruction;
5   program flexibility.

Other studies of effective dropout programs have identified essentially the same set of factors (Merchant, 1987; Olsen and Edwards, 1982; Stern, 1986; Wehlage, Rutter, Smith, Lesko and Fernandez, 1989). Of course, simply following this list of factors does not guarantee an effective program. Moreover, some programs may be better at serving different sorts of dropouts than others — such as those serving Hispanics — which also supports the idea of more rigorous program evaluations.

A couple of other difficulties remain to overcome in programmatic efforts to solve the dropout problem. One is that more attention needs to be focused on early prevention, since many at-risk students are already two or more grade levels behind before they even reach high school (Levin, 1988). Another is that more attention be focused on dropout recovery, since only a small fraction of the more than 40 million adult dropouts are enrolled in regular schools, GED programs, or other education and training programs (Rumberger, 1990).

Systemic Solutions

A different approach to solving the dropout problem is necessary if one views the dropout problem as affecting a sizable number of students, as in some communities, or if one views dropping out as a social as well as an educational problem. Both of these aspects apply to many Chicanos and other minorities.

First, most Hispanics and other minorities attend minority-concentration schools. In California, 70 per cent of all minority students in 1984 were enrolled in minority-concentration schools (Haycock and Navarro, 1988, p. 9). As reported above, 27 per cent of all Hispanic students nationally in 1984 were enrolled in the twenty largest school districts in the United States where minorities represented 70 per cent of student enrollment (US Department of Education, 1987, Table 1:27). In large, urban school systems, in particular, where dropout rates approach 40 or 50 per cent, dropping out is the norm rather than the exception (Carnegie Foundation for the Advancement of Teaching, 1988; Hess and Lauber, 1986). And at least for students in these districts, the solution to the problem may require fundamental, systemic changes in the entire school system rather than simply the type of programmatic solutions described above.

Although such changes are difficult to achieve, some fundamental, systemic changes are currently being undertaken in the United States. Some specific programs are being developed that completely restructure elementary schools with predominantly poor, minority students that promise to bring such students up to the achievement levels of other students, which would reduce the likelihood of dropping out in high school (Comer, 1988; Levin, 1988; Slavin and Madden, 1989). New structural arrangements and forms of decision-making are being tried within some districts and schools to foster improved education (Walberg, Bakalis, Bast and Baer, 1989). And the most radical idea being implemented in a large number of states is to permit parents to choose the schools that their children attend (Nathan, 1987), although such a scheme could increase the segregation of students across schools.

A second reason to argue that only systemic solutions can solve the dropout problem rests on a recognition that dropping out is more of a social than an educational problem. It is a social problem in that many dropouts have a variety of other problems in their lives, such as family problems, problems with drugs and crime, or problems with teenage pregnancy. It also is a social problem in that the earlier discussion suggests that there are three major sources of influence on dropping out and other behaviors of young people — families, schools, and communities. If one views these sources as additive — that is, that each plays a significant role in influencing the attitudes, behavior, and academic performance of young people — then each must play a role in addressing the dropout problem.

Recognition of the important role of families, schools, and communities in influencing the behavior of young people is the basis of several types of reform efforts to help potential and actual dropouts. Many educators have long-argued that parents must be centrally involved in improving the educational performance of their children. Thus many dropout programs are built around parental involvement (Orr, 1987; Wehlage, *et al.*, 1989). Other efforts to reduce the dropout problem involve strengthening the role of community, particularly community organizations and the business community. In fact, some observers argue that community involvement is crucial to the successful education of youth because families and schools cannot and should not shoulder the burden alone (Heath and McLaughlin, 1987). In some dropout programs, for example, such as the Boston Compact, the business community plays an important role in programs designed to improve the relevance and payoff to completing high school (Schwartz and Hargroves, 1986–87).

Although systemic solutions are perhaps the only remedy likely to improve the dropout problem for many students, including Chicano students, they are also more difficult to achieve. Moreover, if one believes that systematic efforts must involve changes in circumstances and influences of families and community, then the task of achieving meaningful change and improvement in the dropout problem becomes even greater.

Ultimately, whether one believes such efforts will be successful and spread throughout the educational system depends on one's belief in the educational system as a catalyst for social change. On the one hand, there is a longstanding faith in this country that education can serve to promote social change and improve the social standing of poor, disadvantaged groups. On the other hand, there are critics of the status quo who point out that schools have historically tended to reinforce and perpetuate social class and ethnic differences rather than eliminate them (Bowles and Gintis, 1976; Carnoy and Levin, 1985; see Pearl, in this volume, for a fuller treatment of the debate over various school reform efforts).

The Economic Rationale for Social Intervention

No matter which category of educational solutions one believes is necessary to solve the Chicano dropout problem, there is a strong economic rationale for increased social investment in dropout programs and all programs for the educationally disadvantaged (Levin, 1989a, 1989b). In general, the argument can be made on the basis that the benefits of increasing spending on dropout programs will far exceed the costs of funding such programs.

Unfortunately, few comprehensive studies have ever been conducted that have examined both the costs and benefits of social investment in dropout programs. Levin (1972) estimated that if expenditures on at-risk students were increased by 50 per cent to insure graduation from high school, then the benefits from higher earnings would exceed the costs by a ratio of 6:1. Or based simply on the increased taxes generated from those earnings, taxpayers would receive almost $2 for every dollar invested in dropout prevention. A more recent replication done in Texas that attempted to account for the additional social benefits of reduced crime, welfare, and training costs associated with dropouts estimated that the benefits of dropout prevention would exceed the costs by a ratio of 9:1 (Ramirez and Del Refugio Robledo, 1987).

In general, it appears that the benefits of social investment in dropout prevention and recovery programs would easily outweigh the costs, even if the benefits were restricted to increased tax receipts from the higher earnings associated with high school completion (Rumberger, 1990). And although Chicano high school graduates have, on average, lower earnings than non-Hispanic, White graduates, the social benefits of reducing the dropout rate for Chicanos would still outweigh the costs.

Conclusions

Dropping out of high school is one visible form of educational failure. While graduating from high school alone will not guarantee social and economic success, failure to graduate from high school will most likely deny it. Because so many Chicanos drop out of high school, the economic and social welfare of the entire Chicano population is unlikely to improve until their educational welfare improves.

Many aspects of this problem warrant attention. First, we need to collect more extensive and accurate data on the educational and social experiences of all students in order to better measure the extent of the dropout problem and its causes. Research clearly has a continued role to play in trying to understand and decipher the nature of this complex educational issue.

Second, we need to better document the full range of individual and social consequences associated with dropping out. In particular, we need better estimates of the social costs of dropping out since the few estimates that have been done suggest significant returns to social investments in education (Levin, 1972).

Third, and most important, we need to get on with development, evaluation, and implementation of programs and reforms to improve the educational outcomes of not just Chicanos, but all minority and disadvantaged groups. At a programmatic level, many promising efforts are already under way (Slavin and Madden, 1989). The more difficult and necessary task is to promote fundamental and systemic changes in the current educational system in the United States.

Yet educational reform may not be enough because Chicano school failure is not simply an educational problem. Thirty per cent of all Chicano families and 40 per cent of all Chicano children live in poverty in this country. Many live in segregated, poor neighborhoods. Without a significant improvement in the economic welfare of Chicano families and the communities in which many of them live, the Chicano dropout problem is unlikely to improve dramatically.

References

AMERICAN COUNCIL ON EDUCATION (1986) *The 1986 GED Statistical Report*, Washington, DC, General Educational Development Testing Service.

ANDERSON, J.G. and EVANS, F.B. (1976) 'Family socialization and educational achievement in two cultures: Mexican-American and Anglo-American, *Sociometry*, **39**, pp. 209–22.

BACHMAN, J.G., GREEN, S. and WIRTANEN, I.D. (1971) *Dropping Out: Problem or Symptom?* Ann Arbor, MI, Institute for Social Research, University of Michigan.

BARRO, S.M. and KOLSTAD, A. (1987) *Who Drops out of High School? Findings from High School and Beyond*, Washington, DC, SMB Economic Research.

BERLIN, G. and SUM, A. (1988) *Toward a More Perfect Union: Basic Skills, Poor Families, and our Economic Future*. New York, Ford Foundation.

BISHOP, J.H. (1989) 'Why the apathy in American high schools?' *Educational Researcher*, **18**, pp. 6–10.

BOWLES, S. and GINTIS, H. (1976) *Schooling in Capitalist America*, New York, Basic Books.

BROWN, G.H., ROSEN, N.L., HILL, S.T. and OLIVAS, M.A. (1980) *The Condition of Education for Hispanic Americans*, Washington, DC, US Government Printing Office.

BRUNO, J.E. and DOSCHER, L. (1979) 'Patterns of drug use among Mexican-American potential school dropouts, *Journal of Drug Education*, **9**, pp. 1–10.

BRYK, A.S. and THUM, Y.M. (1989) *The Effects of High School Organization on Dropping out: An Exploratory Investigation*, CPRE Research Report Series RR-012, New Brunswick, NJ, Center for Policy Research in Education, Rutgers.

BURIEL, R. and CARDOZA, D. (1988) 'Sociocultural correlates of achievement among three generations of Mexican American high school seniors', *American Educational Research Journal*, **25**, pp. 177–92.

CARNEGIE FOUNDATION FOR THE ADVANCEMENT OF TEACHING (1988) *An Imperiled Generation: Saving Urban Schools*, Princeton, NJ, Princeton University Press.

CARNOY, M. and LEVIN, H.M. (1985) *Schooling and Work in the Democratic State*, Stanford, CA, Stanford University Press.

CATTERALL, J.S. (1987) 'On the social costs of dropping out of school, *High School Journal*, **71**, pp. 19–30.

COLEMAN, J.S. (1988) 'Social capital in the creation of human capital', *American Journal of Sociology*, **94**, Supplement, pp. S95–S120.

COMER, J.P. (1988) 'Educating poor minority children', *Scientific American*, **259**, pp. 42–8.

COMMITTEE FOR ECONOMIC DEVELOPMENT (1987) *Children in Need: Investment Strategies for the Educationally Disadvantaged*, New York, Committee for Economic Development.

COUNCIL OF CHIEF STATE SCHOOL OFFICERS (1987) *Children at Risk: The Work of the States*, Washington, DC, Council of Chief State School Officers.

DAUBER, S.L. and EPSTEIN, J.L. (1989) *Parent Attitudes and Practices of Parent Involvement in Inner-city Elementary and Middle Schools*, Report 33, Baltimore, Center for Research on Elementary and Middle Schools, Johns Hopkins University.

DELGADO-GAITAN, C. (1986) 'Adolescent peer influence and differential school performance', *Journal of Adolescent Research*, **1**, pp. 449–62.

DELGADO-GAITAN, C. (1988) 'The value of conformity: Learning to stay in school', *Anthropology and Education Quarterly*, **19**, pp. 354–81.

DELGADO-GAITAN, C. (1990) *Literacy for Empowerment: The Role of Parents in Children's Education*, London, Falmer Press.

DESIGNS FOR CHANGE (1985) *The Bottom Line: Chicago's Failing Schools and How to Save Them*, Chicago, Author.

DORNBUSCH, S.M., ELWORTH, J.T. and RITTER, P.L. (1989) 'Parental Reaction to Grades: A Field Test of the Over-justification Approach', manuscript in process.

DORNBUSCH, S.M., RITTER, P.L., LEIDERMAN, P.H., ROBERTS, D.F. and FRALEIGH, M.J. (1987) 'The relation of parenting style to adolescent school performance', *Child Development*, **58**, pp. 1244–57.

EKSTROM, R.B., GOERTZ, M.E., POLLACK, J.M. and ROCK, D.A. (1986) 'Who drops out of high school and why? Findings from a national study', *Teachers College Record*, **87**, pp. 356–73.

ESPINOSA, R. and OCHOA, A. (1986) 'Concentration of California Hispanic students in schools with low achievement: A research note', *American Journal of Education*, **95**, pp. 77–93.

FERNANDEZ, R.M., PAULSEN, R. and HIRANO-NAKANISHI, M. (1989) 'Dropping out among Hispanic youth, *Social Science Research*, **18**, pp. 21–52.

FINE, M. (1986) 'Why urban adolescents drop into and out of public high school', *Teachers College Record*, **87**, pp. 393–409.

FULLERTON, H.N., JR. (1987) 'Labor force projections: 1986 to 2000', *Monthly Labor Review*, **110**, pp. 19–29.

GRANT, C.A. and SLEETER, C.E. (1986) 'Race, class, and gender in education research: An argument for integrative analysis', *Review of Educational Research*, **56**, pp. 195–211.

HANSON, S.L. and GINSBURG, A.L. (1988) 'Gain ground: Values and high school success', *American Educational Research Journal*, **25**, pp. 334–65.

HAYCOCK, K. and NAVARRO, M.S. (1988) *Unfinished Business: Fulfilling Our Children's Promise*, Oakland, CA, The Achievement Council.

HEATH, S.B. and McLAUGHLIN, M.W. (1987) 'A child resource policy: Moving beyond dependence on school and family', *Phi Delta Kappan*, **68**, pp. 576–80.

HESS, G.A., JR. and LAUBER, D. (1986) *Dropouts from the Chicago Public Schools*, Chicago, IL, Chicago Panel on Public School Finances.

HOLLOWAY, S.D. (1988) 'Concepts of ability and effort in Japan and the US', *Review of Educational Research*, **58**, pp. 327–45.

IANNI, F.A (1989) *The Search for Structure: A Report on American Youth Today*, NY, Free Press.

KIRSCH, I.S. and JUNGEBLUT, A. (1986) *Literacy: Profiles of America's Young Adults*, Princeton, NJ, National Assessment of Educational Progress, Educational Testing Service.

KOLSTAD, A.J. and KAUFMAN, P. (1989) 'Dropouts who complete high school with a diploma or GED', paper presented at the annual meeting of the American Educational Research Association, San Francisco, CA, March.

LAOSA, L.M. (1977) 'Socialization, education, and continuity: The importance of the sociocultural context', *Young Children*, **32**, pp. 21–7.

LAREAU, A. (1987) 'Social-class differences in family-school relationships: The importance of cultural capital', *Sociology of Education*, **60**, pp. 73–85.

LEPPER, M.R. and GREENE, D. (1978) *The Hidden Cost of Reward: New Perspectives on the Psychology of Motivation*, Hillsdale, NJ, Erlbaum.

LEVIN, H.M. (1972) *The Costs to the Nation of Inadequate Education*, study prepared for the select committee on equal educational opportunity, US Senate, Washington, DC, US Government Printing Office.

LEVIN, H.M. (1988) 'Accelerating elementary education for disadvantaged students', in COUNCIL OF CHIEF STATE SCHOOL OFFICERS (Eds) *School Success for Students at Risk*, Orlando, FL, Harcourt Brace Jovanovich, pp. 209–26.

LEVIN, H.M. (1989a) 'Economics of investment in educational disadvantaged students', *American Economic Review*, **79**, pp. 52–6.

LEVIN, H.M. (1989b) 'Financing the education of at-risk students', *Educational Evaluation and Policy Analysis*, **11**, pp. 47–60.

MARKEY, J.P. (1988) 'The labor market problems of today's high school dropouts', *Monthly Labor Review*, **111**, pp. 36–43.

MATUTE-BIANCHI, M.E. (1986) 'Ethnic identities and patterns of school success and failure among Mexican-descent and Japanese-American students: An ethnographic analysis, *American Journal of Education*, **95**, pp. 233–55.

MENSCH, B.S. and KANDEL, D.B. (1988) 'Dropping out of high school and drug involvement', *Sociology of Education*, **61**, pp. 95–113.

MERCHANT, B. (1987) *Dropping Out: A Preschool through High School Concern*, Policy Paper No. PP87-12-13, Berkeley, CA, Policy Analysis for California Education, School of Education, University of California, Berkeley.

NATHAN, J. (1987) 'Results and future prospects of state efforts to increase choice among schools', *Phi Delta Kappan*, **68**, pp. 746–52.

OLSEN, L. and EDWARDS, R. (1982) *Push Out, Step Out: A Report on California's Public School Drop-outs*, Oakland, CA, Open Road Issues Research Project, Citizens Policy Center.

ORR, M.T. (1987) *Keeping Students in School*, San Francisco, CA, Jossey-Bass.

ORTIZ, F.I. (1988) 'Hispanic-American children's experiences in classrooms: A comparison between Hispanic and non-Hispanic children', in L. WEIS (Ed.) *Class, Race, and Gender in American Education*, Albany, State University of New York Press, pp. 63–86.

ORUM, L.S. (1986) *The Education of Hispanics: Status and Implications*, Washington, DC, National Council of La Raza.

PALLAS, A.M., NATRIELLO, G. and McDILL, E.L. (1989) 'The changing nature of the disadvantaged population: Current dimensions and future trends', *Educational Researcher*, **18**, pp. 16–22.

PENG, S., FETTERS, W.B. and KOLSTAD, A.J. (1981) *High School and Beyond: A Capsule Description of High School Students*, Washington, DC, National Center for Education Statistics.

PITTMAN, R.B. and HAUGHWOUT, P. (1987) 'Influence of high school size on dropout rate', *Educational Evaluation and Policy Analysis*, **9**, pp. 337–43.

RAMIREZ, D. and DEL REFUGIO ROBLEDO, M. (1987) *The Economic Impact of the Dropout Problem* (IDRA Newsletter), San Antonio, TX: Intercultural Development Research Association.

RUMBERGER, R.W. (1983) 'Dropping out of high school: The influence of race, sex, and family background, *American Educational Research Journal*, **20**, pp. 199–220.

RUMBERGER, R.W. (1987) 'High school dropouts: A review of issues and evidence', *Review of Educational Research*, **57**, pp. 101–21.

RUMBERGER, R.W. (1990) 'Second chance for high school dropouts: The costs and benefits of dropout recovery programs in the United States', in D. INBAR (Ed.) *Second Chance in Education: An Interdisciplinary and International Perspective*, Basingstoke, UK, Falmer Press, pp. 227–50.

RUMBERGER, R.W., GHATAK, R., POULOS, G., RITTER, P.L. and DORNBUSCH, S.M. (1990) 'Family influences on dropout behavior in one California high school', *Sociology of Education*, **63**, pp. 283–99.

SCHWARTZ, R. and HARGROVES, J. (1986–87) 'The Boston compact', *Metropolitan Education*, **3**, pp. 14–24.

SLAVIN, R.E. (1989) 'PET and the pendulum: Faddism in education and how to stop it', *Phi Delta Kappan*, **70**, pp. 752–8.

SLAVIN, R.E. and MADDEN, N.A. (1989) 'What works for students at risk: A research synthesis', *Educational Leadership*, **46**, pp. 4–13.

STEINBERG, L., BLINDE, P.L and CHAN, K.S. (1984) 'Dropping out among language minority youth, *Review of Educational Research*, **54**, pp. 113–32.

STEINBERG, L., ELMAN, J.D. and MOUNTS, N. (1989) 'Authoritative parenting, psychosocial maturity and academic success among adolescents', *Child Development*, **60**, pp. 1424–36.

STEINBERG, L. and SILVERBERG, S.B. (1985) 'The vicissitudes of autonomy in early adolescence', *Child Development*, **57**, pp. 841–51.

STERN, D. (1986) *Dropout Prevention and Recovery in California*, report prepared for the California State Department of Education, Berkeley, CA, School of Education, University of California, Berkeley.

STERN, D. and PAIK, I.W. (1989) 'Comparing the Labor Market Experience of Hispanic, White, and Black Teenagers with and without High School Diplomas', paper presented at the annual meeting of the American Educational Research Association, San Francisco, CA, April.

THORNBERRY, T.P., MOORE, M. and CHRISTENSON, R.L. (1985) 'The effect of dropping out of high school on subsequent criminal behavior', *Criminology*, **23**, pp. 3–18.

TIDWELL, R. (1988) 'Dropouts speak out: Qualitative data on early school departures', *Adolescence*, **23**, pp. 939–54.

TOLES, R., SCHULZ, E.M. and RICE, W.K., JR. (1986) 'A study of variation in dropout rates attributable to effects of high schools', *Metropolitan Education*, **2**, pp. 30–8.

TRUEBA, H. (1989) *Raising Silent Voices: Educating the Linguistic Minorities for the 21st Century*, New York, Harper and Row.

TRUEBA, H., SPINDLER, G. and SPINDLER, L. (1990) *What Do Anthropologists Have to Say about Dropouts?* Basingstoke, London, Falmer Press.

US BUREAU OF THE CENSUS (1975) *School Enrollment — Social and Economic Characteristics of Students: October 1974*, Series P-20, No. 286, Washington, DC, US Government Printing Office.

US BUREAU OF THE CENSUS (1985) *School Enrollment — Social and Economic Characteristics of Students: October 1980*, Series P-20, No. 400, Washington, DC: US Government Printing Office.

US BUREAU OF THE CENSUS (1988a) *Hispanic Population of the United States: March 1988* (Advance Report), Current Population Reports, Series P-20, No. 431, Washington, DC, US Government Printing Office.

US BUREAU OF THE CENSUS (1988b) *School Enrollment — Social and Economic Characteristics of Students: October 1985 and 1984*, Series P-20, No. 426, Washington, DC, US Government Printing Office.

US BUREAU OF THE CENSUS (1988c) *Educational Attainment in the United States: March 1986 and 1987*, Current Population Reports, Series P-20, No. 428, Washington, DC, US Government Printing Office.

US BUREAU OF THE CENSUS (1988d) *School Enrollment — Social and Economic Characteristics of Students: October 1986*, Series P-20, No. 429 Washington, DC, US Government Printing Office.

US DEPARTMENT OF EDUCATION (1987) *The Condition of Education*, 1987 edition, Washington, DC, US Government Printing Office.

US DEPARTMENT OF LABOR, DEPARTMENT OF EDUCATION, DEPARTMENT OF COMMERCE (1988) *Building a Quality Workforce*, Washington, DC, US Government Printing Office.

US GENERAL ACCOUNTING OFFICE (1987) *School Dropouts: Survey of Local Programs*, GAO/HRD-87-108, Washington, DC, US Government Printing Office.

VALVERDE, S.A. (1987) 'A comparative study of Hispanic high school dropouts and graduates', *Education and Urban Society*, **19**, pp. 320–9.

VELEZ, W. (1989) 'High school attrition among Hispanic and non-Hispanic White youths', *Sociology of Education*, **62**, pp. 119–33.

WALBERG, H.J., BAKALIS, M.J., BAST, J.L. and BAER, S. (1989) 'Reconstructing the nation's worst schools', *Phi Delta Kappan*, **70**, pp. 802–5.

WEHLAGE, G.G., RUTTER, R.A., SMITH, G.A., LESKO, N. and FERNANDEZ, R.R. (1989) *Reducing the Risk: Schools as Communities of Support*. London, Falmer Press.

Language and Classroom Perspectives on Chicano Achievement

Part II contains two chapters. In chapter 4, 'Bilingualism, Second Language Acquisition, and the Education of Chicano Language Minority Students', Eugene Garcia provides insights to the theoretical and empirical knowledge bases regarding bilingualism and second language acquisition in Chicano youngsters. As well, Garcia links such knowledge with educational practice and policy pertinent to Chicano students. Chapter 5, 'Promoting School Success for Chicanos: The View From Inside the Classroom', is written by Barbara Merino. Using a framework of micro-level analysis (i.e., inside the classroom), she presents a thorough examination of the schooling received by Chicano students who are second language learners. A main goal is to outline successful and unsuccessful instructional approaches. Merino's chapter covers programmatic alternatives for instruction, research on how classrooms function *vis-à-vis* bilingual/second language instruction, and the ties between classroom processes in schools and their communities.

Chapter 4

Bilingualism, Second Language Acquisition, and the Education of Chicano Language Minority Students

Eugene E. Garcia

Our understanding of language continues to expand in its utilization of diverse theories of linguistics, cognition, and socialization (August and Garcia, 1988). What was once considered the study of habits and structure (Chomsky, 1959; Skinner, 1957), has become today an interlocking study of linguistic, psychological, and social domains, each independently significant, but converging in a single attempt to reconstruct the nature of language. It is this multifaceted phenomenon which confronts an educator when addressing the educational appropriation of knowledge in classrooms. For the educator of Chicano language minority students as a constituency, the issue of language becomes particularly important.

Within the last few years, research in language acquisition has shifted from the study of one language (Brown, 1973; Gonzalez, 1970) to the comparative study of children from diverse linguistic societies (Bowerman, 1975; Braine, 1976) and to the study of children acquiring more than one language (Garcia, 1983; Hakuta, 1986; Hakuta and Garcia, 1989; Krashen, 1984; McLaughlin, 1984). The following discussion introduces the theoretical and empirical knowledge bases related to an understanding of bilingualism and second language acquisition in Chicano children. In doing so, bilingual and second language acquisition will be addressed as they relate to linguistic, cognitive and social research and theory which has developed over the last two decades. Such contributions have reshaped in a dramatic way our view of bilingualism. For at the turn of the century, bilingualism in children was considered a linguistic, cognitive, and academic liability (Hakuta, 1986). Today's understanding of bilingualism indicates that bilingualism is not a linguistic liability and may even serve as a cognitive advantage.

The schooling initiatives targeted at Chicano students have at times been synonymous with the schooling endeavor aimed at immigrant students. As Gonzalez (1990) has documented, Chicano children are usually perceived as the 'foreigners', 'intruders', and 'immigrants' who speak a different language and hold values significantly different from the American mainstream. This perspective has led policy makers (including the US Supreme Court) to highlight the most salient characteristic of the student, the language difference, in their attempts to address the historical academic low achievement of this population. This chapter will include an expanded discussion of this issue which brings together research, theory, educational practice and educational policy of significance to Chicano students.

Bilingual Acquisition

Relative to native monolingual acquisition research, little systematic investigation has been available regarding children who are acquiring more than one language, simultaneously, during the early part of their lives. Recent work in this area however, has centered separately on the linguistic (Garcia and Gonzalez, 1984), cognitive (Cummins, 1979), and social/communicative aspects (Duran, 1981) of the bilingual. That is, research with young bilingual populations has concentrated independently on three areas: (a) the developmental nature of phonology, morphology and syntax; (b) Piagetian and related cognitive attributes of bilingual students; and (c) the social/discourse characteristics of bilingual development. This section reviews research in these areas with an attempt at highlighting similar and disparate theoretical conceptualizations and empirical findings generated by these research endeavors. These conceptualizations are important in addressing the complexities so necessary in understanding Chicano language minority children.

Bilingualism Defined.

It remains difficult to define any term to the satisfaction of the theoretician, researcher and educator. The term bilingualism here suggests the acquisition of two languages during the first 5 to 7 years of life. This definition includes the following conditions:

1 Children are able to *comprehend and produce* aspects (lexicon, morphology, and syntax) of each language.
2 Children *function 'naturally' in the two languages* as they are used in the form of social interaction. This condition requires a substantive bilingual environment in the child's first 3 to 7 years of life. In many cases this exposure comes from within a nuclear and extended family network but this need not be the case (visitors and extended visits to foreign countries are examples of alternative environments).
3 The *simultaneous character of development* must be apparent in both languages. This is contrasted with the case in which a native speaker of one language, who after mastering that one language, begins on a course of second language acquisition.

It is the preceding combined conditions which define the present bilingual population of interest. It is clear from this definition that an attempt is made to include both the child's linguistic abilities in conjunction with the social environment during an important psychological 'segment' of life (August and Garcia, 1988).

Linguistic Development

It does seem clear that a child can learn more than one linguistic form for communicative purposes in many societies throughout the world. Sorenson (1967) describes the acquisition of three to four languages by young children who live in the Northwest Amazon region of South America. In this Brazilian-Colombian border region, the Tukano tribal language serves as the *lingua franca,* but there continue to exist some twenty-five clearly distinguishable linguistic groups. European colleagues Skutnab-Kangas (1979) and Baetens Beardsmore (1982) have provided expanded discussions regarding the international proliferation of multilingualism. In the United States, Skrabanek (1970), Waggoner (1984) and Hakuta (1986) report that school-age Chicano children in the United States continue to be bilingual with no indication that this phenomenon will be disrupted. By the year 2000 the number of limited-English-speaking Chicano school-age children in the US is estimated to double.

One of the first systematic linguistic investigations of bilingualism in young children was reported by Leopold (1939, 1947, 1949a, 1949b). This author set out to study the simultaneous acquisition of English and German in his own daughter. These initial descriptive reports indicate that as the subject was exposed to both languages during infancy, she seemed to weld both languages into one system during initial language production periods. For instance, early language forms were characterized by free mixing. Language production during later periods seem to indicate that the use of English and German grammatical forms developed independently.

With respect to bilingual development in Chicano children, Padilla and Liebman (1975) report a longitudinal linguistic analysis of Spanish-English acquisition in two 3-year-old children. These researchers followed the model of Brown (1973) in recording linguistic interactions of children over a five-month period. By an analysis of several dependent linguistic variables (phonological, morphological, and syntactic characteristics) over this time period, they observed gains in both languages, although several English forms were in evidence while similar Spanish forms were not. They also report the differentiation of linguistic systems at phonological, lexical and syntactic levels. Padilla and Liebman (1975) conclude:

> the appropriate use of both languages in mixed utterances was evident; that is, correct word order was preserved. For example, there were no occurrences of 'raining esta' or 'a es baby', nor was there evidence for such utterances as 'esta raining' and 'es a baby.' There was also an absence of the redundancy of unnecessary words which might tend to confuse meaning.

Garcia (1983) reports developmental data related to the acquisition of Spanish and English for Chicano preschoolers (3–4 years old) and the acquisition of

English for a group of matched English-only speakers. The results of that study can be summarized as follows: (a) acquisition of both Spanish and English was evident at complex morphological levels for Spanish/English 4-year-old children; (b) for the bilingual children studied, English was more advanced based on the quantity and quality of obtained morphological instances of language productions; and (c) there was no quantitative or qualitative difference between Spanish/English bilingual children and matched English-only controls on English language morphological productions.

Huerta (1977) conducted a longitudinal analysis of a Spanish/English Chicano 2-year-old child. She reports a similar pattern of continuous Spanish/English development, although identifiable stages appeared in which one language forged ahead of the other. Moreover, she reports the significant occurrence of mixed language utterance which made use of both Spanish and English vocabulary as well as Spanish and English morphology. In all such cases, these mixed linguistic utterances were well formed and communicative.

Garcia, Maez and Gonzalez (1979) in a study of Chicano bilingual children 4, 5 and 6 years of age, found regional differences in the relative occurrence of switched language utterances. That is, bilingual Spanish/English children from Texas, Arizona, Colorado and New Mexico, showed higher (15–20 per cent) incidences of language switched utterances than children from California or Illinois, especially at pre-kindergarten levels. These findings suggest that some children may very well develop an 'interlanguage' in addition to the acquisition of two independent language systems later in development.

The above 'developmental' linguistic findings can be summarized as follows for Chicano bilingual:

1 The acquisition of two languages can be parallel, but, need not be. That is, the qualitative character of one language may lag behind, surge ahead, or develop equally with the other language (Huerta, 1977; Padilla and Liebman, 1975).

2 The acquisition of two languages may very well result in an interlanguage, incorporating the attributes (lexicon, morphology and syntax) of both languages. But, this need not be the case. Languages may develop independently (Huerta, 1977; Garcia, Maez and Gonzalez 1979).

3 The acquisition of two languages need not hamper, structurally, the acquisition of either language (Garcia, 1983; Hakuta, 1986).

Intelligence, Cognition and Bilingualism

A separate but significant research approach to the understanding of bilingualism and its effects has focused on the cognitive (intellectual) character of the bilingual. Based on correlational studies indicating a negative relationship between childhood bilingualism and performance on standardized tests of intelligence, a causal statement linking bilingualism to 'depressed' intelligence was tempting and this negative conclusion characterized much early work (Darcy, 1953). Due to the myriad of methodological problems of studies investigating this type of relationship, any conclusions concerning bilingualism and intellectual functioning (as measured by standardized individual or group intelligence tests) are extremely tentative in nature (Darcy, 1963; Diaz, 1983).

With the general shift away from utilizing standardized measures of intelligence with school-age populations of non-English backgrounds, the cognitive character of bilingual children has received attention. Leopold (1939) in one of the first investigations of bilingual acquisition reported a general cognitive plasticity for his young bilingual daughter. He suggested that linguistic flexibility (in the form of bilingualism) was related to a number of non-linguistic, cognitive tasks such as categorization, verbal signal discrimination, and creativity. Peal and Lambert (1962) in a summarization of their work with French/English bilingual and English monolinguals suggested that the intellectual experience of acquiring two languages contributed to advantageous mental flexibility, superior concept formation, and a generally diversified set of mental abilities.

Feldman and Shen (1971), Ianco-Worall (1972), Carringer (1974), and Cummins and Gulatsan (1975) provide relevant evidence regarding such flexibility. Feldman and Shen (1971) report differential responding between Chicano Spanish/English bilingual and English monolinguals across three separate tasks reflecting Piagetian-like problem solving and metalinguistic awareness. Results indicated significantly increased cognitive flexibility for Chicano bilinguals. Ianco-Worral (1972) compared matched bilingual (Afrikaans/English) and monolingual (either Afrikaans or English) on metalinguistic tasks requiring separation of word sounds and word meanings. Comparison of scores on these tasks indicated that bilinguals concentrated more on attaching meaning to words rather than sounds. Ben-Zeev's (1977) work with Hebrew-English bilingual children is also related to the metalinguistic abilities of these children. Subjects in these studies showed superiority in symbol substitution and verbal transformational tasks. Ben-Zeev summarizes: 'Two strategies characterized by thinking patterns of the bilingual in relation to verbal material: readiness to impute structure and readiness to reorganize' (p. 1017).

Recent research specifically with Chicano bilinguals (Kessler and Quinn 1986, 1987) supplies additional empirical support for the emerging understanding that bilingual children outperform monolingual children on specific measures of cognitive and metalinguistic awareness. Kessler and Quinn (1987) had bilingual and monolingual children engage in a variety of symbolic categorization tasks which required their attention to abstract verbal features of concrete objects. Spanish/English, Chicano bilinguals from low socioeconomic status (SES) backgrounds outperformed low SES English monolinguals and high SES English monolinguals on these tasks. Such findings are particularly significant given the criticism by McNab (1979) that many bilingual 'cognitive advantage' studies utilized only high SES subjects of non-US minority backgrounds. It is important to note that findings of metalinguistic advantages have been reported for low SES Puerto Rican students as well (Galambos and Hakuta, 1988).

Theoretical attempts linking bilingualism to cognitive attributes have emerged. In an attempt to identify more specifically the relationship between cognition and bilingualism, Cummins (1979, 1981, 1984) has proposed an interactive theoretical proposition: children who do not achieve balanced proficiency in two languages (but who are immersed in a bilingual environment) may be cognitively 'different' and possibly 'disadvantaged'.

Any detailed conclusions concerning the relationship between the bilingual character of children and their cognitive functioning must continue to remain tentative (Diaz, 1983). However, it is the case that:

1 Bilingual children have been found to score lower than monolingual children on standardized measures of cognitive development, intelligence and school achievement.
2 Bilingual children have been found to score higher than 'matched' monolinguals on specific Piagetian, metalinguistic, concept-formation and creative cognitive tasks.
3 'Balanced' bilingual children have outperformed monolinguals and 'unbalanced' bilinguals on specific cognitive and metalinguistic tasks.

Social/Communicative Aspects of Bilingualism

As previously noted, language is a critical social repertoire. The linguistic component of any social interaction most often determines the general quality of that interaction (Bates, 1976; Canale, 1983; Cole, Dore, Hall and Dowley, 1978; Halliday, 1975; Hymes, 1974; Ramirez, 1985; Shantz, 1977). In doing so, it carries special importance for the bilingual child where social tasks include language choice. Moreover, like other children who acquire the ability to differentially employ linguistic codes determined by social attributes of the speaking context (Ervin-Tripp and Mitchell-Kernan, 1977; Phillips, 1972), bilingual children face the task of multiple code differentiation. Implicit in this discussion is the general notion that languages must not only be mastered in a structural sense and operate in conjunction with cognitive processes, they must be utilized as a social instrument. For Chicano children this means being communicatively competent in Spanish and English cultural contexts.

The study of language acquisition in context is known as *pragmatics* (Bates, 1976). This approach demands that we think of the context of communication as involving information about the speaker, the listener, the speaker's goal in using a particular utterance, the information assumed to be true in a particular speech context, and the rules governing discourse. For example, in considering the controversial rules for discourse, three aspects of language may be considered important: (a) how the child establishes a topic; (b) maintains a topic; or (c) changes the topic across 'turns' in a conversation. Adult speakers are generally adept at introducing a new topic into a conversation, by using such conventional routines as 'Let me tell you about X' or 'You'll never guess what happened today' or 'I want to talk to you about Y'. Adults can also maintain this topic across many turns in conversation, even when the other person participating is not particularly cooperative. Interest in these social contexts has generated studies in Chicano bilingual mother-child, teacher-child, and child-child interaction. Garcia (1983) reports an investigation of mother-child interaction including the description of Spanish/English use by children and adults (the children's mothers) in three different contexts: (a) preschool instruction periods, (b) preschool freeplay periods, and (c) the home. These descriptions pointed out very consistently that children, in particular, were 'choosing' to initiate an interaction in either Spanish or English as a function of the language in which the mother was using to initiate that interaction. A closer qualitative examination of the same mothers and children interacting is reported by Garcia and Carrasco (1981). This analysis suggested that almost 90 per cent of mother-child interactions were initiated by the mother, most often in Spanish. That is, mothers most often did not allow children to initiate. For those small number of instances in which children did initiate, the topic determined language choice. That is, 'what' the child spoke about was highly correlated with the language in which he/she chose to speak.

The richest data on the bilingual children dealing with topic initiation comes from child-child interactions. Ginishi (1981) investigated the use of Spanish and English among first-graders and concluded that the general language initiation rule for these students was: 'Speak to the listener in his/her best language'. Her analysis suggests that children when speaking with other children, first made a choice regarding language of initiation based on their previous language use history with their fellow students. Zentella (1981) agrees that bilingual students do make these decisions. She found, however, another discourse rule operating: 'You can speak to me in either English or Spanish'. Although Genishi's (1981) and Zentella's (1981) discourse rules differ, each observation suggests that bilingual students will make use of their social and language use history to construct guidelines related to discourse initiation. These studies suggest that particular sociolinguistic environments lead bilingual students to be aware of language choice issues related to discourse initiation.

A comprehensive understanding of early childhood bilingualism must, therefore, take into consideration more than the linguistic nature of the bilingual or the child's cognitive attributes. It must consider the child's surrounding environment. Recent data tentatively suggests that social context will determine:

1 The specific social language rules for each language.
2 The roles assigned to each language.

Summary

The linguistic, cognitive and social domains of the bilingual experience have been demonstrated as individually important in understanding the essence of the bilingual child. But, the interaction of these would seem to more clearly describe the ongoing developmental quality of bilingualism. This interactive conclusion suggests the following:

1 The linguistic, cognitive and social characters of the bilingual child are developing simultaneously.
2 Linguistic, cognitive and social development are interrelated. That is, cognitive processing factors may act to influence linguistic and social development. Linguistic development — the ability to operate within the structural aspects of language(s) — may act to influence social and potential cognitive functioning. In turn, the development of social competence influences directly the acquisition of linguistic and cognitive repertoires.

This interactive conceptualization is meant to reflect the interrelationship between linguistic, cognitive and social aspects of bilingual development often missing in educational programming for this population. Changes in each of these domains may be attributed to changes in other domains, and in turn, may further alter the qualitative character of the bilingual. It is recent linguistic, cognitive and social discourse data related to bilingualism that has transformed the study of bilingualism from a purely linguistic framework into one that requires an integrative conceptualization. This integrated research which considers as important the linguistic, cognitive and social aspects of bilingualism promises a greater understanding of this phenomenon than previous non-integrated investigations.

Second Language Acquisition

McLaughlin (1985) traces the reported scholarly interest in second language acquisition to the third millennium BC when Sumerian scholars received the task of translating their Arkadian conquerers' language into their own. Egyptian historical records indicate that by 1500 BC multilingual dictionaries were available. According to McLaughlin (1985), Egyptians and Jews received educational experiences in Greek, and Jewish scholars developed the comparative study of Semitic and non-Semitic languages, the scholarly foundation for modern comparative linguistics.

McLaughlin (1985) and Richards and Rodgers (1986) provide incisive updated reviews of the development of theoretical and instructional contributions related to second language acquisition. These authors agree that several themes characterize the historical treatment of this phenomenon with respect to minority students and Chicano students in particular. These themes include:

1 An interest in the relationship between first language and second language acquisition and input.
2 An understanding that the individual and social circumstances within which a second language is acquired can determine the course of second language acquisition.
3 A concern for psychological/cognitive processes utilized during second language acquisition.

The following discussion will explore these themes in recent research and theoretical contexts.

First and Second Language Acquisition

Learners' errors have been considered significant in proving an understanding regarding the strategies and processes the learner is employing during second language acquisition (Corder, 1967). Dulay and Burt (1974) studied the errors in the natural speech of one hundred and seventy-nine 5 to 8-year-olds (including a sample of Chicano children in California) learning English as a second language. They classified errors as either related to first language ('interference' errors) or related to normal language development ('developmental' errors). Their analysis indicated that 'interference' accounted for only 4.7 per cent of the errors while

87.1 per cent of the errors were similar to those made by children learning English as a first language. They postulated that a universal 'creative construction process' accounts for second language acquisition. The process was creative because nobody had modeled the type of sentences that children produce when acquiring a second language. Furthermore, they suggested that innate mechanisms caused children to use certain strategies to organize linguistic input. Dulay and Burt did not claim that they could define the specific nature of the innate mechanisms. They did claim, however, that these mechanisms have certain definable characteristics that cause children to use a limited set of hypotheses to deal with the knowledge they are acquiring. The strategies parallel those identified for first language acquisition.

Krashen (1981) has developed a conceptualization of second language acquisition which considers as fundamental this innate creative construction process. His 'natural order' hypothesis indicates that the acquisition of grammatical structures by the second language learner proceeds in a predictable 'natural' order, independent of first language experiences and/or proficiency. Such acquisition occurs unconsciously without the learner's concern for recognizing or utilizing structural rules. This 'monitor' hypothesis suggests that conscious learning of a second language can occur when the learner has achieved a significant knowledge of structural rules and has the time to apply those rules in a second language learning situation. Krashen, therefore, extends Dulay and Burt's creative construction and natural order conceptualizations by introducing the notion of the 'monitor' hypothesis, learning a second language by first understanding the grammatical structure and having the time to apply that grammatical knowledge. He concludes, however, that conscious learning of a second language is not as efficient or functional as the natural acquisition of a second language.

Other research has documented a distinct interrelationship between first and second language acquisition. Ervin-Tripp (1974) conducted a study of thirty-one English-speaking children between the ages of 4 and 9 who were living in Geneva and were attending French schools. She found that the errors these children made in French, their second language, were a result of their application of the same strategies that they had used in acquiring a first language. Such strategies as over-generalization, production simplification, and loss of sentence medial items, all predicted the kinds of errors that appeared. In over-generalization the American children acquiring French applied a subject-verb-object strategy to all sentences in French, and thus systematically misunderstood French passives. In production simplification they resisted using two forms if they felt that two forms had the same meaning. Also, medial pronouns were less often imitated than initial, or final pronouns. She believed that interference errors occurred only when the second language learner was forced to generate sentences about semantically difficult material or concepts unfamiliar in the new culture.

Moreover, the strategies children use in acquiring a second language may change as they become more proficient in the second language. At the beginning of second language (L2) acquisition, imitation plays an important role in language learning. As children acquire more of the target language they begin to use first language (L1) acquisition strategies to analyze this input.

Hakuta (1974) demonstrated that the child, through rote memorization, acquires segments of speech called 'prefabricated patterns'. Examples of these prefabricated patterns are various allomorphs of the copula, the segment 'do you' as employed in questions, and the segment 'how to' as embedded in how questions. These patterns are very useful in communication. The child uses these patterns without understanding their structure but rather with knowledge of which particular situations call for what patterns in order to communicate in the target language.

Wong-Fillmore (1976) spent a year observing five Spanish-speaking Chicano children acquiring English naturally, and she noticed the same phenomena. The first thing the children did was to figure out what was being said by observing the relationship between certain expressions and the situational context. They inferred the meaning of certain words they began to use as 'formulaic expressions'. (These expressions were acquired and used as analyzed wholes.) The 'formulaic expressions' became the raw material used by the children to figure out the structure of the language. Wong-Fillmore gave two examples of how children use first language acquisition strategies to begin to analyze these .xpressions:

> The first involves noticing how parts of expressions used by others vary
> in accordance with changes in the speech situation in which they occur.
> The second involves noticing which parts of the formulaic expressions
> are like other utterances in the speech of others (p. 15).

As the children figured out which formulas in their speech could be varied, they were able to 'free' the constituents they contained and use them in productive speech.

In addition, at the beginning of L2 acquisition, children seem to depend much more on first language transfer strategies. As learners acquire more of the second language they depend less on these strategies and more on such strategies characteristic of first language acquisition as over-generalization (Hakuta, 1986).

As McLaughlin (1985) has summarized, children acquiring a second language may depend initially on transfer from the first language and on imitation and rote memorization of the second language. In more practical terms, the less interaction a second language learner has with native speakers, the more likely transfer from the first language to the second language will be observed. As the second language is acquired many of the strategies that children use to acquire the second language seem to be the same as those used in first language acquisition.

The Importance of L2 Input

It is apparent that target-language input provides children with the raw material necessary for language acquisition. In addition, the frequency and salience of forms in the input data influence the presence of these forms in the output. Hatch (1974) found that the frequency of morphemes in the input data appears to influence the sequential acquisition of these morphemes. For example, the order of acquisition of question words appears to parallel their frequency in what children heard. She also noted an interaction between frequency of forms and semantic importance. A form appearing frequently, though of low semantic importance, will be acquired later. Larsen-Freeman (1976) found that in-class teacher talk of ESL teachers showed a similar rank order for frequency of morphemes as found in the learner output. Hakuta (1975) discovered that the auxiliary most often omitted by learners in utterances involving the catenative 'gonna' was 'are'. He found such a construction less perceptually salient to the learner because of its absence. The auxiliary because of its absence in the input resulted in its omission in the learner's output.

These observations make researchers (Hakuta, 1975; Hatch, 1974; Larsen-Freeman, 1976) question whether the invariant order of morpheme acquisition (Dulay and Burt, 1974) is a reaction to the input to which the learner was exposed. The correspondence between input and output suggests that interaction between speakers might be important in structuring language output. Even Krashen (1981), a proponent of the natural order of grammatical acquisition, suggests in his 'input' hypothesis that second language learning is enhanced under conditions in which the learner is provided with input that contains 'the next level of linguistic competence'. Krashen (1981) identifies this enhancement strategy as 'providing comprehensible input'. Paradoxically, however, he cautions against any conscious strategy to provide 'comprehensible input' and instead suggests natural interaction which focuses on meaning. Therefore, even though second language learning may be enriched by providing 'comprehensible input', any attempt to do so without the 'natural' concern for conveying meaning could be linguistically disruptive.

Conversely, Keenan (1976) hypothesizes that the interactions from which syntactic structures develop are determined by the rules of discourse. As indicated earlier in this chapter, certain rules are generally followed in order to carry on a conversation. One must get the attention of the conversational partner. The speaker then nominates a topic and develops it. Partners take turns. Topic clarification, shifting, avoidance, and interruption characterize interactions. Finally the topic is terminated.

Adult-child and child-child conversations are very difficult. Each genre of conversation follows the rules of discourse but the rules are applied differently. As a consequence, the child acquiring another language learns different things from each type of conversation. In adult-child conversations the rules of discourse put both the child and the adult under certain constraints (Garcia, 1986; Hatch, 1978; McLaughlin, 1985). These constraints structure the interaction, and consequently also the output. The child must first get the adult's attention. Once this is accomplished by gestures and verbalizations the child must nominate a topic. The adult is also constrained by the rules of discourse in that the response must be relevant. For the response to be relevant, the information about the topic must be shared by both child and adult. The adult's response usually clarifies the topic that has been nominated by labeling it or asking for more information about it. *What, where, whose, what color, how many, what is x doing, can x verb, is x verbing* are the kinds of questions the adults can use in response to the child's topic nomination and be relevant. The child's response in turn must also be relevant. As a result there is a great deal of what, where, whose, who is verbing, etc. Hatch (1978) hypothesized that this accounted for the order of acquisition of these forms in previous studies. If the child is unable to say something relevant he or she can just repeat what the adult has said, but with the appropriate intonation. He or she will answer a question with rising intonation and a statement with falling intonation.

In summary, current research suggests that natural communication situations must be provided for second language acquisition to occur. Regardless of the differences in emphasis of the theories discussed above, recent theoretical propositions regarding second language acquisition propose that through natural conversations the learner receives the necessary input and structures which promote second language acquisition. This finding suggests that in schooling situations highly segregated Chicano classrooms may significantly limit L2 acquisition while L1–L2 integrated classrooms will promote L2 acquisition.

Social Factors Related to Second Language Acquisition

There are sociocultural variables that contribute to a child's motivation to communicate in the target language. The attitude that the learner has towards members of the cultural group whose language he or she is learning influences language acquisition. Gardner and Lambert (1972) found that the positive attitude of English-speaking Canadians towards French-speaking Canadians led to high integrative motivation to learn French. Oller and colleagues (Oller, Baca and Vigil, 1978; Oller, Hudson and Liu, 1977) investigated the relationship between Chinese, Japanese, and Chicano students' achievement in English with their attitude towards the foreign language group. Positive attitudes toward the target language group corresponded to higher language proficiency.

Schumann (1976) found that Chicano children are more motivated to learn a second language if they do not perceive this learning process as alienation from their own culture. If a child belongs to a family whose integration pattern is preservation of the native language and culture rather than assimilation or acculturation, the child may be less motivated to acquire the second language. There may be less impetus for a cultural group to assimilate or acculturate if that group has its own community in the 'foreign country', or if the duration of residence in the foreign country is short.

Not only is the individual's attitude toward the target culture important, but the perceived positive or negative relationship between two cultures influences second language acquisition. Schumann (1976) hypothesized that the greater the social distance between the two cultures, the greater the difficulty the second language learner will have in learning the target language, and conversely, the smaller the social distance, the better will be the language learning situation. Social distance is determined in part by the relative status of two cultures. Two cultures that are politically, culturally, and technically equal in status have less social distance than two cultures whose relationship is characterized by dominance or subordination. In addition, there is less social distance if the cultures of the two groups are congruent.

A child motivated to learn a second language still needs certain social skills to facilitate his or her ability to establish and maintain contact with speakers of the target language. Wong-Fillmore (1976) and Wong-Fillmore and Valadez (1986) suggest that individual differences in the social skills of the child influence the rate of second language acquisition. Second language learners who seem most successful employ specific social strategies:

1   Join a group and act as if you understand what's going on even if you don't. The learners must initiate interactions and pretend to know what is

going on. As a result they will be included in the conversations and activities.

2   Give the impression with a few well chosen words that you can speak the language. Children must be willing to use whatever language they have and as a result, other children will keep trying to communicate with them.

3   Count on your friends for help. The acquisition of language depends on the participation of both the learner and someone who already speaks the language — the friend. The children's friends helped in several ways. They showed faith in the learner's ability to learn the language, and by including the learner in their activities they made a real effort to understand what the learner was saying. They also provided the learner with natural linguistic input that he or she could understand.

Seliger (1977) has also demonstrated that high-input generators are the most successful L2 learners. High-input generators are learners who place themselves in situations in which they are exposed to the target language and are willing to use it for communication. Therefore they receive the necessary input as well as the opportunity for practice.

In summary, children acquire a second language naturally. Although the underlying cognitive processes used by children in acquiring a second language may be similar in all children, social factors in social skills and the social climate do seem to influence directly and significantly second language acquisition. For Chicano language minority students, a schooling context which promotes L1 and provides the opportunity for L2 interaction is most likely to achieve successful L2 acquisition.

Summary

From the above review of second language acquisition theory and research, 'second language' acquisition:

1   has been characterized as *related* and *not related* to acquisition of L1 linguistic structures;
2   has been related to specific rules of discourse;
3   may be influenced by the motivation to learn a second language; and,
4   has been related to social factors.

Hammerly (1985) has also suggested that it is useful to indicate what second language acquisition is *not*:

1   an intellectual exercise in involving the understanding and memorization of grammar;
2   translation;
3   memorization of sentences;
4   mechanical conditioning; and/or,
5   applying abstract rules.

Our understanding of second language acquisition requires cognizance of similar interrelationship identified in this chapter when discussing the nature of bilingualism. Each phenomenon has been 'diagnosed' as dependent on L1–L2 crosslinguistic effects in combination with the social aspects of language use and the psychological/cognitive processes which serve and guide learning. Certain theoretical emphases and contradictions discussed in this chapter continue to remind us that our understanding of second language acquisition remains incomplete. This is not to suggest that little is known. The above discussion has presented a large body of research and various sophisticated conceptualizations (theories) to guide our understanding of this phenomenon.

From Bilingual Education to Language Minority Education

The debate regarding the education of Chicano students in the United States has centered on the instructional use of the two languages of the bilingual student. With regard to the schooling process, the broader issue has been the effective instruction of a growing population of ethnic minority students who do not speak English and therefore are considered candidates for special educational programming that takes into consideration this language difference. Discussion of this issue has included cross-disciplinary dialogues involving psychology, linguistics, sociology, politics, and education (for a more thorough discussion of these issues see August and Garcia, 1988; Baker and de Kanter, 1983; Cummins, 1979; Garcia, 1983; Hakuta and Gould, 1987; Rossell and Ross, 1986; Troike, 1981; and Willig, 1985). The central theme of these discussions has to do with the specific instructional role of the native language. At one extreme of this discussion, the utilization of the native language is recommended for a significant part of the non-English-speaking student's elementary school years, from 4–6 years, with a concern for native language communicative and academic 'mastery' prior to immersion into the English curriculum (Wong-Fillmore and Valadez, 1986). At the other extreme, immersion into an English curriculum is recommended early — as early as preschool — with minimal use of the native language and a concern for English language 'leveling' by instructional staff to facilitate understanding on behalf of the limited-English-speaking student (Rossel and Ross, 1986).

Each of these disparate approaches argues that the result of its implementation brings psychological, linguistic, social, political and educational benefits. The 'native language' approach suggests that competencies in the native language, particularly as they relate to academic learning, provide important psychological and linguistic foundations for second language learning and academic learning in general — that is, 'you really only learn to read once'. Native language instruction builds on social and cultural experiences and serves to politically empower students in communities that have been historically excluded from meaningful participation in majority educational institutions. The 'immersion' approach suggests that the sooner a child receives instruction in English the more likely that student will acquire English proficiency — 'more time on task, better proficiency'. English proficiency will in turn mitigate against educational failure, social separation and segregation, and, ultimate economic disparity.

As this discussion has unfolded, it is clear that the education of students who come to our schools speaking a language other than English has received considerable research, policy and practice attention in the last two decades. The Departments of Education, Health and Human Services as well as private foundations have supported specific demographic studies and instructional research related to this population of students, preschool through college. The United States Congress has authorized legislation targeted directly at these students on five separate occasions (1968, 1974, 1978, 1984, and 1987) while numerous states have enacted legislation and developed explicit program guidelines. Moreover, Federal District Courts and the US Court have concluded adjudication proceedings that directly influence the educational treatment of language minority students. This significant attention has allowed answers to some questions of importance that were unanswerable less than a decade ago. The following discussion will highlight these questions in light of emerging information regarding Chicano language minority students.

Who Are These Students?

As one searches for a comprehensive definition of the 'language minority' student, a continuum of definitional attempts unfold. At one end of the continuum are general definitions such as 'students who come from homes in which a language other than English is spoken'. At the other end of that continuum are highly operationalized definitions, 'students scored above the first quartile on a standardized test of English language proficiency'. Regardless of the definition adopted, it is apparent that these students come in a variety of linguistic shapes and forms. The language minority population in the United States continues to be linguistically heterogeneous with over 100 distinct language groups identified. For example, some Chicanos are monolingual Spanish speakers while others are to some degree bilingual. Other non-English-speaking minority groups in the United States are similarly heterogeneous. Not inconsequential is the related cultural attributes of this population of students, making this population not only linguistically distinct but also culturally distinct.

Describing the 'typical' Chicano language minority student, as you may have already surmised, is highly problematic. However, put simply, we might agree that the student is one: (a) who is characterized by substantive participation in a non-English-speaking Chicano social environment, (b) who has acquired the normal communicative abilities of that social environment, and, (c) who is exposed to a substantive English-speaking environment, more than likely for the first time, during the formal schooling process. Estimates of the number of language minority students have been compiled by the federal government on several occasions (Development Associates, 1984; O'Malley, 1981). These estimates differ because of the definition adopted for identifying these students, the particular measure utilized to obtain the estimate, and the statistical treatment utilized to generalize beyond the actual sample obtained. For example, O'Malley (1981) defined the language minority student population by utilizing a specific cutoff score on an English language proficiency test administered to a stratified sample of students. Development Associates (1984) estimated the population by utilizing reports from a stratified sample of local school districts. Therefore, estimates of language minority students have ranged between 1,300,000

(Development Associates, 1984) to 3,600,000 (O'Malley, 1981) with the following attributes:

1 The total number of language minority children, ages 5–14, in 1976 approximated 2.52 million, with a projected increase to 3.40 million in the year 2000 (Waggoner, 1984). In 1983, this population was more conservatively estimated to be 1.29 million (Development Associates, 1984). Recall that this divergence in estimates reflects the procedures used to obtain language minority 'counts' and estimates.

2 The majority of these children reside throughout the United States, but with distinct geographical clustering. For example, about 62 per cent of language minority children are Chicano students found in Arizona, Colorado, California, New Mexico, and Texas (O'Malley, 1981; Development Associates, 1984; Waggoner, 1984).

3 Of the estimated number of language minority children in 1978, 72 per cent were of Spanish language background, 22 per cent other European languages, 5 per cent Asians, and 1 per cent American Indian. However, such distributions will change due to differential growth rates, and by the year 2000, the proportion of Spanish language background children is projected to be about 77 per cent of the total (O'Malley, 1981). Estimates by Development Associates (1984) for students in grades K-6 indicate that 76 per cent are Spanish language background; 8 per cent Southeast Asian (Vietnamese, Cambodian, Hmong, etc.); 5 per cent other European; 5 per cent East Asian (Chinese, Korean, etc.); and, 5 per cent other (Arabic, Navaho, etc.).

4 For the national school districts sampled in the nineteen most highly impacted states utilized by Development Associates (1984), 17 per cent of the total K-6 student population was estimated as language minority in these states.

Regardless of differing estimates, a significant number of students from language backgrounds other than English are served by US schools. Moreover, this population is expected to increase steadily in the future. The challenge these students present to US educational institutions will continue to increase concomitantly.

What Types of Educational Programs Serve These Students?

For a school district staff with language minority students there are many possible program options: 'transitional bilingual education', 'maintenance bilingual education', 'English-as-a-second-language', 'immersion', 'sheltered English', 'submersion', etc. (Government Accounting Office, 1987). Ultimately, staff will reject program labels and instead answer the following questions (August and Garcia, 1988):

1 What are the native language (L1) and second language (L2) characteristics of the students, families and community (ies) we serve?

2 What model of instruction is desired?
   (a) How do we choose to utilize L1 and L2 *as mediums of instruction*?
   (b) How do we choose to handle the *instruction* of L1 and L2?
3 What is the nature of staff and resources necessary to implement the desired instruction?

These program initiatives can be differentiated by the way they utilize the native language and English during instruction. A recent report by Development Associates (1984) surveyed 333 school districts in the nineteen states that served over 80 per cent of language minority students in the United States. For grades K–5, they report the following salient features regarding the use of language(s) during the instruction of language minority students:

1 Ninety-three per cent of the schools reported that the use of English predominated in their programs; conversely, 7 per cent indicated that the use of the native language predominated.
2 Sixty per cent of the sampled schools reported that both the native language and English were utilized during instruction.
3 Thirty per cent of the sampled schools reported minimal or no use of the native language during instruction.

Two-thirds of these schools have chosen to utilize some form of bilingual curriculum to serve this population of students. One-third of these schools minimize or altogether ignore native language use in their instruction of language minority students. Recall that some two-thirds to three-fourths of language minority students in this country are of Spanish-speaking backgrounds. Programs which serve these students have been characterized primarily as 'Bilingual Transitional Education'. These programs call for the transition of these students from early-grade, Spanish-emphasis instruction to later-grade, English-emphasis instruction, and, eventually to English-only instruction.

Recent research in transition-type schools suggests that language minority students can be served effectively. These effective schools are organized to develop educational structures and processes that take into consideration both the broader aspects of effective schools reported for English-speaking students (Purkey and Smith, 1983) as well as specific attributes relevant to language minority students (Carter and Chatfield, 1986; Garcia, 1988; Tikunoff, 1983). Of particular importance has been the positive effect of intensive instruction in the native language that focuses on literacy development (Wong-Fillmore and Valadez, 1986). Hakuta and Gould (1987) and Hudelson (1987) maintain that skills and concepts learned in the native language provide a 'scaffold' for acquisition of new knowledge in the second language.

For the one-third of the students receiving little or no instruction in the native language, two alternative types of instructional approaches likely predominate: ESL and immersion. Each of these program types depends on the primary utilization of English during instruction but does not ignore the fact that the students served are limited in English proficiency. However, these programs do not require instructional personnel who speak the native language of the student. Moreover, these programs are suited to classrooms in which there is no substantial number of students from one non-English-speaking group, but instead may have a heterogeneous non-English background student population (Ovando and Collier, 1985).

Both ESL and immersion programs have been particularly influenced by recent theoretical developments regarding the instruction of a second language (Chamot and O'Malley, 1986; Krashen, 1984). These developments have suggested that effective second language learning is best accomplished under conditions that simulate natural communicative interactions and minimize the formal instruction of linguistic structures, e.g., memorization drills, learning grammatical rules, etc. Although ESL programs continue to involve 'pull-out' sessions in which students are removed from the regular classroom to spend time on concentrated language learning activities with specially trained educational staff, the recent theoretical and practice consensus is that such language learning experiences should be communicative and centered around academic content areas (Chamot and O'Malley, 1986).

School district staff have been creative in developing a wide range of language minority student programs. They have answered the above questions differentially for: (a) different language groups (Spanish, Vietnamese, Chinese, etc.), (b) different grade levels within a school, (c) different sub-groups of language minority students within a classroom, and even different levels of language proficiency. The result has been a broad and at times perplexing variety of program models.

What Federal and State Policies Have Been Generated?

The immediately preceding discussion has attempted to lay a foundation for understanding *who* the Chicano language minority student is and *how* that student has been served. This discussion turns now to educational policy: first, federal legislative and legal initiatives, and second, state initiatives.

Federal Legislative Initiatives

The United States Congress set a minimum standard for the education of language minority students in public educational institutions in its passage of Title VI of the Civil Rights Act of 1964 prohibiting discrimination by educational institutions on the basis of race, color, sex or national origin and by subsequent Equal Educational Opportunity Act of 1974 (EEOA). The EEOA was an effort by Congress to specifically define what constitutes a denial of constitutionally guaranteed equal educational opportunity. The EEOA provides in part:

> No state shall deny equal educational opportunities to an individual on account of his or her race, color, sex, or national origin, by ... the failure by an educational agency to take appropriate action to overcome language barriers that impede equal participation by students in its instructional programs. 20 USC ss 1703(f).

This statute does not mandate specific education treatment, but it does require public educational agencies to sustain programs to meet the language needs of their students.

The Congress of the United States on five occasions (1968, 1974, 1978, 1984, and 1987) has passed specific legislation related to the education of language minority students. The Bilingual Education Act (BEA) of 1968 was intended as a demonstration program designed to meet the educational needs of low-income limited-English-speaking children. Grants were awarded to local educational agencies, institutions of higher education, or regional research facilities to: (a) develop and operate bilingual education programs, native history and culture programs, early childhood education programs, adult education programs, and programs to train bilingual aides; (b) make efforts to attract and retain as teachers, individuals from non-English-speaking backgrounds; (c) establish co-operation between the home and the school.

Four major reauthorizations of the BEA have occurred since 1968 — in 1974, 1978, 1984 and 1987. As a consequence of the 1974 Amendments (Public Law 93-380), a bilingual education program was defined for the first time as 'instruction given in, and study of English and to the extent necessary to allow a child to progress effectively through the education system, the native language' (Schneider, 1976, p. 146). The goal of bilingual education continued to be a transition to English rather than maintenance of the native language. Children no longer had to be low-income to participate. New programs were funded, including a graduate fellowship program for study in the field of training teachers for bilingual educational programs, and a program for the development, assessment, and dissemination of classroom materials.

In the Bilingual Education Amendments of 1978 (Public Law 95-561), program eligibility was expanded to include students with limited-English academic proficiency as well as students with limited-English-speaking ability. Parents were given a greater role in program planning and operation. Teachers were required to be proficient in both English and in the native language of the children in the program. Grant recipients were required to demonstrate how they would continue the program when federal funds were withdrawn.

The Bilingual Education Act of 1984 created new program options including special alternative instructional programs that did not require use of the child's native language. These program alternatives were expanded in 1987. State and local agency program staff were required to collect data, identify the population served and describe program effectiveness. Over one billion federal dollars have been appropriated through Title VII legislation for educational activities (program development, program implementation, professional training, and research) for language minority students. In addition, other congressional appropriations (e.g., Vocational Education, Chapter I, etc.) explicitly target language minority students.

Federal Legal Initiatives

The 1974 United States Supreme Court decision in *Lau v. Nichols* (44 US 563) is the landmark statement of the rights of language minority students indicating that limited-English-proficient students must be provided with language support:

[T]here is no equality of treatment merely by providing students with the same facilities, textbooks, teachers, and curriculum: for students who do not understand English are effectively foreclosed from any meaningful discourse.

Basic English skills are at the very core of what these public schools teach. Imposition of a requirement that, before a child can effectively participate in the education program he must already have acquired those basic skills is to make a mockery of public education. We know that those who do not understand English are certain to find their classroom experiences wholly incomprehensible and in no way meaningful (*Lau v. Nichols*, 44 US 563, p. 17).

The fifth Circuit *Castaneda v. Pickard* (1981) court set three requirements that constitute an appropriate program for language minority students:

1 The theory must be based on a sound educational theory.
2 The program must be 'reasonably calculated to implement effectively' the chosen theory.
3 The program must produce results in a reasonable time.

The courts have also required appropriate action to overcome language barriers. 'Measures which will actually overcome the problem', are called for by the *US v. Texas* (506 F. Supp. at 43), or 'results indicating that the language barriers confronting students are actually being overcome' are mandated by the *Castaneda* court (628 F. 2nd at 1010). Therefore, local school districts and state education agencies have a burden to assess the effectiveness of special language programs on an ongoing basis. Other court decisions have delineated staff professional training attributes and the particular role of standardized tests.

State Initiatives

Through state legislation, twelve states named mandate special educational services for language minority students, twelve states permit these services, and one state prohibits them. Twenty-six states have no legislation that directly addresses language minority students.

State program policy for language minority students can be characterized as follows:

1 Implementing instructional programs that allow or require instruction in a language other than English (17 states).
2 Establishing special qualifications for the certification of professional instructional staff (15 states).
3 Providing school districts supplementary funds in support of educational programs (15 states).
4 Mandating a cultural component (15 states).
5 Requiring parental consent for enrollment of students (11 states).

Eight states (Arizona, California, Colorado, Illinois, Indiana, Massachusetts, Rhode Island, and Texas) impose all of the above requirements concurrently. Such a pattern suggests continued attention by states to issues related to language minority students (see August and Garcia, 1988, for details).

General Policy and Practice Implications for Education

The previous discussions of bilingual acquisition and second language acquisition have attempted to highlight important data and theory that serve to provide an understanding of these phenomena. These same data and theory, however, have influenced the educational treatment of Chicano language minority students. As indicated previously, the knowledge based on this area continues to expand, but is in no way to be considered complete or overly comprehensive. In addition, it would be an error to conclude that the data and theory emerged have been a primary factor in determining the educational treatment of language minority students. It does seem appropriate, however, to identify in the present discussion possible program and policy implications derived from research and theory as highlighted by our own discussion and that of Hakuta and Snow (1986), August and Garcia (1988) and Hakuta and Garcia (1989).

1   One major goal of Chicano language minority education should be the development of the full repertoire of linguistic skills in English, in preparation for participation in mainstream classes.

2   Time spent learning the native language is not time lost in developing English. Children can become fluent in a second language without losing the first language, and can maintain the first language without retarding the development of the second language.

3   There is no cognitive cost to the development of bilingualism in children; very possibly bilingualism enhances children's thinking skills.

4   Language minority education programs for Chicanos should have the flexibility of adjusting to individual and cultural differences among children. Furthermore, educators should develop the expectation that it is not abnormal for some students to need instruction in two languages for relatively long periods of time.

5   Educators should expect that young children will take several years to learn a second language to a level like that of a native speaker. At the same time, they should not have lower expectations of older learners, who can typically learn languages quite quickly.

6   Particularly for children who on other grounds are at risk for reading failure, reading should be taught in the native language. Reading skills acquired in the native language will transfer readily and quickly to English, and will result in higher ultimate reading achievement in English.

7   A major problem for minority-group children is that young English-speaking children share the negative stereotypes of their parents and the society at large. Any action that upgrades the status of the minority child and his language contributes to the child's opportunities for friendship with native English-speaking children.

In summary, theoretical (and to some extent, research) support can be identified for educational interventions that choose to utilize language in a variety of distinct ways within an educational program for language minority students. It seems necessary to conclude that the present state of research and theory with respect to the language and the education of Chicano language minority students does allow for some specific conclusions. Of course, it is recommended that educational professionals in their quest to intervene for betterment of Chicano students, carefully scrutinize relevant theory and research and utilize that analysis to design, implement and evaluate interventions of significance to their particular educational circumstances. It is fair to request from such designers and implementers to provide a clear theoretical and research foundation, one which can in turn receive the necessary careful scrutiny.

References

AUGUST, D. and GARCIA, E. (1988) *Language Minority Education in the United States: Research, Policy and Practice*, Chicago, IL, Charles C. Thomas.

BAETENS BEARDSMORE, H. (1982) *Bilingualism: Basic Principles*, Clevedon, UK, Tieto Ltd.

BAKER, K.A. and DE KANTER, A.A. (1983) 'An answer from research on bilingual education', *American Education*, pp. 48–88.

BATES, E. (1976) *Language in Context: The Acquisition of Pragmatics*, New York, Academic Press.

BEN-ZEEV, S. (1977) 'The influence of bilingualism on cognitive strategy and cognitive development', *Child Development*, **48**, pp. 1009–18.

BOWERMAN, M. (1975) 'Crosslinguistic similarities at two stages of syntactic development', in E. LENNENBERG and E. LENNENBERG (Eds) *Foundations of Language Development*, London, UNESCO Press, pp. 47–69.

BRAINE, M.D.S. (1976) 'Children's first word combination', *Monographs of the Society for Research in Child Development*, New York: John Wiley.

BROWN, R.A. (1973) *A First Language: The Early Stages*, Cambridge, MA, Harvard University Press.

CANALE, M. (1983) 'From communicative competence to communicative pedagogy', in J. RICHARDS and R. SCHMIDT (Eds) *Language and Communication*, London, Langman.

CARRINGER, D.C. (1974) 'Creative thinking abilities of Mexican youth: The relationship of bilingualism', *Journal of Cross-Cultural Psychology*, **5**, pp. 492–504.

CARTER, T.P. and CHATFIELD, M.L. (1986) 'Effective bilingual schools: Implications for policy and practice', *American Journal of Education*, **95**, pp. 200–34.

CASTANEDA V. PICKARD (1981) 648 F.2d 989, 1007 5th Cir. 1981; 103 S.ct. 3321.

CHAMOT, A.U. and O'MALLEY, J.M. (1986), *A Cognitive Academic Language Learning Approach: An ESL Content Based Curriculum*, Wheaton, MD, National Clearing House for Bilingual Education.

CHOMSKY, N. (1959) 'Review of B.F. Skinner', *Verbal Behavior and Language*, **35**, pp. 116–28.

COLE, M., DORE, J., HALL, W. and DOWLEY, G. (1978) 'Situation and task in children's talk', *Discourse Process*, **1**, pp. 119–26.

CORDER, S.P. (1967) 'The significance of learner's errors', *International Review of Applied Linguistics in Language Teaching*, **11**, pp. 176–85.

CUMMINS, J. (1979) 'Linguistic interdependence and the educational development of bilingual children', *Review of Educational Research*, **19**, pp. 222–51.

CUMMINS, J. (1981) 'The role of primary language developments in promoting educational

success for language minority students', in CALIFORNIA STATE DEPARTMENT OF EDUCA-
TION (Ed.) *Schooling and Language Minority Students: A Theoretical Framework* Los
Angeles, CA, Evaluation, Dissemination, and Assessment Center, pp. 3–50.

CUMMINS, J. (1984) *Bilingualism and Special Education*, San Diego, CA, College-Hill Press.

CUMMINS, J. and GULATSAN, M. (1975) 'Bilingual education and cognition', *Alberta Journal
of Educational Research*, **20**, pp. 259–69.

DARCY, N.T. (1953) 'A review of the literature of the effects of bilingualism on the
measurement of intelligence', *Journal of Genetic Psychology*, **82**, pp. 21–57.

DARCY, N.T. (1963) 'Bilingualism and the measurement of intelligence: Review of a
decade of research', *Journal of Genetic Psychology*, **103**, pp. 259–82.

DEVELOPMENT ASSOCIATES (1984) *Final Report Descriptive Study Phase of the National Longitudinal Evaluation of the Effectiveness of Services for Language Minority Limited English
Proficient Students*, Arlington, VA, Development Associates, December.

DIAZ, R.M. (1983) 'The impact of bilingualism on cognitive development', in E.W.
GORDON (Ed.) *Review of Research in Education*, Washington, DC, American Educational Research Association, pp. 23–54.

DULAY, H. and BURT, M. (1974) 'Natural sequence in child second language acquisition',
Working Papers on Bilingualism, Toronto, Canada, The Ontario Institute for Studies in
Education.

DURAN, R. (Ed.) (1981) *Latino Language and Communicative Behavior*, Norwood, NJ, Ablex.

ERVIN-TRIPP, S.M. (1974) 'Is second language learning like the first?' *TESOL Quarterly*, **8**,
pp. 111–27.

ERVIN-TRIPP, S. and MITCHELL-KERNAN, C. (1977) *Child Discourse*, New York, Academic
Press.

FELDMAN, C. and SHEN, M. (1971) 'Some language-related cognitive advantages of bilingual five-year-olds', *Journal of Genetic Psychology*, **118**, pp. 235–244.

GALAMBOS, S.J. and HAKUTA, K. (1988) 'Subject-specific and task-specific characteristics of
metalinguistic awareness in bilingual children', *Applied Linguistics*, **9**, pp. 141–62.

GARCIA, E. (1983) *Bilingualism in Early Childhood*, Albuquerque, NM, University of New
Mexico Press.

GARCIA, E. (1986) 'Bilingual development and the education of bilingual children during
early childhood', *American Journal of Education*, **95**, pp. 96–121.

GARCIA, E. (1988) 'Effective schooling for language minority students', in NATIONAL
CLEARING HOUSE FOR BILINGUAL EDUCATION (Ed.) *New Focus*, Arlington, VA, National Clearing House for Bilingual Education.

GARCIA, E. and CARRASCO, R. (1981) 'An analysis of bilingual mother-child discourse', in
Duran (Ed.) *Latino Language and Communicative Behavior*, New York: Ablex, pp. 173–
189.

GARCIA, E. and GONZALES, G. (1984) 'Spanish and Spanish-English development in the
Hispanic child', in J.V. MARTINEZ and R.H. MENDOZA (Eds) *Chicano Psychology*, New
York, Academic Press.

GARCIA, E., MAEZ, L. and GONZALEZ, G. (1979) 'Language switching in bilingual children:
a national perspective', in E. GARCIA (Ed.) *The Mexican-American Child: Language,
Cognition and Social Development*, Tempe Arizona State University, pp. 56–73.

GARDNER, R.C. and LAMBERT, E. (1972) *Attitudes and Motivation in Second Language Learning*, Rowley, MA, Newbury House.

GINISHI, C. (1981) 'Code switching in Chicano six-year-olds', in R. DURAN (Ed.) *Latino
Language and Communicative Behavior*, Norwood, NJ, Ablex, pp. 133–52.

GONZALEZ, G.C. (1970) 'The Acquisition of Spanish Grammar by Native Spanish Speakers', unpublished doctoral dissertation, University of Texas, Austin.

GONZALEZ G.C. (1990) *Chicano Education in the Era of Segregation*, Philadelphia, PA, The
Balch Institute Press.

GOVERNMENT ACCOUNTING OFFICE (1987) *Bilingual Education Policy and Practice*, Washington, DC, Author.

HAKUTA, K. (1974) 'A preliminary report on the development of grammatical morphemes in a Japanese girl learning English as a second language', *Working Papers in Bilingualism*, Toronto, The Ontario Institute for Studies in Education, **3**, pp. 294–316.

HAKUTA, K. (1975) 'Learning to speak a second language: what exactly does the child learn? in D.P. DATO (Ed.) *Georgetown University Round Table on Languages and Linguistics*, Washington, DC, Georgetown University Press.

HAKUTA, K. (1986) *Mirror of Language: The Debate on Bilingualism*, New York, Basic Books.

HAKUTA, K. and GARCIA, E. (1989) 'Bilingualism and education', *American Psychologist*, **44**, pp. 374–9.

HAKUTA, K. and GOULD, L.J. (1987), 'Synthesis of research on bilingual education', *Educational Leadership*, **44**, pp. 39–45.

HAKUTA, K. and SNOW, C. (1986) *The Role of Research in Policy Decisions About Bilingual Education*, Washington, DC, US House of Representatives, Education and Labor Committee (Testimony; January).

HALLIDAY, M. (1975) *Learning How to Mean: Explorations in the Development of Language*, London, Dover.

HAMMERLY, H. (1985) *An Integrated Theory of Language Teaching*, Burnby, Canada, Second Language Publications.

HATCH, E. (1974) 'Second language learning universal?' *Working Papers on Bilingualism*, Toronto, The Ontario Institute for Studies in Education, **3**, pp. 1–16.

HATCH, E. (1978) *Second Language Acquisition: A Book of Readings*, Rowley, MA, Newbury House.

HUDELSON, S. (1987) The role of native language literacy in the education of language minority children', *Language Arts*, **64**, pp. 827–41.

HUERTA, A. (1977) 'The development of codeswitching in a young bilingual', *Working Papers in Sociolinguistics*, **21**.

HYMES, D. (1974) *Foundations in Sociolinguistics: An Ethnographic Approach*, Philadelphia, PA, University of Pennsylvania.

IANCO-WORRAL, A. (1972) 'Bilingualism and cognitive development', *Child Development*, **43**, pp. 1390–400.

KEENAN, E. (1976) 'Conversational competence in children', *Journal of Child Language*, **1**, pp. 163–83.

KESSLER, C. and QUINN, M.E. (1986), 'Positive effects of bilingualism on science problem-solving abilities', in J.E. ALATIS and J.J. STACZEK (Eds) *Perspectives on Bilingual Education*, Washington, DC, Georgetown University Press, pp. 289–96.

KESSLER, C. and QUINN, M.E. (1987) 'Language minority children's linguistic and cognitive creativity', *Journal of Multilingual and Multicultural Development*, **8**, pp. 173–85.

KRASHEN, S.D. (1981) 'Bilingual education and second language acquisition theory', in CALIFORNIA STATE DEPARTMENT OF EDUCATION (Ed.) *Schooling and Language Minority Students: A Theoretical Framework*, Los Angeles, CA, Evaluation, Dissemination, and Assessment Center, pp. 3–50.

KRASHEN, S.D. (1982) *Principles and Practices in Second Language Acquisition*, Oxford, UK, Pergammon Press.

LARSEN-FREEMAN, D. (1976), 'An explanation of the morpheme acquisition order of second language learners', *Language Learning*, **26**, pp. 125–34.

LAU V. NICHOLS (1974) US Supreme Court, 414 US 563.

LEOPOLD, W.F. (1939) *Speech Development of a Bilingual Child: A Linguist's Record, Vol. I. Vocabulary Growth in the First Two Years*, Evanston, IL, Northwestern University Press.

LEOPOLD, W.F. (1947) *Speech Development of a Bilingual Child: A Linguist's Record, Vol. II. Sound Learning in the First Two Years*, Evanston, IL, Northwestern University Press.

LEOPOLD, W.F. (1949a) *Speech Development of a Bilingual Child: A Linguist's Record, Vol. III.*

Grammars and General Problems in the First Two Years, Evanston, IL, Northwestern University Press.

LEOPOLD, W.F. (1949b) *Speech Development of a Bilingual Child: A Linguist's Record, Vol. IV. Diary from Age Two*, Evanston, IL, Northwestern University Press.

McLAUGHLIN, B. (1984) *Second Language Acquisition in Childhood: Vol. I: Preschool Children*, Hillsdale, NJ, Lawrence Erlbaum.

McLAUGHLIN, B. (1985) *Second Language Acquisition in Childhood Vol. II: School Age Children*, Hillsdale, NJ, Lawrence Erlbaum.

MacNAB, G. (1979) 'Cognition and bilingualism: A re-analysis of studies', *Linguistics*, **17**, pp. 231–55.

MOLL, L. (1988) 'Educating Latino students', *Language Arts*, **64**, pp. 315–24.

OLLER, J., BACA, L. and Vigil, J. (1978) 'Language attitudes of Japanese American students', *TESOL Quarterly*, **16**, 163–71.

OLLER, J., HUDSON, R. and LIU C. (1977) 'A comparison of native language attitudes in distinct language groups', *NABE Journal*, **4**, pp. 34–41.

O'MALLEY, M.J. (1981) *Children's and Services Study: Language Minority Children with Limited English Proficiency in the United States*, Rosslyn, VA, National Clearinghouse for Bilingual Education.

OVANDO, C. and COLLIER, V. (1985) *Bilingual and ESL Classrooms: Teaching in Multicultural Contexts*, New York, McGraw Hill.

PADILLA, A.M. and LIEBMAN, E. (1975) 'Language acquisition in the bilingual child', *The Bilingual Review/La Revista Bilingüe*, **2**, pp. 34–55.

PEAL, E. and LAMBERT, W.E. (1962) 'The relation of bilingualism to intelligence', *Psychological Monographs: General and Applied*, **76**, pp. 1–23.

PHILIPS, S.U. (1972) 'Participant structures and communication incompetence: Warm Springs children in community and classroom', in C. CAZDEN, D. HYAMES and W.J. John (Eds) *Function of Language in the Classroom*, New York, Teachers College Press.

PURKEY, S.C. and Smith, M.S. (1983) 'Effective schools: A review', *Elementary School Journal*, **83**, pp. 52–78.

RAMIREZ, A. (1985) *Bilingualism Through Schooling*, Albany, NY, State University of New York Press.

RICHARDS, J. and RODGERS, T.S. (1986) *Approaches and Methods in Language Teaching*, Cambridge, UK, Cambridge University Press.

ROSSELL, C. and ROSS, J.M. (1986) *The Social Science Evidence on Bilingual Education*, Boston, MA, Boston University Press.

SCHNEIDER, S.G. (1976) *Revolution, Reaction or Reform: The 1974 Bilingual Education Act*, New York, Las Americas.

SCHUMANN, J.H. (1976) 'Affective factors and the problem of age in second language acquisition', *Language Learning*, **25**, pp. 209–39.

SELIGER, H.W. (1977) 'Does practice make perfect? A study of interactional patterns and L2 competence', *Language Learning*, **26**, pp. 263–78.

SHANTZ, C. (1977) 'The development of social cognition', in E.M. HETHERINGTON (Ed.) *Review of Child Development Research*, **5**, Chicago, IL, University of Chicago Press.

SKINNER, B.F. (1957) *Verbal Behavior*, Englewood Cliffs, NJ, Prentice-Hall.

SKRABANEK, R.L. (1970) 'Language maintenance among Mexican Americans', *International Journal of Comparative Sociology*, **11**, pp. 272–82.

SKUTNAB-KANGAS, T. (1979) *Language in the Process of Cultural Assimilation and Structural Incorporation of Linguistic Minorities*, Rosslyn, VA, National Clearinghouse for Bilingual Education.

SORENSON, A.P. (1967) 'Multilingualism in the Northwest Amazon', *American Anthropologist*, **69**, pp. 67–8.

TIKUNOFF, W.J. (1983) *Compatability of the SBIF Features with Other Research on Instruction of LEP Students*, San Francisco, CA, Far West Laboratory (SBIF-83-4.8/10).

TRIOKE, R.C. (1981) 'Synthesis of research in bilingual education', *Educational Leadership*, **38**, pp. 498–504.

US GENERAL ACCOUNTING OFFICE (1987) *Research Evidence on Bilingual Education*, Washington, DC, US General Accounting Office, GAO/PEMD-87-12BR, March.

US v. TEXAS (506 F. Supp. at 43).

WAGGONER, D. (1984) 'The need for bilingual education: Estimates from the 1980 census', *NABE Journal*, **8**, pp. 1–14.

WILLIG, A. (1985) 'A meta-analysis of selected studies on the effectiveness of bilingual education', *Review of Educational Research*, **55**, pp. 269–317.

WONG-FILLMORE, L. (1976) 'The Second Time Around: Cognitive and Social Strategies in Second Language Acquisition', unpublished doctoral dissertation, Stanford University.

WONG-FILLMORE, L. and VALADEZ, C. (1986) 'Teaching bilingual learners', in M.S. WITTROCK, *Handbook on Research on Teaching*, Washington, DC, AERA, pp. 648–85.

ZENTELLA, A.C. (1981) 'Ta bien you could answer me en cualquier idioma: Puerto Rican code switching in bilingual classrooms', in R. DURAN (Ed.) *Latino Language and Communicative Behavior*, Norwood, NJ, Ablex, pp. 109–22.

Chapter 5

Promoting School Success for Chicanos: The View from Inside the Bilingual Classroom

Barbara J. Merino

The Hispanic population varies along several dimensions that can have clear implications for its rate of success in school. Although the majority of the Hispanic population is Mexican in origin, many come from Puerto Rico, Cuba, and Central or South America (US Bureau of the Census, 1982). For each group, there has been a somewhat different tradition of immigration. For many Mexicans and Puerto Ricans, immigration is viewed as temporary. For others (e.g., Cubans), immigration is seen as a necessary, permanent step. Hispanics also differ by level of education in the home country. Many Mexican immigrants come from rural backgrounds, with low levels of education in Mexico; Cubans and to a lesser degree Central Americans have typically had higher levels of education. Many Hispanics in the US have lived there for generations. Although some Hispanics speak English fluently when they arrive in school, the unifying characteristic for most is the Spanish language. Eleven million of the close to 15 million Hispanics counted by the 1980 census reported speaking Spanish at home (Lopez, 1982). Most (93 per cent) of Hispanic adults report that Spanish was their primary language when they grew up (US Bureau of the Census, 1982) and only 14 per cent of all Hispanics in the United States report having an English language background (Brown, Rosen, Hill and Olivas, 1980).

The purpose of this chapter is to describe the nature of education for Hispanics of Mexican origin (i.e., Chicanos), as seen from inside the classroom and to outline successful and unsuccessful approaches as well as to propose a research agenda for the future. Almost all of this existing research focuses on the Chicano as a second language learner. First, I will briefly discuss programmatic alternatives for instruction. Second, I will focus on research about how classrooms function with respect to bilingual and second language instruction. Finally, I will explore the relation of the classroom process to schools and their communities and conclude with the implications of classroom process research for other researchers and policy makers.

Programmatic Alternatives for Instruction:
Bilingual Education and Structured Immersion

In North America, two principal program models have been used in designing instruction for children learning a second language: structured immersion and bilingual education. For many researchers, both of these models constitute variations on bilingual education, broadly defined as

> schooling provided fully or partly in the second language with the object of making students proficient in the second language while, at the same time, maintaining and developing their proficiency in the first language and fully guaranteeing their educational development. (Stern, 1975, p. 1)

In the United States, however, bilingual education has been legally defined as

> the use of two languages, one of which is English, as mediums of instruction for the same pupil population in a well organized program which encompasses part or all of the curriculum and includes the study of the history and culture associated with the mother tongue. (Bratt-Paulston, 1980, p. 8)

In operational terms, structured immersion as implemented in Canada to service the needs of English speakers learning French, conforms most to the first definition. Instruction often begins in the second language, with a gradual introduction of the first around the second or third grade (Lambert and Tucker, 1972). Many variations, however, of the model operate in the Canadian context and some programs, sometimes labelled partial immersion, use both languages as mediums of instruction (Swain, 1984).

In the United States, a wide variety of program models also operate. The most common approach, however, is to provide some instruction in both languages from the beginning, with a much quicker transition to instruction wholly in the second language in the later years of schooling. While these definitions very broadly outline the framework in which these programs operate, they do little to concretely operationalize how languages are actually used inside the classroom. In fact, there is wide consensus among practitioners and researchers of bilingual education in the United States that in practice these programs are best defined administratively in fiscal terms. That is, they are seen as programs that receive a certain type of funding, because many seldom, if ever, use the primary language of the children they serve (Wong-Fillmore, Ammon, McLaughlin and Ammon, 1983). Moreover, even within bilingual programs that actually use two languages the distribution patterns may vary a great deal (Legarreta, 1977). Recently, an interest has developed in adopting the structured immersion Canadian model in implementing instruction for language minority students in the United States (Genesee, 1985; Pena-Hughes and Solis, 1982). In the implementation of this model, however, US policy makers have not generally envisioned a systematic effort to continue development of first language skills as in the Canadian model, with a resurgence of instruction in the first language (L1) after the second or third year of schooling. Rather, the US model of structured immersion is perceived as early instruction in the second language (L2), English, with some allowance for instruction in the primary language in the beginning but no instruction after the first few years (Baker and de Kanter, 1981). For this reason, and for others — most notably the dramatically different social context in which the US and Canadian models operate — many educators in the United States have questioned the viability of this model for the education of language minority students in the United Sates (Hernandez-Chavez, 1984).

Classroom Process Studies

Applied research on bilingual education has shown mixed effects for its effectiveness, although a recent meta-analysis of the most robust evaluation studies showed small but positive effects for bilingual education (Willig, 1985). Moreover, so-called primary research (i.e., research that tests the underlying assumptions about bilingual education, such as transfer of learning) clearly supports the viability of bilingual education (Hakuta and Snow, 1986). Structured immersion as an educational alternative has not been studied systematically in the United States, although a five-year study comparing structured immersion and early, late-exit bilingual programs is currently in its final phase (Ramirez, Wolfson, Tallmadge and Merino, 1984). To date, very few studies on bilingual education actually include observational data of program implementation in the classroom. In fact, of the evaluation studies reviewed by Willig, only one (Legarreta, 1979) collected classroom observation data on instruction.

In searching for effective program models for teaching language minority children, recent research has turned away from simple comparisons of students' achievement under different treatments. This shift has come from a rediscovery of a truism in educational research that before program effects can be analyzed, the program treatment must be defined operationally and observed systematically to insure that it is in place (Baker and de Kanter, 1981; Willig, 1985; Wong-Fillmore and Valadez, 1986). Four principal approaches have been used in observational studies of language use in bilingual classrooms. Borrowing from the research paradigms of the teacher effectiveness literature (Dunkin and Biddle, 1974), researchers have focused on: 1) a description of the process in which the two languages are used with bilingual children (Schulz, 1975); 2) the relationship of process to context, for example, distribution of language use in different program models (Legarreta, 1977); 3) the relationship of process to process, for example, how the use of certain behaviors by teachers (e.g., feedback) affect the responses of students (Chaudron, 1977; Nystrom, 1983); 4) the relationship of process to product, in which effective teaching behaviors are identified in relationship to language use and their effect in promoting student achievement (Legarreta, 1979; Politzer, 1980; Ramirez and Stromquist, 1979).

A variety of approaches for data collection have been used in these studies. One approach, borrowing from the tradition of teacher effectiveness studies, (Dunkin and Biddle, 1974), relies on quantifying classroom behavior through the tallying of relevant behaviors. A large number of classroom observation instruments have been developed to record classroom process in second language classrooms. Long (1983) and Chaudron (1988) provide useful syntheses of these instruments and their assumptions. Table 5.1 illustrates some of the principal

Table 5.1: *Classification of instruments to study classroom interaction in Chicanos*

Authors	Type of recording procedure	Recording technique	Focus and sample item
Legarreta, 1977	Sign	Real time	Pedagogical, affective; 'teacher warms'
US Commission on Civil Rights, 1973	Sign	Real time	Pedagogical, affective, cognitive; 'teacher uses student ideas'
Laosa, 1979	Sign	Real time	Affective; student focus — types of feedback; 'teacher disapproves'
Politzer, 1980	Category	Video	Pedagogical; 'questioning-guided response'
Hernandez, 1983	Category	Video	Discourse; 'opening moves'
Schinke-Llano, 1983	Sign	Audio	Pedagogical; 'instructional, managerial, disciplinary'
Ramirez, Yuen, Ramey and Merino, 1986	Category	Audio	Pedagogical; 'procedural explanation'
Ramirez and Merino, 1986	Sign	Real time	Pedagogical; 'referential questions'
Wong-Fillmore, Ammon, McLaughlin and Ammon, 1983	Rating	Audio	Pedagogical, affective; 'teacher asks questions that require extended response'
Hoover, Calfee, Mace-Matluck, 1984a	Sign	Real time	Pedagogical, content; 'instructional focus-letter sound unit'

approaches used in this type of classroom research. Basically, these instruments differ in terms of their unit of analyses: (1) an arbitrary time unit (three seconds and so on), also known as a sign system, (2) or an analytical unit (an exchange, a move) also labelled a category system. A sign system records a behavior if it occurs within a specified time period. Thus for example, Legarreta (1977) recorded classroom behavior every three seconds, noting the language being used, who was talking, who was being addressed, and the pedagogical function of the utterance, commanding and so on. In a category system, every behavior is classified. Thus, Politzer (1980) and his associates Ramirez and Stromquist (1979) and Merino, Politzer and Ramirez (1979) classified every behavior as it occurred according to a system that generated categories based on teacher effectiveness research and L2 acquisition theory. Using videotapes of structured lessons, teacher and student behaviors were classified into one of sixteen categories. The principal advantage of a category system is that it is more likely to record every behavior that occurs. It tends, however, to overemphasize those behaviors that are very frequent and of short duration. The principal advantage of a sign system is that it should be more representative of the different types of behaviors that occur. A sign system, however, assumes that the amount of time a behavior is in place is important and is thus more likely to miss a very rare type of behavior that may have a lot of influence simply because it is appropriate. For example, the author once observed a limited-English-proficient 9-year-old child say, 'Oh, now I get it', after hearing a teacher's explanation of the plural system in English. This kind of event is rare and some observation systems might tally it very simplistically as a student initiation or student comment, when in fact it reveals that for this child that teacher's grammatical explanation was very relevant.

An intrinsic weakness of these systems is that the behaviors observed tend to be 'low inference', that is behaviors that are readily identified and thus more likely to yield high interrater reliabilities. Another disadvantage is that the systems tend to be formulated on the basis of theoretical constructs held by the researcher. These may or may not be relevant and tend to ignore the participants' perceptions of events. An approach that addresses these concerns is the use of ethnography where an individual classroom is studied in detail and over long periods of time by a participant/observer (Trueba and Wright, 1981; van Lier, 1988). This approach has generated fundamental reanalyses of classroom discourse, particularly among minority populations. For example, Phillips (1972) studying Warm Springs Indians has shown that the native American students had different rates of participation in classroom discourse because they were operating under a different set of rules than were the Anglo teachers. Self nomination in a large group, when the teacher was leading the discussion, was simply inappropriate behavior, which violated community mores for participation in large group discussion. An inherent disadvantage of ethnographic research, however, is one of selection. The process by which the ethnographer selects what is reported is not always well articulated and may lead to a bias for the researcher's preconceived assumptions about what is going on.

Process Studies

Studies that focus on describing classroom dynamics have been termed 'process' studies. Much of the early work on observation of bilingual classrooms used a case study approach in which language use was simply described in one classroom or program. For example, Mackey (1972) described language use patterns in the John F. Kennedy School in Berlin. In this prestigious, private school the ratio of native German and English speakers was closely monitored, and bilingual teachers were allowed to switch back and forth from English and German as they saw it necessary to facilitate instruction. This approach labelled 'concurrent translation' was found to be highly effective in promoting balanced bilingualism and high levels of achievement. This approach served as the model of preference in bilingual programs in the United States. It soon became apparent, however, that this approach was not so successful in the context of public schools, with children from families with few resources. Moreover, in United States public schools it has not been possible to ensure a minimal proficiency in the teachers, and the numbers of children from each language group vary greatly from year to year. Schulz (1975), studying a bilingual classroom in Boston through an ethnographic approach, found that teachers tended to favor the use of English, using Spanish principally to control behavior. Students and teachers perceived that it was better not to use Spanish, and most complex academic instruction was conducted in English. Furthermore, some studies have shown that in fact, when using a concurrent approach, students sometimes tune out the teacher when their primary language is not being used (Wong-Fillmore *et al.*, 1983). This type of research is particularly effective in identifying further lines of inquiry for later more controlled studies, where specified systems of language use might be manipulated.

Table 5.2: Language of instruction: process/context studies

Study	Grade	N (teachers)	Context	Results
Legarreta, 1977	K	5 teachers (4 concurrent 1 alternate day)	Bilingual	L1 use ranged from 16–47%; 1 alternate day teacher achieved 50%
Schulz, 1975	K	1		70% English; 30% Spanish
Ramirez, Yuen, Ramey and Merino, 1986	K-3rd	13 K 11 Gr 1 7 K 11 Gr 3	Bi EE Imm Bi EE Imm LE Bi LE Bi	Imm = 93–100% English LE K = 66% L1 EE K = 36% L1
Ramirez and Merino, in press	1st/2nd	37	Immersion Early	Imm = 98% English EE Bi = 68% English in Gr. 1 75% English in Gr. 2 LE Bi = 22% English in Gr. 1 41% English in Gr. 2
Strong, 1986	3rd and 5th	10 10	Bilingual v. submersion	Bi = 47% English; 6% Spanish Sub = 53% English
Nystrom, Stringfield and Miron, 1984	Jr and Sr High	3 5	Bilingual ESL	L1 and L2 used equally in both program settings
Fisher, *et al.*, 1981; Tikunoff and Vasquez-Faria, 1982	Elem.	58 Elem.	Exemplary bilingual teachers	60% English 20% L1 5% Mixed

Note: EE = Early Exit; LE = Late Exit; Bi = Bilingual; K = Kindergarten; Imm = Immersion
      L1 = Spanish; L2 = English.

Process/Context Studies

Studies that attempt to describe classroom process in relation to a particular context, program models, curriculum area, and so on have been labelled 'process/context' studies. The language of instruction — that is the distribution of language use in relationship to the program model — was first studied systematically by Legarreta (1977), who observed five bilingual kindergarten classrooms in California in the early 1970s with a real time observation instrument. She found that teachers using a concurrent translation model often favored English, with many of them speaking English 80 per cent of the time. When the languages, however, were separated by day, with instruction provided in one language one day and in the other the next (the so-called alternate day model used by one teacher), the language use distribution was more nearly equal. It should be noted that one teacher using the concurrent translation approach was also able to effect a near equal distribution of languages. Table 5.2 gives an overview of other studies which have investigated the patterns of language use in bilingual classrooms.

Sapiens (1982), Strong (1983), and Nystrom, Stringfield, and Miron (1984) represent documented examples of many practitioners' perceptions that the label of the program does not guarantee the language of instruction. Sapiens (1982) reported that although the high school civics teacher he observed used Spanish 45 per cent and English 55 per cent of the time, most instructional exchanges were in English. The two studies conducted as part of the longitudinal national study to investigate immersion and early or late exit bilingual programs (Ramirez, Yuen, Demay and Merino, 1986; Ramirez and Merino, in press) used sites in which well articulated bilingual programs were under operation. Strong (1983), on the other hand, studied a very small sample ($N = 10$) of both Spanish and Chinese bilingual classrooms and does not report results separately by language group. The supply of proficient bilingual Chinese teachers is even more limited than for Spanish and this may have resulted in reduced expectations for how the primary language can be used in the classroom. Moreover, he studied third and fifth grade classrooms, which tend to reduce the amount of L1 being used. Finally, his method for data collection involved using three separate clocks, one for each language and one for silence, while reviewing audio or videotapes. Ramirez *et al.* (1986), however, also used audio, and they report 51 per cent use of Spanish and 48 per cent of English for teachers at the third grade, in late-exit bilingual programs and 52 per cent use of English and 47 per cent of Spanish for students. Thus, while grade can clearly have an effect as shown by Ramirez *et al.* (1986), it may be that the bilingual classrooms studied by Strong were simply less committed to the use of L1. Nonetheless, it is clear that in the future, policy makers and researchers cannot assume that the primary language of the students is used unless this use is verified through classroom observation. It is worth noting that in the national, longitudinal study of immersion and bilingual classrooms conducted under J.D. Ramirez' direction, it was the researchers who insisted on including classroom observations as part of the design (see Table 5.2).

Regarding language of instruction and pedagogical function, it is of greater interest, of course, to investigate not simply how much the primary language is used but *how* it is used. In several studies, the analysis of language use in different program models has focused on the issue of specific functions. In most studies the functions have been generated on the basis of second language acquisition or teacher effectiveness research. Thus, Politzer (1980) focused on six kinds of teacher functions: modeling, questioning, commanding, explaining, correcting, and reinforcing. Reflecting the influence of Asher (1969), commanding and modeling were coded with a variety of possible modalities: verbal, visuals, objects, or physical response. Ramirez *et al.* (1986) used the same basic functions, although they collapsed correcting and reinforcing to one category, labelling it 'feedback'. Each one of these categories was then further sub-divided. Explanations, for example, could focus on procedure, on concepts, on labels, or on rules. As can be seen in Table 5.3, explaining, questioning, and commanding are the predominant functions for teacher talk in several studies. Ramirez and Stromquist (1979) report less incidence of explaining and a greater incidence of modeling. Ramirez and Stromquist (1979) asked teachers to teach four lessons related to certain grammatical concepts (e.g., the use of comparative adjectives). Thus, these lessons were possibly skewed to be more like traditional language lessons, with greater use of modeling.

Program comparisons by function are possible in some of these studies. Ramirez *et al.* (1986) report no significant difference in function across programs when teacher utterances are pooled across languages, although commanding tended to be more prevalent among late-exit bilingual programs at kindergarten. These results echo findings from other comparisons of teacher behaviors across programs in non-minority settings, where immersion programs have been compared to monolingual classrooms in Canada (Hamayan and Tucker, 1980). That

Table 5.3: Teacher as focus: functions of teacher talk

Study	Grade	Context	N (teachers)	Results
Legarreta, 1979	K	Bilingual	5	Structuring and questioning predominate
Ramirez, Yuen, Ramey and Merino, 1986	K-3rd	Bilingual + Immersion classes	72	Explanations are predominant in all programs. Questioning and commanding fluctuate in second place.
Ramirez and Merino, in press	1st–2nd	Bilingual Immersion	37 Immersion 39 EE 27 LE	Questioning predominates in Immersion, EE and LE with commanding second; behaviors are comparable in bilingual programs.
Ramirez and Stromquist, 1979	1st–3rd	Bilingual	18	Modeling, explaining, and questioning predominate but vary in prominence by teacher.

Note: EE = Early Exit; LE = Late Exit.

is, teachers in both program models tended to manipulate questioning, reinforcement, and error correction in similar ways. These studies further suggest that teacher classroom discourse, at least when analyzed broadly, tends to be similar across program models in North American settings. Ramirez *et al.* (1986) coded for four different kinds of explanations: procedures, concepts, labels, and rules. The most common type of explanation was procedural (ranging between 57 per cent to 65 per cent), followed by concept explanations, which constituted almost a third of all explanations. Explanations of grammatical rules were very rare and explanations for labels reached their highest level at first grade in both immersion and early exit bilingual programs.

In one of the few studies of Chicanos in a high school bilingual program, Milk (1980) observed teacher behavior in civic classes and found that elicitations and informatives — in a near even split — accounted for almost half of the teachers' discourse with student replies as the next most frequent behavior (19 per cent). Thus the patterns of classroom talk with older Hispanic students appear to display a similar trend to young students. Teacher talk dominates classroom discourse at all levels. (See Table 5.4 for an overview.)

Process/Process Studies

Studies that have sought to establish how particular classroom behaviors affect other classroom behaviors have been labelled 'process/process' studies. In this tradition, researchers have investigated the nature of teachers' and students' language use patterns in the classroom and how they may affect each other. Cases in point are Gaies (1977) and Chaudron (1979) who found that teachers adjust the complexity of their speech to ESL students on the basis of the students' proficiency. Holley and King (1971) reported that increasing the amount of wait time when asking second language students a question, increased the number of correct responses. Table 5.3 provides an overview of this research in relationship

Table 5.4: Teacher as focus: amount of teacher talk

Study	Grade	Context	N (teachers)	Comparison Group	Results
Legarreta, 1977	K	Bilingual classes	5	Concurrent translation v. alternate day	Greater use of English in some concurrent. Teacher talk dominates discourse (70%–89%).
Enright, 1984	K	Bilingual classes	2	Smaller group v. whole class	No difference. Teacher talk dominates (62%–84%).
Ramirez, Yuen Ramey and Merino, 1986	K-3rd	Bilingual and immersion classes	70	Across programs and grades	Teacher talk dominates (60%–80%) in L1 and L2, except in immersion with Spanish
Hernandez, 1981	1st-3rd	Bilingual	8	Teacher v. student	Teacher dominates 62% v. 38% for students

Note: K = Kindergarten.

to Chicanos. First we will discuss research that explores classroom process in relationship to the proficiency or ethnicity of the learner. Then, we will focus on research that relates teacher behaviors to student output.

Schinke-Llano (1983) found that some teachers in elementary classrooms in Illinois treat fluent English-speaking Anglo students and Hispanic limited-English-proficient students differently, for example, addressing fewer academically oriented utterances to the limited-English speakers. This differential pattern of teacher interaction has also been documented in a large scale study of teacher interaction with Chicano and Anglo students (US Commission on Civil Rights, 1973). Chicano students were addressed and praised less and their ideas were incorporated into the discourse of the classroom less frequently. No data were provided, however, on the language proficiency of the Chicano students. Laosa (1979), however, investigated both ethnicity and proficiency and their effects on teacher behaviors. He studied fourteen kindergarten and second-grade classrooms and observed targeted sets of pupils who were matched on social educational status but differed in ethnicity and proficiency. He found that these teachers were not affected by the ethnicity of the students but did tend to direct greater numbers of disapprovals to Chicano limited-English-proficient students.

Ramirez and Merino (in press) investigated the functions of teacher speech in relationship to the language proficiency of the student groups in 103 first-grade and second-grade classrooms in structured immersion, early- and late-exit bilingual programs. Using a real time category system based on their earlier audio sign system, they coded teacher utterances directed to limited-English-proficient (LEP) students, fluent-English-proficient or English only students (FEPs/EOs) and mixed groups. They then tabulated the percentage of behaviors that could be classified in any of the following categories: explaining, questioning, commanding, modeling, feedback, monitoring and other. Explaining and commanding were the only two behaviors directed to LEPs that differed in their distribution by program by a margin of at least 10 percentage points. In the first-grade late-exit programs, teachers tended to command more, and explain less than in the immersion and early-exit bilingual programs. This tendency to favor commanding also appeared more frequently in the behaviors directed to the FEP/EO first-grade students in both early-exit and late-exit bilingual programs as well as in first-grade students in mixed groups in the late-exit bilingual program. Immersion students in mixed groups were also more likely to receive explanations than students in the bilingual programs. Differences by program did not appear at the second grade. Within programs, differences in explanations were also noted. In all instances except in late, exit bilingual first-grade classrooms, explaining was a more frequent behavior when teachers addressed mixed groups than when they addressed LEPs or FEPs/EOs by themselves. Because the coding relied on a pragmatic protocol (that is, classification of a behavior was based on its function and not simply surface structure), these differences should not be due to stylistic differences in English or Spanish nor in the teachers themselves.

The greater use of commands has been noted in teachers with large numbers of working-class students (Wilcox, 1978). The large use of commands, however, is also typical of certain second language teaching methods such as the Total Physical Response (Asher, 1969). The reasons teachers used a higher amount of commands in the bilingual late-exit program may be conscious, based on pedagogical intent or unconscious. In future research the processes by which teachers organize their behavior in the classroom should be investigated, using the techniques of Shulman (1987) or ethnographers such as Trueba (1987) and van Lier (1988).

It is clear that when addressing students of a mixed level of proficiency, teachers provide greater numbers of explanations. Chaudron (1982) has investigated the nature of these explanations in a second language context. He found that teachers paraphrase as well as provide definitions and examples to make their explanations more meaningful to second language speakers. Explanations may be especially necessary in immersion programs in which little Spanish is used.

These differences in patterns of behavior by program and by proficiency and ethnicity of the student need to be further investigated through more qualitative approaches that use ethnographic techniques and discourse analyses. Carrasco (1981) in an ethnographic study, has shown that even a well intentioned, bilingual Chicana teacher had misdiagnosed and subsequently ignored a Spanish-speaking child in her classroom. What factors contribute to the failure to select certain students? How can teachers be trained to recognize inequities in the distribution of student turns? Project EQUALS (Los Angeles Unified School District, 1978) attempts to address some of these concerns by training teachers on peer observation that focuses on allocation of turns. Teachers also need training in providing a greater variety of formats for student response, addressing not only the linguistic but also the cultural needs of the students.

In a second language context, researchers have dedicated considerable effort to identifying how teachers in the classroom, and native speakers outside of it, informally modify speech and interaction patterns when speaking to second language speakers (see Chaudron, 1982, 1988 for reviews). Factors such as simplicity and frequency have been investigated using a variety of approaches. Much of this work, however, is still exploratory in nature. That is, most of this type of research has been conducted mainly with adults in foreign language settings where teachers are usually the only source of input and almost all studies are cross-sectional, conducted at one point in time, rather than longitudinal. Moreover, the aim of most of these studies has been to describe classroom discourse in relationship to the context or the proficiency of the learner and not so much to explore its consequences for students from different cultural backgrounds.

Some studies have focused on the relationship of classroom variables in second language classrooms as they affect student behaviors that are conceived as precursors of eventual student achievement. Some of the behaviors that have been investigated include: student engagement or on-task behavior (Nerenz and Knop, 1982; Tikunoff and Vazquez-Faria, 1982), student perceptions of effectiveness (Moskowitz, 1976; Omaggio, 1982), or student output as it is affected by teacher behaviors, group structure, task characteristics or combinations of these (Cathcart, 1986b; Ramirez and Merino, in press). The fundamental importance of these types of studies is that they strive to understand the process of teaching as it proceeds rather than focusing on the product at the end of the process.

How teachers use the students' time, how successful they are at maintaining students engaged with the academic curriculum, and the method of instruction are the three cornerstones that differentiate effective from ineffective teachers, according to Medley's (1979) review of 289 empirical studies on teacher effectiveness on mainstream classrooms in the United States. Research in second language classrooms with student engagement as a focus is rare. Nerenz and Knop (1982), in an exploratory study, discuss the data collection techniques for this type of research, offering a few examples from a foreign language context. Tikunoff and Vazquez-Faria (1982) using the construct of student engagement, studied fifty-eight 'superior' bilingual teachers at the elementary level in the United States. These teachers were considered effective because: 1) they were nominated by teachers, administrators, parents and students as superior teachers, and 2) they were able to produce high rates of student engagement in their classrooms. The instructional features shared by these classrooms were then identified to generate a template of effective instruction in bilingual classrooms. As outlined by Garcia (1986), the organizational features of effective instruction include: 1) students being instructed as a single group or in small groups for nearly equal portions of the school day; 2) the most common substructure activity consisting of two-thirds of the students working directly with the teacher in a recitation activity; 3) student work on academic tasks was independent 90 per cent of the time (and did not require cooperative work). Successful teachers were described as successful communicators. They could specify task outcomes clearly as well as the necessary steps to complete them. They communicated high expectations for learning and a belief in their own ability to teach. They were clear when giving directions and presenting new information. They promoted student involvement by pacing instruction, monitoring students' progress and expecting success.

The above features are not viewed as unique to bilingual settings. Features that were unique to the bilingual setting included (Garcia, 1986): use of two languages (English for 60 per cent of instruction and the native language by itself or in combination with English 40 per cent of the time.); the use of 'integrative activities' that develop second language skills as a by-product of instruction in a contextualized task and instructional practices that took advantage of students' cultural background. Home and community culture were incorporated through 1) using cultural referents to communicate instructions, 2) observing discourse patterns of the native culture, and 3) respecting the values and norms of the native culture. This study used ethnographic techniques in combination with traditional approaches of classroom observation, thus complementing the strengths of the two methodologies. It also shows, however, some of the weaknesses of the two traditions. Researchers are more likely to observe what they are attuned to. Cooperative work and non-teacher-fronted tasks were rare in these teachers' classrooms. Yet, recent research on the role of learner talk (Swain, 1985) and the positive influence of carefully designed group work (Cathcart, 1986b; Cohen, 1986) suggests that less direct control by the teacher may be particularly effective in promoting second language acquisition. It may be that these teachers are effective because they maintain student engagement and that in the instructional techniques available to teachers at the time of this study, the most prevalent approach to do so, was through tight teacher control. It would be a mistake, however, to assume that tight teacher control is essential to more effective teaching. We turn now to a discussion of research which has investigated the role and promotion of learner talk and autonomy.

The notion that learners will learn to speak by speaking — much as learners of reading and writing improve those skills by using them — has remerged in the second language acquisition literature as proposed by Swain's (1983) theory of 'comprehensible output'. She proposes that when 'there has been a communicative breakdown' and learners are pushed to deliver 'a message that is not only conveyed, but that is conveyed precisely, coherently and appropriately ... [they are pushed] beyond semantic processing to syntactic processing' (p. 19), and as a consequence to greater levels of proficiency. Learners are most likely to experience this kind of pressure in interacting with native-speaking peers. As documentation for this hypothesis, she offers the failure of immersion programs in Canada to produce learners who can compete with native speakers in speaking proficiency. Students in Canadian immersion programs interact in a community of speakers that accepts messages that are clear but not necessarily formally correct.

What kinds of situational and teacher variables lead to high student verbal output? Researchers have investigated this question from a variety of perspectives. Cathcart (1986a, 1986b) sought to identify situations, speakers, and tasks that lead to greater amount of student talk. Through the observation of small numbers of targeted Spanish-speaking kindergarten children (four in one study; eight in the other) over the span of a school year, she found that there was a greater number of student turns when talking to peers than when talking to adults (even in informal situations). Learners were more likely to be pushed to their limits of syntactic complexity by some tasks, for example, when complaining at recess. Requests for action tended to vary in length and complexity depending on the interlocutor and whether that task was in progress or under negotiation (Cathcart, 1986b).

In a more teacher and classroom centered approach, Ramirez and Merino (in press), sought to identify variables that lead to high student output in bilingual and immersion classrooms. Using multiple regression techniques they found that teacher explanations and presentations as well as teacher monitoring and seatwork, resulted in lower student verbalization, while teacher referential questions, drill, and academic content such as science and art resulted in higher student output. Referential questions have been defined in opposition to display questions. Display questions are those in which the student is asked to display previously learned information (e.g., 'What is two times two?'). Referential questions ask for new information (e.g., 'How are you feeling today?'). Referential questions constituted about a third of all questions when pooled across English and Spanish and tended to be most frequent in English (41 per cent) in the early-exit bilingual program at the first grade. Long and Sato (1983) reported that referential questions were rare in the classroom discourse of six ESL lessons for adults but in the majority (76 per cent) in informal native to non-native speaker conversations. This type of question is, by its very nature, communicative and designed to elicit genuine information. It is not surprising then, that it should be so successful in generating student verbalization.

It should be noted that student verbal output appears to be a behavior that is highly influenced by cultural background and home discourse patterns. Philips (1972) found that among Warm Springs Indian children and adults in Oregon, self nomination — particularly in a large group — is considered inappropriate. Sato (1982) analyzed the number of self-selected turns in two adult ESL classes. She found that Asian students (although in the majority) initiated classroom discourse less often than Latin American, European and Middle Eastern students. Differences in interaction patterns may also exist within Asian cultures. Duff (1986) compared pairs of Chinese and Japanese students on a convergent task (problem solving) and a divergent task (a role-played debate). Students were matched for sex, age, proficiency in English, class standing and length of residence in the United States. Chinese subjects dominated 66 per cent of the total number of words and took over a significantly greater number of Japanese turns. Although no cross-cultural research on turn taking is available on Chicanos, there is an extensive literature on Chicano and Anglo dyads and cooperative-competitive behaviors. Kagan (1986), in a synthesis of this research, documents a preference for cooperative task structures among Chicano and Mexican children. This preference was evident in all the Chicano students that he studied but more pronounced among rural, Mexican children. Research that explores patterns of interaction, turn taking in different types of tasks, and the type of language produced in these contexts needs to be conducted among Hispanics, from a variety of backgrounds.

Finally, there is one very provocative ethnographic study on classroom peer interaction, where Chicano learners were the focus, that offers insights about how students perceive the world of the classroom. Delgado-Gaitan (1987) studied Chicano students at home and at school in a San Francisco Bay area community. She found that the teachers' and students' perception of classroom process sometimes differed substantially. Thus, for example, while the teacher perceived as 'cheating' those students who offered assistance to other students while working in a workbook, in the students' view this constituted a logical extension of the cooperative behaviors that were expected at home. It is clear that with all children, but particularly when children of different cultures interact, it is essential to understand students' and teachers' perceptions of classroom dynamics and their relationship to home patterns of socialization. It is unfortunate that there are such few ethnographic studies of Chicanos interacting in the classroom process, for this methodology can do much to enrich our understanding of why students and teachers interact the way they do.

Process/Product Studies

Studies that seek to identify how particular classroom processes affect the learning outcomes of students have been termed 'process/product' studies. The central question in these studies is: What classroom processes actually lead to higher student achievement? Usually the outcome or product has been student achievement, defined as performance on standardized tests (Mace-Matluck, Hoover and Calfee, 1984), oral tests of production and comprehension (Ramirez and Stromquist, 1979), or less frequently, accuracy in morpheme production (Hamayan and Tucker, 1980). More recently, the focus has been on comprehensibility as measured by comprehension tests (Speidel, Tharp and Kobayashi, 1985) and self-rating scales of understanding (Long, 1985). In discussing these studies, it is particularly important to consider the context and data collection procedures used because these factors affect their generalizability. Two basic approaches have been used. In one the focus is the learner; in the other the focus is the teacher interacting with the learner. The latter approach has had a longer tradition and will be discussed first. (Table 5.5 provides an overview of studies conducted with Chicanos.)

Teachers interacting with learners has been one area of research focus. In a

Table 5.5: Learner as focus: process product

Study	Grade	Context	N (teachers)	N (students)	Results
Strong, 1983	K	Bilingual	1	13	Responsiveness (R), Gregariousness (G) and Talkativeness (T) correlated with vocabulary. R and T with grammatical structure, R with pronunciation
Ramirez and Stromquist, 1979	1st–3rd	Bilingual	18	141	Explaining labels, lesson pace, overt correction related to gains.
Johnson, 1983	Bilingual summer prog. 5th–9th	Peer tutoring 7 weeks	1	8 NS — NNS	Student receiving peer instruction improved in comprehension.
Wong-Fillmore et al., 1985	3rd–4th	Bilingual	13 Gr. 3 4 Gr. 4	556	Adjusting complexity of language, encouraging student participation, effects on gains.
Hoover, Calfee and Mace-Matluck, 1984a	K–4th	Bilingual and monolinguals	49	378	Formal language demands, use of primary materials requiring engagement with text resulted in gains in reading.

Note: NS = Native Speakers; NNS = Non-Native Speakers

study conducted under Politzer's direction, Ramirez and Stromquist (1979) videotaped eighteen bilingual elementary classroom teachers teaching four ESL lessons to limited-English-speaking Chicano students between first and third grade. They sought to relate student gains to specific teacher behaviors. Included among the behaviors that were strongly related to student gains in production were: 1) requiring students to manipulate concrete objects following a teacher command, 2) questioning students regarding information previously presented by the teacher, 3) explaining the meaning of new words, 4) correcting students' grammatical errors directly by providing the correct structure, and 5) varying the type of teacher behaviors. Modeling and correction of pronunciation errors were negatively related to student gains. Multiple regression analyses showed that explaining labels as well as overt correction of pupil errors significantly affected performance in oral English production. These behaviors, as well as the pace of the lessons as measured by the frequency of the utterances, significantly affected comprehension. This study represents the first time that specific teacher behaviors were linked with student achievement in a bilingual setting in the United States. It has been influential in supplying a methodological approach for subsequent studies. Because, however, it involved teaching pre-specified lessons on particular grammatical points and not teaching in more naturalistic situations, thus there are some limits to its generalizability to other contexts. Moreover, this type of design only indicates that certain behaviors co-occur with achievement, not that they cause it.

A more naturalistic study was conducted by Wong-Fillmore *et al.* (1983), who looked at classroom processes in thirteen third- and four fourth-grade classrooms in which a mixed group of Hispanic and Chinese limited-English proficient students were enrolled. Half of the classrooms were defined as bilingual. Classroom process was audio taped and ratings were made on a variety of instructional features as well as teacher-student interactions. Although the use of a rating system for coding classroom behaviors is difficult in a research context because of issues of interrater reliability (Long, 1983), the use of audio tapes somewhat mitigated these effects. In this study, growth in English language development was affected by individual differences in the learner. Students who started the treatment with no proficiency in English experienced the most growth with teachers who promoted high levels of teacher and peer interaction. Classroom processes differentially affected students from the two ethnic groups. Hispanic students experienced the most growth in oral English production in classrooms that provided many opportunities to interact with English-speaking peers while Chinese background students fared best in classrooms in which teachers directed instruction. Other classroom features important in promoting growth included adjusting the complexity of language, encouraging student participation, and highlighting English language structure while using it. It is important to recall that the range of L1 use in the bilingual classrooms studied was very low, from 0 to 22 per cent. Thus, this study more properly relates to effective second language teaching techniques. It is an important investigation, however, because it begins to explore the effectiveness of instruction among different kinds of students. This study, moreover, is also correlational. Future research should manipulate teacher or peer centered teaching with other Hispanic and Chinese background students to determine the exact nature of this effect. Furthermore, if it is the case that Chinese background students participate in a more competitive manner in peer instruction (Duff, 1986), such a grouping structure may require additional training in cooperative learning to be successful with Chinese students.

The learner as focus is another tradition of research investigating classroom process and learner outcomes. Such research has focused on the manipulation of peer instruction (Johnson, 1983), on individual interaction patterns in the learner (Chesterfield, Chesterfield, Hayes-Latimer and Chavez, 1983; Strong, 1983) or on the interactions of targeted students in specific areas of the curriculum (e.g., reading and language arts), and eventual gains in proficiency (Hoover, Calfee and Mace-Matluck, 1984a, 1984b; Ramirez and Stromquist, 1978). In this type of study, target children are the focus of observation.

Several studies have investigated whether student production by itself leads to greater proficiency in the learner. Johnson (1983), compared the proficiency of a group of 5 to 9-year-old LEP children receiving peer instruction to that of another comparable group receiving instruction by the teacher over a five-week period, adjusting posttest gains on the basis of pretest performance. There were no significant differences between the groups in oral production (as measured by the Language Assessment Scales [LAS], DeAvila and Duncan, 1977), but the peer instructed students performed better on one measure of comprehension. Chaudron (1988) suggests that the short period of treatment and the wide range in ages could have limited positive effects. An additional factor might have been the use of the LAS which is designed to be a quick screening measure for program placement and is thus less likely to be sensitive to finer increments in proficiency.

Chesterfield *et al.* (1983) followed eleven Spanish-speaking preschool children enrolled in two different bilingual programs in Milwaukee and Corpus Christi over one year using ethnographic techniques. They concluded that interactions with peers were more consistently related to increases in proficiency in classrooms where English-speaking children predominated, while interactions with teachers led to greater gains in proficiency in classrooms where Spanish-speaking students predominated. Gains in proficiency were judged on the basis of increases in the average number of morphemes per utterance in spontaneous speech (MLU), which is a rough measure of grammatical complexity. This study is suggestive of how the psycholinguistic environment in the classroom may result in a differential pattern of effects. This study must be interpreted, however, with a great deal of caution, because a great number of other variables could be confounding the results. The children in Milwaukee had virtually no proficiency in English when the period of observation began, while five of the six children at Corpus Christi began the year with some proficiency in English. The children in Milwaukee made greater gains but one child in Corpus Christi who also started with no proficiency also made greater gains than any of them. There were three classrooms in Corpus Christi and two in Milwaukee. The Texas classrooms encouraged separation of Spanish and English, while the Milwaukee classrooms favored concurrent use of both languages. In both settings, particularly at the beginning of the year, teachers were the principal source of input to students.

Teachers' language use patterns changed to greater use of Spanish over three observations conducted throughout the year for four of the children in Milwaukee and five of the children in Texas. In some cases these fluctuations were dramatic, going from 61 per cent to 23 per cent for José in Corpus Christi and from 56 per cent to 12 per cent for Javier, for example. In another case, Ramona, they went from 40 per cent to 90 per cent and then down to 27 per cent. In addition to the classroom variables, it is important, however, to consider the effect of the two communities on language use patterns in general. Texas communities that are close to the border with Mexico display very different roles for Spanish than would an urban center in the Midwest, such as Milwaukee.

In another longitudinal study of young children's interaction patterns, Strong (1983) focused on social variables (responsiveness, gregariousness and talkativeness) and their relationship to gains in grammatical structure, vocabulary, and pronunciation. Strong found that responsiveness, as measured by the number of responses to other children, correlated with gains in control of structure, vocabulary and pronunciation, while gregariousness (the amount of talk to different children) and talkativeness (total talk) had a significant relationship with at least one measure of proficiency. In this study, it was not interactions with English speakers that affected proficiency but rather a general pattern of responsiveness that often was directed to other Spanish, speaking children.

Ramirez and Stromquist (1978, 1979) found that the six highest achieving ESL teachers in their study (when compared to the four lowest achieving teachers in the production test), had significantly more total student replies, repetitions and comprehensions, as well as greater repetitions with objects and greater comprehending behaviors with visuals. This study adjusted for pretest differences in the students, thus establishing a more direct link between classroom process variables and student gains. In the high achieving classrooms, the learner profile that emerges is one in which the student is actively engaged through a variety of approaches, replies, repetitions, and physical responses that indicate comprehension. Moreover, these responses often are combined with realia, in the form of objects or visuals.

These studies suggest that increasing students' opportunities to use language will result in greater language proficiency. A critical limitation in this research, however, has been the failure to investigate whether participation in tasks in which students must negotiate with the language improve proficiency. This question has largely been explored in process studies only.

Another approach to the study of learner interaction patterns and their effects on learning outcomes has been to focus on targeted children as they develop a skill over time. Such a design was used by Mace-Matluck and her associates (1984) in a cross-sequential study of bilingual and monolingual Spanish- and monolingual English-speaking children learning to read in Texas and northern Mexico. A total of 378 children constituted the sample, entering the study at various points in four different cohorts, beginning at either kindergarten or the first grade and followed from two to five years. A total of forty-nine classrooms from three Texas border sites — one each from central and eastern Texas and one from northern Mexico constituted the initial sample. Although, as students were reassigned to other classrooms, their classes were added to the sample. Students were selected to represent a variety of cognitive styles, along the dimensions of field dependence/independence and reflectivity/impulsivity, as well as varying degrees of proficiency in the two languages for the bilingual sample. Extensive data on the development of oral language and reading skills were collected as well as periodic classroom observations (five a year). The Reading and Mathematics Observation System (RAMOS; Calfee and Calfee, 1978) was used to collect classroom process data. This instrument uses a real time sampling format. The observer at the beginning of the observation records the status of classroom activities and their participants under each RAMOS category, and from that point until the end of the observation, changes in status are noted as these occur. Classroom organizational elements (i.e., who is delivering instruction as well as the content of instruction and responses of the students), are the principal categories of the system.

Data are reported for the bilingual sample in terms of mean percentages for all sites together, separating English and Spanish instruction by year (Hoover *et al.*, 1984a). This approach makes interpretation somewhat difficult, because data from several grade levels, sites, and programs are collapsed, although data from the later years represent higher grade levels. In the first three years, when the largest numbers of students were observed, the number of bilingual students actually receiving instruction in Spanish ranged from 62 to 73 (22 per cent to 32 per cent) in contrast to the number receiving English instruction which ranged from 140 to 244. This represents Texas educational policy current at that time, where Spanish reading instruction was most likely to occur in the border sites even within bilingual programs and where in some programs bilingual students were exited from Spanish reading after one year. In English, reading instruction emphasized letter sound unit correspondence from 49 per cent to 57 per cent of the time for the first three years; teaching focused on word-unit meaning occurred much less frequently (9 per cent to 7 per cent) and sentence text meaning increased after the first year (from 9 per cent to 28 per cent). Standard deviations for each category, however, were quite large indicating that there was a great deal of variability in classroom practice. This allocation of time by activity reflects a natural progression as students shift from decoding to comprehension skills. Most of the time students were found to be listening and responding in groups rather than working individually, although there was a gradual shift towards individual work from year to year. Patterns were very similar in Spanish, although there was greater emphasis on word unit meaning instruction. Individual categories from the observation system were collapsed into seven factors that were used in subsequent analyses. These factors accounted for 57 per cent of the variance as follows: emphasis on reading instruction, or engaged text time (10.3 per cent of the variance); direct group instruction (8.5 per cent); quality of formal language, emphasis on analytic strategies (7.4 per cent); amount of decoding instruction (6.3 per cent). There were two additional factors (which the authors admit are oversimplifications): productivity and secondary materials and the final one which they labelled as the number of students. Finally, when these factor scores were integrated with the reading achievement and language scores, English entry skill and English entry literacy skill were the most highly associated with exit skills. Literacy skills were related to instruction that makes strong formal language demands on students, employs primary materials, and fosters student engagement with text. Growth in vocabulary and comprehension was advanced by increased amounts of time devoted to those skills. Decoding skills, however, showed the opposite relation. The authors speculate that it may be due to the low quality of such instruction in the data set, in that decoding instruction tended to be non-explicit. Instruction in Spanish reading had low negative correlations with reading growth, but this relation seems to have been confounded with initial oral skills in English and is reduced when these are factored in. Students with higher levels of oral English skill were typically not placed in Spanish reading. Moreover, by the fourth year it appears that students who have had Spanish reading throughout this period had higher reading growth in English than those who had limited exposure. Finally, group size appeared to have had no relation to growth, and direct instruction was negatively related to gains in literacy. The authors speculate that the negative relationship of direct instruction may have been due to providing such instruction in large groups. In Spanish, partial correlations between instructional factors and reading growth were lower, although quality of decoding instruction and formal language demands in instruction were positively related to growth. It should be noted that partial correlations between instructional variables and growth were typically low (in the .20 to .40 range).

This study represents a unique attempt to connect systematically the impact of instruction on growth in literacy skills in bilingual students through a longitudinal approach. Observation was frequent and data were collected over a five-year period in a variety of sites. Observation focused on curriculum specific behaviors that were relevant to the teaching of reading. Unfortunately, no formal interrater reliability studies were conducted on the observation procedures, although training continued every year of data collection. Other serious problems that were out of the control of the researchers, were: a) the failure to provide instruction in Spanish reading at several sites, b) a sampling bias that provided Spanish reading instruction largely to those with the lowest English skills, and c) an exiting of the more successful Spanish readers very quickly to an English only program. Moreover, as the number of classes increased when students were reassigned to new teachers after the first year, the influence of the instructional variables were probably reduced. This may have contributed to the relatively low relation of instructional variables on learner growth. Furthermore, the failure to use instructional categories that focused on adjustments made for teaching second language speakers to read in English and to more carefully focus on specific behaviors (such as questioning and feedback techniques) probably reduced the ability to discriminate between poor and effective instruction.

Group structure, classroom process, and curriculum present one other type of investigation. Naturalistic studies of classroom process as it proceeds under the teacher's direction and local school pressures, comprise the vast majority of classroom research with Hispanic children. While this approach captures what teachers and students do in classrooms, it limits findings to practices currently in vogue and often reflects local resistance to mandated changes of instructional practice. Thus, given the negative climate towards bilingual education in the United States in the early 1980s, it does not seem so surprising that in the two recent large-scale studies of bilingual classrooms (Wong-Fillmore *et al.*, 1983; Mace-Matluck *et al.*, 1984), the use of the first language as a medium of instruction was so rare. Similarly, in spite of the fairly conclusive research evidence that teachers should involve second language speakers in peer-focused, jointly negotiated, problem solving tasks with direct manipulation of materials (Long and Porter, 1985), teachers continue to adhere to participant structures where they are in control of classroom process and dominate teacher talk when there is talk (Ramirez and Merino, in press). Alternatively, much instruction in elementary classrooms with limited-English proficient children is conducted in silence, through individualized group structures (Strong, 1983).

Recently two instructional reform efforts have been launched to trigger the use of peer-focused, active problem solving in bilingual classrooms. In the first of these efforts, *Finding Out/Descrubrimiento* (DeAvila and Duncan, 1980) which is a science/math curriculum for second to fifth graders, students work in activity centers using a cooperative approach. The organization of group work in the implementation of the curriculum has been a primary focus. Cohen, DeAvila, and Intili (1981) and their associates have sought to train teachers and their students to rethink their traditional roles, with students taking greater responsibility for their own learning and that of their peers. Individual students are responsible for their own worksheets and are assigned tasks. They must also make sure that any one in the group who needs help gets it. Specific roles (facilitator, checker, and reporter) are assigned to students to facilitate the active engagement of all the students. Materials for the centers are presented bilingually and children with different levels of proficiency in English and Spanish and different types of skills are grouped together in heterogenous groups.

Students instructed through *Finding Out/Descrubrimiento* in a cooperative group structure made significant gains in oral proficiency in English and these gains were most pronounced in children who started out with low proficiency in both languages (DeAvila, 1981). Neves (1983) observed a subset of these children with varying degrees of proficiency and found that the more the monolingual Spanish-speaking children spoke about the task the greater their gains were in English. Much of this talk was conducted in Spanish, but frequently there was interaction with bilingual and English dominant children. Gains were also apparent in standardized tests of math and reading when compared to national norms (Cohen *et al.*, 1981). Cohen (1986) notes that teachers who had difficulty delegating authority and who had supervised and controlled student work too closely did not have gains as large as those who consistently required students to rely on each other. Navarrete (1985) made videotapes of student interaction in one second-grade classroom implementing the curriculum and found that students who engaged in a complete cycle of joint problem solving made the greatest gains. In such a cycle, students sought help, got it and returned to their tasks.

In another curriculum reform effort, Coughran, Merino and Hoskins (1986) developed *BICOMP*, a bilingual science based, interdisciplinary computer assisted curriculum designed to implement a communicative approach. By the authors' definition, this approach required that all lessons involve the manipulation of materials in a problem solving task with peers. Teachers began the lesson with a contextualized demonstration, explanation, and dialogue that used visuals and realia to illustrate concepts and to engage the students in inquiry about their hypotheses. Demonstrations and experiments were designed to be so intrinsically interesting that they would stimulate student talk or comprehensible output (Swain, 1985). Students then began an active period of experimentation or manipulation in a small group. Kagan's (1986) research on cooperative groups and Long's (1983) on negotiation served as the inspiration for organizing group structure. Both convergent and divergent activities were used in the group activities. For example, at times activities involved setting up an experiment to see where the hottest temperatures in the school were; at other times students designed paper airplanes to investigate how paper moves through air. Students studied science lessons for one week in combination with computer lessons related to the science concepts. Limited-English-proficient students worked in pairs with fluent English speakers at the computer. On the second week, students recycled the lesson concepts in art, math and language arts lessons, using the same themes and concepts for the science lessons. Thus, if the students had been investigating causes of hot and cold temperatures and how to measure temperature, they subsequently studied how artists use hot and cold colors in art. The development of the lessons was a collaborative effort between teachers and university-based researchers. Lessons were developed from prototypes by teachers from the participating schools and classroom teachers provided revisions for the lessons before and after they had implemented them in the classroom.

A variety of approaches have been used to determine the effectiveness of the curriculum. The first year of curriculum development was used to collect baseline data for a control; in subsequent years, posttest gains adjusted for pretest differences, language classification and attendance, were compared to the adjusted gains made by students who had received instruction through the curriculum in two subsequent years. Students made significant gains in reading, math and science achievement when instructed through *BICOMP*. Teachers and students were observed as they participated in the curriculum and as they interacted with each other at the computer. The positive effects were particularly pronounced in classrooms of teachers who were 'high' implementers. The teachers were observed through a real time observation instrument (Merino, Legarreta and Coughran, 1984). High implementers made greater use of referential questions, that is questions with a real communicative intent; had higher amounts of student involvement and were skilled at presenting concepts with a variety of visuals and manipulatives.

The research on classroom process and student gains among Chicanos is still very much in its infancy. Observational techniques are seldom replicated, making it more difficult to develop a consensus of what is indeed effective. High school settings and the Chicano who is not limited in English proficiency have been studied to a very limited degree (US Commission on Civil Rights, 1973). Ethnographic research techniques have seldom been applied to investigate classroom process. Several generalizations, however, can be made about the links between classroom process and Chicano students' achievement. It is clear that the selection of a site and community in which research will be conducted is a critical variable. There are many bilingual classrooms for Chicanos that use the label but are otherwise not very different from regular classrooms (Strong, 1983). Border communities function very differently from inland communities in their expectations for language use outside the classroom. Individual schools vary a great deal in the extent to which they create an atmosphere of positive expectations for achievement in the students and community involvement in schooling (Carter and Chatfield, 1986). It is possible, however, to discover effective bilingual classrooms, which are, in fact, delivering bilingual instruction.

What are these classrooms like? They appear to promote a high degree of student involvement (Ramirez and Stromquist, 1979; Strong, 1983;) as well as on task behavior (Tikunoff and Vazquez-Faria, 1982) which nonetheless does not require direct teacher control but is accomplished through grouping strategies and intrinsically interesting materials (Cohen, 1986; Merino and Coughran, in press). Classroom discourse is contextualized (Ramirez and Stromquist, 1979; Wong-Fillmore *et al.*, 1986) and cultural referents are frequent and give positive value to students' cultural background (Garcia, 1986; Tikunoff and Vasquez-Faria, 1982).

How unique are these findings to the Chicano community? In many cases, effective teaching techniques for limited-English-proficient students have been replicated with students of different cultural and linguistic backgrounds. Referential questions as well as on task behavior appear to be positively related to student gains with a variety of populations. In some cases, however, other ethnic groups do not seem to be affected in the same way Hispanics are. Wong-Fillmore and her associates (1983), for example, found that Chinese students functioned best in teacher- rather than peer-focused activities. Tang (1974) found that Chinese parents who wanted Chinese to be used as a medium of instruction in the schools had children who performed better in bilingual programs than those who did not. Spanish-speaking parents generally prefer bilingual instruction, yet not all of them do. Attitudinal factors in the community also need to be explored in identifying effective instruction.

Research and Policy Agendas for the Future

The principal lesson to be learned is that classroom process research — while messy and expensive — is worthwhile and can offer substantive lessons about ways of facilitating student growth. Three other secondary lessons for the researcher should be emphasized. First, almost all of the research conducted to date on classroom process and Chicanos is correlational. Certain behaviors appear to co-occur with growth or student talk but researchers need to manipulate target behaviors and see if these in turn yield greater student gains. Secondly, classroom process research in the traditional mold by necessity tends to focus on easily observable behaviors of low inference. Future research needs to rely on both traditional and ethnographic techniques applied concurrently to provide a more complete picture of classroom process. Thirdly, researchers need to focus on exploring individual differences in ability and attitude and their interaction with a variety of classroom processes. At what level of proficiency and in what kinds of tasks, for example, does negotiating with peers result in growth of proficiency?

The principal lesson for researchers is also for policy makers. Classroom process research should be an essential component of any future evaluation of any program for Chicano students. Recently (1988) California issued a request for proposal (RFP) for yet another evaluation of bilingual education services in the state. The initial version of the RFP did not require classroom observation. Treatments need to be verified in the classroom as they are implemented. Policy makers also need to focus on tracing effects of particular classroom processes over the long term and not simply for one year or less. Merino and Lyons (1988), in a recent longitudinal study of bilingual students schooled in a model bilingual program in Calexico, followed students through the sixth grade. They found that the mean percentile ranks for these students ranged from the fortieth in English reading to the sixtieth in Spanish math. All but 20 per cent of the sample showed growth in percentile rank during the period of observation. Lower oral skills in English, lower reading skills in Spanish and birthplace in Mexico were important predictors in decreasing the chances of growth. Students displayed several different patterns of growth, some growing steadily every year, some pausing after a period of growth, some dropping and then increasing in growth, some simply dropping steadily every year, and yet others grew and then dropped in percentile rank. For particular children, at particular points in their lives, different kinds of factors may be affecting growth. Future research needs to explore in greater detail these patterns of growth and the factors that contribute to them over time.

Perhaps one best way of illustrating a research agenda for the future, is to build some scenarios for studies that would seek to identify effective ways of organizing classrooms for Chicano limited-English-proficient students. What might be some of the essential elements of such studies? In outlining the first study, a manipulative one, we will cast it in modest terms as 'teacher research' in which the teacher is the researcher. This type of research could begin with one teacher by herself or in collaboration with a researcher or with another teacher, followed by many replications with other teachers. The first task would be to identify a theoretically-based range of treatments that are systematically manipulated. These should not be based on the language of instruction alone. Thus, for example, extending the hypotheses of Long (1981) and Swain (1985), what is the effect of providing opportunities for negotiating interaction v. simply producing language? What type of tasks lead to negotiation more easily? Extending the research of Delgado Gaitan (1987), what patterns of negotiating are seen at home and could be adapted easily to a school context? As an exploratory study, teacher/researcher teams could collaborate in peer observation through both traditional observation techniques as well as the ethnographer's methodology of the participant observer. In the context of the fluidity of the schools, the best way to operationalize a treatment is not simply to give guidelines for lesson development, but to actually develop curriculum that concretely illustrates the theoretical intent of the treatment. A time series design, within the same year or from one year to the next could compare the amount and complexity of the language produced by students as they are engaged in tasks designed to provide opportunities for negotiation (e.g., debates in pairs about a controversial issue), compared to tasks in which simple production of language is the focus (e.g., exploration and description in pairs about feelings, scary dreams). As ways of gauging effectiveness, process variables could be the focus: How much language is used? How complex is the language? How evenly are conversational turns distributed across languages and participants? How do these vary depending on the ethnicity and proficiency of the students? In addition, through ethnographic interview techniques, students' perceptions of appropriate ways of interacting, styles of discourse, and attitudes toward the tasks could be explored.

Another more expensive study (using the paradigms of Moskowitz, 1976, and Tikunoff and Vasquez-Faria, 1982), could explore the dimensions of superior teachers in comparable situations and in contrast to typical teachers. There are several existing large data bases of bilingual students across the United States. These could be the starting point for selecting teachers who have been unusually successful in developing student growth. How do superior teachers organize instruction? How do they use their expert knowledge to plan in advance and react in the classroom in order to implement effective instruction? Shulman (1987) and Berliner (1987) have begun to explore expert knowledge in monolingual teachers. Their approach in combination with ethnographic interviews of the students and teachers would be useful in identifying the types of behaviors that subsequently might be tested through systematic manipulation in teacher training programs. It is essential, however, that we recognize that teachers and students interact in a wide range of communities and schools. These vary along many dimensions, some more critical than others. Thus, for example, the way Spanish and English are used in the community and in the school must be considered an integral component of how individual teachers can manipulate language use in the classroom. Addressing these and other important research questions in the very near future will help push a research-driven policy agenda ahead. Notwithstanding the nascent stage of our knowledge base, the promotion of school success for Chicanos inside bilingual classrooms can be demonstrated. Researchers, practitioners, and policy makers need to work together to make such successes occur on a much larger scale.

References

ASHER, J. (1969) 'The total physical response approach to second language learning', *Modern Language Journal*, **53**, pp. 3–17.

BAKER, K. and DE KANTER, A.A. (1981) *Effectiveness of Bilingual Education: A Review of the Literature*, Washington, DC, US Department of Education, Office of Planning, Budget and Evaluation.

BERLINER, D.C. (1987) 'Simple views of effective teaching and a simple theory of classroom instruction', in D.C. BERLINER and B.V. ROSENSHINE (Eds) *Talks to Teachers*, NY, Random House, pp. 93–110.

BRATT-PAULSTON, C. (1980) *Bilingual Education: Theories and Issues*, Rowley, MA, Newbury House.

BROWN, G., ROSEN, N., HILL, S.T. and OLIVAS, M. (1980) *The Condition of Education for Hispanic Americans*, Washington, DC, National Center for Education Statistics.

CALFEE, R. and CALFEE, M. (1978) *RAMOS: The Reading and Mathematics Observation System*, Stanford, CA, Center for Educational Research at Stanford.

CARRASCO, R. (1981) 'Expanded awareness of student performance: A case study in applied ethnographic monitoring in a bilingual classroom', in H.T. TRUEBA, G.P. GUTHRIE and K. AU (Eds) *Culture and the Bilingual Classroom: Studies in Classroom Ethnography*, Rowley, MA, Newbury House, pp. 153–77.

CARTER, T. and CHATFIELD, M. (1986) 'Effective bilingual schools', *American Journal of Education*, **95**, pp. 200–32.

CATHCART, R. (1986a) 'Input generation by young second language learners', *TESOL Quarterly*, **20**, pp. 515–30.

CATHCART, R. (1986b) 'Situational differences and the sampling of young L2 children's school language', in R.R. DAY (Ed.) *Talking to Learn: Conversation in Second Language Acquisition*, Rowley, MA, Newbury House, pp. 118–40.

CHAUDRON, C. (1977) 'A descriptive model of discourse in the corrective treatment of learners' errors', *Language Learning*, **27**, pp. 29–46.

CHAUDRON, C. (1979) 'Complexity of Teacher Speech and Vocabulary Explanation/Elaboration', paper presented at the Annual TESOL Convention, Boston, MA, March.

CHAUDRON, C. (1982) 'Vocabulary elaboration in teachers' speech to L2 learners', *Studies in Second Language Acquisition*, **4**, pp. 170–80.

CHAUDRON, C. (1988) *Second Language Classrooms: Research on Teaching and Learning*, Cambridge, UK, Cambridge University Press.

CHESTERFIELD, R., CHESTERFIELD, K., HAYES-LATIMER, K. and CHAVEZ, R. (1983) 'The influence of teachers and peers on second language acquisition in bilingual preschool programs', *TESOL Quarterly*, **17**, pp. 401–19.

COHEN, E. (1986) *Designing Groupwork: Strategies for Heterogenous Classroom*, NY, Teachers College Press.

COHEN, E., DEAVILA, E. and INTILI, J.A. (1981) 'Multi-cultural Improvement of Cognitive Ability', unpublished manuscript, Palo Alto, CA, Stanford University.

COUGHRAN, C., MERINO, B. and HOSKINS, J. (1986) *BICOMP: A Science Based, Computer Assisted Curriculum for Language Minority Students*, West Sacramento, CA, Washington Unified School District.

DEAVILA, E. (1981) *Multi Cultural Improvement of Cognitive Abilities: Final Report to State of California, Department of Education*, Stanford, CA, Stanford University.

DEAVILA, E. and DUNCAN, S. (1977) *Language Assessment Scales Level I*, Corte Madera, CA, Linguametrics Group.

DEAVILA, E. and DUNCAN, S. (1980) *Finding Out/Descubrimiento*, Corte Madera, CA, Linguametrics Group.

DELGADO-GAITAN, C. (1987) 'Traditions and transitions in the learning process of Mexican children: An ethnographic view', in G. SPINDLER and L. SPINDLER (Eds) *Interpretive Ethnography of Education at Home and Abroad*, Hillsdale, NJ, Lawrence Erlbaum, pp. 333–59.

DUFF, P. (1986) 'Another look at interlanguage talk: Taking task to task', in R.R. DAY (Ed.) *Talking to Learn, Conversation in Second Language Acquisition*, Rowley, MA, Newbury House, pp. 142–81.

DUNKIN, M.J. and BIDDLE, B.J. (1974) *The Study of Teaching*, New York, Holt, Rinehart and Winston.

ENRIGHT, S. (1984) 'The organization of interaction in elementary classrooms', in J. HANDSCOMBE, R.A. OREM and B.P. TAYLOR (Eds) *On TESOL '83: The Question of Control*, Washington, DC, TESOL, pp. 23–38.

FANSELOW, J. (1977 'Beyond Rashomon — Conceptualizing and describing the teaching act', *TESOL Quarterly*, **11**, pp. 17–39.

FISHER, C., TIKUIOFF, W., GEE, E. and PHILLIPS, M. (1981) *Bilingual Instructional Perspectives: Allocation of Time in the Classrooms of the SBIF Study Vol. III*, San Francisco, CA, Far West Laboratory for Educational Research and Development.

GAIES, S.J. (1977) 'The nature of linguistic input in formal second language learning: Linguistic and communicative strategies in ESL teachers' classroom language', in H.D. BROWN, C.A. YORIO, and R.H. CRYMES (Eds) *On TESOL, '77: Teaching and Learning English as a Second Language: Trends in Research and Practice*, Washington, DC. TESOL, pp. 204–12.

GARCIA, E. (1986) Bilingual development and the education of bilingual children during early childhood', *American Journal of Education*, **95**, pp. 96–121.

GENESEE, F. (1985) 'Second language learning through immersion: A review of US programs', *Review of Educational Research*, **55**, pp. 541–61.

HAKUTA, K. and SNOW, C. (1986) *The Role of Research in Policy Decisions about Bilingual Education*, report prepared for the Education and Labor Committee, US House of Representatives.

HAMAYAN, E. and TUCKER, G.R. (1980) 'Language input in the bilingual classroom and its relationship to second language achievement', *TESOL Quarterly*, **14**, pp. 453–68.

HERNANDEZ, H. (1981) 'English-as-a-Second-Language Lessons in Bilingual Classrooms: A Discourse Analysis', unpublished doctoral dissertation, Stanford University.

HERNANDEZ-CHAVEZ, E. (1984) 'The inadequacy of English immersion education as an educational approach for language minority students in the United States', in CALIFORNIA OFFICE OF BILINGUAL EDUCATION (Ed.) *Studies on Immersion Education: A Collection for United States Educators*, Sacramento, CA, California State Department of Education, pp. 144–83.

HOLLEY, F. and KING, J. (1971) 'Imitation and correction in foreign language learning', *Modern Language Journal*, **55**, pp. 494–8.

HOOVER, W., CALFEE, R. and MACE-MATLUCK, B. (1984a) *Teaching Reading to Bilingual Children Study: Instruction, Vol. VI*, Austin, TX, Southwest Educational Development Laboratory.

HOOVER, W., CALFEE, R. and MACE-MATLUCK, B. (1984b) *Language, Literacy and Instruc-*

tion: Integrating the Findings, Vol. VII, Austin, TX, Southwest Educational Development Laboratory.

JOHNSON, D. (1983) 'Natural language learning by design: A classroom experiment in social interaction and second language acquisition', *TESOL Quarterly*, **17**, pp. 55–68.

KAGAN, S. (1986) 'Cooperative learning and sociocultural factors in schooling', in CALIFORNIA BILINGUAL EDUCATION OFFICE (Ed.) *Beyond Language: Social and Cultural Factors in Schooling Language Minority Students*, Los Angeles, CA, Evaluation, Dissemination and Assessment Center, California State University, pp. 231–98.

LAMBERT, W.E. and TUCKER, G.R. (1972) *Bilingual Education of Children: The St. Lambert Experiment*, Rowley, MA, Newbury House.

LAOSA, L. (1979) 'Inequality in the classroom: observational research on teacher-student interaction', *Aztlan*, **8**, pp. 51–67.

LEGARRETA, D. (1977) 'Language choice in bilingual classrooms', *TESOL Quarterly*, **11**, pp. 9–16.

LEGARRETA, D. (1979) 'Effects of program models on language acquisition by Spanish-speaking children', *TESOL Quarterly*, **13**, pp. 521–34.

LONG, M. (1981) 'Input, interaction and second language acquisition', in H. WINITZ (Ed.) *Native Language and Foreign Language Acquisition*, New York, Annals of the New York Academy of Sciences, pp. 259–78.

LONG, M. (1983) 'Inside the "Black Box", Methodological issues in classroom research on language learning', in H. SELIGER and M. LONG (Eds) *Classroom-Oriented Research in Second Language Acquisition*, Rowley, MA, Newbury House, pp. 3–36.

LONG. M. (1985) 'Input and second language acquisition theory', in S.M. GASS and C.G. MADDEN (Eds) *Input in Second Language Acquisition*, Rowley, MA, Newbury House, pp. 377–93.

LONG, M. and PORTER, P. (1985) 'Group work, interlanguage talk and second language acquisition', *TESOL Quarterly*, **19**, pp. 207–28.

LONG, M. and SATO, C. (1983) 'Classroom foreigner talk discourses: Forms and functions of teachers' questions', in H. SELIGER and M. LONG (Eds) *Classroom-Oriented Research in Second Language Acquisition*, Rowley, MA: Newbury House, pp. 268–86.

LOPEZ, D. (1982) *The Maintenance of Spanish over Three Generations in the US*, Los Alamitos, CA, National Center for Bilingual Research.

LOS ANGELES UNIFIED SCHOOL DISTRICT (1978) *EQUALS: Equal Opportunity in the Classroom*, Los Angeles, Los Angeles Unified School District.

MACE-MATLUCK, B., HOOVER, W. and CALFEE, R. (1984) *Teaching Reading to Bilingual Children Study: Design of the Study, Vol. II*, Austin, TX, Southwest Educational Development Laboratory.

MACKEY, W. (1972) *Bilingual Education in a Binational School*, Rowley, MA, Newbury House.

MEDLEY, D. (1979) 'The effectiveness of teachers', in P. PETERSON and H. WALBERG (Eds) *Research on Teaching*, Berkeley, CA, McCutchan, pp. 11–28.

MERINO, B. and COUGHRAN, C. (in press) 'Lesson design for teachers of language minority students', in M. McGROARTY and C. FALTIS (Eds) *In the Interest of Language: Essays in Honor of Robert L. Politzer*, The Hague, Mouton.

MERINO, B., LEGARRETA, D. and COUGHRAN, C. (1984) *Observation Instruments for the BICOMP Curriculum*, West Sacramento, CA, Washington Unified.

MERINO, B. and LYONS, J. (1988) *Effectiveness of Model Bilingual Program: A Longitudinal Analysis of the Interaction of Individual Differences and Exposure to the Program Treatment*, final report submitted to the California Policy Seminar, University of California.

MERINO, B., POLITZER, R. and RAMIREZ, A. (1979) 'The relationship of teachers' Spanish proficiency to pupils achievement', *NABE Journal*, **3**, pp. 21–38.

MILK, R. (1980) 'Variation in Language Use Patterns Across Different Group Settings in

Two Bilingual Second Grade Classrooms', unpublished doctoral dissertation, Stanford University.

MILK, R. (1982) 'Language use in bilingual classrooms: Two case studies', in M. HINES and W. RUTHERFORD (Eds) *On TESOL '81*, Washington, DC, TESOL, pp. 181–91.

MOSKOWITZ, G. (1976) 'The classroom interaction of outstanding foreign language teachers', *Foreign Language Annals*, **9**, pp. 135–43, 146–57.

NAVARRETE, C. (1985) 'Problem Resolution in Small Group Interactions: A Bilingual Classroom Study', unpublished doctoral dissertation, Stanford University.

NERENZ, A. and KNOP, C. (1982) 'Allocated time, curricular content, and student engagement outcomes in the second language classroom', *Canadian Modern Language Review*, **39**, pp. 222–32.

NEVES, A. (1983) 'The Effect of Various Inputon the Second Language Acquisition of Mexican-American Children in Nine Elementary School Classrooms', unpublished doctoral dissertation, Stanford University.

NYSTROM, N. (1983) 'Teacher student interaction in bilingual classrooms: Four approaches to error feedback', in H.W. SELIGER and M. LONG (Eds) *Classroom Oriented Research in Second Language Acquisition*, Rowley, MA, Newbury House, pp. 169–89.

NYSTROM, N., STRINGFIELD, S. and MIRON, L. (1984) 'Policy Implications of Teaching Behavior in Bilingual and ESL Classrooms', paper presented at the TESOL Convention, Houston, TX.

OMAGGIO, A. (1982) 'The relationship between personalized classroom talk and teacher effectiveness ratings: Some research results', *Foreign Language Annals*, **15**, pp. 255–69.

PENA-HUGHES, E. and SOLIS, J. (1982) 'ABCs', unpublished report, McAllen, TX, McAllen Independent School District.

PHILIPS, S. (1972) 'Participant structures and communicative competence: Warm Springs children in community and classroom', in C. CAZDEN, V. JOHN, D. HYMES (Eds) *Functions of Language in the Classroom*, New York: Teachers College Press, pp. 370–94.

POLITZER, R. (1980) 'Foreign language teaching and bilingual education: Research implications', *Foreign Language Annals*, **13**, pp. 291–7.

RAMIREZ, A. (1978) *Teaching Reading in Spanish: A Study of Teacher Effectiveness*, Stanford, CA, Center for Educational Research at Stanford.

RAMIREZ, D. and MERINO, B. (1986) *Protocols for Observing Classroom Interaction: Longitudinal Study of Immersion Programs*, Mountain View, CA, SRA International.

RAMIREZ, J.D. and MERINO, B. (in press) 'Classroom talk in English immersion, early-exit and late-exit transitional bilingual education programs', in R. JACOBSON and C. FALTIS, (Eds) *Language Distribution Issues in Bilingual Schooling*, Clevedon, UK, Multilingual Matters.

RAMIREZ, A. and STROMQUIST, N. (1978) *ESL Methodology and Student Language Learning in Bilingual Elementary Schools*, Stanford University, Center for Educational Research at Stanford.

RAMIREZ, A. and STROMQUIST, N. (1979) 'ESL methodology and student language learning in bilingual elementary schools', *TESOL Quarterly*, **13**, pp. 145–58.

RAMIREZ, J.D., WOLFSON, R., TALLMADGE, G.K. and MERINO, B. (1984) *Final Study Design of the Longitudinal Study of Immersion Programs for Language-Minority Children*, Mountain View, CA, SRA Technologies, Inc.

RAMIREZ, J.D., YUEN, S., RAMEY, D. and MERINO, B. (1986) *First Year Report: Longitudinal Study of Immersion Programs for Language Minority Children*, Arlington, VA, SRA Technologies.

SAPIENS, A. (1982) 'The use of Spanish and English in a high school bilingual civics class', in J. AMASTAE and L. ELIAS-OLIVARES (Eds) *Spanish in the United States, Sociolinguistic Aspects*, Cambridge UK, Cambridge University Press, pp. 386–412.

SATO, C. (1982) 'Ethnic styles in classroom discourse', in M. HINES and W. RUTHERFORD (Eds) *On TESOL '81*, Washington, DC, TESOL, pp. 11–24.

SCHINKE-LLANO, L. (1983) 'Foreigner talk in content classrooms', in H. SELIGER and M. LONG (Eds) *Classroom Oriented Research in Second Language Acquisition*, Rowley, MA, Newbury House, pp. 146–68.

SCHULZ, J. (1975) 'Language Use in Bilingual Classrooms', paper presented at the Annual Convention of Teachers of English to Speakers of Other Languages (TESOL), Los Angeles, CA.

SHULMAN, L. (1987) 'The wisdom of practice: Managing complexity in medicine and teaching', in D.C. BERLINER and B.V. ROSENSHINE (Eds) *Talks to Teachers*, New York, Random House, pp. 93–110.

SHULMAN, L. (1988) 'Knowledge and teaching: Foundations of the new reform', *Harvard Educational Review*, **57**, 1–22.

SPIEDEL, G., THARP, R. and KOBAYASHI, L. (1985) 'Is there a comprehension problem for children who speak nonstandard English: A study of children with Hawaiian-English backgrounds', *Applied Psycholinguistics*, **6**, pp. 83–96.

STERN, H.H. (1975) 'Introduction', in M. SWAIN (Ed.) *Bilingual Schooling: Some Experiences in Canada and the United States*, Toronto, Ontario Institute For Studies in Education, pp. 1–12.

STRONG, M. (1983) 'Social styles and the second language acquisition of Spanish-speaking kindergartners', *TESOL Quarterly*, **17**, pp. 241–58.

SWAIN, M. (1983) 'Communicative Competence: Some Roles of Comprehensive Input and Comprehensible Output in Its Development', paper presented at the Second Language Research Forum, USC, Los Angeles, CA, February.

SWAIN, M. (1984) 'A review of immersion education in Canada: Research and evaluation studies', in CALIFORNIA OFFICE OF BILINGUAL EDUCATION (Ed.) *Studies on Immersion Education: A Collection for United States Educators*, Sacramento, CA, California State Department of Education.

SWAIN, M. (1985) 'Communicative competence: Some roles of comprehensive input and comprehensible output in its development', in S.M. GASS and C.G. MADDEN (Eds) *Input in Second Language Acquisition*, Rowley, MA, Newbury House, pp. 235–53.

TANG, B. (1974) 'A psycholinguistic study of the relationship between children's ethnic linguistic attitudes and the effectiveness of methods used in second language reading instruction', *TESOL Quarterly*, **8**, pp. 233–51.

TIKUNOFF, W. and VAZQUEZ-FARIA, J. (1982) 'Successful instruction for bilingual schooling', *Peabody Journal of Education*, **59**, pp. 234–71.

TRUEBA, H.T. (Ed.) (1987) *Success or Failure: Linguistic Minority Children at Home and in School*, New York, Harper and Row.

TRUEBA, H. and WRIGHT, P. (1981) 'A challenge for ethnographic researchers in bilingual settings: Analyzing Spanish/English classroom', *Journal of Multilingual and Multicultural Development*, **2**, pp. 243–57.

US BUREAU OF THE CENSUS (1982) 'Ancestry and language in the US: November, 1979', *Current Population Reports*, Series P-23, No. 116.

US BUREAU OF THE CENSUS (1983) 'School enrollment: Social and economic characteristics of students: October, 1981', *Current Population Reports*, Population Characteristics Series P-20, No. 373.

US COMMISSION ON CIVIL RIGHTS (1973) *Teachers and Students: Report V: Mexican-American Study: Differences in Teacher Interaction with Mexican-American and Anglo Students*, Washington, DC, US Government Printing Office.

VAN LIER, L. (1988) *The Classroom and the Language Learner: Ethnography and Second Language Classroom Research*, New York, Longman.

WILCOX, K. (1978) 'Schooling and Socialization for Work Roles', unpublished doctoral dissertation, Harvard University.

WILLIG, A. (1985) 'A meta-analysis of selected studies on the effectiveness of bilingual education', *Review of Educational Research*, **55**, pp. 269–317.

WONG-FILLMORE, L., AMMON, P., MCLAUGHLIN, B.P. and AMMON, M. (1983) *Learning Language Through Bilingual Instruction: Final Report* (submitted to the National Institute of Education), Berkeley, CA, University of California.

WONG-FILLMORE, L. and VALADEZ, C. (1986) 'Teaching bilingual learners', in M.C. WITTROCK (Ed.) *Handbook of Research on Teaching'*, 3rd ed., New York, Macmillan, pp. 648–85.

Part III

Cultural and Familial Perspectives on Chicano Achievement

Two chapters comprise Part III. Chapter 6, 'From Failure to Success: The Roles of Culture and Cultural Conflict in the Academic Achievement of Chicano Students', is written by Henry Trueba. He presents an overview of current theories in educational anthropology that attempt to explain the low academic achievement of Chicano students. As well, Trueba discusses interdisciplinary approaches that lead to successful educational interventions for Chicanos. In chapter 7, 'Cognitive Socialization and Competence: The Academic Development of Chicanos', Luisa Laosa and Ronald Henderson examine both theory and research that bear on socialization processes and the development of competence in Chicano children and youth. Such aspects as family interaction, single parenting, home environmental processes, intervention experiments, and parental beliefs are discussed.

Chapter 6

From Failure to Success: The Roles of Culture and Cultural Conflict in the Academic Achievement of Chicano Students

Henry T. Trueba

The emphasis on minority school failure has been pervasive in the educational research literature. The theoretical approaches employed in order to make sense of apparent low achievement of some linguistic minority students attempt to persuade readers that there is something fundamentally wrong with minority cultures, and that there is nothing one can do to change it.

This chapter discusses current theories in educational anthropology attempting to explain Chicano low academic achievement and its change achievement as a result of successful educational interventions. I present first a theoretical discussion of our current thinking on minority achievement and culture, and then offer an interdisciplinary approach to the study of literacy development for Chicano students. Second, I describe the Southern San Diego Bay area literacy project. As other previous studies (Spindler and Spindler, 1987a, 1987b; Trueba, 1989a, Trueba and Delgado-Gaitan, 1988), this project had important implications for applied research because of its empowering effect on minority students.

Achievement Theories in Anthropology

The continuous arrival of new Hispanic immigrants over the last four decades, resulting from war-torn Central America and poverty in Mexico and Latin America, contributes to create an impression of permanence and stagnation in the state of poverty and isolation of Hispanic groups. There does not seem to be an adequate way of measuring upward mobility of Hispanic individuals, though some serious attempts have been made (McCarthy and Burciaga Valdes, 1985, 1986). Government reports on the socioeconomic conditions and school achievement of Hispanics reinforce negative attitudes about Hispanic populations.

According to the US Department of Commerce:

— The Hispanic civilian noninstitutional population increased by 4.3 million (or 30 per cent) from 1980 to 1987.
— The educational attainment of Hispanics has improved since 1982, but lags behind that of non-Hispanics.
— Hispanic men and women continue to earn less than non-Hispanics.
— Hispanic families continue to have less total money income than non-Hispanic families.
— The poverty rate of Spanish-origin families in 1986 was almost three times as high as that of non-Hispanic families.
— The poverty rate for Hispanic families has not changed significantly between 1981 and 1986, but because of population growth, the number of Hispanic families below the poverty level in 1986 was 24 per cent higher than that in 1981 (US Department of Commerce, 1987, p. 1).

Culture and School Failure

Educational researchers have not been able to present adequate justification for the differential achievement levels of minorities. Some have presented controversial theories pinpointing genetic (Dunn, 1987; Jensen, 1981) or cultural ecological arguments (Ogbu, 1978, 1987a, 1987b) to explain low achievement. Attempts have been made to analyze these explanations (Trueba, 1987a, 1988b, 1988c) and consider their application to teacher education (Trueba, 1989a).

Culture plays a similar role in both successful learning and the 'social accomplishment' of academic failure and minority alienation is very similar (Florio-Ruane, 1988). Culture provides the motivation to achieve either success or failure. That is particularly true of the ultimate failure of dropping out and rejecting educational institutions and their knowledge, norms and values. How is this possible? Why is there such a conflict of cultural values? The explanation must be found within the larger sociocultural, historical and political contexts of the minority participation in mainstream social institutions. The indiscriminate use and application of minority group taxonomies (designations of caste-like, autonomous, and immigrant types) by cultural ecologists for entire ethnic or minority groups may have objectionable theoretical and practical consequences (Trueba, 1988b). These taxonomies are based on theories of differential school achievement which do not allow for either individual or collective change in status, and therefore they tend to stereotype entire ethnic groups. Furthermore, these theories do not explain the conversion of failure into success among 'caste-like' minorities described as follows:

> *Castelike* or *involuntary minorities* are people who were *originally brought into United States society involuntarily* through slavery, conquest, or colonization. Thereafter, these minorities were relegated to menial positions and denied true assimilation into mainstream society. American Indians, black Americans, and Native Hawaiians are examples. In the case of Mexican Americans, those who later immigrated from Mexico were assigned the status of the original conquered group in the southwestern United States, with whom they came to share a sense of

peoplehood or collective identity. (Ogbu, 1987b, p. 321; emphasis in original)

For example, the task of empirically documenting that all or most Mexican Americans were colonized or entered this country involuntarily, or that they have been denied true assimilation into mainstream America is enormous. There is abundant evidence of fairly rapid assimilation of many, while many more continue to arrive of their own free will seeking economic and educational opportunities. Thus, while we can seek in the home culture an explanation for the response of a minority to the academic demands placed by school and society, we must search for explanations that do not stereotype minorities or preempt our search. An interdisciplinary approach — as seen in this book — may be one solution.

Failure to learn may be better understood as related to communication skills which develop in the context of culturally congruent and meaningful social exchanges. It is not an individual failure; it is a failure of the sociocultural system that denies a child the opportunity for meaningful social intercourse, and thus for cognitive development. As such, academic failure is fully understandable only in its macro-historical, social, economic and political contexts (see Pearl, this volume). Failure in learning is not caused by a single social institution, such as the school or the family (Cole and Griffin, 1983).

Both academic success and academic failure are socially constructed phenomena. Failure to learn is a consequence of a given sociocultural system:

> Working within pre-existing social norms and role relationships, teachers and students collaborate to create the linguistic and social conditions under which students fail to learn ... Misunderstandings of one another at that time can lead to assessment of students as less than able or interested learners. (Florio-Ruane, 1988, p. 1)

The acquisition of academic knowledge is not necessarily any more difficult than the acquisition of the concrete knowledge required for effective everyday social interaction. Thus, some researchers believe that resistance to learning should be viewed as students' rejection of cultural values and academic demands placed on them by school personnel. For example, Erickson (1984) discussed resistance to academic achievement on the part of alienated students in cultural transition.

Recent studies on English literacy acquisition have analyzed the use of culturally and linguistically congruent instructional approaches that smooth the transition from the home to the school learning environment (e.g., Au and Jordan, 1981; Tharp and Gallimore, 1989, in the Kamehameha Schools of Hawaii and Southern California; Delgado-Gaitan, 1987a, 1987b, with Mexican children in Northern and Central California; and Trueba, 1989a, with Hispanic and Indo-Chinese). In contrast, other studies have shown the consequences of the use of approaches which are culturally incongruent or meaningless (e.g., Richards, 1987, among the Mayan children of Guatemala; Hornberger, 1988, among the Quechua children of Peru; Macias, 1987, among the Papago; and Deyhle, 1987, among the Navajo). What is significant about these studies is that they show the intimate relationship between language and culture in the adjustment of minority students in the schools.

George and Louise Spindler (1982), who have consistently viewed education as a phenomenon of cultural transmission — implying the inculcation of specific values — have recently called our attention to educators' need for *reflective cultural analysis* in order to take into account unconscious biases and cultural ethnocentrism.

In the tradition of the Spindlers' cross-cultural comparisons (1982, 1987a), Fujita and Sano (1988) have compared and contrasted American and Japanese daycare centers, using the Spindlers' reflective cross-cultural interview technique. They elicited and analyzed videotapes of Japanese and American teachers; then they asked one group of teachers to interpret the behaviors of the other group. This study has permitted us to reflect on the ethnocentrism and projection of cultural values reflected in day-care activities; that is, socialization for 'independence' or for 'nurturing tolerance and cooperation' characterizing' respectively; American and Japanese teachers. Another approach in looking at academic socialization for achievement has been the one taken by Borish (1988) who uses the Spindlers' model of 'compression and decompression' cycles. He focuses on the socialization of high school kibbutz young adults getting ready to enter the armed forces who endure intense labor experiences 'in the winter of their discontent'.

DeVos (1973, 1982, 1983; DeVos and Wagatsuma, 1966), for example, has used projective techniques in combination with ethnographic methods to penetrate complex layers of personality structure and motivational processes. Suarez-Orozco (1987, in press), using cultural ecological approaches and projective techniques shows that the success of Central American refugee children is based on a motivation to achieve. This motivation is an expression of their profound commitment to assist and make proud their parents or family members left behind in war-torn Central America. These research methods have been applied at the broader macro-sociological, political and historical levels, as well as at the micro-structural levels of interaction (Ogbu, 1978, 1987a, 1987b; Suarez-Orozco, 1987, in press).

Culture and Cognitive Development

Soviet psychologists led by Vygotsky (1962, 1978), and Neo-Vygotskians (see references in Wertsch, 1985; and in Tharp and Gallimore, 1989) have provided us with forceful arguments for linking the development of higher mental functions to social activities. Vygotsky viewed language as crucial for the development of thinking skills, and language control as a measure of mental development. His emphasis on the learner's role in determining his/her area of most possible cognitive development (or 'zone of proximal development') is related to the role that culture plays in communication during learning activities. Wertsch's position (1987) is that culture is instrumental in the selection and use of specific communicative strategies in adult-child interaction, as well as in the organization of cognitive tasks.

Wertsch (1987) indicates that 'people privilege the use of one mediational means over others' and that 'we need to combine the analysis of collectively organized mediational means with the analysis of interpsychological functioning'. Consequently, if 'choice of mediational means is a major determinant of how thinking and speaking can proceed, then processes whereby groups make decisions (either implicitly or explicitly) about these means should become a focus of our research' (Wertsch, 1987, pp. 20–1). In brief, according to Wertsch, culture either determines or at least it facilitates a conscious, collective choice of communicative strategies. Thus, if we want to study memory, thinking, attention, or other facets of human consciousness 'we must begin by recognizing the sociohistorical and cultural embeddedness of the subjects as well as investigators involved' (1987, pp. 21–2).

Within this theoretical framework, symbolic systems are presumed to mediate between the mind and outside reality, and the development of the higher psychological functions is a necessary condition for school achievement. That reality, however, is determined by cultural knowledge transferred from one generation to another and by universal psychological principles which go beyond the individual. Furthermore, both linguistic and social skills are viewed as developing within the microsociological units in which children grow, such as the family, school and the peer groups.

Culture and Literacy

One can argue that effective English literacy instruction requires the transmission of cultural values and skills as much as the academic knowledge associated with mainstream American culture (Spindler and Spindler, 1982, 1987b). The work by Gumperz and Hymes (1964), Gumperz (1982, 1986), and Cook-Gumperz (1986), has forced us to reconceptualize the interrelationships between communication, literacy, and culture that form a single symbolic system used in adapting to new cultural contexts and changing with the cumulative experiences in people's lives. As such, literacy is seen as a 'socially constructed phenomenon' (Cook-Gumperz, 1986, p. 1) consisting of culture-specific symbols developed for communicative purposes. As such, literacy depends on the economic and political institutions determining power hierarchies and access to resources; technological, industrial and military complexes not only depend on overall levels of literacy in a given society, but they also determine the quality of instruction in schools and the nature of curriculum.

According to Goodenough, culture 'is made up of the concepts, beliefs, and principles of action and organization' that a researcher finds enacted in the daily experiences of the members of that society (1976, p. 5). However, as Frake points out, the problem is not 'to state what someone did but to specify the conditions under which it is culturally appropriate to anticipate that he, or persons occupying his role, will render an equivalent performance' (1964, p. 112).

It follows, therefore, that a good understanding of a culture requires a good theory predictive of behavior in a particular social setting. In other words, cultural knowledge and cultural values are at the basis of reasoning, inferencing and interpreting meanings. There is an important distinction between cultural knowledge and cultural values in the acquisition of literacy skills. The task is to make sense of text as a message whose content takes meaning within the 'concepts, beliefs and principles of action' alluded to by Goodenough (1976). To accomplish this task we must have knowledge of the codes of behavior (the cognitive dimensions of culture), but also we must share in the cultural values (the normative dimensions of culture) which invite us to engage in communication through text.

In order to see the culture-specific cognitive and normative dimensions operating in the literacy activities of Chicano and other minority students it is necessary to observe such literacy activities systematically and not exclusively in the constrained school settings, but also at home (Delgado-Gaitan, 1989). The following discussion of a research project will help to illustrate the difficulties in creating culturally congruent literacy activities in the school setting, and the advantages of an interdisciplinary research approach.

The South San Diego Writing Project

This project consisted of ethnographic data collected over a period of four years (1980–84) in the San Diego South Bay area along the US-Mexican border (Trueba, 1984, 1987b; Trueba, Moll, Diaz and Diaz, 1984). The intent was to explore more effective ways of teaching Chicano youth how to write in English. The two high schools selected for the study had a 45 per cent Chicano population and the lowest academic scores in the school district.

High school Chicano students were not only socially isolated in the community and minimally exposed to English-speaking peers, but they were also economically isolated in barrios where violence and other gang activities frequently occurred. As we gathered the twelve volunteer teachers who wanted to work in our project, we found out that most of them lived away from the community in which they taught. All were eager to become effective writing instructors and teachers, but most of them felt that students were so unprepared and ignorant that the teacher alone was doomed to fail. Only three of the twelve teachers knew Spanish well.

The objectives of this applied research project, discussed with parents and teachers during an orientation, were to 1) improve the student's quantity and quality of English compositions, 2) encourage student participation and cooperation in writing activities, and 3) analyze in detail student response to English writing instruction. The specific demographic, socioeconomic and political characteristics of the barrio, as well as the home language and culture of the students, were generally unknown and viewed as irrelevant by teachers. Given the history of low academic performance of Chicano youth in the local schools, teachers felt that students could not succeed in learning how to write in English. Researchers arranged for parents and teachers to meet and become acquainted with each other's culture.

Teachers were asked to organize their classrooms into small groups that eventually became cohesive work teams with full control of their own writing activities. They would explore possible topics, research them, develop data-gathering instruments such as surveys and interview protocols, conduct actual interviews with peers and adults, discuss findings and finally write cooperatively extended and complex essays. The Chicano students discovered that writing was no longer a futile school exercise designed by teachers for their own purposes, but a meaningful activity and a means for exchanging important ideas with specific audiences and for expressing their own feelings.

Students finally realized that their individual and collective voices can make a difference in public opinion and in the quality of life at school. Thus, Chicano high school students not only significantly sharpened their communicative skills but realized that these skills are a powerful instrument in voicing individual and collective concerns. Teachers would often express their surprise: 'I am impressed. Look!' they said as they shared their students' compositions. A teacher wrote in her diary: 'This [the unexpected high performance of students] was a very successful lesson for me in many ways. It furthers my belief that if what is taught is important in the mind of the learner, much more will truly be learned' (Trueba *et al.*, 1984, p. 131).

Analytical Reflections

The analysis of the project was limited to a theoretical discussion of Vygotsky's cognitive development in the context of writing curriculum, without attempting to account for the psychosocial factors that generated the strong motivation leading to high achievement and literacy levels. The importance of the peer group as a working unit providing moral support during the learning process, especially for young Chicanos undergoing rapid changes at home, would have required more systematic study of the Mexican families' cultural knowledge and values, as well as the processes of integration of school knowledge and values.

Writing gradually became easier and more rewarding to students. Teachers and researchers learned more about students' home life and their aspirations through the English compositions. Then, we celebrated our success and enthusiastically assumed the role of 'experts' on writing focusing on technical matters. As one teacher noticed: 'The more controversial and relevant they make the topic, the more willing the students are to unite and write well. The more complicated the assignment is, the better the responses' (Trueba, 1987b, p. 246). In our analysis we forgot an important psychological principle advanced by anthropologists; that in order to understand motivation behind expressed values, 'one must deal with the universal emotions of love, fear, and hate' and that 'culture, from one psychological viewpoint, is a mode of expressing, in all their complexity, these primary emotions, which are aroused by inner biological urges or occur as reactions to specific outer stimuli' (DeVos, 1973, p. 63).

It has taken several years to realize that it is precisely in young Chicanos' need to express their feelings of love, hate and fear that their motivation to write began to develop. More importantly, this need was most appropriately met within the peer group, because cooperation and team work is culturally the preferred mode of academic activity for Mexican-origin youth. Writing groups offered Chicano students a unique opportunity to express both their collective feelings and to reinforce a cultural value acquired in the home. Furthermore, there was a positive side-effect: high academic performance in an English writing class impacted positively their overall performance in school, thus stimulating student motivation to produce better English compositions.

In the end, writing became a vehicle for restoring the credibility Chicanos lacked among other students, and, further, a means for gaining political representation in the school. Violence or other gang activities, low-riding and other conspicuous activities of 'cholos' or 'vatos locos' which had been the common expressions of Chicano youth power, were effectively replaced by writing as a legitimate expression of power. This was not done by brute force power, but of intellectual power to function within the existing social institutions. Here is the essence of empowerment in a democratic society.

Mexican and Mexican American families often find themselves isolated from mainstream society, yet they must face drastic changes in a new world whose language and culture is not understandable to them. Children growing up in these families are subject to high levels of anxiety related to their status as 'illegal aliens' in extreme poverty and their inability to communicate in English with mainstream society. The dramatic change from failure to success in acquiring English literacy cannot be explained in terms of 'caste-like' concepts and cultural ecological theory that would have predicted permanent failure of these students (Ogbu, 1978, 1987a, 1987b).

The explanation for the unexpected academic success of 'vatos locos' rests on their newly discovered meaning of English literacy activities if used for purposes of genuine communication and political representation within the social institutions in which they live, particularly within the school. It was indeed a discovery for the researchers and teachers as well. Writing can become a powerful instrument in the hands of students precisely because it gives them a voice in an academic world in which they have little control of their lives. The recognition, status and personal satisfaction embedded in the ability to communicate well through writing were a joint accomplishment of students, teachers and researchers all working together within the political arena of school achievement. This is how the internal rewards for English literacy acquisition function. The journey from failure to success should help us understand the social construction of failure. The next section examines an aspect of the social construction of the dropout, the ultimate academic failure.

Action Research and Empowerment

The conversion of failure into success is empirically demonstrable, whether we can explain it theoretically or not. Unfortunately, it is a rare fact. However, it is important to revise not only the theories of failure and success, but their very components, especially the concepts created by academicians and imposed on students. The concept of 'dropout' is particularly inadequate because it misrepresents the social reality of students' school experience.

The literature does not distinguish the diverse types of dropouts, nor their views of school and reasons for abandoning school within the context of their home culture. Ethnographic fieldwork among dropouts, however, seems to indicate that minority students distinguish clearly different types of dropouts. A study conducted in the San Joaquin Valley (Trueba, 1988a) suggests that Chicano students make conscious and deliberate decisions to withdraw permanently from school for reasons beyond their control (e.g., relocation of family, economic need, personal safety, etc.). These students are referred to as 'discontinuers' in contrast to those pressured to leave school against their will who are called 'pushedouts'. In general, both discontinuers and pushedouts tend to leave school permanently and are presumed by educators to be deprived of the economic opportunities given to individuals with higher educational levels. We do not have good studies of the actual outcomes. We know that some of the discontinuers are doing well economically and plan to return to school later on. There is a profound difference between pushedouts and discontinuers with regard to their degree of alienation and their views of school. The cycles of alienation, marginality, and illiteracy for some minority students are clearly related to their experience and interpretation of cultural conflict within the school, which are also guided by parental perceptions of schools (Wilson, 1989).

Culture is closely related to the acquisition of knowledge and motivation to achieve, both at the social level (as it affects the family, school and society), as well as at the personal level (as it affects the structure of participation in learning events within specific contexts). The role of culture in students' perception of school activities as enhancing cultural goals and values acquired in the home is instrumental in converting failure into success. But students' cultural perceptions of school as oppressive and destructive of the home culture can have devastating effects (Wilson, 1989). Therefore, culture must be recognized by researchers as a key factor in the study of Chicano achievement.

Implications for Literacy and Dropout Research

What should be the focus of dropout research? Where and how should we explore the role of culture in literacy and dropout phenomena? What is the expected impact of such research? Researchers are often overwhelmed with these questions and opt for a detached and safe position; they become 'pure researchers' and reject applied research as unscientific. Others explore intervention-oriented research convinced that science can also grow from the study of interventions. The work of many anthropologists and psychologists suggests that intervention and explanatory research are complementary and that the dichotomy between basic and applied research was the result of a political and historical accident more than the logical distribution of research activities (Trueba, 1988a).

Applied and basic research must be conducted in both formal and informal learning settings where students manipulate symbolic systems within their sociocultural environment. The immediate as well as the broader contexts of academic activities in specific learning settings must be studied. They are essential in understanding the organization of behavior and the type of student participation in learning activities. The analysis of literacy activities, for example, and the patterns of student participation should lead us to a more comprehensive view of the 'cultural embeddedness' of Chicano dropout and alienation problems. Teacher's knowledge of the home language and culture of Chicanos can be highly instrumental in understanding any communication gaps between the parents or students and school personnel. The school cultural environment and the organization of classroom work should reflect sensitivity to the ethnic cultures of minority students and this way maximize their participation in learning activities. Chicano and other minority children can generate their own text materials based on their home experiences as a bridge to engaging in the school culture (Trueba, 1989b). The analysis of learning activities in the home is most important because there inquiry strategies, logical inferencing and cultural congruence occur naturally (see studies by Delgado-Gaitan, 1987a, 1987b, 1989). This analysis can provide insights into possible linkages between self-empowerment efforts on the part of Chicano students and their parents and the role of school personnel in such empowerment through literacy activities.

Concluding Thoughts

Several years ago, Erickson (1982) called our attention to the need for inter-disciplinary approaches to the study of learning:

> Individual cognitive functioning has been largely the purview of cogni-tive psychologists who have often attempted to study thinking apart from the naturally occurring social and cultural circumstances. The anthropology of education often has studied *anything but* deliberately taught cognitive learning. Clearly, some rapprochement is needed, from the direction of the (more cognitively sophisticated) psychology of learning to the (more contextually sophisticated) anthropology of learning. (p. 173)

Empowerment research has developed in the last five years through the integration of cultural anthropology and the Vygotskian school of psychology. Interdisciplinary research on dropouts can become a powerful tool in the imple-mentation of educational reform provided it reflects genuine concern for the culture of minorities. Researchers' understanding of the role of culture in con-verting minority failure into success is constituted by the following ingredients:

1 Compassion for Chicano and other linguistic minority children who are not responsible for their academic predicament and their struggles in adjusting to a new cultural and linguistic environment.
2 Commitment to the principles of educational equity, particularly to that of respect for the home language and culture of linguistic minority children.
3 Theoretical flexibility and persistence in the pursuit of the elusive role of culture in both the acquisition of knowledge and values both in school and away from school.

We find ourselves at an educational crossroad of research approaches on Chicano achievement. Anthropology and psychology can offer important con-tributions to educational reform, but only if researchers can internalize pedago-gical principles capitalizing on children's culture and language. The approaches are an example of action research whose ultimate purpose is to enhance our understanding of democratic empowerment processes through learning, as a means to understand American democracy and to share in the American dream. Isn't this precisely what thousands of immigrants seek as they face the dangers and tribulations in crossing our borders?

References

Au, K.H. and Jordan, C. (1981) 'Teaching reading to Hawaiian children: Finding a culturally appropriate solution', in H. Trueba, G. Guthrie and K. Au (Eds) *Culture and the Bilingual Classroom: Studies in Classroom Ethnography*, Rowley, MA, Newbury House, pp. 139–52.

BORISH, S. (1988) 'The winter of their discontent: Cultural compression and decompression in the life cycle of the kibbutz adolescent', in H. TRUEBA and C. DELGADO-GAITAN (Eds) *School and Society: Teaching Content Through Culture*, New York, Praeger, pp. 181–99.

COLE, M. and GRIFFIN, P. (1983) A socio-historical approach to remediation, *The Quarterly Newsletter of the Laboratory of Comparative Human Cognition*, **5**, pp. 69–74.

COOK-GUMPERZ, J. (Ed.) (1986) *The Social Construction of Literacy*, Cambridge, MA, Cambridge University Press.

DELGADO-GAITAN, C. (1987a) 'Parent perceptions of school: Supportive environments for children', in H. TRUEBA (Ed.) *Success or Failure?: Learning and the Language Minority Student*, Cambridge, MA, Newbury House, pp. 131–55.

DELGADO-GAITAN, C. (1987b) 'Traditions and transitions in the learning process of Mexican children: An ethnographic view', in G. SPINDLER and L. SPINDLER (Eds) *Interpretive Ethnography of Education: At Home and Abroad*, Hillsdale, NJ, Lawrence Erlbaum, pp. 333–59.

DELGADO-GAITAN, C. (1989) 'Literacy for Empowerment: Role of Mexican Parents in Their Children's Education', unpublished manuscript, Graduate School of Education, University of California, Santa Barbara.

DEVOS, G. (1973) 'Japan's outcastes: The problem of the Burakumin', in B. WHITAKER (Ed.) *The Fourth World: Victims of Group Oppression*, New York, Schocken Books, pp. 307–27.

DEVOS, G. (1982) 'Adaptive strategies in US minorities', in E. JONES and S.J. KORCHIN (Eds) *Minority Mental Health*, New York, Praeger, pp. 74–117.

DEVOS, G. (1983) 'Ethnic identity and minority status: Some psycho-cultural considerations', in A. JACOBSON-WIDDING (Ed.) *Identity: Personal and Socio-Cultural*, Uppsala, Almquist and Wiksell Tryckeri AB, pp. 135–58.

DEVOS, G. and WAGATSUMA, H. (1966) *Japan's Invisible Race: Caste in Culture and Personality*, Berkeley, CA, University of California Press.

DEYHLE, D. (1987) 'Learning failure: Tests as gatekeepers and the culturally different child', in H. TRUEBA (Ed.) *Success or Failure?: Learning and the Language Minority Student*, NY, Newbury Publishers, pp. 85–108.

DUNN, L.M. (1987) *Bilingual Hispanic Children on the US Mainland: A Review of Research on Their Cognitive, Linguistic, and Scholastic Development*, Circle Pines, MN, American Guidance Service.

ERICKSON, F. (1982) 'Taught cognitive learning in its immediate environments: A neglected topic in the anthropology of education', *Anthropology and Education Quarterly*, **13**, pp. 149–80.

ERICKSON, F. (1984) 'School literacy, reasoning, and civility: An anthropologist's perspective', *Review of Educational Research*, **54**, pp. 525–44.

FLORIO-RUANE, S. (1988) 'The Relation of Family, Community, and Schooling in Tomorrow's Schools', unpublished manuscript, Holmes Group, Michigan State University, East Lansing.

FRAKE, C.O. (1964) 'A structural description of Subanum "religious behavior"', in W.H. GOODENOUGH (Ed.) *Explorations in Cultural Anthropology*, New York, McGraw-Hill.

FUJITA, M. and SANO, T. (1988) 'Children in American and Japanese day-care centers: Ethnography and reflective cross-cultural interviewing', in H. TRUEBA and C. DELGADO-GAITAN (Eds) *School and Society: Teaching Content Through Culture*, New York, Praeger, pp. 73–97.

GOODENOUGH, W.H. (1976) 'Multiculturalism as the normal human experience', *Anthropology and Education Quarterly*, **7**, pp. 4–7.

GUMPERZ, J. (Ed.) (1982) *Language and Social Identity*, Cambridge, MA, Cambridge University Press.

GUMPERZ, J. (1986) 'International Sociolinguistics in the study of schooling', in J. COOK-

GUMPER (Ed.) *The Social Construction of Literacy*, Cambridge, MA, Cambridge University Press, pp. 45–68.

GUMPERZ, J. and HYMES, D. (Eds) (1964) 'The ethnography of communication', *American Anthropologist*, **66**.

HORNBERGER, N. (1988) 'Iman Chay?: Quechua children in Peru's schools', in H. TRUEBA and C. DELGADO-GAITAN (Eds) *School and Society: Teaching Content Through Culture*, New York, Praeger, pp. 99–117.

JENSEN, A.R. (1981) *Straight Talk about Mental Tests*, New York, The Free Press.

McCARTHY, K.F. and BURCIAGA VALDEZ, R. (1985) *Current and Future Effects of Mexican Immigration in California: Executive Summary*, The Rand Corporation Series (R-3365/1-CR), Santa Monica, CA, Rand Corporation.

McCARTHY, K.F. and BURCIAGA VALDEZ, R. (1986) *Current and Future Effects of Mexican Immigration in California*, The Rand Corporation Series R-3365-CR, Santa Monica, CA, Rand Corporation.

MACIAS, J. (1987) 'The hidden curriculum of Papago teachers: American Indian strategies for mitigating cultural discontinuity in early schooling', in G. SPINDLER and L. SPINDLER (Eds) *The Interpretive Ethnography of Education: At Home and Abroad*, Hillsdale, NJ, Lawrence Erlbaum, pp. 363–80.

MEHAN, H. (1979) *Learning Lessons*, Cambridge, MA, Harvard University Press.

OGBU, J. (1978) *Minority Education and Caste: The American System in Cross-Cultural Perspective*, New York, Academic Press.

OGBU, J. (1987a) 'Variability in minority responses to schooling: Nonimmigrants vs. immigrants', in G. SPINDLER and L. SPINDLER (Eds) *The Interpretive Ethnography of Education: At Home and Abroad*, Hillsdale, NJ, Lawrence Erlbaum, pp. 255–78.

OGBU, J. (1987b) 'Variability in minority school performance: A problem in search of an explanation', *Anthropology and Education Quarterly*, **18**, pp. 312–34.

RICHARDS, J. (1987) 'Learning Spanish and classroom dynamics: School failure in a Guatemalan Maya community', in H. TRUEBA (Ed.) *Success or Failure?: Learning and the Language Minority Student*, New York, Newbury Publishers, pp. 109–30.

SPINDLER, G. and SPINDLER, L. (1982) 'Roger Harker and Schonhausen: From the familiar to the strange and back again', in G. SPINDLER (Ed.) *Doing the Ethnography of Schooling*, New York, Holt, Rinehart and Winston.

SPINDLER, G. and SPINDLER, L. (1987a) 'Teaching and learning how to do the ethnography of education', in G. SPINDLER and L. SPINDLER (Eds) *The Interpretive Ethnography of Education: At Home and Abroad*, Hillsdale, NJ, Lawrence Erlbaum, pp. 17–33.

SPINDLER, G. and SPINDLER, L. (1987b) 'Cultural dialogue and schooling in Schoenhausen and Roseville: A comparative analysis', *Anthropology and Education Quarterly*, **18**, pp. 3–16.

SUAREZ-OROZCO, M. (1987) 'Towards a psychosocial understanding of Hispanic adaptation to American schooling', in H. TRUEBA (Ed.) *Success or Failure: Learning and the Language Minority Student*, New York, Newbury Publishers, pp. 156–68.

SUAREZ-OROZCO, M. (in press) *In Pursuit of a Dream: New Hispanic Immigrants in American Schools*, Stanford, CA, Stanford University Press.

THARP, R. and GALLIMORE, R. (1989) *Rousing Minds to Life: Teaching, Learning and Schooling in Social Context*, Cambridge, MA, Cambridge University Press.

TRUEBA, H.T. (1984) 'The forms, functions and values of literacy: Reading for survival in a barrio as a student', *Journal of the National Association for Bilingual Education* **9**, pp. 21–38.

TRUEBA, H. (Ed.) (1987a) *Success or Failure?: Learning and the Language Minority Student*, New York, Newbury Publishers.

TRUEBA, H. (1987b) 'Organizing classroom instruction in specific sociocultural contexts: Teaching Mexican youth to write in English', in S. GOLDMAN and H. TRUEBA (Eds) *Becoming Literate in English as a Second Language: Advances in Research and Theory*, Norwood, NJ, Ablex, pp. 235–52.

TRUEBA, H. (1988a) 'Peer socialization among minority students: A high school dropout prevention program', in H. TRUEBA and C. DELGADO-GAITAN (Eds) *School and Society: Learning Content Through Culture*, New York, Praeger, pp. 201–17.

TRUEBA, H. (1988b) 'Culturally-based explanations of minority students' academic achievement', *Anthropology and Education Quarterly* **19**, pp. 270–87.

TRUEBA, H. (1988c) 'English literacy acquisition: From cultural trauma to learning disabilities in minority students', *Journal of Linguistics and Education*, **1**, pp. 125–52.

TRUEBA, H. (1989a) *Raising Silent Voices: Educating the Linguistic Minorities for the 21st Century*, New York, Harper and Row.

TRUEBA, H. (1989b) 'Report on the Multicultural Bilingual Special Education Program of California State University, Bakersfield', unpublished Manuscript, Office for Research on Educational Equity, University of California, Santa Barbara.

TRUEBA, H. and DELGADO-GAITAN, C. (Eds) (1988) *School and Society: Learning Content Through Culture*, New York, Praeger.

TRUEBA, H., MOLL, L., DIAZ, S. and DIAZ, R. (1984) *Improving the Functional Writing of Bilingual Secondary School Students* (Contract No. 400-81-0023), Washington, DC, National Institute of Education, ERIC, Clearinghouse on Languages and Linguistics, No. ED 240 862.

US DEPARTMENT OF COMMERCE (1987) *The Hispanic Population in the United States: March 1986 and 1987 (Advance Report)*, Washington, DC, Government Printing Office.

VYGOTSKY, L.S. (1962) *Thought and Language*, Cambridge, MA, MIT Press.

VYGOTSKY, L.S. (1978) *Mind in Society: The Development of Higher Psychological Processes*, M. COLE, V. JOHN-TEINER, S. SCRIBNER and E. SOUBERMAN (Eds), Cambridge, MA, Harvard University Press.

WERTSCH, J. (1985) *Vygotsky and the Social Formation of the Mind*, Cambridge, MA, Harvard University Press.

WERTSCH, J. (1987) 'Collective memory: Issues from a sociohistorical perspective', *The Quarterly Newsletter of the Laboratory of Comparative Human Cognition*, **9**, pp. 19–22.

WILSON, S. (1989) 'Cultural Conflict and Academic Achievement of Cree Indian Students: Perceptions of Schooling from Opasquia Ininiwuk', unpublished doctoral dissertation, University of California, Santa Barbara.

Chapter 7

Cognitive Socialization and Competence: The Academic Development of Chicanos

Luis M. Laosa and Ronald W. Henderson

It is now well known that Chicanos,[1] as a group, attain considerably lower levels of academic achievement than the national average (Orum, 1986; Valencia, chapter 1, this volume). This is a serious and persistent problem facing educators at all levels of the US educational system. More than an educational problem, however, this state of affairs has become a pressing social issue of growing significance and urgent public concern, given that this ethnic group represents a rapidly expanding proportion of the US population (US Bureau of the Census, 1988). Nevertheless, there is little agreement about the causes of the problem. Our goal in this chapter is to provide a context that we hope contributes toward a constructive understanding of these causes. To this end, we relate the question of causes to theory and research bearing on socialization processes and the development of competence in children and youth.

Socialization

Although there is some variation in how scholars of different disciplines and theoretical orientations conceptualize it, current definitions of *socialization* can be summed up as the process whereby the individual acquires the values, beliefs, ways of thinking, behavior patterns, and other personal, yet social, attributes that will characterize the person in the next phase of his or her development. Most concisely put, the study of socialization focuses on the development of the person as a participant in society (for a review of the evolution of the concept see Clausen, 1968).

Socialization may be viewed from the perspective of the individual or from that of a collectivity — be it the larger society or a constituent group. Some writers put the stress on the individual's learning or development; others emphasize the social apparatus that influences such learning and that defines for the individual the range of what is acceptable. In either case, socialization implies that the individual is induced in some measure to conform to the ways of the society or of a particular group. Socialization and social control therefore go hand in hand; they are complementary processes. Social control rests largely on the transmission of norms through socialization. Moreover, as Clausen further reminds us, the effectiveness of social control depends 'on the recruitment and socialization of (witting or unwitting) control agents' (1968, p. 6). As an underlying basis for social control socialization leads the new member to adhere to the norms of the society or of the group and to become committed to its future (Clausen, 1968).

The process of socializing the growing child takes place through many avenues, including schools, television, and peers; but the family generally is, at least for young children, the primary arena for socialization. In recent years, there has been a growing awareness that socialization is not always a unidirectional process; there is evidence that children influence their parents or teachers as well as vice versa (for reviews of research see Brophy and Good, 1974; Dusek and Joseph, 1983; Henderson, 1980; Laosa, 1977a; Maccoby and Martin, 1983; Peterson and Rollins, 1987; Sigel, Dreyer and McGillicuddy-DeLisi, 1984). But, as Maccoby and Martin (1983) caution us, this idea should not lead us to lose sight of the enormous differential in power that exists between an adult and a child, and the potential for asymmetry thus involved.

Although the point is seldom clearly made, socialization is by no means always a purposive endeavor. It comprises, of course, situations in which a socialization agent consciously seeks to modify or mold the individual toward more or less clearly envisioned outcomes. But the concept also includes the kinds of incidental learning, or experiencing, that occur, often unwittingly, when one lives among others. Some dimensions of the socialization process are indeed quite subtle, and only with difficulty can they be brought into awareness. This characteristic does not make them insignificant or inconsequential. On the contrary, it is just because they are frequently subtle and outside of our immediate awareness that the study of socialization process and outcomes becomes a particularly challenging endeavor.

Social and behavioral scientists are not alone in their sensitivity to the implications of the individual's experience for his or her development and public behavior as a member of the society. Parents, educators, and other socialization agents generally have in mind some conception of what the child is 'supposed to become' and of the role that any child-rearing or educational practice may play in achieving or hindering the desired outcome (Inkeles, 1968b; Laosa, 1983). This sensitiviy is also evident in the growing public concern over the impact on the future of the society of persistent poor academic achievement by an ever expanding Chicano population. That is, there is an urgent concern with the ability of the present generation of young children in the United States — an increasing proportion of whom are Chicanos and similarly situated minorities — to maintain, upon becoming adults, the nation's technological and economic competitiveness and to support adequately the aging mainstream population. This is a well-founded concern, and it is reflected perhaps nowhere better than in the recent spate of reports by national and regional commissions on the status of youth and education in the United States (Board of Inquiry, 1985; National Commission on Excellence in Education, 1983; Regional Policy Committee on Minorities in Higher Education, 1987; Youth and America's Future, 1988).

Competence

Whereas socialization refers to the process whereby attributes are acquired, the concept of *competence* stresses the end product, namely, the person as he or she is after having been socialized. Socialization and competence are thus intimately linked concepts (Inkeles, 1968a; Laosa, 1979/1989, 1983). Generally, the goal of socialization is to produce competent people. But, specifically, what is competence? Lay conceptions of competence are generally broad and evaluative. Thus, the *American Heritage Dictionary* defines a competent person as one who is '1. Properly or well qualified; capable.... 2. Adequate for the purpose; sufficient' (1982, p. 301). On the other hand, theoretical definitions of competence vary considerably, as differing conceptions of the term have been advanced in both the psychological and sociological literatures.

In the sense that White (1959, 1979) has used the term, for example, competence refers to the exercise of behaviors that lead to a feeling of efficacy and thus to a source of gratification that is universally and spontaneously sought by all humans. Thus, for White, competence is primarily a biological concept. Humans, he argued, have an urge to act effectively on the environment, and a primary factor in developing competence is how self-gratifying or intrinsically rewarding one's behavioral initiatives are to the individual. On the other hand, in Inkeles' (1968a, b) conception, which is rooted in the structural tradition of role-status theory, the emphasis is upon acquired information, skills, motives, and styles of thinking and of expressing affect. For Inkeles, then, competence is largely a matter of acquired capacities for role performance. In his view, competent performance is measured against the role requirements of the various statuses or positions in the social structure that a person may occupy. From yet another perspective, which stems from the symbolic-interactionist and neo-Freudian traditions, the focus is on the interactional process in role relationships; in this formulation, role relationships are conceived primarily in interpersonal rather than social-structural terms (e.g., Foote and Cottrell, 1955; see also Smith, 1968).

Vygotsky's writings, which have attracted considerable attention among developmental psychologists in recent years, provide still another conception of competence. An attractive feature of the Vygotskyan perspective is the attempt it represents to avoid the intellectual isolation across disciplines that frequently separates studies of individual psychology from research on the social and cultural environment in which individuals live (Wertsch, 1985). For Vygotsky, the individual's development is an integral part of the sociocultural setting in which the person functions. Indeed, a central tenet of his formulation is that mental processes have their origin in social processes. *Mediation* is a key concept in understanding this relation. Specifically, Vygotsky defined development in terms of the emergence or transformation of forms of mediation, and his notion of social interaction and its relation to mental processes involves mediational mechanisms. He argued that mental processes can be understood only if we understand the 'tools and signs' that mediate them. *Tools* and *signs* in this formulation refer to habits and forms of cultural behavior, cultural methods of reasoning, and the cultural meanings of particular stimuli. In short, for Vygotsky the psychological characteristics of persons are a joint, interactive function of the biological features and potentialities of the human species, on the one hand, and, on the other, of the forms of psychological functioning and possible sources of development existing in a given culture or subculture at a particular point in its history. It thus follows that the repertoire of psychological processes and outcomes available as possibilities for individual development can vary across cultures or subcultures, and that alterations in social or cultural conditions can bring about decisive changes in forms of behavior and modes of thought (Vygotsky, 1929, 1978; the same line of theorizing is found in the work of Luria, 1928, 1976).

In some respects, Vygotsky's views are similar to the longstanding tradition in psychological anthropology that argues that different environmental demands lead to the development of different patterns of ability (see, e.g., Laboratory of Comparative Human Cognition, 1983). These conceptions are compatible with Laosa's (1979/1989) *developmental, socioculturally relativistic paradigm*. From the perspective of Laosa's paradigm, social competence involves functional adaptations to specific environments. Each environment may have its own specific demand characteristics for functional adaptation, and a person's success in two different environments may depend on the degree of overlap in the demand characteristics of the environments. This paradigm is particularly appealing because it provides a useful way of approaching the problems that arise in defining competence in complex, changing, and culturally diverse societies — such as the United States — in which individuals, at virtually every phase of their life span, find themselves in environments with very different demand characteristics.

Finally, in considering our topic, we must continually remind ourselves of the conceptual distinction between *proficiency* and *performance*. This distinction acknowledges the difficulty of making inferences about capability without regard for the cultural context and analogous factors that can play as large a role as capability in determining the level of response in any given situation (Anderson and Messick, 1974; Laosa, 1979/1989). A child's performance in a particular classroom setting, for example, may not always be a sign of his or her potential competence in an environment better suited to that child.

The Environmental Ecology

Participation in society means participation in a complex social order; yet the dominant conceptions in the study of human development and education have tended to separate not only the individual from the family for independent examination but also the family from the society. Exceptions to these conceptions include the theoretical formulations of such ecologically oriented psychologists as Bronfenbrenner (1979), Laosa (1979/1989), and Sameroff (1983).

Within developmental psychology, the most visible and systematic emphasis on the need to formulate ecological models for the understanding of human behavior has been the work of Bronfenbrenner (1977, 1979, 1988). Bronfenbrenner emphasizes 'the progressive accommodation, throughout the life span, between the growing human organism and the changing environments in which it lives and grows' (1977, p. 513). This emphasis is found also in Laosa's (1979/1989) developmental, socioculturally relativistic paradigm and in Sameroff's (1983) general systems approach.

Bronfenbrenner's (1979, 1988) conception has much in common with our ideas, and it contributes a useful framework and vocabulary. He conceives of the environment as a set of four nested structures, each inside the next. At the innermost level (the *microsystem*) is the immediate setting — an environment with particular features, activities, and roles — containing the developing person. This can be the home, the classroom, the testing room, and so on. The next level, or *mesosystem*, comprises the relations among one's major settings at a particular point in one's development. In the present view, such interconnections can be as decisive for development as events taking place within a given setting. A child's ability to learn to read in school, for instance, may depend as much on the existence and nature of linkages or continuity of experiences between the school and the home as on a particular teaching technique (Laosa, 1977c, 1982b).

The third level of the ecological environment evokes the hypothesis that the person's development is profoundly affected by events occurring in settings in which the person is not even present. This is the *exosystem*, in which the mesosystem is embedded (Bronfenbrenner, 1979, 1988). It includes, for example, the parents' experiences in the world of work as factors indirectly influencing the child's immediate context.

Finally, pertaining to all three former levels, there is the overarching *macrosystem*, which refers to the 'blueprint' that every society, culture, or subculture has for the organization of every type of setting. This blueprint can be changed, with the result that the structure of the settings in a society can become markedly altered and produce corresponding changes in human behavior and development (Bronfenbrenner, 1979). For example, an economic crisis occurring in a society can have an impact on the child's immediate settings and thence a longstanding influence on children's subsequent development. Similarly, a change in a society's policies affecting the relations between the home and the school may produce effects detectable in the child years later.

The primary focus of the remainder of this chapter is on the first level in Bronfenbrenner's classification, namely, the microsystem; more specifically, the focus is on the innermost aspect of the microsystem level — the family. Space considerations preclude an exhaustive review of the research literature on Chicano children's socialization in the family. We have selected for review, therefore, studies that illustrate principal strands in this literature. When necessary for placing these works in context, we also refer to research on other ethnic groups.

Family Interaction

The innermost level in the environmental ecology of the child is, as we just saw, the household family. Beginning at this level of the ecological system, one of the basic units of analysis is the dyad, or two-person system (Bronfenbrenner, 1979).

In keeping with the traditional focus of collecting research information on individuals, behavioral and social scientists typically gather data on only one person at a time. Partly because of the difficulties and expense involved in conducting reliable observations of people in interaction, research on Chicanos has seldom included observations of actual family interactions using systematic samples of adequate size. Among the few exceptions is Laosa's work on maternal teaching strategies. A principal aim of these studies was to contribute empirical data that might help explain, at least partly, ethnic group differences in academic performance.

As Laosa (1981a) makes clear, the choice of maternal behavior in these studies does not reflect a belief that the mother's behavior is the only important source of influence in the development of the young child or that only biological mothers, or women, are or should be responsible for the care of children. Many relationships can and do play influential roles in the course of a child's life. Certainly the father, although ignored in much of the available research, plays a substantial role in the lives of many children. The same can be said of sibling relationships. Nevertheless, in most cultural settings one finds that, of all the relationships during the child's early years, the ordinary everyday interactions between mother and child constitute a paramount — or at least a very important — aspect of the social environment of childhood. A fundamental assumption is that the mother, in her everyday interactions with her child, continually functions (wittingly or unwittingly) as a teacher. Thus, much of the implicit curriculum and instructional method to which the child is exposed in the home, especially during the early years, is mediated by maternal teaching strategies. A primary focus of the study of mother-child relationships is on identifying diverse patterns of mother-child interaction, how these different styles of mother-child relationship develop, and how they are related to particular child behaviors outside of the maternal relationship (Laosa, 1981a).

Research on non-Chicano populations has shown that depending on the family's social class, mothers use different strategies to teach their young children (for a review of research see Laosa, 1981a). Traditionally in such studies, specific socioeconomic status variables (e.g., mother's and father's occupational status and education) have been either employed interchangeably or aggregately subsumed under a general index of social class or a global measure of socioeconomic status. But Deutsch (1973) and Laosa (1978, 1981a, 1982b) argue that it may be more appropriate and useful to view social class or socioeconomic status not as a unitary dimension but as a conglomerate of different variables, such as occupation, education, and income, that must be examined separately. One of the issues addressed by Laosa (1978), therefore, centered on the relationship between particular socioeconomic status variables, on the one hand, and maternal teaching behaviors, on the other. Thus, one aim of Laosa's (1978) study was to 'unpackage' different components of what is commonly labeled either social class or socioeconomic status, an exosystem factor, and then to examine the influence of these particular components of the exosystem upon the microsystem dimensions of mother-child interaction.

In one study, Laosa (1978) conducted direct observations of Chicano mothers in their homes while they taught cognitive-perceptual tasks to their own 5-year-old children. The sample consisted of forty-three Chicano families residing in Los Angeles; the sample was selected to be as representative as possible of Chicano families in the United States with regard to the distributions of socioeconomic and parental schooling levels. Using the Maternal Teaching Observation Technique (Laosa, 1980b), trained observers recorded the frequency of occurrence of nine categories of maternal behavior. Reliability and short-term stability analyses indicated that these measurements represented adequately reliable and moderately stable attributes of maternal behavior (Laosa, 1980b).

Laosa's (1978) analyses revealed significant correlations of substantial magnitude between the mothers' teaching behaviors and their own level of schooling (i.e., years of formal schooling). In contrast, there was very little relationship between these maternal teaching behaviors and either the mothers' or the fathers' occupational statuses. These results indicate that the schooling level attained by a Chicana is a strong predictor of the strategies that she, once she becomes a mother, will use in teaching her own children.

Specifically, the correlations obtained by Laosa (1978) between the mothers' schooling level and their own teaching strategies were as follows. The mothers' schooling level was positively related to their frequent use of *inquiry*, which refers to the use of questions as a teaching modality. The mothers' schooling level was also positively related to their frequent use of *praise*, namely, verbal expressions of approval of the child's activity or product. In contrast, the mothers' schooling level was inversely related to their use of modeling as a teaching strategy; *modeling* here refers to the mother's doing parts of the task for the child's observation and imitation. Thus, the frequency of use of each of these three distinct maternal teaching strategies varied widely as a function of maternal schooling level. In short, the Chicana mothers with fewer years of education taught more frequently through a modeling or demonstration approach. That is, they tended to demonstrate the solutions so that the child could learn through observation. In contrast, the more highly schooled Chicana mothers taught more often through a style characterized by the frequent use of questions and verbal praise.

In discussing the results of this study by Laosa (1978), LeVine (1980) has called attention to the striking similarity between the approach to teaching employed by the more highly educated Chicana mothers and the academic style of school classrooms. The more educated Chicana mothers taught through a more conversational style (i.e., *inquiry*) rather than motoric demonstration (i.e., *modeling*), and they especially included verbal reinforcement (i.e., *praise*). One might say the more highly schooled Chicana mothers 'imitated' the academic style of the school classrooms in which they had spent so much of their lives (Laosa, 1982b).

Although these findings are correlational, they suggest that, at least among Chicanas, schooling has a marked impact on certain behavioral dispositions that determine the manner in which they, once they become mothers, interact with their children. These findings raise provocative questions about the role that schooling plays in influencing the evolution of culture, and, specifically, in influencing the evolution of cultural patterns of family interaction. (By *evolution* is meant change through adaptation and not progression toward some superior stage.)

Some of these questions were posed in a subsequent study, in which Laosa (1980a) compared the teaching strategies of Chicana mothers to those of non-Hispanic White mothers. The results showed significant differences in the maternal teaching strategies of these two groups. In general, compared to the Chicana mothers, the teaching strategies of the non-Hispanic White mothers were more similar to the academic teaching style that one expects to find in school classrooms. These ethnic group differences in mothers' teaching strategies virtually disappeared, however, when the analyses controlled statistically for the mothers' years of education.

Taken together, the results of these studies led Laosa (1982b) to propose a hypothetical model to explain the high frequency of scholastic failure among Chicanos and other populations in which parents, on the average, have completed relatively few years of schooling. The general hypothetical model can be summarized as follows: the children of the more highly schooled parents learn to master in their homes the form and dynamics of teaching and learning processes that 'take after' those of the school classroom. Because of this relative similarity, the interactional processes that these children learn to master at home will have adaptive value in the classroom. Insofar as the children of the more highly schooled parents learn to master classroom-like interactional processes in their homes, therefore, they will have a decided academic advantage over the children of the less-schooled parents since the latter, by contrast, learn to master in their homes the form and dynamics of teaching and learning processes that have comparatively little adaptive value in the classroom (Laosa, 1982b). To the extent that the relational systems of family and school differ from one another, the child and the classroom teachers will be unable to draw on a shared process of teaching and learning. As a result of this *discontinuity* between the family and the school, the child and the teachers will spend a great portion of their time simply attempting to make sense out of one another's behavior. Hence, school failure for many Chicanos probably occurs, at least partly, because they and their teachers are unable to make sense of each other's relational systems. The Laosa (1982b) model further posits — and his data suggest — that the extent to which the family and the school will share in common a relational system for teaching and learning depends, at least in part, on the length of the parents' schooling experience.

Family Constellation

Another feature of a child's microsystem is the *family's constellation*, that is, such characteristics as the child's family size and sibling structure. Family constellation is relevant to the topic of this chapter for two related reasons. First, demographic statistics show that Chicanos, as a group, differ from non-Hispanic Whites in family constellation (Bean and Tienda, 1987). Second, some researchers have suggested that family constellation influences children's cognitive development (e.g., Zajonc, 1976, 1986). Thus, the question arises: Does family constellation explain the difference in academic performance between Chicano and non-Hispanic White students?

Chicanos, on the average, produce a relatively large number of offspring. Demographic studies demonstrate clearly and consistently that the fertility level of Mexican Americans exceeds those of all other major ethnic or racial groups in the United States, including other Hispanic groups (Bean and Tienda, 1987). Moreover, the fertility difference between Mexican Americans and non-Hispanic Whites is reduced, but not eliminated, when such factors as age, education, income, labor force participation, and generational status are held constant (Bean and Tienda, 1987). Compared to other ethnic groups, therefore, Chicanos have more siblings and, consequently, are less likely to be the firstborn or the only child. Now, juxtapose these demographic differences to the large body of theory and data suggesting that sibling structure and family size influence children's cognitive development, including academic achievement (for reviews see Cicirelli, 1978; Henderson, 1981; Marjoribanks, 1979; Zajonc, 1983, 1986). Indeed, numerous studies, including a few on Chicano families, have examined the relationship between family constellation and children's development. Several family constellation variables have been studied, particularly sibship size (the total number of siblings in a family), birth order (the relative rank of a child in terms of the age hierarchy among siblings), and the presence or absence of a father in the household. This literature, to which we now turn, provides a context for examining the question of whether and how family constellation, among Chicanos, might influence the foundations of intellectual performance that are likely to predict academic achievement.

Sibship size   Many studies have shown an inverse correlation between sibship size and indices of children's cognitive development (e.g., Belmont and Marolla, 1973; Blake, 1989; Breland, 1974; Kellaghan and Macnamara, 1972). Unfortunately, much of the research on the effects of family size on cognitive development has been subject to confounding. A frequent confounding variable is socioeconomic status (SES), because there is generally a correlation between SES and sibship size; that is, lower SES families generally tend to have more children than the more affluent and better educated families (Westoff, 1986). Because usually there is also a correlation between SES and cognitive test performance (Deutsch, 1973; Hess, 1970), it is difficult to isolate the statistical effects of SES and family size, respectively, on cognitive scores. Kellaghan and Macnamara (1972) addressed this problem by studying Catholic families in Ireland, where large families tend to be valued at all SES levels. Significantly, even in this cultural setting, where it was possible to limit the confounding of sibship size and SES, there was the typical correlation between sibship size and cognitive test performance.

A notable exception to the typical inverse correlation between sibship size and cognitive performance was reported by Rankin, Gaite, and Heiry (1979). These researchers tested the hypothesis that the frequently observed correlation between sibship size and cognitive test performance can be explained on the basis of cultural expectations and values. Their sample consisted of elementary-grade children in American Samoa, a cultural setting where large families are the norm. An instrument especially designed for this cultural population was used to measure cognitive ability. Rankin and his associates did observe an association between sibship size and cognitive performance among Samoan children, but this relationship was curvilinear. Children from families closest to the sibship size that is the norm within Samoan culture attained the highest cognitive performance. In a culture where large sibships are the norm, children in families near the average size showed superior cognitive performance than those from either small or very large families. This finding suggests that cultural values mediate the association between family size and cognitive performance. This conclusion raises the question of whether the large body of published research on family constellation is generalizable to Chicanos, since Chicano culture is largely different from that of the samples in most of this research. Only a few studies of Chicanos have given explicit attention to the relation of family size to cognitive performance. This research is discussed below.

Some of the early research suggested that the inverse association between sibship size and cognitive performance observed in non–Hispanic White samples may indeed generalize to Mexican American families. Henderson and Merritt (1968), for example, compared the family characteristics of Mexican American children who scored particularly high on two tests of cognitive ability with the families of children of the same ethnicity who scored particularly low. Both groups of children attended the first grade in schools in Tucson, Arizona. Henderson and Merritt (1968) found that the low-scoring group had significantly larger sibship sizes than did the higher-scoring group.

The above finding must be interpreted cautiously, however, because household family size among Chicanos is heavily confounded with socioeconomic status and home language. Indeed, Henderson and Merritt's (1968) analyses revealed that their two groups of Mexican American children differed not only in the number of siblings, but also in maternal schooling level and socioeconomic status. Valencia, Henderson and Rankin (1981) attempted to untangle such confounding of variables in a study of Mexican American preschoolers and found that when statistical controls were applied to cope with the problem of covariation among predictor variables, the hypothesis of an association between sibship size and the children's cognitive development was not supported. This finding is congruent with results obtained by Laosa (1984a) in a study comparing Chicano and non-Hispanic White toddlers. Let us examine these two studies in some detail.

Given that the Mexican American population is one in which children typically score below the norms on measures of intellectual performance (although there is substantial variation within the population — Duran, 1983; Ramist and Arbeiter, 1986; Sawyer, 1987), and because in this population relatively large families are the norm (US Bureau of the Census, 1988) and seem to be valued (Bradshaw and Bean, 1972), Valencia and his colleagues (1981) set out to ascertain how much of the variance in Mexican American children's cognitive performance they could explain (statistically) by family constellation, compared with other family characteristics. Their sample consisted of 190 Mexican American preschool enrollees in various cities and towns in southern California; only very poor families with both parents present were included. Data were gathered on the following variables: the child's age, sex, sibship size, and ordinal position in the sibship, the parents' schooling attainment level and country of schooling, the language (English or Spanish) spoken in the home and used in the test administration, and the Hollingshead indices of socioeconomic status and social class. In order to cope with the colinearity that is common to such data, the variables were reduced to three factors by means of a factor analysis. The first factor had the highest loadings for the language and parental schooling variables; the second, for the socioeconomic and social class indices; and the third factor was defined by the child's sibship size and ordinal position.

Factor scores were used as independent variables in multiple regression analyses in order to identify the most powerful one-, two-, and three-variable models for the (concurrent) prediction of the Mexican American children's scores on the General Cognitive Index of the McCarthy Scales of Children's Abilities. The best single predictor (it accounted for 6.8 per cent of the variance in cognitive scores) was the factor defined by parental education and language. The SES factor accounted for an additional 3.6 per cent of the variance when added to the first factor to form the most powerful two-variable model. Finally, in the best three-variable model, the sibling constellation factor explained only an additional 2.8 per cent of the variance in cognitive scores.

This research by Valencia *et al.* (1981) suggests that, for Mexican Americans, the number of children in the household and birth order account for a very small proportion of the variance in young children's cognitive development. The results further suggest that parental schooling level and other socioeconomic characteristics together account for much more of this variance. These findings are harmonious with those obtained by Laosa (1984a).

Laosa (1984a) studied the family characteristics and various abilities of young children in two different ethnic groups — Chicano and non-Hispanic White. The purpose of this study was to test several hypotheses about the possible causes and origins of the frequently observed difference in academic achievement between these two populations. One of the hypotheses centered on whether ethnic group differences in family size and sibling structure explain the corresponding group difference in children's cognitive performance. Juxtaposing (a) the demographic evidence indicating that Chicanos on the average produce a relatively large number of offspring and also are likely to reside in households with more adults than do members of the other ethnic group (Bean and Tienda, 1987; US Bureau of the Census, 1988) to (b) the large body of literature — mentioned above — suggesting that family size and sibling structure influence cognitive development, Laosa (1984a) set out to assess the relative contribution of several variables, including family constellation, to variance in young children's cognitive performance. Laosa's focus in this study was on very young children (2.5 years old), because an additional purpose of the research was to determine how early in the life course any such effects on cognitive performance commence to show palpably their impact.

Laosa's (1984a) sample consisted of 171 Chicano and non-Hispanic White families with a toddler. The samples were selected to be representative of their respective ethnic populations with regard to the distributions of socioeconomic status and parental schooling level; in order to control for the potentially confounding effects of single parenting, the sample only included households with both parents. Both ethnic samples were drawn from the same geographic area — a large urban center in south-central Texas. The variables measured in the study were: household income, each parent's schooling attainment level, father's occupation, child's birth order, whether the child was an only child, the number of children residing in the household, and the number of adults residing in the household in addition to the parents. Language variables also were measured — the percentage of household verbalizations in English (v. Spanish or a dialect that mixes/switches between the two languages) for each of the following dyads and directionalities: mother to child, child to mother, father to child, child to father; and the percentage of English verbalizations during testing, also by directionality, namely, examiner to child and child to examiner. The child's performance in each of five ability areas was measured, respectively, by the Verbal, Perceptual-Performance (nonverbal reasoning), Quantitative, Memory, and Motor scales of the McCarthy Scales of Children's Abilities. Ethnicity and sex of child were the major independent variables.

The zero-order (i.e., uncontrolled) intercorrelations among the variables were similar for the two ethnic groups. Interestingly, for neither ethnic group was there a significant zero-order correlation between any of the child performance variables, on the one hand, and, on the other, the number of children in the household, the child's birth order, or whether the child was an only child. These findings strongly suggest that any effects of these sibling structure variables on children's development do not occur, or at least do not become visible, before the third year of life.

A comparison between the above finding by Laosa (1984a) and the data reported by Valencia *et al.* (1981) permits pinpointing the specific age at which the frequently observed zero-order correlation between sibling structure and cognitive performance can first be observed. The average age of the Valencia *et al.*'s (1981) sample was 4.5 years, and they report zero-order correlations of –.24 and –.21, respectively, for the number of children in the home and the child's birth order with the child's cognitive score — in spite of the restricted SES range of their sample. In contrast, the age of Laosa's (1984a) samples was 2.5 years, and he obtained a mean zero-order correlation of only .08 between the four cognitive scales in his analyses and these two sibling structure variables for the Chicano sample. These results are all the more impressive when one considers that the SES range in Laosa's (1984a) sample was not restricted, whereas the range of the Valencia *et al.* sample was highly curtailed. Taken together, these differences between Laosa's (1984a) and the Valencia *et al.* (1981) data suggest that the frequently observed (zero-order) correlation between sibling structure and cognitive performance emerges initially during the third and fourth years of the child's life.

By means of a principal-components analysis of the fourteen variables for the combined ethnic sample, Laosa (1984a) uncovered three clearly defined factors. (Orthogonal and oblique solutions were obtained, revealing no difference between rotation methods.) Factor 1 was defined by the language variables; Factor 2, by the family constellation variables; and Factor 3 was defined by the socioeconomic and parental schooling measures.[2]

Laosa's (1984a) analyses of the children's test scores revealed significant ethnic group differences in the children's verbal, quantitative, and memory performance (no differences in nonverbal reasoning or motor performance). Laosa then performed a series of analyses of covariance in order to ascertain whether these ethnic group differences in children's performance could be explained (statistically) by the three aforementioned factors, either individually or in combination. The results showed that the family constellation factor explained very little, if any, of the ethnic group differences in the children's performance on the ability scales. In contrast, the SES and home language factors accounted for significant portions of the between-group variance in this performance; indeed, the ethnic group differences in children's performance became nonsignificant when the SES and home language factors were simultaneously controlled.

Laosa (1984a) also found that there were no significant *within*-group correlations of scores on any of the five ability scales with the number of household children, the child's birth order, or whether the child was an only child; this was true in both ethnic groups. It should be noted, however, that Laosa (1984a) obtained significant (positive) correlations between the number of adults (in addition to the parents) residing in the Chicano households and the children's scores on two ability scales — Quantitative and Motor. As Laosa (1984a) notes, the latter finding bears on the confluence theory proposed by Zajonc and Markus (1975), a theory discussed in the next section.

In sum, both Laosa (1984a) and Valencia *et al.* (1981) found that, at least during early childhood, neither the number of children in the home nor the child's birth order has much of an impact on Chicano children's cognitive development. The results of both studies are also congruent in clearly pointing to the family's socioeconomic level and home language as being significantly related to Chicano children's performance on cognitive tests; this relationship was even prior to the third birthday and thus long before school entry.

Confluence model The *confluence model* gained much attention when it first appeared in the research literature in the mid 1970s. This theoretical model was proposed by Zajonc and Markus (1975) in an attempt to explain research data showing an association between family constellation and children's cognitive performance. The model, acclaimed for its parsimony, proposes that the intellectual environment of a family has a direct influence on the intellectual development of the children born into it. As defined by the model, the intellectual environment consists of the average intellectual ability of all family members. (The intelligence construct employed in this theoretical model is more akin to the concept of mental age than to IQ.) Adults are cognitively more advanced than children, and therefore they contribute more intellectual stimulation to the family environment by virtue of their greater experiences and accumulated learning opportunities; conversely, the arrival of an infant can worsen the intellectual environment by lowering the average intellectual ability of its members. Thus, according to the confluence model, a child's intellectual environment is 'diluted' by the presence of younger siblings. The model, however, also proposes that children with younger siblings are able to engage in teaching them and thereby perhaps to improve their own intellectual ability. Research on family interaction does suggest that older siblings can serve as effective intellectual resources for their younger siblings (Laosa, 1982a; Norman-Jackson, 1982; Stewart, 1983); it also suggests that teaching itself can benefit teachers as much as learners (Bargh and Schul, 1980; Cohen, Kulik and Kulik, 1982).

In part, the extraordinary interest generated by the confluence model was stimulated by Zajonc's (1976) suggestion that the observed declines in national Scholastic Aptitude Test (SAT) scores merely reflected a population bulge of children from large families who were heavily represented in the pool of test takers. Zajonc (1976, 1986) predicted that the average scores would begin to rise as children from a generation of smaller families approached college age and entered the pool. Although the predicted rise in SAT scores did indeed occur (Zajonc, 1986), the confluence model is the subject of considerable scientific controversy.

Tests of the model on other types of data have been attempted with greater (e.g., Berbaum and Moreland, 1985) and lesser success (Melican and Feldt, 1980; Page and Grandon, 1979; Velandia, Grandon and Page, 1978), and the model has been criticized on several grounds. Critics of the model raise questions about the appropriateness of the populations studied, the levels of data aggregation, the details of the calculations, and the logical basis of the model (Henderson, 1981; Scott-Jones, 1984; Steelman, 1985), while proponents of the model refute criticisms and question the suitability of the statistical analyses techniques and the omission of certain variables (Zajonc, 1983).

Most studies of the confluence model are based on samples of non-minority populations in the United States and Western Europe. Given the restricted cultural variability represented in such studies, it is important to establish whether the empirical findings apply to other cultural groups. The question of whether the model is generalizable to other populations was addressed in a study of a large sample of college applicants in Colombia, South America (Velandia *et al.*, 1978). Neither the predicted associations between birth order and intelligence nor the relation of intelligence to family size were upheld. In a follow-up study with a large national sample in the United States, Page and Grandon (1979) found that the apparent effects of family size were best explained by ethnic group and social class variables. These results are consistent with those obtained by Laosa (1984a) and Valencia *et al.* (1981) for Mexican American young children. The little research that exists on Mexican American samples shows no significant effects of sibship size or birth order on intellectual development once proper controls for other background variables are taken into account (Laosa, 1984a; Valencia *et al.*, 1981) — more precisely, if any such effects occur, they are not evident in early childhood.

Single Parenting

The aforementioned studies of Chicano families by Laosa (1984a) and Valencia *et al.* (1981) focused on *two-parent* families — that is, on households in which the child resided with both mother and father. By designing their sampling plans in this manner, these investigators successfully avoided confounding their results with possible effects due to differences between one- and two-parent families. Although a large majority of Chicano children reside with two parents, some of them live in solo-parent households; in 1988, 18.5 per cent of the Mexican-origin families in the United States were headed by a woman with no husband present (US Bureau of the Census, 1988; see also Laosa, 1988a).[3]

The issue is important because the research literature suggests that compared with children in two-parent households, those in single-parent homes are more likely to develop academic and conduct problems in school (for a research review see Hetherington, Camara and Featherman, 1983). Because almost all of this research is based on non-Hispanic White or Black samples, the question arises as to whether these findings generalize to Chicanos. Do Chicano children in solo-parent families develop differently from those in two-parent households? Is the scholastic performance of Chicano children affected by whether they live with one or two parents? Are there features of Chicano culture that serve to buffer or moderate the effects of solo parenting observed in children from other cultural groups?

These questions were addressed by LeCorgne and Laosa (1976) in a study designed to test the null hypothesis of no effects due to solo mothering on Mexican American children's cognitive and psychosocial development. The sample consisted of 248 fourth-grade students in a predominantly Mexican American, urban area in south-central Texas. About half of the children were selected for the sample because they did not have a father or male father surrogate (other than an older sibling) living at home, whereas the other half were randomly selected from among those living in two-parent households. Only Mexican American families at or below the poverty level were included. The data were analyzed using a 2 × 2 (father presence/absence by child's sex) analysis of covariance (child's chronological age covaried). LeCorgne and Laosa's analyses uncovered important differences between Mexican American children of the two family types.

Among the dependent variables examined by LeCorgne and Laosa were classroom teachers' ratings of the students' psychosocial adjustment. The teachers were instructed that school achievement was not to be a consideration in making the personal adjustment ratings, but that the child's 'self-concept and relationship to others' (p. 470) should be the major consideration. The analyses revealed that both the main effect of family type and the interaction with child's sex were significant for this variable. Specifically, the teachers' ratings showed more signs of school maladjustment in boys of solo mothers than in boys of two-parent homes or in girls of either family type. This finding suggests a differential effect of father absence on boys and girls.

LeCorgne and Laosa's (1976) finding of a significant family-type-by-child's-sex interaction for teachers' ratings of Mexican American children's school adjustment is consonant with data on other populations suggesting that boys are more susceptible to certain forms of stress than girls (e.g., Rutter, 1979). Although little is known about the reasons for this sex difference, recent reviews of the research literature do indeed point to the conclusion that boys may respond more negatively than girls to some forms of psychosocial stress, including the stresses from divorce (Hetherington *et al.*, 1983; Zaslow, 1987; Zaslow and Hayes, 1986). LeCorgne and Laosa's (1976) findings add confirmatory evidence for this general hypothesis and extend it by showing that the sex difference in vulnerability to certain forms of psychosocial stress, a vulnerability that has been observed in research on other ethnic populations, is generalizable to Mexican Americans. Specifically, LeCorgne and Laosa's data show that solo mothering appears to have no deleterious effect on Mexican American girls' psychosocial adjustment to school (at least during middle childhood), whereas something as yet undetermined about the experiences associated with solo mothering seems to affect negatively the school adjustment of Mexican American boys.

A plausible explanation for this sex difference, offered by Hetherington *et al.* (1983), is that separation from the father may represent a more important loss for a male than for a female, both as a figure of identification and as a disciplinarian. Research indeed suggests that girls in father-custody families exhibit some of the same difficulties in social behavior as do boys in mother-headed, one-parent families (Camara and Resnick, 1988; Santrock and Warshak, 1979; Santrock, Warshak and Elliott, 1982). This finding suggests that separation from the same-sex parent may be particularly difficult for children. Given the present, most common custodial arrangements (Maccoby, Depner and Mnookin, 1988), there-fore, boys may be at higher risk for deleterious outcomes from family disruption and divorce than are girls.

LeCorgne and Laosa's (1976) study also included three measures of the children's cognitive-perceptual development — the Raven Coloured Progressive Matrices, the Goodenough-Harris Drawing Test, and the Bender-Gestalt Test. There were no significant differences between family types (and no interactions with sex) for either Raven or Bender-Gestalt developmental scores. There was, however, a significant difference in Goodenough-Harris scores, suggesting a higher level of conceptual development for the group of two-parent children. In interpreting this result, LeCorgne and Laosa point out that, although the sample included only poor families, this difference in cognitive performance could be the outcome of very small differences in socioeconomic level between the two family types. National statistics show lower average incomes for solo-mother than for two-parent households (Laosa, 1988a); and the lower a family's economic status, the more important small dollar differences may become. Indeed, Harris and Roberts (1972) found a noticeable increase in mean Goodenough-Harris scores between children from families with incomes of less than $3,000 and those of $3,000 to $4,999.

The latter observation brings forward yet another effect of diversity in family structure, namely, family income. Laosa (1988a) recently examined the economic implications of single parenting. His analyses, as mentioned above, clearly show that solo mothers and the children living with them are, on the average, economically disadvantaged compared with those in two-parent families; this is true irrespective of ethnicity or race. This situation is partly the result of sex inequalities in income, as the average woman earns lower wages per hour than does the average man (Fuchs, 1986). Even when all of the variance predicted by family structure can be explained by the socioeconomic level of the family, however, we should not ignore the causal links in the process (Hetherington *et al.*, 1983). Divorce, separation, or death of a spouse may create low socioeconomic conditions in the home, and such conditions in turn can influence the child's academic attainment.

Environmental Processes in the Home

Whereas some studies of socialization, such as those discussed in the preceding section, focus on the influence of 'molar-level' sociodemographic variables on children's development — such as household income, parental education and occupation, family size and structure — other studies attempt to examine the effects of 'micro-level' processes. Such micro-level processes are often hypothesized to act as intervening or mediating variables that may explain the association between the molar-level factors and the child's development. A good example of micro-level processes are the data on teaching strategies that Laosa (1978, 1980a, 1982b) obtained through direct observations of the interactions between Chicana mothers and their own children, discussed elsewhere in this chapter. In this section the focus is on research in which interviews — rather than direct observations — are used to obtain data on micro-level processes in the home.

Among the early research on environmental process variables is the work stimulated by Benjamin Bloom, who recognized the need for knowledge about the learning processes that occur in the home and other features of the home environment that facilitate intellectual development. Two of Bloom's doctoral students — Davé (1963) and Wolf (1964) — hypothesized several home effects on intellectual performance on the basis of an extensive literature review, and they devised a focused interview approach to measure them. Davé and Wolf found that the home environmental process variables that they measured through interviews with (non-Hispanic) parents of elementary-grade children were remarkably good concurrent predictors of both academic achievement (multiple $R = .80$) and IQ (multiple $R = .70$). These associations have been replicated in different countries (Marjoribanks, 1979) and with different cultural groups, including Mexican Americans (Henderson, 1966; Henderson and Merritt, 1968).

The principal environmental process variables in these studies are represented by those employed in Davé's (1963) research; among them are 'achievement press', 'language models', 'academic guidance', 'activeness of family', and 'intellectuality in the home'. The measurement procedures are intended to identify specific parental behaviors rather than statements of attitudes or intentions. For example, parents' goals and aspirations for their children are subsumed under the 'achievement press' variable. Interview items and probes relevant to this variable are designed to identify and quantify such parental behaviors as the reinforcement practices for the child's academic performance and the achievement standards on which these practices are based. Additional indices of this variable are derived from interview questions tapping into parents' concrete knowledge of the developmental and educational progress of their children and into the specific plans and preparations they have made to accomplish the educational goals they claim to hold for their children. The influence of role models, too, is taken into account in composing the 'achievement press' variable; this is done by incorporating information on the educational and occupational attainments of family members and friends. Further exemplifying Davé's and Wolf's measurement procedures, the 'language model' variable is based on ratings of the parent's own language during the interview, including such language characteristics as richness and variety of vocabulary, fluency of expression, and the organization of thought as expressed through speech. This variable also comprises information on the parent's awareness of specific features of the child's use of language and on the nature of the parent's direct efforts to influence the child's language development.

Building on the work of Davé and Wolf, Henderson and Merritt (1968) demonstrated that the aforementioned kinds of environmental process variables can distinguish the families of Mexican American children who perform well on cognitive measures from those who do poorly. Henderson (1972) later showed that, for the same children, these environmental process variables predicted academic achievement over a three-year period. Specifically, Henderson and Merritt (1968) studied eighty Mexican American Spanish-speaking first-grade children in Tucson, Arizona. Two groups comprised the sample: half of the children were selected because of their very high scores on the Goodenough-Harris Drawing Test — a measure of general conceptual development — and the Van Alstyne Picture Vocabulary Test; the other half were chosen because of their very low scores. From individual interviews with the mothers, the researchers obtained ratings on thirty-three characteristics of the home that defined nine environmental process variables generally similar to those that Davé and Wolf had identified earlier. The analyses revealed significantly higher means on the environmental process variables for the group scoring higher on the cognitive tests. Thus, the processes taking place in the homes of the Mexican American children who scored high on these cognitive tests apparently differed in specific ways from the homes of those who scored low. It should be pointed out, too, that the analyses also revealed that the mothers of the high-scoring children had, on the average, more formal education and a higher socioeconomic status than did the mothers of the low-scoring children.

In a follow-up study, Henderson (1972) administered the California Reading Test to thirty-five children of the original Mexican American sample when they were in the third grade and correlated these third-grade reading achievement scores with the home environmental process measures obtained two years earlier.

Henderson (1972) reports a predictive bivariate correlation of .55 between the reading achievement scores and the combined score for the various home environmental process variables. This finding is congruent with that obtained by Wolf (cited in Henderson, 1981), who followed his aforementioned (non-Hispanic) sample over a four-year period and found that the multiple correlation between IQ at this time and the environmental process variables measured earlier was only slightly lower than the original, concurrent coefficient. These findings do not establish cause, but they do demonstrate reasonably long-term predictive stability for the measures of environmental processes in the home.

The approach that Davé (1963) and Wolf (1964) developed for the measurement of environmental processes in the home thus proved to be an exceptionally good predictor of intellectual performance, but the method is time consuming and requires the services of skilled interviewers. For this reason, Henderson, Bergan and Hurt (1972) set out to develop an interview schedule, adapted from Davé's (1963) and Wolf's (1964) method, that could be more easily administered and coded. The resulting instrument — the Henderson Environmental Learning Process Scale (HELPS) — is a structured questionnaire using a Likert-type response format. It is designed to provide measures of educationally relevant processes in the home that can be subject to change through intervention programs in the school and in the home. The items composing this instrument focus primarily on specific experiences provided for the child in the home and on patterns of interaction among family members, but they also tap parental attitudes and such factors as the parent's aspirations and expectations for the child. Although the information yielded by the HELPS is less detailed than that provided by focused interview procedures, it has the advantage of requiring less than twenty minutes to administer, and little training is required for its administration.

In order to assess the predictive validity and other psychometric properties of the measures obtained by the HELPS, Henderson *et al.* (1972) administered the Stanford Early Achievement Test and the Boehm Test of Basic Concepts to sixty low-income Mexican American and sixty-six middle-SES non-Hispanic White first-grade children in Tucson, and the HELPS to their mothers. The analyses in this study were performed on the combined ethnic sample. A principal-components analysis of the twenty-five HELPS items yielded five factors. The HELPS items loading on the first factor reflected opportunities taken by parents to expand their own and their child's social and intellectual interests and experiences. Specific items tapped such parental behaviors as having discussions with the child about programs viewed on television, seeking answers to the child's questions by consulting a book (in the child's presence), encouraging the child to read, and extending interpersonal contacts via participation in clubs or organizations and visits with friends in neighborhoods other than one's own. The second factor was characterized by the label, 'Valuing Language and School Related Behavior'. Specific parental behaviors identified by items loading on this factor included such interactions as explaining the sequence of steps for performing particular tasks, praising the child for approved behavior at school, and talking with the child at mealtimes. The third factor, labeled 'Intellectual Guidance', was defined by such items as helping the child with homework, pointing out features of intellectual interest during outings, and reading to the child during the pre-school years. The items loading on Factor 4 appeared to involve attempts to prepare the child to function well in school without attempting to duplicate directly the functions of a school teacher. Included here were opportunities to obtain school-related information through such community resources as libraries and museums, providing an intellectual atmosphere by modeling the use of printed materials, communicating verbally with the child, and being aware of specific features of the child's language development. The final factor, labeled 'Attention', reflected a variety of ways in which parents attend to behaviors that seem likely to stimulate intellectual development. Mothers who scored high on the items loading on this factor were likely to provide attention by showing interest in the child's learning and by calling attention to the child's use of language.

In order to ascertain whether the home environmental process variables as measured by the HELPS correlate with academic performance, Henderson *et al.* (1972) performed stepwise regressions (for the combined ethnic sample), using HELPS factor scores as predictors (concurrent) and the test scores as criteria. The results showed that together the HELPS factors accounted for the majority of the variance in cognitive test scores (e.g., a multiple R of .72 for the Boehm). The Henderson *et al.* (1972) HELPS is, then, a practical questionnaire that can be administered to large samples and scored with relative ease and that identifies variables reflecting environmental processes in the home that correlate highly with measures of children's academic achievement and conceptual development. The measure has demonstrated good qualities of reliability and predictive validity when adapted for use with varied populations in different community settings (e.g., Kitonyi, 1980; Prior, 1974; Valencia, Henderson and Rankin, 1985).

The HELPS was used in a study by Valencia and associates (1985) to assess the relative contributions of socioeconomic status, parental schooling level, home language, sibship size, and home environmental processes to the cognitive performance of Mexican American preschool enrollees from low-income, two-parent households. Multiple regression analyses revealed that the home environmental processes, as measured by the HELPS total score, accounted for more unique variance in performance on the General Cognitive Index of the McCarthy Scales of Children's Abilities than did any of these other variables. The next largest portion of unique variance in cognitive scores was explained (statistically) by a composite variable comprising parental schooling level and use of English over Spanish in the home. Finally, parental occupational status and sibship size did not add significantly to the prediction (concurrent) of cognitive scores. These findings provide support for Laosa's theoretical model (Laosa, 1982b; Marjoribanks, 1984), according to which parental schooling level exerts an indirect influence on children's developmental trajectories by affecting how parents interact with their children.

Another influential approach to the measurement of home environments was developed by Bettye Caldwell and her associates. Caldwell's Home Observation for Measurement of the Environment (HOME) Inventory has been used in numerous studies of the relation of home environments to the development of competence, and it has proven to be a good predictor of (non-Hispanic) children's intellectual performance (e.g., Bradley *et al.*, 1989; Bradley, Caldwell and Rock, 1988; Elardo, Bradley and Caldwell, 1977). This instrument is designed to assess the stimulation and support available to a child in the home environment. Information needed to score the Inventory is obtained through observation and interview done in the home with the child and the child's primary caregiver (Caldwell and Bradley, 1984). As is the case with variables based on the measurement approach developed by Davé (1963) and Wolf (1964), the HOME Inventory has been found to be a more effective predictor of mental test performance than have global indices of SES (e.g., Bradley et al., 1989). The HOME Inventory is not, however, an equally effective measure for all ethnic groups.

In one study (Elardo et al., 1977), the predictions of intellectual performance at age 3 years from HOME scores obtained a year earlier held up for samples of both Black and non-Hispanic White families. Although intellectual performance scores were significantly associated with HOME scores in both ethnic groups, the relation was not as strong for Black as for non-Hispanic White families. The investigators speculated that the attenuated association between HOME and intellectual performance scores for Black families might have been the result of a range restriction in the intellectual performance scores for the Black sample or of a lower validity of HOME scores for Blacks than for non-Hispanic Whites. More recently, Bradley et al. (1989) examined the relationship between HOME scores and measures of children's intellectual development in Black, Mexican American, and non-Hispanic White samples; the samples were matched on HOME scores. Importantly, the results of this major study showed that, whereas the HOME scores significantly predicted intellectual performance for the non-Hispanic White and Black samples, the corresponding coefficients for the Mexican American sample were nonsignificant and near zero. These findings add support to Laosa's argument that there is a need to assess the measurement properties of data separately by ethnic group (Laosa, 1977b, 1982c). The findings also contribute to the growing evidence justifying Laosa's exhortations to practitioners and policy-makers cautioning them against generalizing research results across different ethnic populations in the absence of supporting empirical evidence (Laosa, 1981b, 1988b, 1990).

In sum, studies of relations between home environmental processes and intellectual development show that measures of specific characteristics of home environments account for a statistically and educationally significant portion of the variance in children's intellectual performance, and that they provide stable predictions over time. With children of varied ages, and spanning a number of cultural groups and socioeconomic statuses, it has been shown that experiences and expectations in the family setting are associated with children's intellectual development. Measures of home environments can provide information of a specific nature about the actual experiences that differentiate between intellectual-ly higher and lower performing children. At the same time, a small but growing number of studies underscore the need for caution in assuming — in the absence of appropriate evidence — that research findings obtained for a particular cultural population generalize to different ethnic groups.

The studies discussed thus far in this chapter offer correlational information and are therefore suggestive of — but not definitive about — causation. A few studies have been conducted to identify causal connections between home environment variables and intellectual performance, either by testing causal hypotheses using special statistical procedures (e.g., Bradley, Caldwell and Elardo, 1979; Laosa, 1982a) or by experimentally manipulating parenting behaviors. An example of the latter is a study by Henderson and Garcia (1973), discussed below.

Intervention Experiments

For obvious reasons, it is impossible to assign children randomly to different kinds of home environments at birth and observe the results. It is possible, however, to manipulate selected aspects of parental behavior on the basis of causal hypotheses derived from correlational findings. It then becomes possible to determine if the manipulated home practices influence the children's development in the predicted direction. This approach differs from large-scale parent training programs of the type that were popular in the 1970s (for reviews see Goodson and Hess, 1975; Haskins and Adams, 1983; Zigler and Weiss, 1985), because those intervention programs commonly manipulate several aspects of parental practice simultaneously, in ways that make it impossible to compare systematically the particular outcomes of specific practices. In contrast to such interventions with global objectives, a few studies have manipulated and assessed the effects of a narrow range of specific variables suggested by the research on family environments.

In one such study, Henderson and Garcia (1973) tested the hypothesis that parents can be trained to adopt the kinds of behavior that may facilitate their children's academic performance. Mexican American mothers of first-grade children in a low-income neighborhood in Tucson, Arizona were selected to participate in the experiment. Half of the mothers in a sample of sixty families were randomly assigned to the experimental group; the remainder served as controls and received no treatment. The mothers in the experimental group were trained by the experimenter to model, cue, and reinforce their children's inquiry skills — inquiry skills being defined as asking causal questions. These mothers received instruction in small groups, which consisted of participating in discussions of the rationale for the experiment, viewing demonstrations in which project staff modeled parent and child behavior, learning to code question-asking behavior, and engaging in role playing activities to learn techniques designed to promote their children's production of causal questions. Each mother participated in a total of five weekly sessions. Following each training session, the mother spent at least two brief (ten minute) periods with her child in the home, attempting to apply the procedures that she had learned during the training.

Before and after this intervention, data on the children's question-asking were collected for the experimental and control groups under three conditions, as follows. In the baseline condition, the experimenter showed the child a set of pictures and prompted him or her to ask questions about them. This was followed by an instructional condition, in which the experimenter used modeling procedures in an attempt to foster the child's tendency to ask causal questions. Immediately following this instructional session, the experimenter again measured the child's tendency to ask causal questions, using the same pictorial stimuli employed in the baseline condition. In the final data-collection condition, generalization was tested as the experimenter prompted the children to apply their question-asking skills to another, unfamiliar, set of pictorial stimuli. Henderson and Garcia's (1973) results showed that compared to the control group, the children whose mothers participated in the intervention displayed significantly superior performance on every one of these measures at posttest.

The differences in performance between the children in the two groups resembled the differences one would expect to find between two groups differing in aptitudes for question-asking skills. That is, in the posttest data, not only did the performance of the children in the experimental group exceed that of the controls on the baseline condition, but also the performance improvement in response to the instruction condition was greater for the experimental children than for the controls. Moreover, this advantage was maintained during the generalization condition. These results, obtained with Mexican American families, have been replicated, with a slightly modified design, in a study with Papago families (Henderson and Swanson, 1974).

The relevance of the above findings by Henderson and Garcia (1973) is magnified when considered in light of Laosa's (1982b) theoretical model — which he supports with empirical data — regarding the use of questions as a teaching strategy by Chicano mothers with their own children. To illustrate the implications of their findings for education, Henderson and Garcia offer the following analogy. The experimental and control children, drawn randomly from a single population, appear in the posttests to represent two different populations: high achievers and low achievers on the specific tasks of the study. This difference, however, is not attributable to a corresponding difference in the aptitudes of the children. Rather, it is attributable to the fact that the experimental group of children received a particular kind of instruction and support at home, whereas the controls did not. This situation may be parallel to the natural circumstances in which children's school performance is facilitated by the types of interaction that take place in their homes.

Field experiments have demonstrated also that environmental processes modeled on those investigated in correlational studies of home environments can influence specific components of academic motivation. Swanson and Henderson (1976), for example, conducted such a study in response to a request from Papago parents. These parents were interested in learning to influence their children to become more interested in, and successful at, reading. Swanson and Henderson, therefore, designed a field experiment to test the hypothesis that children would choose activities of the sort that were reinforced through the overt approval or attention of a significant person in the home environment. Specifically, these investigators hypothesized that students whose mothers were trained in procedures to influence children's preferences for reading activities would (a) show an increase in their selection of reading materials over attractive alternatives, and (b) display generalization of this preference to the classroom. The participants in the experiment were families with a second-grader on the Papago Indian Reservation in Arizona. During a series of training sessions, the mothers in the experimental group were taught a series of behavior sequences for interacting with their children. After each session, they practiced at home, interacting in a warm, supportive way with their own children in situations focused on children's books, as follows. At designated intervals, the mother laid out reading materials, together with other toys and games that were attractive to children. She provided differential reinforcement by expressing her approval and engaging in affectionate interactions whenever her child approached and examined the reading materials; the mother merely continued her household routines when the child chose other materials.

Two different tests of the effects of the intervention were conducted. A pre-post situational measure involved bringing each child to a room where materials were attractively displayed in three distinct interest areas; one containing books, one with puzzles, and one with various kinds of blocks. Observational records were kept of the amount of time the child spent engaged with each type of activity. Swanson and Henderson's (1976) analyses of these observations showed that the children in the experimental group displayed significant pre-to-post increases in the amount of time spent interacting with the reading materials, whereas the control group children did not. The second test was conducted in the regular classroom, to determine if treatment effects generalized beyond the situational tasks. Teachers set up a free choice situation in which children could select from a range of normal classroom activities. Observational data demonstrated that the experimental group children selected reading materials more often than did the control children, whose parents had not participated in the training or home intervention. We anticipate that findings such as these generalize to Chicanos, since the experimental procedures were based on data and theory on the nature of intellectually stimulating home environments, which available data suggest are applicable to Chicano families (e.g., Henderson *et al.*, 1972; Henderson and Merritt, 1968; Valencia *et al.*, 1985); moreover, the experimental manipulation was an extension and elaboration of a design that proved effective with Mexican American children (i.e., Henderson and Garcia, 1973; Swanson and Henderson, 1976). The results of the experiments reviewed in this section of the chapter show that parents can be trained effectively to teach specific intellectual skills to their children and to influence their motivation toward academic activities.

As we conclude this section, recall that in a previous section of the chapter we reviewed correlational research showing substantial and stable relationships between experiences provided naturalistically to children in the home environment and the children's intellectual performance. Field experiments such as those conducted by Henderson and his colleagues (Henderson and Garcia, 1973; Henderson and Swanson, 1974; Swanson and Henderson, 1976), on the other hand, are intended to examine the mechanisms hypothesized to mediate the relations identified in correlational studies. In this manner, field experiments can help illuminate the ways in which particular skills and motives acquired in the home environment interact with the demand characteristics of instructional settings.

Further insights into the nature of relations between the family environment and scholastic achievement can be gleaned from research on parental beliefs and expectations, to which we now turn.

Parental Beliefs, Mathematics Achievement, and Sex Differences

Some investigators are focusing their research on parental belief systems (e.g., Sigel, 1985). Among the questions being asked is whether parents' beliefs about their children's ability influence intellectual performance. Evidence is accumulating that parents' ideas about their children's ability may be a potent force in determining the children's ideas of themselves as academic performers (Alexander and Entwisle, 1988; Parsons, Adler and Kaczala, 1982; Phillips, 1987), and that children's ideas of themselves may, in turn, affect their achievement level (Stevenson and Newman, 1986). This influence may be especially salient in mathematics, a domain in which parental belief systems are likely to influence children's self-concepts of ability and expectancies of success, their future achievement in this subject, and their course enrollment plans (Eccles, 1983).

Public concern about the school achievement of Chicanos has tended to focus largely on literacy and literacy-related skills, perhaps because of a general belief that the academic obstacles facing this ethnic group stem only from linguistic factors. Because the symbols and operations associated with mathematics are assumed to be common across languages, mathematics learning may receive less attention than other subjects. Whatever the cause for this neglect, the fact is that Chicano students are as much 'at risk' for law achievement or failure in mathematics as they are in other subjects (Durán, 1983; Educational Testing Service, 1989; Laosa, 1985; Sawyer, 1987).

Competence in mathematics is especially important for achievement in scientific and engineering fields and, increasingly so, for adequate functioning in other professions as well. Nevertheless, Mexican American pupils perform below norm in mathematics, as a group, and are less likely than the average student to enroll in mathematics courses (as they are in academic courses generally) that prepare them for college study toward these careers (Ramist and Arbeiter, 1986). The High School and Beyond study of high school sophomores and seniors is a valuable source of information on this point, because it included a sample of 4,016 Mexican Americans who were oversampled randomly from the general population of high school students. Analyses of these data by Nielsen and Fernandez (1981) revealed that Mexican Americans performed lower than non-Hispanic Whites in every achievement area that was assessed, including mathematics. Non-Hispanic Whites showed about a one standard deviation advantage over Mexican Americans in tested mathematics, reading, and vocabulary. Other relevant, and more recent, data come from college-bound seniors who take the Scholastic Aptitude Test (SAT) for college admissions, which is intended to measure developed ability in the use of language and in simple mathematics reasoning as might be expected of students in undergraduate college coursework. Analyses of SAT scores in 1989 reveal a sixty-five-point advantage for non-Hispanic Whites over Mexican Americans on the verbal section, and a sixty-one-point advantage in mathematics (Educational Testing Service, 1989) — these are differences of about two thirds of a standard deviation (Ramist and Arbeiter, 1986). The American College Testing Program (ACT) college-admissions test shows the same pattern of ethnic-group differences for first-year college students — non-Hispanic Whites outperform Mexican Americans by about one standard deviation on every ACT subtest (i.e., English, mathematics, natural sciences, and social studies; Sawyer, 1987). These various data sets likely underestimate the true achievement differences, because they exclude school dropouts — who are usually among the lowest achievers (Steinberg, Blinde and Chan, 1984) — and the dropout rate is higher for Mexican Americans than for non-Hispanic Whites (Orum, 1986; Rumberger, this volume).

Not only do Mexican American students as a group score lower than the norm on achievement tests of quantitative skills, but they also take fewer courses in mathematics than the average pupil; this is true even considering only seniors who seem to be planning to enter college (MacCorquodale, 1988; Ramist and Arbeiter, 1986). The relatively low participation of Mexican American students in advanced high school electives in mathematics is troublesome, because it constitutes a pattern of choice that closes off options to participate in science-related occupations and in many of the social science or business college courses that require quantitative backgrounds as well.

Direct evidence on the nature of the processes that contribute to the observed poor achievement in mathematics and low participation in elective mathematics courses among Mexican Americans is scant, but one wonders whether studies of factors that contribute to sex differences in intellectual performance in other populations might yield some insights into the kinds of processes responsible for the ethnic group differences as well. The study of sex differences has a long history in psychology, and gender is a widely used variable in psychological research. Because most research with children involves both boys and girls, and investigators typically carry out at least perfunctory tests for sex differences, the body of research on sex differences is large (Jacklin, 1989). The earlier research comparing male and female performance averages on intellectual tasks showed sex differences in verbal, mathematical, and other abilities, but trend data point to a gradual narrowing or closing of these gaps during the last two decades (for a recent review of research see Wilder and Powell, 1989). The historical advantage of females in the verbal domain appears to have been virtually eliminated, and the superiority of males in certain mathematical areas seems less substantial now than in the past. A notable exception to this converging trend is in the upper ranges of tested mathematics performance, where the ratio of boys outscoring girls has remained fairly constant over the years (Feingold, 1988; see also Educational Testing Service, 1989). This sex difference emerges around the time of adolescence (cf. Laosa and Brophy, 1970, 1972; Wilder and Powell, 1989), as exemplified by the higher average scores of males than of females on the mathematics sections of college-admissions tests. Among high school seniors in 1989 (combined ethnic groups), the mean SAT mathematics score of males was forty-six points higher than that of females — a difference of more than one-third of a standard deviation — which contrasts with a sex difference of only thirteen points on the test's verbal section (Educational Testing Service, 1989). Course-taking patterns also differ by sex. Males take a greater number of advanced mathematics courses on the average than females, even in high school (Barton, 1989). Significantly, this pattern of sex differences in standardized test scores and in course-taking, which we see among non-Hispanic Whites, is also present among Mexican Americans, although Mexican Americans, whether male or female, score lower and take fewer math courses on the average than non-Hispanic Whites of either sex (MacCorquodale, 1988; Ramist and Arbeiter, 1986; Sawyer, 1987).

Several hypotheses have been advanced in attempts to explain the observed sex differences in mathematics performance and course participation (for reviews see Eccles and Hoffman, 1984; Wilder and Powell, 1989). Among these hypotheses is a plausible explanation that focuses on the cumulative effects of early socialization patterns and that implicates parents and teachers as expectancy socializers. A growing body of research is accumulating on the role of attitudes and expectations in creating or promoting sex differences in mathematical attainment, although these studies are largely on non-Hispanic samples. The existence of a sex difference in expectancy for success in mathematics and in self-concept of mathematical ability from middle childhood on is now well documented (Dossey, Mullis, Lindquist and Chambers, 1988; Eccles, 1983; Entwisle and Baker,

1983; Stevenson and Newman, 1986), but the developmental origins of this difference remain unclear. Eccles (formerly Parsons) and her colleagues argue that parents (Parsons, Adler and Kaczala, 1982) and teachers (Parsons, Kaczala and Meece, 1982) may be perpetuating, if not creating, these sex differences. These investigators designed a study to test the hypothesis that parents contribute to the sex differences in achievement expectancy and self-concept of mathematical ability through their beliefs about their children's abilities, the difficulty of math itself, and the importance of taking math courses (Parsons, Adler and Kaczala, 1982). The data provided confirmatory evidence for the hypothesis. The results showed that both mothers and fathers held sex-differentiated perceptions of their children's mathematics aptitude despite the similarity of the actual performance of boys and girls (non-Hispanic fifth to eleventh graders from middle- to upper-class homes). Parents of daughters believed their child had to work harder to do well in math than did parents of sons, whereas parents of sons thought advanced math was more important for their child than did parents of daughters. Moreover, parents' perceptions of and expectations for their children were related to the children's self- and task-perceptions. Similar results have been reported for younger children (Alexander and Entwistle, 1988; Entwisle and Baker, 1983). These findings point to the potential importance of parents' roles as expectancy socializers. Research further suggests that children's self-concepts of mathematical ability may, in turn, influence their actual performance (Stevenson and Newman, 1986). Other studies suggest a similar, though less substantial, influence by teachers (Eccles, 1983; Parsons, Kaczala and Meece, 1982). In sum, a number of studies suggest an influence on children's attitudes toward mathematics and hence on their mathematical attainment by parents' and teachers' gender-stereotyped beliefs and expectations. Such influences appear to be at the root of sex differences in mathematics attainment. These findings are based on non-Hispanic samples, and one may hypothesize similar processes for Mexican Americans; however, this remains an empirical question. It is for future research to ascertain whether or not the processes that account for sex differences in non-Hispanic Whites also explain the sex differences among Mexican Americans.

A different generalizability question is whether or not the processes that account for sex differences also explain the ethnic group differences. Berryman's (1983) study suggests a negative answer. She studied the causes of representation of women and of certain ethnic groups — including Chicanos — among holders of BA, MA, and PhD degrees in the quantitatively based disciplines. Berryman's analyses suggest 'fundamentally different causes of women's and minorities' underrepresentation' among recipients of quantitative degrees. For women, the causes 'seem to be the familiar motivational factors that shift girls' interests away from the sex atypical careers and the high school mathematical sequence associated with quantitative postsecondary training'. For Chicanos, on the other hand, 'the major factors seem to be family socioeconomic status, especially parental education, with its: (1) ... effects on educational aspirations and high school mathematical and science achievements, and (2) ... effects on career information and career preferences' (1983, pp. 105–6). Berryman's findings seem consistent with MacCorquodale's (1988) hypotheses regarding parental influences on Mexican American children's mathematics achievement and general educational attainment. Also germane to the issue of generalizability are the findings of a number of studies suggesting that teachers respond more to a student's racial and ethnic characteristics and socioeconomic status than to gender and that teachers alter their expectations of student achievement accordingly (for a review of research see Dusek and Joseph, 1983).

In an attempt to uncover the determinants of school success among Chicanas, Gándara (1982) interviewed seventeen Chicanas and twenty-eight Chicanos who had attained the PhD, MD, or JD degree. Gándara reasoned that much of the research on Chicanos has focused on low academic achievement, thus yielding numerous hypotheses about educational failure but contributing few insights into the processes associated with success; therefore, knowledge of the kinds of family experience that contribute to success would be especially important.

The high-achieving Chicanas studied by Gándara reported that their mothers played an especially important role in fostering their motivation to achieve academically. Contrary to Gándara's predictions, the majority of the women in the study reported that their mothers had influenced their educational aspirations and attainment at least as much as had their fathers; this was true also of the men. Further, most of these high-achieving Chicanas and Chicanos described their parents as nonauthoritarian in discipline styles and as placing emphasis on independent behavior. Indeed, one of the surprising results was how similarly parents had treated the males and females in the sample. This finding, too, is contrary to the widely held stereotype of male authoritarianism and female submission in families of Mexican descent. Even though most of them had received strong support from their families, particularly their mothers, about 25 per cent of the women reported they did not know what educational aspirations their parents held for them; in contrast, the men generally felt that parental aspirations had been conveyed clearly to them. It is also worth noting that whereas Chicanos tended to credit their own inner strength and abilities for their educational successes, Chicanas most often attributed their accomplishments to the support of their families. Finally, it is also significant that at the age when most Chicanas have married and begun to take on new familial roles, all the high-achieving Chicanas studied by Gándara remained unmarried and childless; there were no marriage or parenthood responsibilities that might have impeded their educational attainment.

Consistent with Gándara's findings, a survey by Chacón, Cohen, and Strover (1986) revealed a high degree of parental support for attending college among both male and female Mexican American college students. These researchers administered mail questionnaires to 508 women and 160 men of Mexican descent enrolled in five California colleges. Over 60 per cent of each sex sample rated their parents as very supportive of their attending college, and only a small fraction reported any kind of parental opposition. Also consistent with Gándara's data, both the men and the women in the Chacón *et al.* study reported at least as much support for college attendance from their mothers as from their fathers. Although the degree of parental support was thus good for both sexes, slightly more college men than women rated their parents as very supportive.

Of the various components of socioeconomic status, the level of formal education attained by parents was identified earlier in this chapter as a significant factor associated with their children's intellectual development. The parents' educational aspirations and expectations for their children, too, have been found to be associated with the parents' own educational level (Laosa, 1982b). These three variables may be especially influential in regard to children's development in quantitative-related areas (e.g., Berryman, 1983; Marjoribanks, 1979). For example, Berryman (1983) points to parental education level as a major influence on Chicano students' curricular choices. Berryman's analyses showed that Chicanos were indeed generally underrepresented in college mathematics, science, and engineering courses, but those Chicanos with a college-educated parent were almost as well represented in these courses as non-Hispanic Whites — in contrast to the pattern for Chicanos who were the first in their families to attend college.

In sum, research on the socialization processes influencing Chicanos' achievement in mathematics or their participation in this subject is scant. It does seem clear, however, that the level of formal education attained by parents constitutes an important influence on their attitudes toward and expectations for their children's participation and performance in mathematics. At the same time, the literature on sex differences in other ethnic populations indicates that women's relatively low participation and achievement in mathematics is related to the expectations and perceptions that their parents held about the women's early mathematical ability, with parents of girls generally expressing lower expectations and making lower ability estimates than those of boys. Beyond the importance of this knowledge in its own right, it has been suggested that an awareness of the research on the processes that affect the participation and achievement of women in mathematics and quantitative-related fields might contribute to our understanding of the kinds of influences involved in opening or closing avenues of opportunity for Chicano students. Although they do have an intuitive appeal, we strongly caution against making such generalizations, given the research evidence (e.g., Berryman, 1983) suggesting that the variables and mechanisms accounting for sex differences are fundamentally different from those determining ethnic group inequalities.

Concluding Comments

The focus of this chapter is primarily on the innermost level in Bronfenbrenner's (1979, 1988) four-level conception of the human environmental ecology, namely, the microsystem — and, more specifically, the child's socialization in the family. We reviewed and discussed selected research studies attempting to illuminate various factors within the family setting that may influence Chicano children's academic development. In addition to the family, the microsystem contains settings that, too, can be important socializers and determinants of academic development — including the school itself, the peer group, and the media. Similarly, the other levels of the environmental ecology — the mesosystem, the exosystem, and the macrosystem — exert their own important, although indirect, influences on the child. These other socialization settings and ecological levels must be examined along with the family in any attempt at a comprehensive analysis of Chicano children's academic development — if such a task were possible. The point is that the family is important, but the other settings and levels of the human ecology should not be ignored.

Indeed, the results of the research reviewed and discussed in this chapter implicate all four levels of Bronfenbrenner's ecological system. As an illustration, consider Laosa's research on maternal teaching strategies. It will be recalled that Laosa (1978, 1980a, 1982b) conducted direct observations of Chicana mothers in their homes while they taught their own children. Among Laosa's findings was a substantial relationship between the kinds of teaching strategy employed by the mothers and the number of years of formal schooling that they themselves had attained. Although correlational, these data suggest that a mother's choice of strategies for teaching her children in the home is determined by the mother's own schooling level. Laosa's data revealed that the higher a mother's schooling level, the more her teaching strategies resemble those that one generally expects to find in school classrooms, thereby likely facilitating her child's adaptation to school. This finding thus implicates all four levels of Bronfenbrenner's ecological framework in the academic development of Chicanos, as follows. The mother's years of schooling correspond to an *exosystem* variable; that is to say, the events that in the past the mother had herself experienced as a student in school are now indirectly affecting her child's immediate environment, or *microsystem*. Further, the findings bearing on home-school similarities in teaching strategies suggest a *mesosystem* relation between home and school.

Finally, any policy implications that one might draw from these findings point to *macrosystem* considerations. On the level of Bronfenbrenner's macrosystem belong a society's policies. Many aspects of the present-day social and educational inequalities affecting Chicanos can be understood only in light of the caste-like structures that have evolved out of the earliest contacts and inter-relationships between this population and other US ethnic groups (Carter and Segura, 1979; Laosa, 1984b). As Bronfenbrenner (1979, 1988) reminds us, the macrosystem can be altered through policy change, with the result that there will be change bearing on the society's exosystem, mesosystem, and microsystem structures.

The study of Chicano children's socialization is still in its infancy — so much so that no attempt is made here to list the myriad research questions that need to be addressed in future research. Many of these questions are raised, however, throughout the chapter — implicitly or explicitly. As shown here, the research literature has moved some distance — both empirically and theoretically — toward specifying the variables and mechanisms in the socialization process that seem to mediate, at least partly, Chicano children's intellectual development and academic attainment; but much remains to be done. We require more studies that illuminate how the socialization process interacts with other levels of the environmental ecology to create and maintain patterns of ethnic group differences in academic learning, scholastic motivation, and movement through the schooling process. It is hoped that this chapter will point researchers in interesting directions toward work that further specifies these mechanisms and that traces their precise effects on Chicano children's academic development.

A large proportion of the academic achievement effects of ethnic group membership appears to be transmitted by mechanisms that in principle are susceptible to control by educators and policy makers. By broadening and deepening our understanding of the nature and action of these mechanisms, research programs such as those reviewed in this chapter can increase our capacity 'to make wise, effective policy in pursuit of an equitable distribution of life chances' (Bidwell and Friedkin, 1988, p. 468).

Notes

1 In this chapter, we interchangeably use the terms *Chicano* and *Mexican American* to refer to persons of Mexican origin or descent in the United States. In the Spanish language, *Chicana* corresponds to a female referent, and *Chicano*, the male; *Chicano* is also the appropriate term for the gender aggregate. In describing and discussing particular studies, we generally use the terms chosen by their authors in reference to their respective samples.

2 The difference in factorial structure between Laosa's (1984a) and the Valencia *et al.* (1981) data is likely the result of the difference in the sampling designs of the two studies.

3 Only a very small proportion of families are headed by a man with no wife present: as counted in the 1980 US census, only 3.1 per cent of the Mexican-origin families with own children under 18 years of age were headed by a man with no wife present (Laosa, 1988a).

References

ALEXANDER, K.L. and ENTWISLE, D.R. (1988) 'Achievement in the first 2 years of school: Patterns and processes', *Monographs of the Society for Research in Child Development*, **53**, (2, Serial No. 218).

American Heritage Dictionary (1982), 2nd college ed., Boston, Houghton Mifflin.

ANDERSON, S. and MESSICK, S. (1974) 'Social competency in young children', *Developmental Psychology*, **10**, pp. 282–93.

BARGH, J.A. and SCHUL, Y. (1980) 'On the cognitive benefits of teaching', *Journal of Educational Psychology*, **72**, pp. 593–604.

BARTON, P.E. (1989) *What Americans Study*, Princeton, NJ, Policy Information Center, Educational Testing Service.

BEAN, F.D. and TIENDA, M. (1987) *The Hispanic Population of the United States*, New York, Russell Sage Foundation.

BELMONT, L. and MAROLLA, F.A. (1973) 'Birth order, family size, and intelligence', *Science*, **182**, pp. 1096–101.

BERBAUM, M.L. and MORELAND, R.L. (1985) 'Intellectual development within transracial adoptive families: Retesting the confluence model', *Child Development*, **56**, pp. 207–16.

BERRYMAN, S.E. (1983) *Who Will Do Science?* New York, Rockefeller Foundation.

BIDWELL, C.E. and FRIEDKIN, N.E. (1988) 'The sociology of education', in N.J. SMELSER (Ed.) *Handbook of Sociology*, Newbury Park, CA, Sage, pp. 449–71.

BLAKE, J. (1989) 'Number of siblings and educational attainment', *Science*, **245**, pp. 32–6.

BOARD OF INQUIRY (1985) *Barriers to Excellence: Our Children at Risk*, Boston, MA, National Coalition of Advocates for Students.

BRADLEY, R.H., *et al.* (1989) 'Home environment and cognitive development in the first 3 years of life: A collaborative study involving six sites and three ethnic groups in North America', *Developmental Psychology*, **25**, pp. 217–35.

BRADLEY, R.H., CALDWELL, B.M. and ELARDO, R. (1979) 'Home environment and cognitive development in the first 2 years: A cross-lagged panel analysis', *Developmental Psychology*, **15**, pp. 246–50.

BRADLEY, R.H., CALDWELL, B.M. and ROCK, S.L. (1988) 'Home environment and school performance: A ten-year follow-up and examination of three models of environmental action', *Child Development*, **59**, pp. 852–67.

BRADSHAW, B.S. and BEAN, F.D. (1972) 'Some aspects of the fertility of Mexican-Americans', in C.F. WESTOFF and R. PARKE, JR. (Eds) *Demographic and Social Aspects of*

Population Growth (Reports of the US Commission on Population Growth and the American Future, Vol. 1) Washington, DC, US Government Printing Office, pp. 139–64.

BRELAND, H.M. (1974) 'Birth order, family configuration, and verbal achievement', *Child Development*, **45**, pp. 1011–19.

BRONFENBRENNER, U. (1977) 'Toward and experimental ecology of human development', *American Psychologist*, **32**, pp. 513–31.

BRONFENBRENNER, U. (1979) *The Ecology of Human Development: Experiments by Nature and Design*, Cambridge, MA, Harvard University Press.

BRONFENBRENNER, U. (1988) 'Ecological Systems Theory', unpublished manuscript.

BROPHY, J.E. and GOOD, T.L. (1974) *Teacher-Student Relationships: Causes and Consequences*, New York, Holt, Rinehart and Winston.

CALDWELL, B.M. and BRADLEY, R.H. (1984) 'Home Observation for Measurement of the Environment', unpublished manuscript, Little Rock, University of Arkansas.

CAMARA, K.A. and RESNICK, G. (1988) 'Interparental conflict and cooperation: Factors moderating children's post-divorce adjustment', in E.M. HETHERINGTON and J.D. ARASTEH (Eds) *Impact of Divorce, Single Parenting, and Stepparenting on Children*, Hillsdale, NJ, Erlbaum, pp. 169–95.

CARTER, T.P. and SEGURA, R.D. (1979) *Mexican Americans in School: A Decade of Change*, New York, College Entrance Examination Board.

CHACÓN, M.A., COHEN, E.G. and STROVER, S. (1986) 'Chicanas and Chicanos: Barriers to progress in higher education', in M.A. OLIVAS (Ed.) *Latino College Students*, New York, Teachers College Press, pp. 296–324.

CICIRELLI, V.G. (1978) 'The relationship of sibling structure to intellectual abilities and achievement', *Review of Educational Research*, **48**, pp. 365–79.

CLAUSEN, J.A. (Ed.) (1968) *Socialization and Society*, Boston, MA, Little, Brown.

COHEN, P.A., KULIK, J.A. and KULIK, C.C. (1982) 'Educational outcomes of tutoring: A meta-analysis of findings', *American Educational Research Journal*, **19**, 237–48.

DAVÉ, R.H. (1963) 'The Identification and Measurement of Environmental Process Variables That are Related to Educational Achievement', unpublished doctoral dissertation, University of Chicago.

DEUTSCH, C.P. (1973) 'Social class and child development', in B.M. CALDWELL and H.N. RICCIUTI (Eds) *Review of Child Development Research* (Vol. 3) Chicago, IL, University of Chicago Press, pp. 233–82.

DOSSEY, J.A., MULLIS, I.V.S., LINDQUIST, M.M. and CHAMBERS, D.L. (1988) *The Mathematics Report Card: Are We Measuring Up?* Princeton, NJ, National Assessment of Educational Progress, Educational Testing Service.

DURÁN, R.P. (1983) *Hispanics' Education and Background: Predictors of College Achievement*, New York, College Entrance Examination Board.

DUSEK, J.B. and JOSEPH, G. (1983) 'The bases of teacher expectancies: A meta-analysis', *Journal of Educational Psychology*, **75**, pp. 327–46.

ECCLES, J.S. (1983) 'Expectancies, values, and academic behaviors', in J.T. SPENCE (Ed.) *Achievement and Achievement Motives: Psychological and Sociological Approaches*, San Francisco, CA, Freeman. pp. 75–146.

ECCLES, J.S. and HOFFMAN, L.W. (1984) 'Sex roles, socialization, and occupational behavior', in H.W. STEVENSON and A.E. SIEGEL (Eds) *Child Development Research and Social Policy* (Vol. 1) Chicago, IL, University of Chicago Press, pp. 367–420.

EDUCATIONAL TESTING SERVICE (1989) *College-bound Seniors: 1989 Profile of SAT and Achievement Test Takers. National Report*, New York, College Entrance Examination Board.

ELARDO, R., BRADLEY, R. and CALDWELL, B.M. (1977) 'A longitudinal study of the relation of infants' home environments to language development at age three', *Child Development*, **48**, pp. 595–603.

ENTWISLE, D.R. and BAKER, D.P. (1983) 'Gender and young children's expectations for performance', *Developmental Psychology*, **19**, pp. 200–9.

FEINGOLD, A. (1988) 'Cognitive gender differences are disappearing', *American Psychologist*, **43**, pp. 95–103.

FOOTE, N.N. and COTTRELL, L.S., JR. (1955) *Identity and Interpersonal Competence: A New Direction in Family Research*, Chicago, University of Chicago Press.

FUCHS, V.R. (1986) 'Sex differences in economic well-being', *Science*, **232**, pp. 459–64.

GÁNDARA, P. (1982) 'Passing through the eye of the needle: High-achieving Chicanas', *Hispanic Journal of Behavioral Sciences*, **4**, pp. 167–79.

GOODSON, B.D. and HESS, R.D. (1975) *Parents as Teachers of Young Children: An Evaluative Review of Some Contemporary Concepts and Programs*, Stanford, CA, Stanford University.

HARRIS, D.B. and ROBERTS, J. (1972) *Intellectual Maturity of Children: Demographic and Socioeconomic Factors* (Vital and Health Statistics, Series 11, No. 116) Washington, DC, US Government Printing Office.

HASKINS, R. and ADAMS, D. (Eds) (1983) *Parent Education and Public Policy*, Norwood, NJ, Ablex.

HENDERSON, R.W. (1966) 'Environmental Stimulation and Intellectual Development of Mexican-American Children', unpublished doctoral dissertation, University of Arizona, Tucson.

HENDERSON, R.W. (1972) 'Environmental predictors of academic performance of disadvantaged Mexican-American children', *Journal of Consulting and Clinical Psychology*, **38**, pp. 297.

HENDERSON, R.W. (1980) 'Social and emotional needs of culturally diverse children', *Exceptional Children*, **46**, pp. 598–605.

HENDERSON, R.W. (1981) 'Home environment and intellectual performance', in R.W. HENDERSON (Ed.) *Parent-child Interaction: Theory, Research, and Prospects*, New York, Academic Press, pp. 3–32.

HENDERSON, R.W., BERGAN, J.R. and HURT, M., JR. (1972) 'Development and validation of the Henderson Environmental Learning Process Scale', *Journal of Social Psychology*, **88**, pp. 185–96.

HENDERSON, R.W. and GARCIA, A.B. (1973) 'The effects of a parent training program on the question-asking behavior of Mexican-American children', *American Educational Research Journal*, **10**, pp. 193–201.

HENDERSON, R.W. and MERRITT, C.B. (1968) 'Environmental background of Mexican-American children with different potentials for school success', *Journal of Social Psychology*, **75**, pp. 101–6.

HENDERSON, R.W. and SWANSON, R. (1974) 'Application of social learning principles in field settings', *Exceptional Children*, **40**, pp. 53–55.

HESS, R.D. (1970) 'Social class and ethnic influences on socialization', in P.H. MUSSEN (Ed.) *Carmichael's Manual of Child Psychology* (Vol. 2) New York, Wiley, pp. 457–557.

HETHERINGTON, E.M., CAMARA, K.A. and FEATHERMAN, D.L. (1983) 'Achievement and intellectual functioning of children in one-parent households', in J.T. SPENCE (Ed.) *Achievement and Achievement Motives: Psychological and Sociological Approaches*, San Francisco, CA, Freeman, pp. 205–84.

INKELES, A. (1968a) 'Social structure and the socialization of competence', in *Socialization and Schools* (Reprint Series No. 1 of the *Harvard Educational Review*) Cambridge, MA, Harvard Educational Review, pp. 50–68.

INKELES, A. (1968b) 'Society, social structure, and child socialization', in J.A. CLAUSEN (Ed.) *Socialization and Society*, Boston, MA, Little, Brown, pp. 73–129.

JACKLIN, C.N. (1989) 'Female and male: Issues of gender', *American Psychologist*, **44**, pp. 127–33.

KELLAGHAN, T. and MACNAMARA, J. (1972) 'Family correlates of verbal reasoning ability', *Developmental Psychology*, **7**, pp. 49–53.

KITONYI, P.N. (1980) 'An Investigation of Predictive Value of the Henderson Environmental Learning Process Scale for Achievement of Black-American Children', unpublished doctoral dissertation, State University of New York at Albany.

LABORATORY OF COMPARATIVE HUMAN COGNITION (1983) 'Culture and cognitive development', in W. KESSEN (Ed.) *Handbook of Child Psychology: Vol. 1. History, Theory, and Methods*, New York, Wiley, pp. 295–356.

LAOSA, L.M. (1977a) 'Inequality in the classroom: Observational research on teacher-student interactions', *Aztlán International Journal of Chicano Studies Research*, **8**, pp. 51–67.

LAOSA, L.M. (1977b) 'Nonbiased assessment of children's abilities: Historical antecedents and current issues', in T. OAKLAND (Ed.) *Psychological and Educational Assessment of Minority Children*, New York, Brunner/Mazel, pp. 1–20.

LAOSA, L.M. (1977c) 'Socialization, education, and continuity: The importance of the sociocultural context', *Young Children*, **32**, pp. 21–7.

LAOSA, L.M. (1978) 'Maternal teaching strategies in Chicano families of varied educational and socioeconomic levels', *Child Development*, **49**, pp. 1129–35.

LAOSA, L.M. (1979/1989) 'Social competence in childhood: Toward a developmental, socioculturally relativistic paradigm', in M.W. KENT and J.E. ROLF (Eds) *Primary Prevention of Psychopathology: Vol. 3. Social Competence in Children*, Hanover, NH, University Press of New England, pp. 253–79. Reprinted on the occasion of the article's tenth anniversary in *Journal of Applied Developmental Psychology* (1989) **10**, pp. 447–68.

LAOSA, L.M. (1980a) 'Maternal teaching strategies in Chicano and Anglo-American families: The influence of culture and education on maternal behavior', *Child Development*, **51**, pp. 759–65.

LAOSA, L.M. (1980b) 'Measures for the study of maternal teaching strategies', *Applied Psychological Measurement*, **4**, pp. 355–66.

LAOSA, L.M. (1981a) 'Maternal behavior: Sociocultural diversity in modes of family interaction', in R.W. HENDERSON (Ed.) *Parent-child Interaction: Theory, Research, and Prospects*, New York, Academic Press, pp. 125–67.

LAOSA, L.M. (1981b) 'Statistical Explorations of the Structural Organization of Maternal Teaching Behaviors in Chicano and Non-Hispanic White Families', invited paper presented at the Conference on the Influences of Home Environments on School Achievement, Wisconsin Research and Development Center for Individualized Schooling, School of Education, University of Wisconsin, Madison, October.

LAOSA, L.M. (1982a) Families as facilitators of children's intellectual development at 3 years of age: A causal analysis', in L.M. LAOSA and I.E. SIGEL (Eds) *Families as Learning Environments for Children*, New York, Plenum, pp. 1–45.

LAOSA, L.M. (1982b) School, occupation, culture, and family: The impact of parental schooling on the parent-child relationship', *Journal of Educational Psychology*, **74**, pp. 791–827.

LAOSA, L.M. (1982c) 'The sociocultural context of evaluation', in B. SPODEK (Ed.) *Handbook of Research in Early Childhood Education*, New York, The Free Press, pp. 501–20.

LAOSA, L.M. (1983) 'Parent education, cultural pluralism, and public policy: The uncertain connection', in R. HASKINS and D. ADAMS (Eds) *Parent Education and Public Policy*, Norwood, NJ, Ablex, pp. 331–45.

LAOSA, L.M. (1984a) 'Ethnic, socioeconomic, and home language influences upon early performance on measures of abilities', *Journal of Educational Psychology*, **76**, pp. 1178–98.

LAOSA, L.M. (1984b) 'Social policies toward children of diverse ethnic, racial, and language groups in the United States', in H.W. STEVENSON and A.E. SIEGEL (Eds) *Child Development Research and Social Policy* (Vol. 1) Chicago, University of Chicago Press, pp. 1–109.

LAOSA, L.M. (1985) 'Ethnic, Racial, and Language Group Differences in the Experiences of Adolescents in the United States', invited paper presented at the Workshop on Adoles-

cence and Adolescent Development, convened by the Committee on Child Development Research and Public Policy of the National Academy of Sciences, Woods Hole,
MA, July.

LAOSA L.M. (1988a) 'Ethnicity and single parenting in the United States', in E.M.
HETHERINGTON and J.D. ARASTEH (Eds) *Impact of Divorce, Single Parenting, and Stepparenting on Children*, Hillsdale, NJ, Erlbaum, pp. 23–49.

LAOSA, L.M. (1988b) *Population Generalizability and Ethical Dilemmas in Research, Policy, and
Practice: Preliminary Considerations* (ETS Research Report No. 88-18), Princeton, NJ,
Educational Testing Service.

LAOSA, L.M. (1990) 'Population generalizability, cultural sensitivity, and ethical dilemmas',
in C.B. FISHER and W.W. TRYON (Eds) *Ethics in Applied Developmental Psychology*,
Norwood, NJ, Ablex, pp. 227–51.

LAOSA, L.M. and BROPHY, J.E. (1970) 'Sex x birth order interaction in measures of
sex typing and affiliation in kindergarten children', *Proceedings of the 78th Annual
Convention of the American Psychological Association*, **5**, Washington, DC, American
Psychological Association, pp. 363–4.

LAOSA, L.M. and BROPHY, J.E. (1972) 'Effects of sex and birth order on sex-role development and intelligence among kindergarten children', *Developmental Psychology*, **6**,
pp. 409–15.

LECORGNE, L.L. and LAOSA, L.M. (1976) 'Father absence in low-income Mexican-
American families: Children's social adjustment and conceptual differentiation of sex
role attributes', *Developmental Psychology*, **12**, pp. 470–1.

LEVINE, R.A. (1980) 'Influence of women's schooling on maternal behavior in the third
world', *Comparative Education Review*, **24** (2, Part 2), pp. S78–S105.

LURIA, A.R. (1928) 'The problem of the cultural behavior of the child', *Journal of Genetic
Psychology*, **35**, pp. 493–506.

LURIA, A.R. (1976) *Cognitive Development: Its Cultural and Social Foundations*, Cambridge,
MA, Harvard University Press.

MACCOBY, E.E., DEPNER, C.E. and MNOOKIN, R.H. (1988) 'Custody of children following
divorce', in E.M. HETHERINGTON and J.D. ARASTEH (Eds) *Impact of Divorce, Single
Parenting, and Stepparenting on Children*, Hillsdale, NJ, Erlbaum, pp. 91–114.

MACCOBY, E.E. and MARTIN, J.A. (1983) 'Socialization in the context of the family:
Parent-child interaction', in E.M. HETHERINGTON (Ed.) *Handbook of Child Psychology:
Vol. 4: Socialization, Personality, and Social Development*, New York, Wiley, pp. 1–101.

MACCORQUODALE, P. (1988) 'Mexican-American women and mathematics: Participation,
aspirations, and achievement', in R.R. COCKING and J.P. MESTRE (Eds) *Linguistic and
Cultural Influences on Learning Mathematics*, Hillsdale, NJ, Erlbaum, pp. 137–60.

MARJORIBANKS, K. (1979) *Families and Their Learning Environments: An Empirical Analysis*,
London, UK, Routledge and Kegan Paul.

MARJORIBANKS, K. (1984) 'Occupational status, family environments, and adolescents'
aspirations: The Laosa model', *Journal of Educational Psychology*, **76**, pp. 690–700.

MELICAN, G.J. and FELDT, L.S. (1980) 'An empirical study of the Zajonc-Markus hypothesis for achievement test score declines', *American Educational Research Journal*, **17**,
pp. 5–19.

NATIONAL COMMISSION ON EXCELLENCE IN EDUCATION (1983) *A Nation at Risk: The
Imperative for Educational Reform*, Washington, DC, US Government Printing Office.

NIELSEN, F. and FERNANDEZ, R.M. (1981) *Hispanic Students in American High Schools:
Background Characteristics and Achievement*, Washington, DC, US Government Printing
Office.

NORMAN-JACKSON, J. (1982) 'Family interactions, language development, and primary
reading achievement of Black children in families of low income', *Child Development*,
53, pp. 349–58.

ORUM, L.S. (1986) *The Education of Hispanics: Status and Implications*, Washington, DC,
National Council of La Raza.

PAGE, E.B. and GRANDON, G.M. (1979) 'Family configuration and mental ability: Two theories contrasted with US data', *American Educational Research Journal*, **16**, pp. 257–72.

PARSONS, J.E., ADLER, T.F. and KACZALA, C.M. (1982) 'Socialization of achievement attitudes and beliefs: Parental influences', *Child Development*, **53**, pp. 310–21.

PARSONS, J.E., KACZALA, C.M. and MEECE, J.L. (1982) 'Socialization of achievement attitudes and beliefs: Classroom influences', *Child Development*, **53**, pp. 322–39.

PETERSON, G.W. and ROLLINS, B.C. (1987) 'Parent-child socialization', in M.B. SUSSMAN and S.K. STEINMETZ (Eds) *Handbook of Marriage and the Family*, New York, Plenum, pp. 471–507.

PHILLIPS, D.A. (1987) 'Socialization of perceived academic competence among highly competent children', *Child Development*, **58**, pp. 1308–20.

PRIOR, D.R. (1974) 'Inner City Elementary Pupil Mobility, Reading Achievement, and Environmental Process Variables', unpublished doctoral dissertation, Fordham University, New York.

RAMIST, L. and ARBEITER, S. (1986) *Profiles, College-Bound Seniors, 1985*, New York, College Entrance Examination Board.

RANKIN, R.J., GAITE, A.J.H. and HEIRY, T. (1979) 'Cultural modification of effect of family size on intelligence', *Psychological Reports*, **45**, pp. 391–7.

REGIONAL POLICY COMMITTEE ON MINORITIES IN HIGHER EDUCATION (1987) *From Minority to Majority: Education and the Future of the Southwest*, Boulder, CO, Western Interstate Commission for Higher Education.

RUTTER, M. (1979) 'Protective factors in children's responses to stress and disadvantage', in M.W. KENT and J.E. ROLF (Eds) *Primary Prevention of Psychopathology: Vol. 3. Social Competence in Children*, Hanover, NH, University Press of New England, pp. 49–74.

SAMEROFF, A.J. (1983) 'Developmental systems: Contexts and evolution', in W. KESSEN (Ed.) *Handbook of Child Psychology: Vol. 1. History, Theory, and Methods*, New York, Wiley, pp. 237–94.

SANTROCK, J.W. and WARSHAK, R.A. (1979) 'Father custody and social development in boys and girls', *Journal of Social Issues*, **35**, pp. 112–25.

SANTROCK, J.W., WARSHAK, R.A. and ELLIOTT, G.L. (1982) 'Social development and parent-child interaction in father-custody and stepmother families', in M.E. LAMB (Ed.) *Nontraditional Families: Parenting and Child Development*, Hillsdale, NJ, Erlbaum, pp. 289–314.

SAWYER, R.L. (1987) *College Student Profiles: Norms for the ACT Assessment* (1987–88 ed.), Iowa City, IA, American College Testing Program.

SCOTT-JONES, D. (1984) 'Family influences on cognitive development and school achievement', in E.W. GORDON (Ed.) *Review of Research in Education* (Vol. 11) Washington, DC, American Educational Research Association, pp. 259–304.

SIGEL, I.E. (Ed.) (1985) *Parental Belief Systems: The Psychological Consequences for Children*, Hillsdale, NJ, Erlbaum.

SIGEL, I.E., DREYER, A.S. and McGILLICUDDY-DeLISI, A.V. (1984) 'Psychological perspectives of the family', in R.D. PARKE, R.N. EMDE, H.P. McADOO and G.P. SACKETT (Eds) *Review of Child Development Research: Vol. 7. The Family*, Chicago, IL, University of Chicago Press, pp. 42–79.

SMITH, M.B. (1968) 'Competence and socialization', in J.A. CLAUSEN (Ed.) *Socialization and Society*, Boston, MA, Little, Brown, pp. 270–320.

STEELMAN, L.C. (1985) 'A tale of two variables: A review of the intellectual consequences of sibship size and birth order', *Review of Educational Research*, **55**, pp. 353–86.

STEINBERG, L., BLINDE, P.L. and CHAN, K.S. (1984) 'Dropping out among language minority youth', *Review of Educational Research*, **54**, pp. 113–32.

STEVENSON, H.W. and Newman, R.S. (1986) 'Long-term prediction of achievement and attitudes in mathematics reading', *Child Development*, **57**, pp. 646–59.

STEWART, R.B. JR., (1983) 'Sibling interaction: The role of the older child as teacher for the younger', *Merrill-Palmer Quarterly*, **29**, pp. 47–68.

SWANSON, R. and HENDERSON, R.W. (1976) 'Achieving home-school continuity in the socialization of an academic motive', *Journal of Experimental Education*, **44**, pp. 38–44.

US BUREAU OF THE CENSUS (1988) *The Hispanic Population in the United States: March 1988 (Advance Report)* (Current Population Reports, Series P-20, No. 431) Washington, DC, US Government Printing Office.

VALENCIA, R.R., HENDERSON, R.W. and RANKIN, R.J. (1981) 'Relationship of family constellation and schooling to intellectual performance of Mexican American children', *Journal of Educational Psychology*, **73**, pp. 524–32.

VALENCIA, R.R., HENDERSON, R.W. and RANKIN, R.J. (1985) 'Family status, family constellation, and home environmental variables as predictors of cognitive performance of Mexican American children', *Journal of Educational Psychology*, **77**, pp. 323–31.

VELANDIA, W., GRANDON, G.M. and PAGE, E.B. (1978) 'Family size, birth order, and intelligence in a large South American sample', *American Educational Research Journal*, **15**, pp. 399–416.

VYGOTSKY, L.S. (1929) 'The problem of the cultural development of the child', *Journal of Genetic Psychology*, **36**, pp. 415–34.

VYGOTSKY, L.S. (1978) *Mind in Society: The Development of Higher Psychological Processes*, Cambridge, MA, Harvard University Press.

WERTSCH, J.V. (1985) *Vygotsky and the Social Formation of Mind*, Cambridge, MA, Harvard University Press.

WESTOFF, C.F. (1986) 'Fertility in the United States', *Science*, **234**, pp. 554–9.

WHITE, R.W. (1959) 'Motivation reconsidered: The concept of competence', *Psychological Review*, **66**, pp. 297–333.

WHITE, R.W. (1979) 'Competence as an aspect of personal growth', in M.W. KENT and J.E. ROLF (Eds) *Primary Prevention of Psychopathology: Vol. 3. Social Competence in Children*, Hanover, NH, University Press of New England, pp. 5–22.

WILDER, G.Z. and POWELL, K. (1989) *Sex Differences in Test Performance: A Survey of the Literature* (College Board Report No. 89-3, ETS Research Report No. 89-4) New York, College Entrance Examination Board.

WOLF, R.M. (1964) 'The Identification and Measurement of Environmental Process Variables Related to Intelligence', unpublished doctoral dissertation, University of Chicago.

YOUTH AND AMERICA'S FUTURE: THE WILLIAM T. GRANT FOUNDATION COMMISSION ON WORK, FAMILY, AND CITIZENSHIP (1988) *The Forgotten Half: Non-College Youth in America. An Interim Report on the School-to-work Transition*, Washington, DC, Author.

ZAJONC, R.B. (1976) 'Family configuration and intelligence', *Science*, **192**, pp. 227–36.

ZAJONC, R.B. (1983) 'Validating the confluence model', *Psychological Bulletin*, **93**, pp. 457–80.

ZAJONC, R.B. (1986) 'The decline and rise of scholastic aptitude scores: A prediction derived from the confluence model', *American Psychologist*, **41**, pp. 862–7.

ZAJONC, R.B. and MARKUS, G.B. (1975) 'Birth order and intellectual development', *Psychological Review*, **82**, pp. 74–88.

ZASLOW, M.J. (1987) 'Sex Differences in Children's Response to Parental Divorce', paper commissioned by the Committee on Child Development Research and Public Policy of the National Academy of Sciences, Washington, DC, National Research Council.

ZASLOW, M.J. and HAYES, C.D. (1986) 'Sex differences in children's response to psychosocial stress: Toward a cross-context analysis', in M.E. LAMB, A.L. BROWN and B. ROGOFF (Eds) *Advances in Developmental Psychology*, (Vol. 4) Hillsdale, NJ, Erlbaum, pp. 285–337.

ZIGLER, E. and WEISS, H. (1985) 'Family support systems: An ecological approach to child development', in R.N. RAPOPORT (Ed.) *Children, Youth, and Families: The Action-research Relationship*, Cambridge, UK, Cambridge University Press, pp. 166–205.

Part IV

Educational Testing and Special Education Issues Vis-à-Vis Chicano Students

Part IV contains two chapters. Chapter 8, 'The Uses and Abuses of Educational Testing: Chicanos as a Case in Point' is written by Richard Valencia and Sofia Aburto. After describing the functions of testing, the authors cover issues of test abuse in the two broad areas of intelligence and competency testing (i.e., minimum competency and teacher competency). The focus is on concerns about the psychometric integrity of tests as well as the problem of using tests as the primary or sole data source in educational decision-making. Valencia and Aburto offer numerous suggestions about improving testing that could help promote Chicano school success. Robert Rueda wrote chapter 9, 'An Analysis of Special Education as a Response to the Diminished Academic Achievement of Chicano Students'. Rueda begins his coverage by raising a number of questions dealing with the relationship between special education and Chicano students (e.g., questions about historical relationships, the referral process, emerging issues, and so on). In his critical analysis of how special education has served Chicanos, Rueda structures the discussion so as to examine ways in which a tighter, more responsive connection can be developed between theory, research, policy, and practice in the area.

Chapter 8

The Uses and Abuses of Educational Testing: Chicanos as a Case in Point

Richard R. Valencia and Sofia Aburto

One of the most persistent problems in educational research in the United States has been how to explain the continuing low performance on standardized tests by certain racial/ethnic minority-group students, such as Chicanos. Second, the potential uses and abuses of educational tests with Chicanos and other minorities have generated tremendous controversy over the years. These two major testing issues — correlates and consequences of testing performance *vis-à-vis* Chicano students — conform one of the most profound and controversial debates in the annals of education, a debate that has spilled beyond the confines of the academic community. The media, public, courts, and legislative bodies have all entered the fray in one form or another. In short, these testing issues are historically rooted, controversial and — by their pervasiveness — important within and outside the institution of education.

Although the correlates associated with standardized test performance of Chicano students are important to examine in reaching some understanding of Chicano school failure and success, they will only be lightly touched upon in this chapter (see Laosa and Henderson, this volume, for a discussion of socialization and competence aspects of cognitive performance). Our goal here is to identify and discuss a number of abusive practices stemming from standardized testing that we believe help shape school failure among Chicano students.[1] We will not, however, dwell entirely on the negative. Given the spirit and charge of the present book, our focus will also be on the identification of proactive ideas about educational testing, particularly in the form of research and policy strategies that are likely to enhance school success among Chicano students.

The discussion begins with a brief overview of the functions of testing. This follows with the chapter's core — an analysis of test abuse with respect to Chicano students. To do this, we employ a 'test typology' format. That is, our focus on abusive practices is placed in the context of the two following types of tests: 'intelligence' and 'competency' based.[2] The section on intelligence testing covers a brief history, the early period of nondiscriminatory assessment, test bias research and Chicano students, the responsibility of test publishers and school psychologists in helping to promote nondiscriminatory assessment, and the need to link nondiscriminatory assessment with nondiscriminatory schooling. The section on competency testing examines the various types of competency tests (e.g., minimum competency tests; teacher competency examinations), and discusses their impact on Chicanos. Following this is a discussion of the notion of 'educability'. The chapter closes with a presentation of eight research and policy ideas about improving educational testing in order to help promote Chicano school success.

Functions of Testing

Before any analysis of test abuse is undertaken, a logical question to ask is, what functions do educational tests serve? There are a number of frameworks that have been advanced to address this concern (e.g., Cronbach, 1984; Resnick, 1979; Salvia and Ysseldyke, 1988; Thorndike and Hagen, 1977).[3] The analysis we find particularly useful for the issues discussed here is the framework advanced by Resnick, who presents a lucid discussion on current test use in the schools.[4] Resnick identifies three broad test functions: 1) the management of instruction, 2) public accountability, and 3) the legitimization of the schooling process.

Management of Instruction

This is the rubric for several purposes of testing — the sorting, monitoring, and grading functions. In the sorting function, tests are given before the instructional process begins. Here, educational tests serve as mechanisms to assist in the assignment of students to special education and, as Resnick (1979) notes, for 'tracking' in the educational mainstream. With respect to the monitoring function, tests are administered during the course of the instructional process and provide information that can be used to make curriculum adjustments so as to improve student achievement. The third purpose of testing within the management of instruction area is the grading function. Here, tests are given at the end of the instructional process and serve as sources of evaluating a student's academic performance.

In the case of the Chicano, as well as other minority students (e.g., Black), the sorting function has created the most controversy. For example, the issue of overrepresentation of racial/ethnic minority children in classes for the educable mentally retarded (EMR) was particularly explosive during the 1970s (Henderson and Valencia, 1985; see also Rueda, this volume). With respect to Chicano students, the EMR misclassification of many children from this ethnic population during the 1970s was likely the outgrowth of a long taproot. There is historical evidence from the 1920s that IQ tests were routinely used as sorting instruments to place large numbers of Chicano pupils in classes for the 'mentally defective' (Gonzalez, 1974a). More on the abuses of intelligence testing will be presented in the section, 'Intelligence Testing and Chicano Students: A Brief History'.

Public Accountability

The general notion of accountability in education is that public schools should be held accountable to the public (the logic being that the public financially supports the schools). Milliken (1970) describes this idea as a collective sense '... that people are increasingly demanding to know how their children are learning, what they are learning, and why they are being taught whatever they are being taught' (p. 17). Norm-referenced achievement and aptitude tests are typically used to meet the public's demands for accountability. In a later section, we will discuss the abuses of competency-based testing *vis-à-vis* Chicanos. (Competency testing, broadly conceptualized, refers to the testing of examinees for the acquisition of basic skills. Often such tests are used as gatekeepers for determining grade-to-grade promotion, graduation, entry to pre-professional training programs, and so on.)

Legitimization of the Schooling Process

This is the third broad function of educational testing that Resnick (1979) discusses in her framework. In that the legitimization function of testing is linked to our broader analysis of test abuse, an expanded discussion of this function is necessary at this time. We will take intelligence testing as a case in point.

Each of our nation's 16,000 public school districts maintains and supports a program of standardized testing. The testing movement in the United States, beginning in the second decade of the twentieth century, is deeply rooted in our desire for efficiency, our ideas of equality, and our need to have national standards (Resnick, 1981). The notions and values of 'rational management', 'scientific management', and 'efficiency reform' as applied to public education at the turn of the century stem from the larger influence of the business ideology and the application of modern business methods during the Progressive period from 1890 to 1920 (Callahan, 1962). These values of rationality and efficiency were initially reactions to corruption and inefficiency in government, but because of huge problems in public schools (e.g., high rates of dropouts, overcrowding), '... schools became a central target for the efficiency reformers in the decade before World War I' (Resnick, 1981, p. 625). The scientific management ethos and the use of intelligence testing in the schools took on massive proportions as seen in the creation of numerous bureaus of research and measurement from 1912 to 1922 in urban school systems (Resnick, 1981).

In a lucid account of how the intelligence testing movement transformed administrative policies in public schools, Tyack (1974) notes that one survey in 1926 reported thirty-seven out of forty cities with populations of 100,000 or more were using intelligence tests for ability grouping in some or all elementary and secondary schools. By 1932, three-fourths of 150 large cities made curricular assignments of pupils by using the results of intelligence tests. Historical case examinations of selected cities (e.g., Gonzalez's (1974a), study of the testing program of Los Angeles City School District and its effect on Chicano students from 1920 to 1930) illustrate the inner workings and powerful influences of early intelligence testing and research departments on the educational bureaucracies of urban school systems. As Resnick (1981) concludes on this topic:

> The present use of testing to support decisions about ability and curriculum grouping affirms traditions of practice that have been in existence for more than 60 years ... The American use of tests reflects our

culture's interest in qualified and 'objective judgments, part of the rational management ethos'. (p. 626)

In light of this marriage of scientific management and the intelligence testing movement, it becomes clearer why Resnick (1979) believes that intelligence testing has served a 'legitimization of the schooling process' function. The point is that in addition to having a practical function in schooling, intelligence tests also play symbolic roles through their aura of science and objectivity.[5] The implications here are important. If intelligence tests are indeed objective (in content and use of results), then our highly differentiated and tracked public school system is sanctioned. Bowles and Gintis (1976), writing from a neo-Marxist perspective, have taken the legitimization function of intelligence testing a bit further. In brief, these scholars offer the following argument: (a) evidence shows that test scores (IQ) are poor predictors of individual economic success; (b) the meritocratic mechanism — test scores — are assumed to be objective; (c) because economic success, however, cannot be accounted for by cognitive scores of students, then the technocractic-meritocratic ideology is largely symbolic and is used to legitimize economic inequality.

In summary, the notion that intelligence and other forms of educational testing perform a legitimization function is a powerful idea. Its utility as an analytical tool in understanding the abusive practices of education testing with respect to Chicanos will be discussed in the next section.

Abuses of Educational Testing

As Linn, Madaus and Pedulla (1982) underscore, 'When properly used, a test can be a valuable educational tool' (p. 1). The extent tests contribute to improving schooling for students depends on their psychometric integrity (i.e., reliability and validity) as well as their proper interpretation and use. As do Linn *et al.*, we also support test use along certain lines, but we are as strongly opposed to test misuse — and the resultant abusive consequences. Our primary criticisms of test misuse center on two concerns. First is the issue of administering tests that lack good, intrinsic quality — that is, the administration of unreliable tests and tests that have not been validated for specific uses (a subject we later discuss in some detail). Second, there is concern that tests are often used as the sole or major determinant in educational decision-making. A number of scholars and professional organizations have denounced this exclusive, or almost exclusive, reliance of a single test source in decision-making as an improper use of educational testing (e.g., International Reading Association, 1979; Linn *et al.*, 1982).

In this section, we will focus on test abuse with respect to Chicanos in the two broad areas of intelligence testing and competency testing. The latter will cover issues pertinent to minimum competency tests used as standards for high school graduation and teacher competency tests. Throughout the discussion, we will weave in the above concerns about the psychometric integrity of tests and the reliance on tests as the sole or primary data source in the making of educational decisions. Following this section there will be a discussion of the notion of 'educability', a concept we argue that is quite central in the analysis of educational testing and Chicano students.

Intelligence Testing

Intelligence Testing and Chicano Students: A Brief History
In the twentieth century, the construct of intelligence has been given more research attention by psychologists than any other dimension of individual differences (Peterson, 1982). Aside from the sheer volume of this research, more significant have been the long-lasting debates on the 'origins' of intelligence (especially racial/ethnic group differences) and the uses and abuses of intelligence testing results.

It is not the intent here to add further analysis, in any great detail, to the questions and research dealing with the correlates and possible influences on Chicano intellectual performance. Our discussion will be largely confined to an overview of the consequences of test abuse (for a much broader and sustained analysis of Chicano intellectual performance with respect to research, theory, and schooling implications, see Valencia, 1990). This is an attempt to shed some light on questions, such as, in general, what have been the psychological and social consequences of intelligence testing for Chicano students? Assuming that some of this impact has been negative, how has it contributed in part to Chicano school failure? To address these concerns, it is first necessary to look back in time, and then to place our eyes on the contemporary scene.

In that group-administered intelligence tests have been widely banned across the nation for nearly two decades, it is necessary to examine history to understand the foundations of oppressive test use. There is abundant evidence from scholarly work that the results of intelligence tests — particularly during the 1920s and 1930s — were used in racially discriminatory ways *vis-à-vis* Chicano and other racial/ethnic minority students (e.g., Blum, 1978; Gonzalez, 1974a, 1974b; Henderson and Valencia, 1985; Hendrick, 1977; Kamin, 1974; Valencia, 1990). During the heyday of testing in the 1920s and 1930s, practically all large cities in the United States had massive educational bureaucracies routinely administering group-based intelligence tests.

For example, Gonzalez (1974a, 1974b) found that the institutionalization of IQ testing, tracking, curriculum development, and counseling programs were used in ways that effectively stratified students along socioeconomic and racial/ethnic lines.[6] Given their typically and consistently low performance on intelligence tests,[7] Chicano students were often funnelled into slower tracks that frequently led to a low-grade 'vocational education' curriculum.[8] Furthermore, Gonzalez notes that Chicano children who scored below an IQ of 70 on standardized intelligence tests were referred to 'development centers' for the 'mentally retarded'.[9] In short, it appears that Chicano students in the Los Angeles public schools in the 1920s and 1930s routinely faced one of two equally unattractive educational paths — non-academic vocational education that emphasized low-level skills or dead-end special education. Offering a macrolevel analysis of the linkages between intelligence testing and consequences for Chicanos, Gonzalez (1974b) ties up matters this way:

> On the basis of IQ tests administered by guidance counselors, inordinate numbers of Mexican-American children were placed in coursework which prepared them for a variety of manual operations ... This movement was a reaction of the privileged classes to the rising numbers of the

working classes. Schools were redefined in the era of monopoly capitalism to be instruments through which social order could be preserved
and industrialization expanded. Thus American schools were not and
still are not agents of change, but rather bolster the social stratifications
and values of our society. In such an educational system, Mexican-
Americans were not provided with opportunities to improve their lot
but instead were subjected to a socialization process that reinforced the
status quo and was opposed to social change. (p. 301)

In sum, historical research provides some evidence about the abusive practices of intelligence testing with respect to Chicano students. It would be incor-
rect to argue that the invidious misclassifications and channeling of Chicanos into
unchallenging, low-status curricula depended *exclusively* on IQ tests. Yet, such
tests did have a role — along with other elements (e.g., preconceived notions
about Chicano children's educability; forced school segregation of Chicanos by
the White community) — in helping shape inferior schooling for Chicanos.
Whether intelligence testing in later years has negatively affected the 'quality of
life' for Chicanos to the great degree some have claimed (e.g., Aguirre, 1979a,
1979b), is certainly a claim open for debate (a point we will return to later when
we discuss 'educability').

Before moving on to a discussion of contemporary intelligence testing issues
with respect to Chicano students, we need to provide a brief description for the
period sandwiched between the heyday of IQ testing during the 1920s and 1930s
and the group IQ testing ban of the 1970s. The period from the 1940s to the early
1960s represents a time in which intelligence testing did not receive much attention in either scholarly or popular writings (Haney, 1981). Part of this inattention, we think, is likely related to the notion that group-based intelligence testing
after the 1930s became widely implemented in the nation's schools and took on a
life of its own — a life relatively free of controversy.[10]

To some degree, the entrenchment and solidification of group-administered
intelligence testing in the middle of the twentieth century had its curricular roots
in the nascent period of testing. Fass (1980) notes that the purpose and direction
of the intelligence testing movement during the early decades of the century were
driven by a rapidly changing complex society and educational system in serious
need of a socially '. . . powerful organizing principle' (p. 432). Urbanization,
industrialization, and massive immigration combined to force the schools to
address a critical issue of democratic schooling, which was, as Fass argues: '. . .
how to educate the mass without losing sight of the individual' (p. 446). Stated in
another manner, how could the United States educate a presumably intellectually
diverse student population while sorting, selecting, and rewarding individual
talent in a democratically and scientifically defensible manner? The answer, according to Fass, was the idea of IQ and intelligence testing, which coincidentally,
were becoming available at a time when an organizing mechanism for selection
was so much desired.

As time progressed, intelligence testing became widely used, serving as a
sorting mechanism in the educational mainstream as well as the tributary of
special education (see Rueda, this volume, for an analysis and critique of special
education with respect to Chicano students). In the absence of hard data, it is not
possible to claim unequivocally that group-based IQ tests during the 1940s, 50s,

and 1960s were used as unambiguous instruments to stratify students along lines of differentiated curricula. There is no denial that such testing played a role in ability grouping at the elementary level and in tracking at the secondary level. What is not known is how the day-to-day process of curriculum differentiation was influenced by IQ testing, particularly the *degree* to which teachers and counselors relied on test results to make placement and instructional decisions. What we can say, however, is that intelligence testing — along with other institutionalized mechanisms, such as school segregation — helped to limit the learning opportunities for Chicano students and thus contributed in shaping Chicano school failure.

Around 1960, public attention to testing peaked once again (Haney, 1981). Spurred by the launching of Sputnik in 1957 and the subsequent beginning of the 'space race', the identification of 'academically talented' youth became a national obsession. Large-scale testing proliferated, and soon after articles critical of intelligence and other testing (e.g., National Merit Scholarship) appeared in the popular literature.

In the late 1960s, one of the hottest debates of modern time related to IQ testing dealt with the issue of racial differences. Although the 'nature' v. 'nurture' debate over intelligence has occupied the annals of science for over a century (Blum, 1978), it was rekindled with new force by Jensen's (1969) controversial monograph on Black-White differences in intellectual ability. In a lengthy treatise, Jensen hypothesized that the lower intellectual performance of Black Americans was largely due to genetic influences. With a seeming momentum of its own, the nature v. nurture controversy keeps rolling along, as indicated by numerous works in the 1970s and even more recently (e.g., Dunn, 1987; Eysenck and Kamin, 1981; Flynn, 1980; Mercer, 1988). For example, Dunn recently wrote that Hispanic-Anglo differences in intellectual performance are largely due to genetic differences in intelligence. (For a critique of Dunn's position, see the entire issue of the *Hispanic Journal of Behavioral Sciences*, 1988, **10**, 3.)

Nondiscriminatory Assessment and Chicano Students: The Early Years
In 1964, the Society of Social Issues (Division 9 of the American Psychological Association) presented one of the first attempts in modern times to clarify discriminatory assessment issues (Deutsch, Fishman, Kogan, North and Whiteman, 1964). The authors called for greater sensitivity, responsibility, and goodwill on the part of those who test minority children. Concern about discriminatory assessment continued to some degree, but it was not until the early 1970s that the issues of cultural bias in intelligence tests and misclassification of minority children arrived on the national scene. Professional associations, litigation, and legislation were three major influences that helped define the issues and helped fashion more appropriate psychoeducational assessment and services for handicapped and racial/ethnic minority children (Henderson and Valencia, 1985; Oakland and Laosa, 1977; Reschly, 1980).

The first lawsuit regarding the overrepresentation of minority children in special education (i.e., EMR classes) involved Chicano children. In *Diana v. Board of Education* (1970), nine Chicano children, ages 8 to 13 years and attending schools in Monterey County, California, were plaintiffs (see Henderson and Valencia, 1985, for details). The pupils — all from Spanish-speaking homes — claimed they were inappropriately assigned to EMR classes on the basis of IQ scores. Based on widely used IQ tests, the children's IQs ranged from 30 to 72 with a mean score of 64; all tests were administered in English. Upon retest in Spanish, seven of the nine children performed higher than the cutoff point for EMR placement; the other two children's retest scores were only a few points below the cutoff. The plaintiffs contended their placements were inappropriate because the tests administered (a) were standardized on White, native-born children, (b) contained cultural bias, and (c) placed heavy emphasis on English verbal skills (Weintraub and Abeson, 1972; cited in Henderson and Valencia, 1985). *Diana* was settled by consent decree and the final order contained a number of nondiscriminatory provisions — some that later would be part of federal law.

Following the *Diana* case, several other significant and similar cases involving Chicano, Black, and American Indian children were filed in California and Arizona. Each case had a 'piggy-back' effect in which new elements of logic and strategy were added — eventually helping to shape guidelines for psychoeducational assessment and services for Chicano and other racial/ethnic minority children. As Henderson and Valencia (1985) underscore, these lawsuits brought forth by minority plaintiffs proved to be extremely instrumental in molding the future of nondiscriminatory assessment. Out of this judicial crossfire evolved the eventual banning of group-based and some individually administered intelligence tests. The implementation of significant legislature reform (e.g., Public Law 94-142, the Education for All Handicapped Children Act of 1975 [*Federal Register*, 1977]) was also influenced by these lawsuits. In that test bias was a central issue in the preceding minority cases, it is not surprising that of the nine major mandates seen in PL 94-142, three are especially germane to minority children. That is, nonbiased assessment is required (meaning that evaluation and testing materials must not be racially or culturally discriminatory), tests and other evaluation measures must be validated for specific use, and if possible, psychoeducational assessment must be in the child's native language (Henderson and Valencia, 1985). In sum, the quality of the test instrument and how it is administered were key concerns in legislative reform. We now turn to a closer examination of the topics of test bias research and nondiscriminatory assessment during the post PL 94-142 years.

Test Bias Research and Chicanos

With the banning of group-administered intelligence tests and their pernicious sorting consequences, the focus of actual and potential test abuse with respect to Chicanos shifted to individually administered intelligence tests that were used in part for possible special education placement (e.g., EMR; learning disabilities; gifted and talented). The major question researchers asked was: Are the widely used individually administered, standardized intelligence tests biased against Chicano and other racial/ethnic minority children? For example, does the Wechsler Intelligence Test for Children — Revised (WISC–R; Wechsler, 1974) have differential predictive validity of academic achievement for White and Chicano students? Does the Kaufman Assessment Battery for Children (Kaufman and Kaufman, 1983) have differential construct validity for Whites and Chicanos?

Although research on text bias existed prior to the implementation of PL 94-142 (see Jensen, 1980 for a review of pertinent studies), it was not until the late 1970s and into the 1980s that bias research became a noticeable area of concern. Before discussing some of this research that is germane to Chicano students, it is important to clarify a few terms and to provide a backdrop. Jensen (1980) notes the importance of making distinctions between the concepts of 'cultural loading', 'culture biased', and 'test unfairness'. Cultural loading, according to Jensen, basically refers to test items that '... consist of artifacts peculiar to a particular period, locality, or culture ...' (p. 133) or are items that make use of school knowledge or skills (e.g., reading). Given this definition, all tests are culturally loaded to a certain degree. Cultural bias, which is bias involving racial/ethnic group membership, is concerned with psychometric bias.[11] As Jensen comments, this notion of bias is strictly statistical — that is it refers to the systematic errors (e.g., in the predictive validity) of test scores of individuals that are linked to group membership. As such, the assessment of cultural bias is purely objective, statistical, empirical, and quantifiable. On the other hand, the term test unfairness (and its reciprocal, test fairness) are subjective value judgments involving the use of test results (e.g., selection procedures).[12]

Since the advent of intelligence testing of minority children over seventy-five years ago, the issue of test bias and unfairness has been raised and addressed in a number of ways. During the 1970s, the test bias question concerning minority children was one of the most heated issues discussed in the educational assessment literature. Some scholars during that period contended without equivocation that conventional intelligence tests were biased against minorities (e.g., Alley and Foster, 1978; Williams, 1971). Debates on the definition of test bias and fairness became commonplace (e.g., Cleary, 1968; Green, 1975; Thorndike, 1971). Although the concept of test bias was still being debated in the 1980s, the current focus of mental testing research is primarily psychometric investigations of possible test bias in intelligence tests and other tests of mental ability. A number of scholars in the 1980s came to the conclusion that currently used intelligence tests generally are *not* biased against minority children. A good example of this view is the work of Jensen (1980), who states with strong conviction in his preface to *Bias in Mental Testing*:

> Many widely used standardized tests of mental ability consistently show sizable differences in the average scores obtained by various native-born racial and social subpopulations in the United States. Anyone who would claim that all such tests are therefore culturally biased will henceforth have this book to contend with.
>
> My exhaustive review of the empirical research bearing on this issue leads me to the conclusion that the currently most widely used standardized tests of mental ability — IQ, scholastic aptitude, and achievement tests — are, by and large, *not* biased against any of the native-born English-speaking minority groups on which the amount of research evidence is sufficient for any objective determination of bias, if the tests were in fact biased. For most nonverbal standardized tests, this generalization is not limited to English-speaking minorities. (p. ix)

In addition to Jensen, other researchers (e.g., Dean, 1980; Miele, 1979; Reynolds, 1982, 1983; Reschly, 1979; Sandoval, 1979) have provided evidence that certain intelligence tests (e.g., WISC–R) are not biased against minority children. This recent activity of test bias research and debate has generally been healthy for the testing movement, because issues of delineation, detection, and minimization of bias in testing have been opened to wider, and even conflicting, perspectives (e.g., Berk, 1982; Bigelow, 1982; Gould, 1980; Jensen, 1980; Lambert, 1981; Reynolds, 1982; Reynolds and Brown, 1984; Reschly, 1979; Valencia and Rankin, 1985). Let us now move to a brief overview of test bias research pertinent to Chicano students, but first, this point of clarification.

Test bias research across racial/ethnic groups is different from single population validity investigations. Although validity coefficients are useful in the assessment of test bias, they are limited in scope. As Jensen (1980) notes, the concepts of validity and bias are separate questions. Whereas validity can apply to a single population (e.g., Valencia, 1984, 1985a, 1985b), the study of bias always involves a comparison of two or more populations — typically called 'major' and 'minor' groups. With respect to racial/ethnic minority students and test bias research, a study would require a major (e.g., White) and a minor (e.g., Chicano) group (see, for example, Valencia and Rankin, 1986, 1988). There can be, of course, variations of the major-minor group design in investigating cultural bias in tests. For example, in Valencia and Rankin (1985), the major and minor groups were English-speaking Chicano and Spanish-speaking Chicano children, respectively. In summary, the comparison of two or more racial/ethnic groups is the preferred strategy in investigating cultural bias in mental and other tests. Yet, although single population validity studies cannot examine cultural bias directly, they are still valuable in providing insights if validity coefficients are of sufficient magnitudes to conclude that an instrument has clinical utility for a particular minority group (e.g., see Valencia, 1988).[13]

In that the WISC–R is the most frequently individually administered intelligence test for school-age children, it is not surprising that this measure has also been one of the most heavily researched for racial/ethnic (i.e., 'cultural') test bias (Reynolds, 1983). Regarding WISC–R test bias investigations in which Chicano children have been compared to White children, there has been considerable research.[14] Because these studies have been reviewed elsewhere (e.g., Reynolds, 1982, 1983, and to some degree Jensen, 1980), we will only touch on the highpoints.

Test bias research on the WISC–R using Chicano and White samples has been conducted in the areas of construct validity, predictive validity, content validity, and reliability. With respect to construct validity, the basic approach compares the similarity of the factor structure of the WISC–R across Chicanos and Whites. If one finds that the test has factorial similarity for both groups, than it can be concluded, to some degree, that the WISC–R is not biased in construct validity. Investigations by Dean (1980), Gutkin and Reynolds (1980), Oakland and Feigenbaum (1979), and Reschly (1978) have supported the consistent similarity of WISC–R factor analyses across Chicanos and Whites. In short, based on these specific investigations (and of course, the populations sampled), one can conclude that the WISC–R measures the same constructs with approximately equal accuracy for Chicanos and Whites (Reynolds, 1982).

Chicano and White comparisons for potential bias in predictive validity have also been undertaken. In such studies, it is typical to test for homogeneity of regression across Chicanos and Whites (nonbiased prediction).[15] If statistical differences in the two groups' slopes, or intercepts, or standard error of estimates are found, then this would suggest bias in prediction if a common regression line

(Chicano and White combined) is used. Studies by Reschly and Reschly (1979), Reschly and Sabers (1979) and Reynolds and Gutkin (1980) have shown that the WISC–R does not have differential predictive validity (i.e., is not a biased predictor) across Chicanos and Whites.

On the subject of potential bias in content (item) validity on the WISC–R, Sandoval (1979) found the items x groups interaction to account for a very small percentage of the variance in WISC–R performance across Chicano and White children. Based on this investigation, it can be concluded that for the populations studied, WISC–R items were relatively not more difficult for Chicanos than for Whites. Finally, with respect to reliability estimates of the WISC–R across Chicanos and Whites, there is some evidence that the internal reliability of the WISC–R demonstrates an acceptably high degree of consistency for both groups (Oakland and Feigenbaum, 1979; Sandoval, 1979).

The preceding brief overview of WISC–R test bias studies indicates that this popular and widely used individually-administered intelligence test is, by and large, not psychometrically biased against *English-speaking, native-born,* Chicano children.[16] Does this mean, however, that *other* individually-administered intelligence tests are likewise nonbias when used with the Chicano school-age population? Although there is scattered evidence to indicate that some such instruments are free of bias with respect to Chicanos (see, for example, reviews by Jensen, 1980), the best answer to the above question is: given the paucity of test bias studies (i.e., investigations involving instruments other than the WISC–R), it is not possible to draw conclusions one way or the other. That is, in light of the very small number of non-WISC–R bias studies involving Chicanos and Whites, one simply does not know whether the instrument in question is bias or nonbias. Certainly, this pushes the point further along that research on test bias with White and Chicano populations is sorely needed.

The necessity for vigorously undertaking test bias research regarding Chicano children has been recently underscored in a series of studies that provide evidence on the complex nature of test bias findings and interpretation (Valencia and Rankin, 1986, 1988, 1990). The subjects in the Valencia and Rankin investigations were White and Chicano fifth- and sixth-grade boys and girls, and the instrument under examination for potential bias was the Kaufman Assessment Battery for Children (K–ABC). The K–ABC contains an intelligence scale (Mental Processing Scale) and a separate Achievement Scale. Four investigations of possible test bias (against the minor group — Chicanos) were undertaken by Valencia and Rankin. Using a variety of test bias statistical analyses to study potential bias in the K–ABC along lines of three types of validity (construct; content, i.e., item; predictive) as well as reliability, some mixed results were found. Bias *was not* found in construct validity and reliability (Valencia and Rankin, 1986), but bias *was* identified in content validity (Valencia and Rankin, 1990) and predictive validity (Valencia and Rankin, 1988).[17] In the predictive validity study, Valencia and Rankin (1988) offer this conclusion regarding the complicated K–ABC bias findings:

> ... the K–ABC appears to be flawed or biased when used with Mexican American students, because the test does not have the same predictive efficiency with the majority and minority students. Finally it is worth

noting, as does Jensen (1980), that a test could have the same degree of construct validity in both the majority and minority groups (i.e., as seen with the K–ABC in Valencia and Rankin, 1986), even when the pre-dictor variable has comparable reliabilities in both groups (i.e., as seen in Valencia and Rankin, 1986 ...), and yet be a biased predictor of achievement. (p. 263)

It is important to keep in mind that the above 'mixed bag' of test bias research on Chicanos is only a small sliver of the potential research that could be undertaken. It is important to keep in mind that evidence presented in the Valencia and Rankin studies is for *one* instrument (K–ABC), *one* age group (11-year-olds), *one* location in *one* state (central California city), and so forth.[18] It is not difficult to imagine that given the number of intelligence tests available and the variation in possible test bias research focuses and designs, there are indeed a large number of research investigations that are in the realm of possibility.

Unfortunately, at a time when more research is needed on test bias with Chicanos and other racial/ethnic minorities, there appears to be a gradual decline in interest — and thus investigatory activity — by researchers. Peaking in the late 1970s and early 1980s, test bias research (especially on individually-administered intelligence measures used in the assessment of school-age children) began to decrease in the mid 1980s and even into the 1990s. This nosedive in research activity and publication could be related, in part, to the work of some scholars who may have helped close the door to test bias research by prematurely drawing broad conclusions that most mental measures are relatively free of cultural bias (e.g., see Jensen, 1980). A second contributing factor to the decline in test bias research is likely related to the very nature of test bias. As Reschly (1979) comments, test bias is an issue filled with emotion — and for a long time at that. To some degree, the contemporary period from the late 1970s to the present can be viewed as a moody reflection of the public and scholarly waxing and waning toward the test bias controversy seen over the decades. Third, perhaps the decrease in test bias research is connected to a more general climate of apathy toward minority children in the US. For example, in speaking to the need for further theoretical understanding with respect to the widespread issue of poor schooling perform-ance of minority children, Boykin (1986) observes: 'The question is particularly crucial today, at a time of declining political interest in minority affairs. Minority children no longer enjoy national attention, but their educational problems persist' (p. 57).

Whatever the probable reasons might be for the diminished attention to test bias research, it is certainly not because the measurement community lacks the technology. From the advent of mental testing up to the 1960s, there was considerable confusion in test bias research and literature. According to Jensen (1980), much of this disorder was due to inconsistencies in terminology and a lack of clarity in conceptualizing and differentiating bias (a statistical notion) and unfairness (an abuse of test results). In the last ten or so years, however, a number of publications have appeared discussing statistical and methodological approaches for measuring test bias. This body of research — in both theoretical treatises and actual empirical investigations — has greatly enhanced the state-of-the-art of test bias conceptualization, methodological detection, and interpreta-tion (see, for example, Berk, 1982). In short, given what current measurement technology can offer, it seems to us that there is no excuse for Chicano and other minority children to be tested on mental measures that have not been scrutinized for potential cultural bias. And, of course, it would be unpardonable to administer tests to children in which cultural bias has been identified (e.g., see Valencia and Rankin, 1988).

The Responsibility of Test Publishers

There is no doubt that the 'stuff' of the measurement community — that being psychometric theory, knowledge, and application — is continually needed to push along the realization of nondiscriminatory testing and assessment. But, what about the role of test publishers — those who develop and market tests. Should they also have a responsibility to ensure that their products are free of cultural bias and to help prevent the abusive practice (albeit frequency unknown) of examiners who administer tests with poor or unknown psychometric integrity? To even get a sense of this issue, we need to go beyond the topic of individually-administered intelligence tests and into the broad field of test publishing.

Mitchell's (1984) paper on 'Testing and the Oscar Buros lament: From knowledge to implementation to use' provides an incisive look into the many problems of published tests. As Mitchell notes, Buros (the founder of *The Mental Measurements Yearbook*, the world's richest source on the quality of published tests) years back had some harsh words on tests. In the *Eighth Mental Measurements Yearbook* (*MMY*; Buros, 1978), Buros charged, that by and far, the publishers of tests continue to sell tests that do not meet the minimal standards of the *MMY* and test reviewers. According to Buros, 'At least half of the tests currently on the market should never have been published' (see, Mitchell, 1984, p. 113).

Mitchell (1984) cites a small descriptive study conducted by the Buros Institute of Mental Measurements staff that affirms Buros' lament about published tests. The test reviews in *The Eighth Mental Measurements Yearbook* were examined in order to see how well test publishers attended to providing critical test data (i.e., evidence of reliability, validity, and norms). The results of this investigation were discouraging to Mitchell. Key findings were:

1   As a whole, about 41 per cent of the tests listed in the *MMY* '... were lacking reliability and/or validity data in some important respect. Tests in the areas of reading, vocations, and speech and hearing were the worst offenders' (pp. 114–15).
2   Regarding norms, 'All told, 28 per cent of the tests listed ... were inadequately normed in some important respect' (p. 115).

A few other specific points that Mitchell (1984) cites about test publishing further support Buros' disappointment with the quality of tests. To wit,

3   There has been a proliferation of tests. Based on an analysis of *Tests in Print II* (Buros, 1974), there are 496 test publishers listed. Although less than 2 per cent of the publishers publish 26 per cent of all tests, Mitchell notes that the majority of publishers (58 per cent) have just a single test listed, about 75 per cent have three or less tests, and 85 per cent have five or fewer. Mitchell concludes:

> ... there is much of the cottage industry to the test publishing
> business, and there are many test publishers distributing their
> own tests or very small test publishers with single or extremely
> limited test offerings or book or instructional materials who
> have acquired a few tests and publish them in a manner almost
> incidental to their major interest and thrust. (p. 113)[19]

The impact of such an uneven industry is quite revealing. First, according to
Mitchell, there is the fact that more and more tests are being published, but of
poorer and poorer quality. Second, the developmental and marketing costs
— and of course, the huge profits of sales from poor and marginal tests — all
indicate that the measurement community is losing ground in trying to maintain
some semblance of test quality. Third, as more poor tests appear on the market,
it becomes more difficult for test users and the public to become discriminating
consumers.

4 Claims about validity evidence are often overstated. Mitchell (1984) notes
   that it is not uncommon for test publishers to shunt aside modest to
   weak validity evidence and to create illusions than a great deal more
   benefits from tests can be offered. As such, it is irresponsible for test
   publishers to promote test utility in the absence of strong validity
   evidence.

With the broader issue of 'Buros' lament' in mind, it becomes exceedingly
clear that test publishers indeed have a major responsibility and challenge in
developing nonbiased tests (intelligence and otherwise) when such instruments
are to be used in the assessment of Chicano and other culturally and/or linguistically diverse populations. Reynolds (1982) fittingly describes this mandate as
such:

> Test developers are ... going to have to become more sensitive to the
> issues of cultural bias to the point of demonstrating on publication
> whether their tests have differential content, construct, or predictive
> validity across race or sex *prior* [italics added] to publication ... With the
> exception of some recent achievement tests, *this has not been common
> practice* [italics added], yet it is at this stage where tests can be altered
> through a variety of item-analysis procedures to eliminate any apparent
> racial or sexual bias. (p. 208)

Summarizing matters thus far, we have provided some historical and contemporary insights to the uses and abuses of intelligence testing with respect to
Chicano students. Historically, there is some rather convincing evidence that
group-based intelligence testing was used, in part with other educational practices, to help shape limited educational opportunities for Chicanos, both in the
educational mainstream and special education. With the demise of group-
administered intelligence tests, the contemporary spotlight is now on individually-
administered intelligence instruments with respect to potential test bias and the
abusive practice of using psychometrically poor tests. As we have discussed,

despite a substantial technology the measurement community has failed in recent years to muster enough continued interest and energy to pursue the needed research into the question of test bias. By no means is the issue of test bias with respect to Chicanos and other racial/ethnic minority groups a closed issue. The resolution of the test bias question lies in the 1990s, and perhaps beyond.

The researcher, however, does not stand alone in his or her responsibility to bring further light to the question of potential test bias. We have seen that the test publishing community also needs to share in providing bias-free psychoeducational instruments. The Buros lament becomes even graver when one includes the issue of potential test bias. Certainly, for test publishers not to meet minimal standards of adequate reliability, validity, and norming in their educational tests is unjustifiable. For such publishers to also market their poor or marginal quality tests without having undertaken investigations to ensure nonbias across racial/ethnic groups is unconscionable. Indeed, in view of the major abuses at the test publishing level, 'a call to action' for the improvement of test development is in order (see Mitchell, 1984, for several recommendations).

The Responsibility of School Psychologists

In addition to the research/measurement and test publishing communities, there is also a third, significant sector that has responsibility in insuring nonbiased testing and assessment — the practitioners (school psychologists). With respect to intelligence testing, an important traditional task of the school psychologist has been to test children who may be suspected of functioning subnormally in intellectual behavior. Nowadays, this role of the school psychologist presents some serious problems. Henderson and Valencia (1985) capture the issues this way:

> School psychologists were able to go about that task confident that the instruments they used were reliable and valid for their use. The intelligence test, sometimes thought of by educators as a sort of appendage to the school psychologist, was widely regarded as the single most impressive achievement of psychological science. Today, school psychologists are less confident of their assessment tools, ensnarled in an ethical and professional dilemma. (p. 340)

The ethical and professional fix in which school psychologists find themselves is this: on one hand, school psychologists are required by law (e.g., PL 94–142) to search actively for and identify children who may need special educational services or programs. On the other hand, the same legislative mandate requires nondiscriminatory assessment. As these dual (but obviously connected) responsibilities have intensified, school psychologists find themselves more and more troubled (Henderson and Valencia, 1985). Traditional assessment tools, especially the individually-administered intelligence test, are increasingly being called into question for use with children whose racial/ethnic or social class backgrounds fall outside the modal configuration (i.e., English-speaking, middle-class White mainstream).

As such, school psychologists are placed in a difficult position. They need to scrutinize their test arsenals by asking two vital questions. First, do the tests meet the minimal standards for acceptable levels of reliability and validity, as well as for appropriate norming? Second, and an extension of the first concern, is there evidence that the tests in question are free of cultural bias along lines of reliability and the various types of validity? If the answers to these questions are 'no', and if a particular test is administered nevertheless, in our opinion this would constitute an abusive practice of testing.

Inappropriate and deleterious testing practices are not only confined to administering tests that lack good psychometric quality (in general, and with respect to nonbias). First, abuses can also occur by school psychologists when administering intelligence tests, or other various types of educational tests, to students who are not proficient enough in English to handle the verbal demands (see Valencia, 1990, for a discussion of how inattention to this issue has created and continues to create, assessment problems for Chicano students; as well, he presents an overview of how methodologically confounded intelligence testing research with Chicanos was shaped because of the language issue). Second, there is the problem of not attending to multiple data sources of assessment. Salvia and Ysseldyke (1988) underscore that '... testing and assessment are not synonymous' (p. 5). Unfortunately, the belief that testing and assessment are identical has led some school psychologists astray and has caused inappropriate diagnosis and intervention for some students, especially minorities. There is, however, some optimism as the field of school psychology has gradually become more sensitive to the need for expanded ways and models to be used in identifying and providing services for children with learning difficulties (e.g., see Oakland and Goldwater, 1979, for a discussion of assessment and intervention models for mildly retarded children; see Henderson and Valencia, 1985, for a general discussion on expanded assessment and intervention strategies for minority children).

A third area of potential abuse in the testing of Chicanos and other minority students has to do with the failure of school psychologists to *go beyond* bias-free testing. There is no doubt that in the work of school psychology, nonbiased testing is crucial. But, as Henderson and Valencia (1985) contend, 'nonbiased testing is useless unless it results in nondiscriminatory education' (p. 342). It is important for the school psychologist (in a consultative model) to work with teacher and parent in connecting testing and assessment to instructional services and programming.

Along these lines, Henderson and Valencia (1985) argue that despite the limitations of current tests and practices, nondiscriminatory psychological assessment and services are attainable if school psychologists adhere to certain principles. Some examples are:

1 Be knowledgeable about the cultural backgrounds of children and the demand characteristics of the home and school environments.
2 Function as problem solvers. That is, be open to multiple sources of assessment data. Be sensitive to possible cultural influences on the performance in question. Use the gathered data at hand as the basis for testing hypotheses in the context of intervention.
3 Employ a 'consultation' model rather than the traditional 'refer-test-report' model. For example, under the former model, the school psychologist looks for the underlying causes of learning and remediation in the

classroom, rather than in superficial analysis and intervention through potentially meaningless contingency management.

4   In the absence of well-trained psychologists (especially the absence of minority school psychologists), assessment and service delivery could profit from having a cultural informant or ombudsperson.

Beyond Nonbiased Assessment

In closing this section on intelligence testing, we wish to expand the preceding discussion on the relation between nondiscriminatory testing (and assessment) and nondiscriminatory schooling. We do this by placing the discussion in the context of a major focus of our discussion thus far, that is, test bias. Conceptualizing test bias as a psychometric notion has proven to be a valuable contribution to the measurement and interpretation of bias. This contribution is largely so because the psychometric approach defuses, to some degree, the emotional debate often associated with the question of bias. Furthermore, this approach can and does lead to empirically defined and testable definitions of bias (in the case of Chicano students, see for example, Valencia and Rankin, 1985, 1986, 1988, 1990). In recent years, however, reservations have been voiced about the strict statistical approach to understanding bias. The major criticism of statistical, or psychometric, test bias is that it is rather exclusive in its conceptualization. One sub-criticism of this exclusivity area is that there is a muddling of the terms bias and unfairness — a topic we discuss next.

As discussed previously, a number of scholars (e.g., Jensen, 1980) make a sharp distinction between 'bias' and 'unfairness'. While bias and nonbias are empirical and statistical matters, unfairness and fairness are moral and legal issues dealing with how test scores are used in a selection situation. According to Shepard (1982), the distinction between bias and unfairness, however, is problematic. First, the intended difference between the two terms is not unequivocally conveyed in everyday communication. Shepard notes: 'To be biased is to be unfair, unjust, prejudiced. Calling your test "biased" conveys nearly the same message as a placard calling an employer "unfair"' (p. 10).

Second, the distinction between the notions of bias and unfairness presents some awkwardness in the psychometric sense. Shepard (1982) notes that although authors generally conceptualize bias as a form of invalidity, bias '... is now being taken as an inherent feature of a test, while its opposite, validity, has always been considered to be a property of test use, not of the test itself' (p. 10). An example of this disorder is that the difference in the two terms is confused by the bias-in-selection literature (see Peterson and Novick, 1976; cited in Shepard, 1982), which definitely pertains to test use but suggests different models of predictive validity as bias indicators. In this context, bias is thought of as a specific type of invalidity that is *outside* of the test instrument rather than being an inherent feature of the test itself. Notwithstanding the confusion between bias and unfairness, Shepard argues that it is worthy to maintain the distinction intended by some authors, because the difference between bias in tests and unfair test use is critical to an understanding of bias detection. Shepard (1982) does, however, raise this helpful suggestion:

> It is possible to be faithful to the rule that validity must always pertain
> to the particular inferences made from a test, yet still admit different

degrees of externality through which bias may be more or less closely associated with the *use* of a test, rather than its internal characteristics. There is a validity continuum, anchored at one end by unbiased tests that measure what they were designed to measure and do so equally well for all groups. Further along the continuum are tests that provide equal predictive validity in particular contexts. At the farthest end of the continuum are tests for which validity is established by resolving issues of justice and values, as well as scientific arguments over what statistical model of fairness to apply and what the criterion will be. (p. 11)

Given the obviously different points of view, what definition or conceptualization of test bias should be adopted? Henderson and Valencia (1985) ask: 'Is it best defined as the poor match between test content and cultural experiences of minority and poor children, the influence of situational factors on performance, or technical validity?' (p. 350). Regarding the latter (i.e., statistical conceptualization), there is some value in it because, as Shepard (1982) notes, it helps us to study and understand how to detect bias. Furthermore, as we have discussed earlier, such an approach has greatly assisted in providing some evidence that the more well-developed tests (e.g., WISC–R) are relatively nonbias. The existing corpus of statistical research on test bias is significant in advancing our knowledge base and certainly needs to be encouraged. Yet, as we have underscored, the test bias question with respect to Chicano students and other minority groups is far from being resolved.

Notwithstanding the value and contributions of the statistical paradigm in identifying and measuring cultural bias on individually-administered tests (as well as other psychoeducational instruments), we think it is misleading to adhere to such an exclusive conception. Bersoff (1984), Henderson and Valencia (1985), Messick (1989), Reschly (1979), Shepard (1982) and others have come to the heart of the matter with the observation that *tests do have social consequences*. Since the seminal period of testing, tests have been used to open doors for some, and close doors for others. Abusive school testing practices *vis-à-vis* Chicanos, other minorities, and the poor often constitute institutional racism in which self-perpetrating, unquestioned testing practices within school systems diminish learning opportunities for children (Henderson and Valencia, 1985).

In sum, the subject of test bias is complex and controversial. In our opinion, as well as others, it is scientifically and ethically inappropriate not to tie testing/assessment with schooling and its consequences. The statistical notion of bias is useful, but alone it has little meaning. On this, Bersoff (1984) voices: '... reliance on psychometric models for test bias without consideration of the social and ethical consequences of test use ignores the concerns of significant segments of society' (p. 105). Or, as Reschly (1979) points out: '... to defend tests on the basis of evidence of common regression systems or to attempt to separate the issues of technical adequacy from those of social consequences is insufficient' (p. 235). In the final analysis, the administration of intelligence *and* other educational tests to Chicano students should be considered in the context of the broad institutional processes that help shape school problems for them. The wider implications of testing/assessment and the schooling context for Chicanos need to be considered in any effort to envision nondiscriminatory school services.

Reschly (1979) grasps the fundamental nature of this matter in his assertion that

> The ultimate criteria that should guide our evaluations of test bias are the implications and outcomes of test use for individuals. Succinctly stated, test use is fair if the results are more effective interventions leading to improved competencies and expanded opportunities for individuals. Test use is unfair if opportunities are diminished or if individuals are exposed to ineffective interventions as a result of tests. (p. 235)

Competency Testing

As we previously discussed, the issue of 'accountability' in education is a widespread concern in our society. The current 'competency testing' movement is part of the broader public demands for accountability in the nation's schools. In a nutshell, the notion of competency testing carries with it a gatekeeping function in which examinees are tested to see who will be promoted, graduated, admitted, or certified. In this section we begin with a description of the types of competency testing. Following this is a discussion of minimum competency testing and teacher competency testing and their negative impact on Chicanos.

Types of Competency Testing

In our conceptualization of the nature of competency testing, we see three broad forms. First, there is 'minimum competency testing' (MCT). As Jaeger (1987) notes, MCT began in a big way in the early 1970s. Oregon's State Board of Education mandated the school systems in 1972 to develop and implement a statewide program to measure student 'competence' (also see Herron, 1980). Soon after, MCT spread nationwide. Baratz (1980) comments that by 1977, eighteen states jumped into the MCT movement. By 1987, forty states had climbed the bandwagon (Jaeger, 1987). It appears that a primary use of MCT is to award or deny students a high school diploma. After nearly a decade of MCT, in 1980 about 50 per cent of the states used the passage of a test of minimum competence as a prerequisite for the earning of a diploma (Lerner, 1981; cited in Bersoff, 1984). As we enter the 1990s, many states use MCT in such a way. Based on what little data are available, Chicanos and other racial/ethnic minority student groups have higher failure rates than their White peers on these measures, and thus are denied high school diplomas at higher proportions. Later, we will return to the controversial MCT and the resultant abusive practices.

A second major type of competency testing is what we call 'school-based competency testing'. This form of testing typically involves a required statewide system of student evaluation of minimum skills in basic schooling areas (e.g., reading). These mandates are top-down in which state legislatures commonly require school districts throughout the state to administer broad-based achievement tests (e.g., mathematics, reading, writing) to elementary and secondary students (usually at selected grade levels). It is typical for such testing programs to be part of an omnibus school 'reform' package passed by the legislature. Examples of school-based competency testing are the California Assessment Program (CAP) and the Texas Educational Assessment of Minimum Skills test (TEAMS). Typically, a state educational agency provides, after testing, all school districts with aggregated test results (e.g., the unit of analysis is the individual school).[20] In some states, the actual testing, analysis, and reporting of results has spawned bureaucracies. For example, a recent report of TEAMS results in Austin, Texas, contained great detail of test score comparisons for a section of the local district (Christner and Moede, 1988–89). TEAMS scores were compared between schools, grade levels, and racial/ethnic groups.[21]

In sum, it appears that the results of school-based competency testing are filling an accountability function of a sort. By far, compared to the other types of competency testing, school-based testing results are made the most public. It is quite common for local newspapers to report, in some detail, the outcomes of local testing. Depending on the scores of these 'public report cards', local super-intendents — or in some cases the highest ranking state public educational official — may flaunt the test results, contending that 'real progress' is being made and tests score 'are up' from the previous year (Phillips, 1989; Watson and Kramer, 1989). Sometimes, school officials will even discuss problems, underscoring the percentage of students (and often naming the schools) who have 'failed' the competency testing (Graves and Breaux, 1989). We do not find fault with the public's right to know the results of school-based competency testing. We do, however, find disturbing, misleading, and abusive the manner in which test reporting is done in some instances. For example, in some cases school officials in bi- or multiracial communities will report test results in such a way that minority parents are misled to believe that their children are achieving at satisfactory levels.[22]

The third form of competency testing can be placed under the rubric of 'teacher competency testing'. As another child of the parental accountability movement, the teacher competency testing movement began in 1978 and has now swept the country (Valencia and Aburto, in press, a). The term 'teacher tests' is an umbrella for three forms of paper-and-pencil teacher competency tests. An 'admissions' test is a basic skills test required as an entry criterion to a teacher education program. A 'certification' test is also a basic skills test and/or a professional knowledge test and/or a subject matter test required as a condition for earning an initial teaching credential granted by the state. A 'recertification' test is a basic skills test required of incumbent teachers. Based on the most recent data there are twenty-four states that require some type of teacher competency test for admission to a teacher education program; thirty-six states require such testing only upon graduation as part of state certification, and eighteen states mandate both entrance (admissions) and exit testing (certification) (Eissenburg and Rudner, 1988). There are three states that require teacher competency testing for teachers currently practicing (recertification) (Shepard and Kreitzer, 1987).

Approximately a decade ago, concern was raised at public, political, and school levels about the preparedness and effectiveness of beginning teachers. Because of the continuing criticisms of America's teachers and schools (e.g., *A Nation at Risk* by the National Commission on Excellence in Education), the public is demanding some assurance from its state agencies that teachers who become licensed are actually competent — hence the introduction of competency tests. The central idea behind such testing is that before people be allowed to teach, they must demonstrate 'basic skills' (e.g., mathematical ability, reading, writing) that are believed to be necessary to carry on day-to-day instructional activities. Although the motive underlying teacher competency testing is clear (i.e., the need to upgrade teacher quality), the nature of teacher testing is fraught with conceptual, measurement, and social problems. In the case of prospective Chicano teachers, they (and other racial/ethnic minority groups, particularly Blacks) have been forced to carry a very disproportionate burden of teacher reform efforts. That is, Chicanos and other minority examinees, compared to their White peers, have failed teacher tests at very high rates — to such a degree that the minority teacher shortage is at a crisis situation (Valencia and Aburto, in press, a). As will be elaborated later, the sharp decline of Chicano and other minority teacher comes at a time in which the minority school-age population is growing at dramatic rates.

In short, competency testing with respect to Chicanos is filled with controversy. Specifically, these issues include: (a) conceptual confusion about the distinction between 'competence' and 'incompetence' (e.g., Jensen, 1980); (b) arbitrariness and scientific indefensibility of standard setting (i.e., arriving at a cut score to determine who passes, who fails; (see Valencia and Aburto, in press, b); (c) 'high-stakes' nature of competency testing in that one's future rides on a single score (e.g., Madaus, 1986); (d) dire social and educational consequences for Chicano examinees and Chicano school children (e.g., Valencia and Aburto, in press, a). Given the paucity of research in the area of school-based competency testing and because of space limitations, the above issues will only be examined in the areas of MCT and teacher competency testing.

Minimum Competency Testing

As part of major educational reform efforts aimed at improving the quality of our schools, many lay boards of education and state legislatures have responded over the last sixteen years by implementing MCT programs in their states. MCT is primarily based on a belief that testing of essential skills and competencies (e.g., math, reading, and writing) will help raise academic standards, increase educational achievement, and restore public confidence in education. The passage of a minimum competency test for high school graduation and/or grade-to-grade promotion is currently required in at least forty states (Haney and Madaus, 1978; Paulson and Ball, 1984). A 1985 *Education Week* survey indicated twenty states require high school students to show mastery on a state-mandated exit test as a prerequisite to receipt of a regular high school diploma (Airasian, 1988). In this section, we will discuss: (a) criticisms of MCT, (b) adverse impact on Chicano and other minority students, and (c) the effect of MCT on the operation and structure of schooling.

Criticisms of MCT

Boasting strong public and political support, MCT proponents contend that students will benefit by mastering the basic skills, raising their self-confidence, and enhancing their career opportunities. While the MCT movement addresses a variety of social and political purposes, its most widely recognized goal is the improvement of students' basic skills. Ideally, the test's main function is to identify deficiencies that may be treated through remediation. A critical feature in some programs is the use of test results as a screen for high school graduation (Serow, 1984). In general, students are required to pass a test demonstrating 'minimum competency' in basic academic skills and their practical application to 'real-life' demands before receiving their diplomas (Jensen, 1980). Supporters argue that racial/ethnic minority students will particularly benefit from MCT because it will reveal inequities in their education so they may be rectified (Paulson and Ball, 1984; Serow, 1984). In that most students are believed capable of attaining the requisite level of competency before graduation day, the diploma sanction is not considered by some as an act of discrimination against Chicanos, other minority students, or the poor (Serow, 1984).

Yet while competency tests appear simple, straightforward, and are widely used, their overall quality and intentions have been criticized from the start. Numerous writers view the almost exclusive reliance on MCT for awarding a high school diploma, for determining grade-to-grade promotion, or for assigning students automatically to remedial classes as classic examples of improper uses of tests. If in fact the tests were established in recognition of problems in the educational system, then to withhold diplomas, for example, simply punishes the victim (Linn *et al.*, 1982). Opponents also contend competency tests and standards serve more as short-sighted symbolic and political gestures than instrumental reforms (e.g., Airasian, 1988; Ellwein, Glass and Smith, 1988) and simply represent another area of potential discrimination against minorities and the poor, creating an additional obstacle to the attainment of social and economic equality in American life (Serow, 1984). Other critics sum up MCT as simply an effort to legislate educational success without concern for methods or modes of achievement (Jaeger and Tittle, 1980). Finally, there are some scholars who believe that because 'competence' is such a relative concept, it makes no psychometric sense to dichotomize students as being either 'competent' or 'incompetent' (Jensen, 1980).

Unfortunately, a brief survey of recent literature in the area shows that many of the early criticisms and fears raised over competency testing remain unresolved and few expectations or promises have been fulfilled. We now move to one major criticism of MCT — negative impact on Chicanos and other minorities.

Adverse Impact on Chicano and Other Minority Students
Of the many criticisms leveled against MCT, several relate to questions concerning its impact on minorities. From the start, opponents argued that MCT programs posed substantial risks for students from racial/ethnic minority backgrounds, who, through no fault of their own, experience school failure. Rather than forcing those students who fail competency tests to take their education more seriously, some critics believed the diploma sanction would instead lower students' motivation for attending schools, thus causing increased academic and disciplinary problems and higher dropout rates (Serow, 1984). Unless tied to an effective remediation program monitored by sensitive administrators, MCT could also be used to justify a new sort of segregation by placing failing students with the worst teachers or in less effective curriculum tracks (Paulson and Ball, 1984). Above all, competency testing further reinforces a stigma of failure for low-achieving students, and in the long run perpetuates racial and economic inequality (Serow, 1984). Though few studies have

examined the consequences of MCT it appears many negative premonitions have come to pass.

Failure rates on minimum competency tests for minorities, particularly Blacks, Chicanos, and other Latinos, are much higher than they are for White students. For example, early MCT trial run information from Florida showed that of 115,901 students taking the state's MCT in 1977, 36 per cent failed. Of those who failed, 78 per cent were Black, even though Blacks constituted only about 20 per cent of those taking the exam (Paulson and Ball, 1984). In 1978 it was reported that some 77 per cent of Blacks, 39 per cent of Latinos, and 24 per cent of Whites 'failed' the arithmetic test; furthermore, 26 per cent of Blacks, 7 per cent of Latinos, and 3 per cent of Whites 'failed' the reading test and writing portions (Jensen, 1980). Those students failing received a certificate of completion rather than a standard diploma. This is a significant impact when one considers that a certificate of completion is not considered a diploma for purposes of employment in the state of Florida or for purposes of admission to one of Florida's nine state universities. It was estimated that the denial of a diploma to Black students who failed the competency test resulted in a 20 per cent decline in Black enrollment in the state's universities and colleges (Paulson and Ball, 1984). Competency test performance data from the states of California, Florida, North Carolina and Virginia, also confirm the expectation that minority students experience greater difficulty in passing such tests than Whites (Serow, 1984). Supplementary data from the state of North Carolina revealed that students from lower-socioeconomic status (SES) backgrounds were about one-third less likely to pass the exam on their first attempt than students from higher SES backgrounds (Serow). As is well known, racial/ethnic minorities are usually concentrated in the lower SES categories.

Other studies have shown that even for students who stay in school, many fail to meet course and proficiency test requirements established at the district level. In 1981–82, minority high school seniors in California were three times less likely to complete the course requirements for graduation than were other students. Among those students that completed the district's course requirements for graduation, racial/ethnic group differences existed in passing the proficiency examinations required for graduation. As of December 1981, 17 per cent of the White students in this category did not pass one or more of the proficiency tests required for high school graduation, compared with 36 per cent of Black seniors and 25 per cent of Chicano and other Latino senior students (Brown and Haycock, 1985).

The effect of the MCT movement may be especially adverse for students who have previously suffered school failure because it places higher academic demands on those already at risk of dropping out (Archer and Dresden, 1987). It is difficult to distinguish between students who would have dropped out regardless of MCT requirements and those who became dropouts specifically because of their failure to pass competency tests. Data from Archer and Dresden's study, however, suggest that a significant number of Texas students already at a late junior or senior level will not receive high school diplomas as a result of failing the minimum competency test. This situation creates a new kind of dropout — students with a poor academic background who have the willingness to stay in school and graduate, but who will be denied a high school diploma because they do not meet the minimum standards.

Statistics from a 1985 administration of the Texas Educational Assessment of Minimum Skills (TEAMS) test taken their junior year indicates 12 per cent (22,485) of the examinees failed the mathematics section and 9 per cent (16,921) failed the English language arts section (Archer and Dresden, 1987). The demographic data suggest that failure to master the tests and attain diplomas will be disproportionately high for some groups. Those most effected by the exit level requirement will be students with limited-English proficiency being served in bilingual programs (48 per cent failing in language arts on their first try) and 'disadvantaged' students in Chapter I programs (39 per cent failing in mathematics). Blacks failed the mathematics portion at a rate of 28 per cent, and the failure rates for Chicano and White students were 18 per cent and 6 per cent, respectively. Language arts failure rates were 19 per cent for Blacks, 16 per cent for Hispanics, and 4 per cent for Whites. Additional students at risk of not receiving a diploma were almost 12,000 students who did not sit for this examination or any subsequent make-up administrations. Failure to master either subtest results in failure to receive a diploma. Unfortunately, this group of students will only join others from economically disadvantaged and racial/ethnic minority backgrounds who already traditionally have disproportionately high rates of truancy, dropping out, and school discipline problems (McDill, Natriello, and Pallas, 1985).

Very few states provide information on final diploma denial figures, especially with respect to the racial/ethnic or socioeconomic backgrounds of the pupils. The Texas data suggest, however, that MCT diploma sanctions are imposed disproportionately on Chicano and Black students (Archer and Dresden, 1987). Projections from California based on 1981 test results similarly show that Chicano and Black students are overrepresented among potential diploma denials (Brown and Haycock, 1985). Available data probably underestimate minority students' share of diploma denials because they fail to account for retest performances (Serow, 1984). North Carolina figures based on final results show Blacks made up about 25 per cent of the 1980 graduates but received more than 75 per cent of all diploma sanctions. In all, 4.4 per cent of all Black graduates were denied a diploma because of MCT failure, compared to 1.8 per cent of other minorities, and .5 per cent of White graduates (Serow, 1984).

Effect on the Operation and Structure of Schooling
At the onset, the hurried implementation of MCT could only allow for speculation about its effectiveness. Yet, fifteen years later, expediency is no longer a viable excuse for not knowing the effect of MCT on the operation and structure of our schools. Even a cursory search through the literature, however, shows that attention is still primarily focused on questions of competency definition, test development, standard setting, and program operations. Ellwein *et al.* (1988) note that over 60 per cent of the MCT research published between 1977 and 1987 is primarily rhetorical. Only 10 per cent of the entire literature could be classified as systematic, empirical research. Two perspectives examining the benefits of MCT reform are presented here. One discusses the effects of MCT on multiple school sites across the nation from an empirical perspective, and the other is a teacher's personal lament on the status of MCT in one school. Both indicate that the amount of attention given to minority issues or the remedial efforts aimed at offsetting the poor showing of all students who fail competency tests appears to

be minimal. We seem to have accepted these high-stakes examinations on what Airasian (1988) calls 'symbolic validation' without demanding that they justify their existence on any sort of empirical ground.

Aware of the need for an empirical view of MCT and standard-setting, Ellwein *et al.* (1988) studied five sites across the country. These researchers were guided by three major questions: For whom and for what purposes are test standards set? How and by whom are standards established? What consequences follow from the setting of standards? Results from the Ellwein *et al.*, investigation led to the formulation of five propositions that address the nature of competency testing reforms. Of special interest are the propositions noting (a) lopsided organizational activity, (b) nominal attention to minority issues witnessed at all five sites, and (c) the assertion that competency tests and standards function more as symbolic and political gestures than instrumental reforms.

Ellwein *et al.* (1988) note that organizational efforts are most visible, intense, and detailed during early phases of competency testing reforms — with similar efforts conspicuously absent in later stages. Intense efforts are concentrated in the development and administration of the instruments, but the amount of time invested contrasts sharply with the attention given to gauging and evaluating the effects of what the tests produced. In general, sites routinely figured only initial pass rates, with only a few collecting and reporting ultimate pass rates. Planned evaluations in general did not go beyond the tangible, technical outcomes of such rates.

The study also found that agency attention to minority issues is most prominent in efforts to build unbiased tests and most inconspicuous in efforts to assess adverse impact. In spite of differential pass rates at each site, issues of impact beyond the test themselves were left unexamined. Efforts for the most part centered on judgmental and technical reviews of items with no measure of the tests' impact. Only one site kept track of failure rates, number of repeat attempts, and the number and type of test-related decisions concerning retention or graduation. Given that some sites have large racial/ethnic minority student populations, failure to report such obviously important data is cause for concern (Ellwein *et al.*, 1988).

Of special importance is the conclusion by Ellwein *et al.* (1988) that '... competency tests and standards function as symbolic and political gestures, not as instrumental reforms' (p. 8). Two of five observed themes underpinning this conclusion are the loose coupling of test performance and subsequent decisions and the striking contrast between early and late phases of competency testing reforms. While information on the numbers of students who fail and do not graduate may exist within local institutions, such figures are not calculated or available at the state level and thus are not a matter of routine or public information. In addition, the attention given to test development, standard-setting, and general implementation contrasts sharply with the lack of attention to questions of impact, utility, and the value of competency tests and standards. In short, there seems little to say about the instrumental value of MCT and standards because it simply has not been examined in any of these sites. A lack of attention to these larger issues only further conceals any instrumental benefits or dangers these reforms may bring (Ellwein *et al.*, 1988).

A second reality check on what MCT has accomplished at the school level is offered by Forney (1989), an English teacher in a California high school requiring the passage of a competency test for graduation. Forney reports that students are given a choice of seven topics (two days before the exam) in order to organize their materials and to practice writing the essay. Even though they are not allowed to bring anything with them the day of the test, the examination ends up being a memorized essay that an English teacher has already approved or that another student has written. While the exercise models the five-paragraph essay taught in preparation sessions, the students fail to write an essay showing any sort of individualized style or creativity. Problems also arise when students view passing the test not as evidence of possessing minimum competency, but as proof that their need for formal education no longer exists. Forney notes that little evidence exists showing the tests do anything towards guaranteeing that illiterate students are not continuing to pass through the system. Furthermore, no effective measures are being formulated to replace MCT, the only acceptable action possibly justifying its continued use. The only observable change noted is the placing of more and more emphasis on preparing the students for the test. Forney concludes by acknowledging the charge that high school diplomas continue to have practically no value because schools are unable to demonstrate that the holders of these diplomas even have minimum skills.

Serow (1984) further cautions that even when students initially fail a competency examination and are subsequently able to obtain a passing grade, the data do not by themselves constitute evidence of the remedial effectiveness of MCT programs. While many states point to reduced failure rates in subsequent testing attempts as evidence of remedial effectiveness, what appears to be an indication of improvement in pupils' basic skills could simply be an artifact of repeated testing. Rather than reflecting true academic increases, score gains may reflect familiarity with test items (i.e., a practice effect) or the tendency of extreme scores (in this case extreme low scores) to move toward the mean in repeated testing (i.e., regression to the mean effect).

That MCT failure rates are much higher for certain racial/ethnic minority groups than they are for White students is not surprising. The adverse impact is likely a result of prior and current discrimination, tracking, poor quality education, and other social and economic factors, over many of which neither the school nor pupil has control (Linn *et al.*, 1982). What is especially disheartening, however, is that a majority of MCT programs have chosen to emphasize the punitive aspects of testing through diploma denials, rather than maximizing their potential as diagnostic and remedial tools. The use of mandatory diploma sanctions by states having relatively large minority and low-income populations (e.g., California, New York, North Carolina, Virginia, Florida) simply confirms and perpetuates existing inequities by providing minority students with yet another educational failure (Serow, 1984).

It is not difficult to see stigmatizing tendencies within MCT — that is, the setting of minimum standards without also assuming the social responsibility for helping those who fall below them is a concern. As noted by Cohen and Haney (1980) Florida's MCT scheme, for example, gave little if any attention to the issue of remediation before the startling finding in 1977 that 40 to 50 per cent of the students failed portions of the test. MCT has also gained momentum at a time when educational funds are scarce and in light of scant evidence that it is successful in achieving any positive aims. Not only are the MCT instruments of doubtful quality, but at the moment they merely serve to identify and not remedy the failures they define (Cohen and Haney, 1980).

Given that Chicano and other minority students are the ones most affected by MCT programs, it is the responsibility of the research and policy communities to continue to raise and seek resolutions to a number of issues concerning the use of these tests. While they initially were adopted with high levels of uncertainty, we now know that MCT has delivered little reform improvements in exchange for the severe blow it has dealt students, particularly those of racial/ethnic minority background. As noted by Airasian (1987), Ellwein *et al.* (1988) and stressed throughout this chapter, the crucial issues of testing are not only technical but also involve the allocation of privileges and opportunities. If MCT instruments are to continue in use, evidence must be shown of their effectiveness in raising standards and providing equitable learning opportunities for all children.

In conclusion, MCT is a topic of serious debate. As a major arm of the accountability movement, MCT continues to grow — but not without controversy. As we have discussed, there are far more weaknesses with MCT than there are strengths. Taking all criticisms together, it is quite clear that MCT constitutes an abuse of tests with respect to a substantial number of Chicano students. On the broad issue of MCT abuse, we agree with the issues Jensen (1980) raises:

> Although the results of MCT undoubtedly highlight a serious educational problem, I cannot see MCT as in any way contributing to the solution of the problem. It appears to me to be an unnecessary stigmatizing practice, with absolutely no redeeming benefits to individual pupils or to society. I say this not because I do not believe that individual differences in scholastic attainments cannot be reliably measured, but because I seen no utility whatsoever in drawing an arbitrary, imaginary line between 'minimal competence' and 'incompetence'. 'Competence' is an entirely relative concept. What is competence for one purpose may be incompetence for another. There can be no single all-purpose demarcation between 'competence' and 'incompetence'. *The notion is psychometrically nonsensical* [italics added].... So who would possibly benefit from the extremely costly and occupationally and socially stigmatizing minimal competency testing of all graduating high school pupils? MCT is surely one of the most futile proposals to come along in public education in a decade.... The role of standardized tests ... is to monitor pupil achievement periodically so as to assure its fullest development, to whatever level that might be for a given individual. *It is an abuse of tests* [italics added] to use them to assign general labels of 'competent' or 'incompetent' (pp. 724–5).

MCT is not the only form of competency testing that adversely effects Chicanos. There is also teacher competency testing, a subject we turn to next.

Teacher Competency Testing Within the larger crisis faced by the majority of Chicano students, there is brewing a smaller, but critical situation — the low and falling proportion of Chicano teachers. To best understand this grave problem, it is helpful to place this 'crisis within a crisis' situation in a broader perspective of the minority schooling experience. In 1980, the total racial/ethnic minority elementary and secondary public school enrollment nationally was 27 per cent (Orfield, 1988). By the year 2000, the combined minority kindergarten through twelfth grade (K-12) enrollment is predicted to be 33 per cent of the total, national public school population (Smith, 1987) — a growth of 22 per cent in two decades. During the same time period, the total racial/ethnic minority teaching force in grades K-12 is projected to *decline* by 60 per cent — from 12.5 per cent in 1980 to less than 5 per cent in the year 2000 (Smith, 1987). In this section we discuss two issues pertinent to teacher competency testing and Chicanos: the Chicano teacher shortage, and technical aspects of teacher tests.

Teacher Testing and the Chicano Teacher Shortage

Orum (1986) has identified three significant factors that contribute to the small and declining percentage of the Chicano and other Latino K-12 teaching force. These influences are: (a) Latinos' low and declining college-going rate, (b) their declining preference for choosing and pursuing careers in teaching, and (c) the very high failure rate of Latinos on state-required, standardized teacher competency tests. In one of the most sustained analyses to date of the factors related to competency testing and Latino access to the teaching profession, we have identified the teacher competency test as the major obstacle in Latino teacher production (Valencia and Aburto, in press, a, b). The evidence is unequivocal: the Chicano failure rate on teacher competency tests is considerably higher compared to their White peers. For example, in 1986–87 the failure rate on the California Basic Educational Skills Test (CBEST) was 41 per cent for Chicanos (compared to only 19 per cent for White examinees (Smith, 1987). In Texas, in the period from March 1984 to June 1987, the majority (53 per cent) of Chicano students who desired to enroll in teacher education programs failed the admissions test (Pre-Professional Skills Test; PPST). The White failure rate was quite lower at 19 per cent (Smith, 1987). Based on some very recent data, the high failure rate of Chicanos on teacher tests continues unabated. In Texas, for example, nearly 3,000 teacher education program candidates took the Texas Academic Skills Program test (TASP, a recent replacement for the PPST) in September, 1989. The failure rates for Chicanos and Whites were 39 per cent and 14 per cent, respectively (Garcia, 1989).

An immediate consequence of the high fail rates of Chicano examinees on teacher tests can be seen in the growing Chicano student/Chicano teacher disparity. For example, in the mammoth Los Angeles City Unified School District, a few years ago Latino students comprised one of every two K-12 students, yet only one in ten teachers were Latinos (Crawford, 1987). On a state-wide analysis of California, Latinos fared no better. In the 1987–88 school year, Latino K-12 students were 30 per cent of the total public school enrollment in the state, but only 7 per cent of the K-12 teachers were Latino (Watson, 1988) — a Latino student/Latino teacher disparity of 77 per cent (that is, Latino teachers were underrepresented by 77 per cent). This disparity figure, by the way, is very close to the national disparity percentage (75 per cent) for Latino teachers (Valencia and Aburto, in press, a).

The predominant view is that the growing shortage of Chicano and other minority teachers contribute negatively to the education of all students in a pluralistic society (e.g., Bass de Martinez, 1988; Nava, 1985). An additional concern is the absence of teacher role models for minority youngsters, and all what that entails — for example, passing on cultural heritage, instilling minority pride, promotion of racial understanding among all students, and so on (see Valencia and Aburto, in press, a, for an extended rationale for the value of having Latino teachers).

An especially serious consequence of the Chicano teacher shortage is the severe and worsening shortage of bilingual/multicultural teachers and the resultant impact in meeting the needs of Chicano students who are limited- or non-English-speaking. For instance, in California (the state with the largest Chicano student population) it is predicted that in the year 2000, there will be about 18,000 bilingual teachers. Yet, the actual demand to meet the needs of the thousands and thousands of linguistic minority students will be about 30,000 bilingual teachers — a projected shortfall of about 12,000 teachers (Olsen, 1988). The bilingual teacher shortage is also acute in Texas, the state with the second largest Chicano student enrollment. In 1985, Nava had this to say about the severe bilingual teacher shortage in Texas with respect to meeting the needs of over 600,000 language minority students (99 per cent of them Latino, predominantly Chicano): 'An additional 20,000 bilingually certified/endorsed teachers are needed to provide adequate equal education opportunities for these linguistically and culturally different children' (p. 34). Summing matters up, Valencia and Aburto (in press, a) observe,

> ... the high failure rate of Latinos on teacher tests will continue to be a major contributing factor in blocking access to teaching careers in bilingual education — unless this obstacle to access is vigorously dealt with. In any event, the negative effects of teacher testing on the Latino community are here and now. (p. 21)

Technical Aspects of Teacher Tests

What is particularly distressing about the low and falling proportion of Chicanos and other minorities in the teaching profession is that the main barrier — teacher competency tests — are very questionable in how they are constructed and in what they purportedly predict. Valencia and Aburto's (in press, b) analysis of these issues center on two concerns: (a) the reliability and validity of existing paper-and-pencil teacher competency tests, and (b) the decision-making aspects of teacher testing — standard setting, that is how a predetermined cut score of a particular test is developed and used to decide who passes and fails.

Regarding reliability and validity of these tests, the existing psychometric evidence is weak and irrelevant. Also, research on the question of potential racial/ethnic bias on teacher tests is sorely needed. Based on their evaluation of the available literature and pertinent reviews, Valencia and Aburto (in press, b) come to this conclusion:

> ... while psychometric evidence exists on current certification examinations, none of it is strong. In the case of reliability, while internal consistency estimates are high, cut score reliability has not been thoroughly examined. Criterion-related validity is extremely weak and, as has been pointed out by Haertel (1988), much of the content validity evidence is irrelevant to the uses made of licensure tests. Although

current item bias studies and sensitivity review panels contribute to removing bias from existing examinations, no test bias research (defined as differential criterion validity for different groups) exists. (p. 21)

With respect to the cut score in standard setting on teacher tests, it has become the linchpin of the decision-making process along technical, political, and equality lines. Valencia and Aburto (in press, b) note that the cut score has two sides — one strong, one weak. One side represents omnipotence in deciding who passes and who fails a particular teacher competency test. The other side, however, is brittle and open to charges that the cut score standard cannot be defended on how it is technically decided. In that standard-setting methods use a great deal of human judgment in trying to capture and measure the notion of 'competence' during setting, there is a resultant variability in accuracy. In reference to judges being asked to speculate on the competence of unknown test-takers and to give some probability statements of item accuracy, Haertel (1988) states, 'There is simply no evidence that people can perform this kind of task with accuracy' (p. 60). As such, there are major problems in the methods and steps used to develop the linchpin of teacher testing. From a measurement and technical perspective, Haertel offers this critique of the cut score determination:

> I see absolutely no basis for asserting that the judgments of individual panelists about individual items are unbiased estimates of performance for the imagined target population of minimally competent teachers. I consider attempts to derive a meaningful cutting score by aggregating panelists' judgments to be at best a meaningless misapplication of statistical theory. (p. 61)[23]

To summarize matters, teacher competency testing as a measurement tool of the accountability movement contains some serious problems. The available reliability and validity evidence for teacher tests is weak and not particularly relevant. Regarding the development and use of cut scores, there is a growing controversy in the measurement community about their technical defensibility. Finally, there is the arbitrariness of how cut scores are set by school officials (we did not cover this issue here; see Valencia and Aburto, in press, b). As Haney and Madaus (1978) contend, the point at where the cut score on basic skills-type tests is eventually set often comes about as a compromise between apparently acceptable expectations of pass and failure rates that are politically tolerable.

With the above problems in mind, it is not difficult to conclude that the sole or near sole use of teacher competency tests to determine admissions to teacher education programs or to grant state license is a practice difficult to justify. Given all the concerns raised — coupled with the high-stakes nature of teacher testing — we argue that such testing constitutes an abusive practice. There is little doubt in the high-stakes game of teacher competency testing that a substantial number of prospective Chicano teachers are clear and big losers. Within a five-year period alone, Smith's (1987) study of nineteen states documented the alarming teacher test failure of 10,142 Latinos.[24]

How will prospective Chicano and other Latino teachers fare in the 1990s and beyond? Zapata (1988) offers this assessment of the ever-growing Latino student/Latino teacher gap, 'Projections for the future are generally bleak' (p. 20).

Such pessimism, of course, is embedded in the presumption that the status quo of teacher testing will go undisturbed as we approach the twenty-first century — a belief, we contend, that has to be challenged. We agree with Smith (1988) who voices, 'For the nation to plunge headlong into the 21st century with a public school system devoid of minority teachers is unacceptable' (p. 168). At this chapter's end we offer some research and policy ideas how educational testing and assessment might be strengthened to help promote far greater access for prospective Chicano teachers.

On Educability and Chicano Students

Up to this point in our analysis, we have concentrated on two major abusive practices of educational testing with respect to Chicano students — the adminis-tration of tests that lack good technical qualities (particularly administering instru-ments that have not been examined for potential cultural bias), and the use of high-stakes testing (i.e., relying on a single test or score) in educational decision-making. To conclude our discussion on this note would not only be premature but misleading. It is easy to 'blame the tests', and certainly there has been a great deal of test-bashing over the last two decades. The issue is not that *all* educational testing is invalid and leads to discriminatory outcomes. The real issue is to identify those tests that are psychometrically poor, biased, and used in unfair ways. In short, the issue is documentation, not imputation. Madaus (1986) puts matters in a way that make most sense to us: '. . . the decision is inherently linked to the tool. The question that we need to consider is what line of evidence needs to be gathered to counter critics who blame poor results on the use of an invalid test' (p. 12).

Indeed, what kind of evidence needs to be gathered? Should the evidence be only in the form of statistical, quantifiable (particularly psychometrically-driven) data? Certainly, scientifically grounded evidence derived from reliability, valid-ity, and bias investigations are essential. We also argue, however, for the ex-amination of extrascientific evidence, that is, understanding people's perceptions of an individual's and group's presumed ability to learn and the connection of educational testing to these perceptions.

Historically, and to some degree presently, tests have been widely used by schools in helping to decide whom — and how much — to educate. But the linkage between the measurement of scholastic aptitude of school children and their presumed capacity for scholastic learning is very shaky in its theoretical underpinnings. According to the dominant view, school learning ability is in-fluenced primarily by the child's intellectual ability. What have risen from this perspective are institutionalized different school curricular policies and practices allegedly based on the belief that students can be hierarchically arranged as 'advanced', 'average', or 'slow' learners. The belief in this 'normal' distribution of educability — or scholastic learning ability — is one of the most entrenched assumptions in education today. Such an assumption potentially carries grave implications for Chicano students. Some scholars would have us believe that educability is largely dependent on individual intellectual ability and that social, political, and economic conditions within the schools and society are largely unrelated to '. . . *why* some of our children are so much more educable than others' (Hawkins, 1984, p. 375). So, we contend, an additional fruitful way to discuss the abuses of educational testing regarding Chicano students lay in the concept of 'educability'.

Educability is not a new notion. The belief that the quality and quantity of schooling should be dictated by a person's perceived and/or measured abilities and other background characteristics can be seen in the writings of Plato (*ca.* 348 BC) over 2,000 years ago. Plato's educational philosophy emphasized the training of an élite, that is the offspring of the guardians or statesmen who directed the policy of the commonwealth were those who had opportunities to be formally educated. On the other hand, the 'common people', that is the business and working classes who were at the bottom of the Athenian caste system, would be directed to practical and vocational jobs (Ulich, 1950).

There is also longstanding evidence that the concept of educability cut deeply into racial questions. For example, Lyons' (1975) *To Wash An Aethiop White: British Ideas About Black African Educability, 1530–1960*, gives an evolutionary account of the belief that Black Africans were intellectually inferior to White Europeans, and the influence that idea had upon British attitudes and policies toward the education of Africans during the colonization of Africa. He is able to show strong connections between British attitudes about the alledged African intellectual inferiority and the implementation of school policies directed toward simpler, less demanding education for Black Africans. These practices were based on the belief that the presumed 'deficient mental capacity' of Black Africans placed severe limitations on how much they could benefit from education. Lyons underscores the point that ideas about human mental ability and educability superseded the testing movement by centuries:

> ... attitudes about human mental ability long antedate the concept of 'IQ' ... Britons began to formulate opinions about capacity for learning or educability at least as far back as the seventeenth century. In many respects the psychological testing movement of the twentieth century represents less a startlingly new departure and more a continuation of a type of investigation which had been going on for at least three centuries. (pp. xi–xii)

In more recent history, it is interesting to note that Alfred Binet (the co-developer of the first intelligence tests) used the term 'educability' in his 1910 book, *Modern Ideas About Children*, whose first chapter was entitled 'The Educability of Intelligence'. Binet, one of the early remedial educators, was a firm believer that intelligence could be 'trained'. His classes for the mentally retarded in Paris in 1909 consisted of a curriculum that emphasized the training of memory, attention, judgment, and other factors of intelligence he believed important (Kirk, 1973).

Ironically, Binet, the father of mental testing and a strong believer in the modifiability of intelligence, held a minority opinion with respect to educability. The dominant position held by early psychologists at the turn of the century was: intelligence is fixed at the point of conception; intelligence (as measured by IQ) is constant over time; intelligence is unalterable by the environment (Kirk, 1973). How this notion of educability influenced views on the relations among intelligence, school learning, and vocational guidance was exemplified by Lewis

Terman, a dominant figure during the advent of the testing movement in the United States.

> ... the grade of school work which a child is able to do depends chiefly upon the level of mental development he has attained ... *The limits of a child's educability can be fairly accurately predicted in the first school year* [italics added]. By repeated tests these limits can be determined accurately enough for all practical purposes by the end of the child's fifth or sixth school year.
>
> Vocational guidance is not, and may never be, an exact science. Nevertheless, *intelligence tests will be of value even if they tell us nothing more than that reasonable success in a given vocation is or is not compatible with the general mental ability which a particular individual possesses* ... [italics added] (Terman, 1920, p. 21)[25]

Anastasi (1984) offers some sharp insights to common misconceptions about how measured aptitude and achievement were believed to be related during the 1920s. A case in point Anastasi refers to is a popular and widely used textbook of the times — Frank N. Freeman's *Mental Tests* (1926). Anastasi comments on two unwarranted assumptions discussed in Freeman's book. First, intelligence tests gave a measure of innate capacity (i.e., not dependent on training). Second, all school achievement depended on the same, singular intellectual capacity.

Beliefs in fixed intelligence and the minimal impact of the environment on modifying intelligence were entrenched in the intelligence testing movement up to about World War II. Beginning in the 1940s and up to the present, however, mounting theory and evidence have challenged beliefs about the immutability of intelligence (Hunt, 1972). For example, the works of Hunt (1961) and Piaget (1952) represent prominent research with respect to new conceptions of intelligence and the malleability of intellectual development.

In summary, thoughts on the relation between intelligence and school learning — like the debate about the relative contributions of nature and nurture to intelligence — have hit peaks and valleys for decades. Dabney (1980) has explained the historical essence of the educability issue in this way:

> The historical emphasis upon capacity for learning has been to perceive school learning as primarily dependent upon the presumed ability of the student, rather than upon the quality of the learning environment. However, there appears to be a growing recognition that school failure and student achievement are socially determined. Even so ... such recognition has not prevented new interpretations of these failures which blame the victims and often co-exist with arguments about innate or class deficiencies. (p. 13)

In the case of Chicanos, as we moved year by year into the nascent period of the intelligence testing movement of the twentieth century, stronger and stronger connections are seen between American attitudes about alleged Chicano intellectual inferiority and the implementation of school policies directed toward simpler, less challenging education (cf. Gonzalez, 1974a). Those policies were based, in part, on the pseudo-scientific, even racist beliefs, that the presumed deficient mental capacity of Chicanos and other racial/ethnic minority groups placed severe limitations on how much they could benefit from schooling.

More recently, the issue of educability of Chicano students has recently received national exposure in the inspiring 1988 motion picture, *Stand and Deliver*, in which the character of East Los Angeles teacher Jaime Escalante was brought to life by the widely acclaimed performance of actor Edward James Olmos. In the beginning of their tough, intellectual odyssey, Escalante speaking slowly and unflinchingly warns his Chicano students: 'You already have two strikes against you. There are some people in this world who will assume that you know *less* than you do, because of your name and your complexion'. Later in the movie, Escalante's foreboding words materialize. Because his Advanced Placement Calculus students score extremely high on the calculus test, have very similar errors, and finish the test with plenty of time to spare, the Educational Testing Service suspects these irregularities to be evidence that Escalante's students cheated. In a very dramatic scene, Escalante confronts the two psychometricians from the ETS who are in charge of the investigation. Escalante demands to see the evidence of cheating, but the investigators refuse to accommodate him. Furiously, Escalante lashes out at the two men: 'These scores would have never been questioned if my kids did not have Spanish surnames and come from barrio schools! You know that!'

Let us now conclude by placing the notion of educability in its proper place regarding educational testing and the schooling of Chicano students. Granted, it is very difficult to pin down precisely an intangible idea as educability and its relationship to the education of Chicanos. We do speculate, however, that in light of our discussion thus far, the concept of educability as a value-laden, extrascientific notion has helped to mold historical and current thought on the nature of schooling for Chicanos. A major feature of this analysis is that the abusive practices of educational testing have been partially instrumental in creating school inequality. We contend that the ideological configuration of educability *also* needs to be taken into consideration why barriers to educational opportunities for Chicanos exist. The perspective that educational tests have served as oppressive, sorting tools in the schools has some value in theory building. This thesis, however, as currently structured is essentially mechanistic, deterministic, and simplistic in scope. It gives too much credit to tests as sole forgers of inequality while failing to understand that a great deal of oppression also lies in a fundamentally unequal society that views the educability of working-class and Chicano students as limited.

Improving Educational Testing for Chicanos

Now, let us shift gears and travel into a brighter territory. In this concluding section of the chapter, we offer a number of research and policy oriented ideas how educational testing — particularly test use — might be improved to help promote Chicano school success. These suggestions cover eight topics: test bias research, test translation, performance v. capability, multiple data sources, criterion-referenced testing, short-term solutions, science and ethics, and educability.

Test Bias Research

As we have seen, there are some individuals in the measurement community who contend that the question of cultural bias in educational testing — particularly intelligence tests — is a closed issue. On the contrary, we disagree. The subject of cultural bias with respect to Chicano students remains an open issue whose resolution lies in the years ahead.

We advocate continued research into the subject of cultural bias of various educational tests, hopefully with more sophisticated paradigms and designs that cover the complex relations among the testing situation, such as the actual item, the instructions, the examiner, and aspects of the examinee including at least attitudes toward the task, motivation, and the finer grained mental processes (e.g., attention, memory; information processing; cf. Scheuneman, 1984).

Test Translation

The number of non-English-speaking (NEP) and limited-English-speaking (LEP) Chicano students will continue to increase as we enter the 1990s, and their dramatic growth is predicted to continue as we move into the twenty-first century.[26] The psychoeducational assessment of these students presents a difficult problem and challenge for the field of school psychology (Figueroa, Sandoval and Merino, 1984). An especially troubling area is the lack of standardized intelligence and achievement tests that can be administered to NEP and LEP students.

A recent approach to this shortage issue has been the development of translated versions of extensively used, individually administered cognitive tests (see Valencia and Rankin, 1985, for a brief discussion). Although we applaud the development of such tests (including a variety of psychoeducational assessment tests), 'It is critical that these tests meet the minimal psychometric properties of reliability and validity and are free of bias. Thus, intensive comparative research on these translated tests and their English equivalents is strongly encouraged' (Valencia and Rankin, p. 206).

Performance v. Capability

The educational community will have taken a big step forward if those who are in the business of undertaking the individualized psychoeducational assessment of Chicano students would understand and acknowledge the critical distinction between *performance* and *capability*. What students *do* in a testing situation (their observed *performance*) is not always congruent what they *could do* (their *capability*). Factors helping to create this discrepancy during testing are referred to as situational influences. Interindividual differences, for example, in examinees' test-taking skills, motivational level, responses to time pressures of speeded tests, and so on, can and do account for variability in test performance among students (Henderson and Valencia, 1985). For Chicano and other students from culturally/

237

linguistically diverse backgrounds, their familiarity with the language and cultural content of the test (i.e., the degree of cultural loading) is a particularly important factor to consider during testing. In sum, school psychologists and others who routinely administer tests should be vigilant of the potential situational influences that may lower the test performance of Chicano students.

Multiple Data Sources

'In all ... educational decisions, test scores provide just one type of information and should always be supplemented by past records of achievement and other types of assessment data. *No major educational decision should ever be based on test scores alone*' (Gronlund, 1985, p. 480).

We daresay by now the above version of an admonishment we have been reiterating throughout should be quite familiar to the reader. We cannot repeat it enough. It should be kept in mind that testing is only one component of three types of information that can be collected during the process of psychoeducational assessment. The other two sources of diagnostic information are 'observations' and 'judgments' (Salvia and Ysseldyke, 1988). Each of the three types can be collected by a diagnostician or another person, whom Salvia and Ysseldyke refer to as 'direct information' and 'indirect information' sources, respectively.

Suffice it to say that conceptualizing psychoeducational assessment as a tripartite structure and process can greatly enhance the gathering of data, diagnosing interindividual strengths and weaknesses based on these multiple sources, and making decisions on how to improve schooling for students. The use of multiple, informed data sources (e.g., tests; parental and teacher informants; classroom observations; medical records) have the potential to provide a rich database and also to improve the credibility of the various sources (Valencia, 1982). We strongly encourage that multi-measurement efforts be utilized in the psychoeducational assessment of Chicano students.

Criterion-Referenced Testing

Although the notion of an absolute versus a relative standard of testing can be traced to about 1913, research investigations and practical applications of criterion-referenced testing did not truly begin until the early 1960s (Berk, 1984). In the simplest sense, such tests '... are designed expressly for interpreting an individual's performance in terms of what he or she can and cannot do irrespective of the performance of other students ... ' (Berk, 1984, p. 1). Or, a more precise definition: 'A criterion-referenced test is one that is deliberately constructed to yield measurements that are directly interpretable in terms of specified performance standards' (Glaser and Nitko, 1971, p. 653; cited in Nitko, 1984).

The use of tests to identify learning problems and to utilize such results to modify instruction of individual students is a very commendable educational practice. Furthermore, it is a form of testing that the schools should use more of (particularly teacher-made tests). The payoffs for school learning appear to be quite substantial. We share Nitko's (1984) call for research in criterion-referenced testing, as it seems important for the advancement of both instructional theory and practice. With respect to Chicano students, given their typically low academic performance, well-developed criterion-referenced tests that provide useful diagnostic feedback could be a bonanza in improving these students' academic progress.[27]

Short-Term Solutions

Until the time comes when broad-based, workable, nondiscriminatory testing and assessment *vis-à-vis* Chicano students materialize, it is necessary to identify and implement short-term solutions to the abuses of educational testing. As a case in point, let us take teacher competency testing.

In a recent analysis, we discuss numerous practical strategies of test reform and other means to improve access for Chicano and other Latino students who aspire to become teachers (Valencia and Aburto, in press, b). Examples include the modifing (i.e., lowering) of cut scores of existing paper-pencil teacher tests, implementing multiple data sources of assessment (including performance-based assessment), and using numerous ways to identify, recruit, test diagnostically, and offer remediation for perspective Latino teachers. Taken together, some of these suggestions require monetary commitments, others mean institutional-wide commitment, while others require convincing policymakers that such ideas will work.

Science and Ethics

We have argued repeatedly that tests do not exist in a vacuum. They have social consequences. As such, there needs to be a striving for a unified view of test validity that integrates both the *science* and the *ethics* of assessment. In a recent treatise, Messick (1989) presented a very thoughtful paper on the importance and necessity for the integration of science and ethics. In brief, Messick contends that test validity and values are one imperative, not two. Thus, test validation implicates both science and ethics. This unified conceptualization of validity, according to Messick, integrates both the scientific and ethical underpinnings of how tests are interpreted and used. The following, we believe, gets to the fundamental nature of this inherent tie between meaning and values in test validation:

> ... it is simply not the case that values are being added to validity in the unified view. Rather, values are intrinsic to the meaning and outcomes of the testing ... This makes explicit what has been latent all along, namely, that validity judgments *are* value judgments. (Messick, 1989, p. 10)

It is easy to see that in the case of Chicanos — and other groups who have at times been victimized by abusive testing practices — such a unified view of test validity, if universally accepted, would certainly help to promote nondiscriminatory assessment.

Educability

Our list of ideas for improving educational testing for Chicanos ends with a reference to a previously discussed notion — educability. The main point posited here is difficult to attain, but relatively simple to grasp. Those in the educational system (e.g., teachers, school psychologists, administrators, elected officials) who have direct and indirect contact with Chicano students must come to grips with any preconceived, negative notions they hold of the educability of Chicanos. It would be wonderful if all educators (especially kindergarten through twelfth-grade teachers) would embrace the proposition that *every Chicano student has an infinite capacity to learn*. If this fundamental premise becomes widely accepted in the schools, then it would not be so easy to explain away low test performance as simply due to a perceived learning problem inside the Chicano student or to an alledgedly impoverished home environment.

Conclusions

We leave the reader with two final observations. First, as we make the transition into a new decade and move slowly into the twenty-first century, it is likely that educational testing will increase in frequency and in its variants. In particular, the accountability movement with its emphasis on measuring 'competence' will continue to be driven by an 'If it moves, test it!' mentality. If 'the more testing the better' philosophy of the 1970s and 1980s remains unchallenged in the 1990s, then such an ideology is likely to become more deeply entrenched. On the optimistic side, a serious challenge to the status quo in educational testing can be mounted. This reform effort will likely include a number of features we have discussed throughout this analysis — for example, the development of test instruments that are nonbiased, the use of multiple data sources of assessment, and a unified conceptualization of test validity. In that '. . . testing of abilities has always been *intended* as an impartial way to perform a political function — that of determining who gets what' (Cronbach, 1984, p. 5), we urge those who are interested in Chicano students to become vigilant and active in bringing about the needed shifts in educational testing reform in the very near future.

Our second and last observation flows from the first one. Reform in educational testing with respect to Chicanos needs to be placed in the broader subject of school reform. To a very large extent, the typically low performance of Chicano students on norm-referenced achievement tests, on MCT, on school-based competency tests, and so on, is just one manifestation of the poor schooling they receive. We argue that given the massive schooling problems Chicanos face (e.g., school segregation; curriculum differentiation; disparities in school financing), their low test performance is not surprising.

To understand this linkage between low test performance and schooling inequalities, it is helpful to mention 'opportunity to learn', a construct which is receiving some attention in the measurement community (Tittle, 1982). Basically, the notion of opportunity to learn deals with the fit — or lack of fit — between the content of a test (i.e., those samples of behavior that are measured), and the formal curriculum (i.e., that which is taught and learned in school). The implication for the testing of Chicano students is clear: if Chicanos are not given the opportunity to learn the test material on which they later will be tested, then it is not surprising that their test scores will be low. As such, there are increasing instances in which claims as the following are being voiced: 'Testing children on what they have not been taught and then stigmatizing their "failure to learn" is a fundamental form of discrimination' (Hanson, Schutz, and Bailey, 1980, p. 21).

In the final analysis, it is refreshing to see a renewed interest in educational issues regarding Chicano students. Let us hope that as we begin the short trek to the next century there will be more light than heat. The abusive testing practices that we have described and discussed here can be remedied with better scientific work and ethical judgments. As reform in educational testing takes shape and evolves, it is vital to link it inextricably with broad-based school reform, lest such testing reform efforts become mere palliatives. The many issues we have outlined demand to be answered and present the research, educational, measurement, and policymaking communities with significant challenges in the years ahead.

Notes

1 The focus is on standardized (norm-referenced) tests. At the chapter's end, there will be a brief discussion of criterion-referenced tests.

2 Standardized, group-administered 'achievement' tests form a third major category of educational tests. Such tests are '... designed to measure the amount of knowledge and/or skill a person has acquired usually as a result of classroom instruction ...' (Lyman, 1986, p. 158). By far, achievement tests are the most widely administered tests in the nation's schools. It is typical for school districts to administer such tests on a routine basis (usually during the spring). The purposes of standardized, group-administered tests include the following: to determine a pupil's developmental level so instruction can be adapted to individual needs, to diagnose a pupil's strengths and weaknesses, and to provide meaningful data that can be reported to parents (Wiersma and Jurs, 1985).

Achievement tests, as described above, have been at the center of controversy *vis-à-vis* Chicano and other minority students for some time. A frequent charge is that the results from such tests are used, in part, to sort students into ability groups for instructional purposes (e.g., see Oakes, 1985). In that Chicano students typically score lower on achievement tests, it is claimed that these students often end up in the 'low-ability' groups or tracks and thus receive inferior schooling. Although there are data to support the contention that Chicano students are disproportionately overrepresented in low-ability groups and underrepresented in high-ability groups throughout schools in the southwestern United States (e.g., US Commission on Civil Rights, 1974), it is difficult to ascertain the direct link between test performance and grouping practices. That is, there are few hard data showing that teachers *actually use* the scores from standardized, group-administered achievement tests as a major mechanism in deciding who is placed in which instructional groups. In short, there is no argument that ability grouping at the elementary school level and tracking at the secondary level exist. The issue is, how are achievement test scores used (if indeed they are used) to help shape the teacher's decision-making when it comes to grouping? In the absence of empirical findings, we have elected not to focus on the potential abuses of achievement tests.

3 In some cases these functions or purposes are discussed in the context of 'assessment', that is the process of collecting test information as well as other forms of data (see, for example, Salvia and Ysseldyke, 1988).

4   Resnick's (1979) framework centers on IQ testing. Yet, we think the functions discussed by Resnick can be generalized, in part, to other types of tests (i.e., achievement and competency).

5   In that group-administered intelligence tests have been for the most part banned throughout the nation, their 'practical function in schooling' is confined to psycho-educational assessment in special education. Yet, one can argue (as does Resnick) that intelligence tests historically have played, and contemporarily play, symbolic roles. The present authors contend that most — if not all — of educational testing also has symbolic roles, as well as practical purposes as earlier described.

6   There is, however, a recent publication that challenges this thesis. In a provocative article, Rafferty (1988) contends that educational historians have greatly exaggerated the role intelligence testing played in ability grouping placements of Chicano and other minority students in the 1920s and 1930s in Los Angeles. Rafferty's case study does shed some light on the role of IQ testing — particularly how classroom teachers may or may have not used test results for grouping purposes. We think, however, that her thesis and final analysis are misleading. Rafferty criticizes other educational historians for stating that IQ tests were used *exclusively* for educational placement. Our reading of the same material (e.g., Gonzalez, 1974a) leads us to believe that such historians *did* speak to *other* discriminatory factors than just IQ testing.

7   In the early years of intelligence testing, Chicano students — as a whole — typically performed about 10–20 IQ points lower than their Anglo peers (Valencia, 1990).

8   It is important to add that there is evidence indicating a marriage between the local industry (in this case, Los Angeles) and the school. Gonzalez (1974b) states '... the vocational courses were incorporated into the curriculum on the basis of labor needs of business and industry.... Counselors were the link between the requirements of industry and the school' (p. 299; also see Gonzalez, 1974a). These self-serving connections between business and education are good examples, we believe, of the negative social consequences that intelligence testing indirectly helped promote for Chicanos.

9   Gonzalez (1974b) reports that by 1929, there were 2,500 children enrolled in eleven development centers in Los Angeles schools. Ten of the centers were in 'laboring class communities', and of the total enrollment, Chicano children were '... highly represented in five of them, constituting the entire population of one, one-third in two, and one-fourth in two others' (p. 298). The development centers were geared to training unskilled and semi-skilled workers for industry (e.g., menial occupations in restaurants, laundries, and agriculture). Gonzalez offers an interesting insight to the development center business connection by quoting a school administrator who viewed the centers as bonanzas to local industry:

> ... several employers have told us that a dull girl makes a very much better operator on a mangle than a normal girl. The job is purely routine and is irksome to persons of average intelligence, while the sub-normal seems to get actual satisfaction out of such a task. Fitting the person to the job reduces the 'turn over' in an industry and is, of course, desirable from an economic point of view. (p. 298)

10 For valuable insights to the waxing and waning of intelligence and other forms of testing over the decades, see Cronbach (1975) and Haney (1981).

11 Cultural bias is just one form of 'bias', a general term. Psychometric bias can also occur along other group memberships — e.g., social class, sex, and age.

12 The dichotomized framework of test bias and test unfairness is not without critics. For example, Hilliard (1984) states: 'The important demonstration that is needed is not an empirical demonstration of test bias, but of test utility. None of the discussion over the presence or absence of bias should be allowed to obscure that central matter' (p. 166).

13 Valencia (1988) reviewed psychometric research with respect to the McCarthy Scales of Children's Abilities (McCarthy, 1972) and Latino children (predominantly Chicano). The investigations reviewed were primarily single population studies. In such reviews, statements are drawn whether or not the observed validity and/or reliability coefficients in the individual studies are of acceptable magnitudes to conclude that the instrument has sound psychometric properties. For example, Valencia (1988) concluded:

> In the case of Puerto Rican children, the psychometric knowledge base is simply too sparse to allow any recommendation about the McCarthy's use as an assessment tool . . . For Mexican American children, our knowledge of the McCarthy's psychometric properties is considerable. Recent research has produced a good variety of studies and a solid base of knowledge from which to build. For English-speaking Mexican American children, particularly preschoolers, the McCarthy generally appears to be psychometrically sound. Based on the available evidence, it appears justified to recommend the McCarthy as an instrument in the psychoeducational assessment of these children. It is admonished that performance on the Verbal Scale, however, be interpreted with extreme caution for reasons cited earlier. (p. 100)

14 In a number of these cross-racial/ethnic studies, other minorities (e.g., Black and American Indian children) have also been subjects of WISC–R research (e.g., Oakland and Feigenbaum, 1979; Reschly and Sabers, 1979). For a review of test bias research involving Chicanos and Whites who were administered intelligence measures other than WISC–R, see Jensen (1980) and Valencia (1990).

15 In such studies, the criterion variable is typically a standardized measure of academic achievement.

16 We underscore the terms 'English-speaking' and 'native-born' as this is the context in which most conclusions about nonbiased tests are made. For example, Jensen (1980) when bringing *Bias in Mental Testing* to an end, places this caveat about the existence of bias-free mental tests:

> These conclusions are confined to native-born subpopulations within the United States, not because of any evidence on immigrant groups or on populations outside the United States that is at odds with the present conclusion, but only because of the lack of relevant studies that would warrant broader conclusion. (p. 715)

17 In the content (item) validity study (Valencia and Rankin, 1990), only very negligible amounts of bias against Chicanos were found on the Mental Processing Scale. On the other hand, pervasive item bias was observed on the Achievement Scale.

18 Incidentally, with respect to K–ABC bias research involving Chicanos, no investigations other than those by Valencia and Rankin could be located.

19 However, it is important to comment, as does Mitchell (1984) that the test publishing business is an odd mixture of positive and negative features. On one hand, there are the major, large test companies, some which employ highly capable measurement specialists. Conversely, there are the numerous publishers in the 'cottage industry' of test publishing where quality control is typically lacking.

20 In some states (e.g., Texas) variants of the school-based competency testing can also serve as MCT used for diploma award or denial (see Graves, 1989).

21 It is also common for state school officials to report test results that compare scores *across* districts. For example, in 1989 a news article in the *San Jose Mercury News* (Watson, 1989) compared CAP scores of twenty-two school districts in four counties in the peninsula location of the Bay area (California). Another example — in Texas a

1989 report by the Texas Education Agency compared TEAMS test scores for the eight largest urban school districts in the state (Effective Schools Data Resource Unit, 1989).

22 For example, in the CAPs in California,

> Schools throughout the state are ranked by two methods: one compares them to each other on a scale of one to 99. The other organizes schools into groups based on students' background information including socioeconomic level, percent of students with limited English-language ability, student mobility and percent of students from families receiving Aid to Families with Dependent Children. (Watson and Kramer, 1989, p. 2B)

It is well known that some of the variables (e.g., socioeconomic level) in the second method above (sometimes called the 'band' comparison) are often proxies for racial/ethnic backgrounds of students. In short, in light of these variables — coupled with the high degree of racial/ethnic segregation in California's schools — it is typical in the band comparison that a working-class Chicano district (or school) be compared to another 'similar' district (or school). Likewise, more affluent White districts are compared to other 'similar' districts. In the case of Chicano working-class districts, such CAP percentile rank comparisons between similar districts tend to show relatively good rankings because comparisons are made only between them and not relative to higher socioeconomic, White districts. If Chicano working-class districts were to be compared with more affluent White districts, then the *real* status (i.e., low-achieving levels) of the former would be revealed.

We have no quarrel with CAP fulfilling its public accountability function. We do, though, find the band comparison indefensible. In our opinion, CAP comparisons as such may actually be harmful to Chicano and other working-class students enrolled in predominantly minority schools. That is, by using this method of comparison, school districts may be creating false impressions of satisfactory progress for these students and their parents. Compared to students in White, middle-class and more affluent districts, working-class minority students are — in reality — performing academically at very low levels. Perhaps this illusory sense of satisfactory academic achievement helps to shape perceptions among students, parents, and educators that schooling is fine and the status quo need not be challenged. Although speculative on our part, it is likely that school-based competency testing programs that use the band comparison may become nothing more than substitutes for the educational barriers erected by past abuses in group-administered intelligence tests. (Finally, for a measurement critique of the band comparison, see Cronbach, 1984.)

23 In addition to this limitation of technical indefensibility, there are two additional criticisms of standard setting: the nonexistent evidence for the establishment of a decision rule with respect to classification errors, and the arbitrariness — or political nature — of cut score determination. In that space does not permit an overview of these two limitations, see Valencia and Aburto (in press, b) for a discussion.

24 Those candidates failing were individuals attempting to enter teacher education programs or trying to obtain a teaching credential. Smith's survey documented nearly 38,000 members of minority groups failing teacher tests. In addition to the over 10,000 Latinos who failed during the five-year period, there were: 21,515 Blacks, 1,626 Asian Americans, 716 American Indians, and 3,718 members of other minority groups. Smith admonishes that the data are likely underestimations in that some states do not disaggregate test results by racial/ethnic group and because some states were not able to provide data for all test administrations.

25 Terman's thoughts about the predictive nature of IQ indicated a rather tight fit between measured intelligence of a child and the subsequent, attained occupational status during adulthood. Note the specificity of the following:

Preliminary investigations indicate that an IQ below 70 rarely permits any-thing better than unskilled labor; that the range from 70 to 80 is preeminent-ly that of semi-skilled labor, from 80 to 100 that of the skilled or ordinary clerical worker, from 100 to 110 or 115 that of the semi-professional pur-suits; and that above all these are the grades of intelligence which permits one to enter the professions or the larger fields of business. Intelligence tests can tell us whether a child's native ability corresponds approximately to the median for: (1) the professional classes; (2) those in the semi-professional classes; (3) ordinary skilled workers; (4) the semi-skilled laborers; or (5) unskilled laborers; and *this information is of great value in planning a child's education* [italics added]. (Terman, 1920, p. 31)

26 Pallas *et al.* (1988) discuss long-term projections for the growth of children who speak a primary language other than English. In 1982, there were just under 2 million of such children. The number of NEP/LEP children is projected to triple (to about 6 million) by 2020.

27 We also highly encourage further research and classroom utilization of the principles of mastery learning theory. In brief, this instructional strategy uses tests in a monitoring fashion to guide closely a student's learning. All pupils are expected to have high mastery of material in all course objectives. In regular classroom instruction, time allotted for learning is generally held constant and classroom achievement is expected to have a wide variance. In mastery learning instruction, however, time for learning becomes variable and achievement is expected to have a restricted range (i.e., little variance, high performance) (see Gronlund, 1985).

References

AGUIRRE, A., JR. (1979a) 'Chicanos, intelligence testing, and the quality of life', *Educational Research Quarterly*, **4**, pp. 3–12.

AGUIRRE, A., JR. (1979b) 'Intelligence testing and Chicanos: A quality of life issue', *Social Problems*, **27**, pp. 186–95.

AIRASIAN, P.W. (1987) 'State-mandated testing and educational reform: Context and con-sequences', *American Journal of Education*, **95**, pp. 393–412.

AIRASIAN, P.W. (1988) 'Symbolic validation: The case of state-mandated, high stakes testing', *Educational Evaluation and Policy Analysis*, **10**, pp. 301–13.

ALLEY, G. and FOSTER, C. (1978) 'Nondiscriminatory testing of minority and exceptional children', *Focus on Exceptional Children*, **9**, pp. 1–14.

ANASTASI, A. (1984) 'Aptitude and achievement tests: The curious case of the indestructible strawperson', in B.S. PLAKE (Ed.) *Social and Technical Issues in Testing: Implications for Test Construction and Usage*, Hillsdale, NJ, Erlbaum, pp. 129–40.

ARCHER, E.L. and DRESDEN, J.H. (1987) 'A new kind of dropout. The effect of minimum competency testing on high school graduation in Texas', *Education and Urban Society*, **19**, pp. 269–79.

BARATZ, J.C. (1980) 'Policy implications of minimum competency testing', in R.M. JAEGER and C.K. TITTLE (Eds) *Minimum Competency Achievement Testing: Motives, Models, Measures and Consequences*, Berkeley, CA, McCutchan, pp. 49–68.

BASS DE MARTINEZ, B. (1988) 'Political and reform agendas' impact on the supply of Black teachers', *Journal of Teacher Education*, **39**, pp. 10–13.

BERK, R.A. (Ed.) (1982) *Handbook of Methods for Detecting Test Bias*, Baltimore, MD, Johns Hopkins University Press.

BERK, R.A. (Ed.) (1984) *A Guide to Criterion-referenced Test Construction*, Baltimore, MD, Johns Hopkins University Press.

BERSOFF, D.N. (1984) 'Social and legal influences on test development and usage', in B.S.

PLAKE (Ed.) *Social and Technical Issues in Testing: Implications for Test Construction and Usage*, Hillsdale, NJ, Erlbaum, pp. 87–109.

BIGELOW, R.A. (1982) [Review of *Bias in Mental Testing*] *Educational Researcher*, **11**, pp. 21–3.

BINET, A. (1910) *Modern Ideas about Children*, Paris, E. Flamarion.

BLUM, J. (1978) *Pseudoscience and Mental Ability: The Origins and Fallacies of the IQ Controversy*, New York, Monthly Review Press.

BOWLES, S. and GINTIS, H. (1976) *Schooling in Capitalist America: Education Reform and the Contradictions of Economic Life*, New York, Basic Books.

BOYKIN, A.W. (1986) 'The triple quandary and the schooling of Afro-American children', in U. NEISSER (Ed.) *The School Achievement of Minority Children: New Perspecives*, Hillsdale, NJ, Erlbaum, pp. 57–92.

BROWN, P.R. and HAYCOCK, K. (1985) *Excellence for Whom?* Oakland, CA, The Achievement Council.

BUROS, O.K. (1974) *Tests in Print II*, Highland Park, NJ, Gryphon Press.

BUROS, O.K. (1978) *The Eighth Mental Measurements Yearbook*, Highland Park, NJ, Gryphon Press.

CALLAHAN, R.E. (1962) *Education and the Cult of Efficiency: A Study of the Social Forces that have Shaped the Administration of the Public Schools*, Chicago, IL, University of Chicago Press.

CHRISTNER, C. and MOEDE, L.H. (1988–89) *Priority Schools: The Second Year*. Austin, TX, Department of Management Information, Office of Research and Evaluation, Austin Independent School District.

CLEARY, T.A. (1968) 'Test bias: Prediction of grades of Negro and white students in integrated colleges', *Journal of Educational Measurement*, **5**, pp. 115–124.

COHEN, D.K. and HANEY, W. (1980) 'Minimums, competency testing, and social policy', in R.M. JAEGER and C.K. TITTLE (Eds) *Minimum Competency Achievement Testing: Motives, Models, Measures and Consequences*, Berkeley, CA, McCutchan.

CRAWFORD, J. (1987) 'Bilingual education: Language, learning, and politics', *Education Week*, **6**, pp. 19–50.

CRONBACH, L.J. (1975) 'Five decades of public controversy over mental testing', *American Psychologist*, **30**, pp. 1–14.

CRONBACH, L.J. (1984) *Essentials of Psychological Testing*, 4th ed., New York, Harper and Row.

DABNEY, M.G. (1980) 'The Gifted Black Adolescent: Focus upon the Creative Positives', paper presented at the Annual International Convention of the Council for Exceptional Children, Philadelphia, PA, April (ERIC Document Reproduction Service No. ED 189 767).

DEAN, R.S. (1980) 'Factor structure of the WISC–R with Anglos and Mexican-Americans', *Journal of School Psychology*, **18**, pp. 234–9.

DEUTSCH, M., FISHMAN, J., KOGAN, L., NORTH, R. and WHITEMAN, M. (1964) 'Guidelines for testing minority group children', *The Journal of Social Issues*, **20**, pp. 127–45.

DIANA V. BOARD OF EDUCATION (1970) Civil action no. C-70-37 (N.D. Cal.).

DUNN, L.M. (1987) *Bilingual Hispanic Children on the US Mainland: A Review of Research on their Cognitive, Linguistic, and Scholastic Development*, Circle Pines, MN, American Guidance Service.

EFFECTIVE SCHOOLS DATA RESOURCE UNIT (1989) *Executive Summary for the Analysis of Texas Educational Assessment of Minimum Skills Test Results from the 1987–88 Test Cycle: A Comparison of San Antonio Independent School District with the State and Seven Urban School Districts*, Austin, TX, Texas Education Agency, Division of Accreditation.

EISSENBURG, T.E. and RUDNER, L.M. (1988) 'State testing of teachers: A summary', *Journal of Teacher Education*, **39**, pp. 21–2.

ELLWEIN, C.M., GLASS, G.V. and SMITH, M.L. (1988) 'Standard of competence: Propositions on the nature of testing reforms', *Educational Researcher*, **17**, pp. 4–9.

EYSENCK, H.J. and KAMIN, L. (1981) *The Intelligence Controversy*, New York, Wiley.

FASS, P.S. (1980) 'The IQ: A cultural and historical framework', *American Journal of Education*, **88**, pp. 431–58.

FEDERAL REGISTER (1977) 'Education of Handicapped Children', Regulations Implementing Education of All Handicapped Children Act of 1975, August, pp. 42474–518.

FIGUEROA, R.A., SANDOVAL, J. and MERINO, B. (1984) 'School psychology and limited-English-proficiency (LEP) children: New competencies', *Journal of School Psychology*, **22**, pp. 131–43.

FLYNN, J.R. (1980) *IQ and Jensen*, London, Routledge and Kegan Paul.

FORNEY, W. (1989) 'Striving for mediocrity? When MCTS become the maximum', *Thrust*, **18**, pp. 31–3.

FREEMAN, F.N. (1926) *Mental Tests: Their History, Principles, and Applications*, Boston, Houghton Mifflin.

GARCIA, G.X. (1989) '74% of graduates pass TASP tests: Failure rate among Black students 52%', *Austin American-Statesman*, November 25, pp. A1, A8.

GLASER, R. and NITKO, A.J. (1971) 'Measurement in learning and instruction', in R.L. THORNDIKE (Ed.) *Educational Measurement*, 2nd ed., Washington, DC, American Council on Education, pp. 625–70.

GONZALEZ, G.C. (1974a) 'The System of Public Education and Its Function within the Chicano Communities, 1910–1930', unpublished doctoral dissertation, University of California, Los Angeles.

GONZALEZ, G.C. (1974b) 'Racism, education, and the Mexican community in Los Angeles, 1920–1930', *Societas*, **4**, pp. 287–301.

GOULD, J. (1980) 'Jensen's last stand', *New York Review of Books*, May 1.

GRAVES, D. (1989) '10,000 students fail TEAMS twice', *Austin American-Statesman*, November 21, pp. B1, B4.

GRAVES, D. and BREAUX, B.J. (1989) '18 Austin schools receive low rating from state agency: District trustee plans to review results of minimum skills tests taken last year', *Austin American-Statesman*, September 6, p. B2.

GREEN, D.R. (1975) *What Does It Mean to Say a Test is Biased?* paper presented at the meeting of the American Educational Research Association, Washington, DC, March/April (ERIC Document Reproduction Service No. ED 106 348).

GRONLUND, N.E. (1985) *Measurement and Evaluation in Teaching*, 5th ed., New York, Macmillan.

Gutkin, T.B. and REYNOLDS, C.R. (1980) 'Factorial similarity of the WISC–R for Anglos and Chicanos referred for psychological services', *Journal of School Psychology*, **18**, pp. 34–9.

HAERTEL, E.H. (1988) 'Validity of Teacher Licensure and Teacher Education Admissions Tests', paper prepared for the National Education Association and Council of Chief State School Officers.

HANEY, W. (1981) 'Validity, vaudeville, and values: A short history of social concerns over standardized testing', *American Psychologist*, **36**, pp. 1021–34.

HANEY, W. and MADAUS, G. (1978) 'Making sense of the competency test movement', *Harvard Educational Review*, **48**, pp. 462–84.

HANSON, R.A., SCHUTZ, R.E. and BAILEY, J.D. (1980) *What Makes Achievement Tick: Investigation of Alternative Instrumentation for Instructional Program Evaluation*, Los Alamitos, CA, Southwest Regional Laboratory for Educational Research and Development.

HAWKINS, T. (1984) 'Vote of confidence. Commentary in "Backtalk"', *Phi Delta Kappan*, **65**, p. 375.

HENDERSON, R.W. and VALENCIA, R.R. (1985) 'Nondiscriminatory school psychological services: Beyond nonbiased assessment', in J.R. BERGAN (Ed.) *School Psychology in Contemporary Society*, Columbus, OH, Charles E. Merrill, pp. 340–77.

HENDRICK, I. (1977) *The Education of Non-whites in California, 1849–1979*, San Francisco, R & E Associates.

HERRON, M.D. (1980) 'Graduation requirements in the state of Oregon: A case study', in R.M. JAEGER and C.K. TITTLE (Eds) *Minimum Competency Achievement Testing: Motives, Models, Measures and Consequences*, Berkeley, CA, McCutchan, pp. 258–63.

HILLARD, A.G. (1984) 'IQ testing as the emperor's new clothes: A critique of Jensen's *Bias in Mental Testing*', in C.R. REYNOLDS and R.T. BROWN (Eds) *Perspectives on Bias in Testing*, New York, Plenum, pp. 139–69.

HUNT, J. McV. (1961) *Intelligence and Experience*, New York, Ronald Press.

HUNT, J. McV. (1972) 'The role of experience in the development of competence', in J. McV. HUNT (Ed.) *Human Intelligence*, New Brunswick, NJ, Transaction Books, pp. 30–52.

INTERNATIONAL READING ASSOCIATION (1979) 'A position on minimum competencies in reading', *Journal of Reading*, **23**, pp. 50–1.

JAEGER, R.M. (1987) 'Two decades of revolution in educational measurement!?' *Educational Measurement: Issues and Practice*, **6**, pp. 6–14.

JAEGER, R.M. and TITTLE, C.K. (Eds) (1980) *Minimum Competency Achievement Testing: Motives, Models, Measures and Consequences*, Berkeley, CA, McCutchan.

JENSEN, A.R. (1969) 'How much can we boost IQ and scholastic achievement?' *Harvard Educational Review*, **39**, pp. 1–123.

JENSEN, A.R. (1980) *Bias in Mental Testing*, New York, The Free Press.

KAMIN, L.J. (1974) *The Science and Politics of IQ*, Potomac, MD, Erlbaum.

KAUFMAN, A.S. and KAUFMAN, N.L. (1983) *Kaufman Assessment Battery for Children*, Circle Pines, MN, American Guidance Service.

KIRK, S.A. (1973) 'The education of intelligence', *Slow Learning Child*, **20**, pp. 67–83.

LAMBERT, N.M. (1981) 'Psychological evidence in *Larry P. v. Wilson Riles*: An evaluation by a witness for the defense', *American Psychologist*, **36**, pp. 937–52.

LERNER, B. (1981) 'The minimum competence testing movement: Social, scientific and legal implications', *American Psychologist*, **36**, pp. 1057–66.

LINN, R.L., MADAUS, G.F. and PEDULLA, J.J. (1982) 'Minimum competency testing: Cautions on the state of the art', *American Journal of Education*, **91**, pp. 1–35.

LYMAN, H.B. (1986) *Test Scores and What They Mean*, 4th ed., Englewood Cliffs, NJ, Prentice-Hall.

LYONS, C.H. (1975) *To Wash an Aethiop White: British Ideas about Black African Educability, 1530–1960*, New York, Teachers College Press.

McCARTHY, D. (1972) *Manual for the McCarthy Scales of Children's Abilities*, New York, Psychological Corporation.

McDILL, E.L., NATRIELLO, G. and PALLAS, A.M. (1985) 'Raising standards and retaining students: The impact of the reform recommendations on potential dropouts', *Review of Educational Research*, **55**, pp. 415–33.

MADAUS, G.F. (1986) 'Measurement specialists: Testing the faith — a reply to Mehrens', *Educational Measurement: Issues and Practices*, **5**, pp. 11–20.

MERCER, J.R. (1988) 'Ethnic differences in IQ scores: What do they mean?' (A response to Lloyd Dunn) *Hispanic Journal of Behavioral Sciences*, **10**, pp. 199–218.

MESSICK, S. (1989) 'Meaning and values in test validation: The science and ethics of assessment', *Educational Researcher*, **18**, pp. 5–11.

MIELE, F. (1979) 'Cultural bias in the WISC', *Intelligence*, **3**, pp. 149–54.

MILLIKEN, W.G. (1970) 'Making the school system accountable', *Compact*, **4**, pp. 17–18.

MITCHELL, J.V. (1984) 'Testing and the Oscar Buros lament: From knowledge to implementation to use', in B.S. PLAKE (Ed.) *Social and Technical Issues in Testing: Implications for Test Construction and Usage*, Hillsdale, NJ, Erlbaum, pp. 111–26.

NATIONAL COMMISSION ON EXCELLENCE IN EDUCATION (1983) *A Nation at Risk: The Imperatives for Educational Reform*, Washington, DC, US Government Printing Office.

NAVA, R. (1985) 'Caveat: Teacher competency tests may be hazardous to the employment of minority teachers and the education of language minority students', *Thrust*, **14**, pp. 33–4.

NITKO, A.J. (1984) 'Defining "criterion-referenced test"', in R.A. BERK (Ed.) *A Guide to Criterion-referenced Test Construction*, Baltimore, MD, Johns Hopkins University Press, pp. 8–28.

OAKES, J. (1985) *Keeping Track: How Schools Structure Inequality*, New Haven, CT, Yale University Press.

OAKLAND, T. and FEIGENBAUM, D. (1979) 'Multiple sources of test bias on the WISC–R and the Bender-Gestalt test', *Journal of Consulting and Clinical Psychology*, **47**, pp. 968–74.

OAKLAND, T. and GOLDWATER, D.L. (1979) 'Assessment and interventions for mildly retarded and learning disabled children', in G.D. PHYE and D.J. RESCHLY (Eds) *School Psychology: Perspectives and Issues*, New York, Academic Press, pp. 125–55.

OAKLAND, T. and LAOSA, L.M. (1977) 'Professional, legislative and judicial influences on psychoeducational assessment practices in schools', in T. OAKLAND (Ed.) *Psychological and Educational Assessment of Minority Children*, New York, Brunner/Mazel, pp. 21–51.

OLSEN, L. (1988) *Crossing the Schoolhouse Border: Immigrant Students and the California Public Schools*, Boston, MA, California Tomorrow.

ORFIELD, G. (1988) 'The Growth and Concentration of Hispanic Enrollment and the Future of American Education', paper presented at the National Council of La Raza Conference, Albuquerque, NM, July.

ORUM, L.S. (1986) *The Education of Hispanics: Status and Implications*, Washington, DC, National Council of La Raza.

PALLAS, A.M., NATRIELLO, G. and McDILL, E.L. (1988) 'Who falls behind: Defining the 'at-risk' population — current dimensions and future trends', paper presented at the meeting of the American Educational Research Association, New Orleans, LA, April.

PAULSON, D. and BALL, D. (1984) 'Back to basics: Minimum competency testing and its impact on minorities', *Urban Education*, **19**, pp. 5–15.

PETERSEN, N.S. and NOVICK, M.R. (1976) 'An evaluation of some models for culture-fair selection', *Journal of Educational Measurement*, **13**, pp. 3–29.

PETERSON, P.L. (1982) 'Individual differences', in H.E. MITZEL (Ed.) *Encyclopedia of Educational Research*, 5th ed., New York, McMillan, pp. 844–51.

PHILLIPS, J. (1989) 'Students' test scores improve in AISD', *Austin American-Statesman*, August 28, pp. B1, B4.

PIAGET, J. (1952) *The Origins of Intelligence in Children*, New York, W.W. Norton.

RAFFERTY, J.R. (1988) 'Missing the mark: Intelligence testing in Los Angeles public schools', *History of Education Quarterly*, **28**, pp. 73–93.

RESCHLY, D.J. (1978) 'WISC–R factor structures among Anglos, Blacks, Chicanos, and Native American Papagos', *Journal of Consulting and Clinical Psychology*, **46**, pp. 417–22.

RESCHLY, D.J. (1979) 'Nonbiased assessment', in G.D. PHYE and D.J. RESCHLY (Eds) *School Psychology: Perspectives and Issues*, New York, Academic Press, pp. 215–53.

RESCHLY, D.J. (1980) 'Assessment of exceptional individuals: Legal mandates and professional standards', in R.K. MULLIKEN and M.R. EVANS (Eds) *Assessment of Children with Low-incidence Handicaps*, Washington, DC, National Association of School Psychologists, pp. 8–23.

RESCHLY, D.J. and RESCHLY, J.E. (1979) 'Validity of WISC–R factor scores in predicting achievement and attention for four sociocultural groups', *Journal of School Psychology*, **17**, pp. 355–61.

RESCHLY, D.J. and SABERS, D. (1979) 'Analysis of test bias in four groups with the regression definition', *Journal of Educational Measurement*, **16**, pp. 1–9.

RESNICK, D.P. (1981) 'Testing in America: A supportive environment', *Phi Delta Kappan*, **62**, pp. 625–8.

RESNICK, L.B. (1979) 'The future of IQ testing in education', *Intelligence*, **3**, pp. 241–53.

REYNOLDS, C.R. (1982) 'The problem of bias in psychological assessment', in C.R.

REYNOLDS and T.B. GUTKIN (Eds) *The Handbook of School Psychology*, New York, Wiley, pp. 178–208.

REYNOLDS, C.R. (1983) 'Test bias: In God we trust; all others must have data', *Journal of Special Education*, **17**, pp. 241–60.

REYNOLDS, C.R. and BROWN, R.T. (Eds) (1984) *Perspectives on Bias in Testing*, New York, Plenum.

REYNOLDS, C.R. and GUTKIN, T.B. (1980) 'A regression analysis of test bias on the WISC–R for Anglos and Chicanos referred to psychological services', *Journal of Abnormal Child Psychology*, **8**, pp. 237–43.

SALVIA, J. and YSSELDYKE, J.E. (1988) *Assessment in Special and Remedial Education*, 4th ed., Boston, MA, Houghton Mifflin.

SANDOVAL, J. (1979) 'The WISC–R and internal evidence of test bias with minority children', *Journal of Consulting and Clinical Psychology*, **47**, pp. 919–27.

SCHEUNEMAN, J.D. (1984) 'A theoretical framework for the exploration of causes and effects of bias in testing', *Educational Psychologist*, **19**, pp. 219–25.

SEROW, R.C. (1984) 'Effects of minimum competency testing for minority students: A review of expectations and outcomes', *The Urban Review*, **16**, pp. 67–75.

SHEPARD, L.A. (1982) 'Definitions of bias', in R.A. BERK (Ed.) *Handbook of Methods for Detecting Test Bias*, Baltimore, MD, Johns Hopkins University Press, pp. 9–30.

SHEPARD, L.A. and KREITZER, A.E. (1987) 'The Texas teacher test', *Educational Researcher*, **16**, pp. 22–31.

SMITH, G.P. (1987) *The Effects of Competency Testing on the Supply of Minority Teachers*, a report prepared for the National Education Association and the Council of Chief State School Officers.

TERMAN, L.M. (1920) 'The use of intelligence tests in the grading of school children', *Journal of Educational Research*, **1**, pp. 20–32.

THORNDIKE, R.L. (1971) 'Concepts of cultural fairness', *Journal of Educational Measurement*, **8**, pp. 63–70.

THORNDIKE, R.L. and HAGEN, E. (1977) *Measurement and Evaluation in Psychology and Education*, New York, Wiley.

TITTLE, C.K. (1982) 'Use of judgmental methods in item bias studies', in R.A. BERK (Ed.) *Handbook of Methods for Detecting Test Bias*, Baltimore, MD, Johns Hopkins University Press, pp. 31–63.

TYACK, D. (1974) *The One Best System: A History of American Urban Education*, Cambridge, MA, Harvard University Press.

ULICH, R. (1950) *History of Educational Thought*, New York, American Book Co.

US COMMISSION ON CIVIL RIGHTS (1974) *Mexican American Education Study, Report 6: Toward Quality Education for Mexican Americans*, Washington, DC, Government Printing Office.

VALENCIA, R.R. (1982) 'Psychoeducational needs of minority children: The Mexican American child, a case in point', in S. HILL and B.J. BARNES (Eds) *Young Children and Their Families: Needs of the 90s*, Lexington, MA, Lexington Books, D.C. Heath, pp. 73–87.

VALENCIA, R.R. (1984) 'Concurrent validity of the Kaufman Assessment Battery for Children in a sample of Mexican American children', *Educational and Psychological Measurement*, **44**, pp. 365–72.

VALENCIA, R.R. (1985a) 'Stability of the Kaufman Assessment Battery for Children in a sample of Mexican American Children', *Journal of School Psychology*, **23**, pp. 189–93.

VALENCIA, R.R. (1985b) 'Predicting academic achievement with the Kaufman Assessment Battery for Children in Mexican American children', *Educational and Psychological Research*, **5**, pp. 11–17.

VALENCIA, R.R. (1988) 'The McCarthy Scales and Hispanic children: A review of psychometric research', *Hispanic Journal of Behavioral Sciences*, **10**, pp. 81–104.

VALENCIA, R.R. (1990) *Chicano Intellectual Performance: Theory Research, and Schooling Implications*, manuscript in progress.

VALENCIA, R.R. and ABURTO, S. (in press, a) 'Competency testing and Latino student access to the teaching profession: An overview of issues', in J. DENEEN, G.D. KELLER and R. MAGALLAN (Eds) *Assessment and Access: Hispanics in Higher Education*, Albany, NY, State University of New York Press.

VALENCIA, R.R. and ABURTO, S. (in press, b) 'Research directions and practical strategies in teacher testing and assessment: Implications for improving Latino access to teaching', in J. DENEEN, G.D. KELLER and R. MAGALLAN (Eds) *Assessment and Access: Hispanics in Higher Education* Albany, NY, State University of New York Press.

VALENCIA, R.R. and RANKIN, R.J. (1985) 'Evidence of content bias on the McCarthy Scales with Mexican American children: Implications for test translation and nonbiased assessment', *Journal of Educational Psychology*, **77**, pp. 197–207.

VALENCIA, R.R. and RANKIN, R.J. (1986) 'Factor analysis of the K–ABC for groups of Anglo and Mexican American children', *Journal of Educational Measurement*, **23**, pp. 209–19.

VALENCIA, R.R. and RANKIN, R.J. (1988) 'Evidence of bias in predictive validity on the Kaufman Assessment Battery for Children in samples of Anglo and Mexican American children', *Psychology in the Schools*, **22**, pp. 257–63.

VALENCIA, R.R. and RANKIN, R.J. (1990) 'Examination of Content Bias on the K–ABC with Anglo and Mexican American Children', manuscript submitted for publication.

WATSON, A. (1989) 'Minority teachers sought', *San Jose Mercury News*, December 31, pp. 1A, 6A.

WATSON, A. and KRAMER, P. (1989) 'CAP math scores up, reading down in state: Honig pleased to see overall trend rising', *San Jose Mercury News*, April 26, pp. 1B–2B.

WECHSLER, D. (1974) *Manual for the Wechsler Intelligence Scale for Children — Revised*, New York, Psychological Corporation.

WEINTRAUB, F.J. and ABESON, A.R. (1972) 'Appropriate education for all handicapped children: A growing issue', *Syracuse Law Review*, **23**, pp. 1037–58.

WIERSMA, W. and JURS, S.G. (1985) *Educational Measurement and Testing*, Boston, MA, Allyn and Bacon.

WILLIAMS, R. (1971) 'Abuses and misuses in testing black children', *The Counseling Psychologist*, **2**, pp. 62–73.

ZAPATA, J.T. (1988) 'Early identification and recruitment of Hispanic teacher candidates', *Journal of Teacher Education*, **39**, pp. 19–23.

Chapter 9

An Analysis of Special Education as a Response to the Diminished Academic Achievement of Chicano Students

Robert Rueda

In the face of overwhelming evidence of diminished academic achievement by Chicano and other minority students in the United States (Valencia, chapter 1, this volume), an increasing number of research and intervention efforts have begun to focus on the prevention of school failure. In much of this work, the primary unit of analysis consists of the individual student or his/her family. For example, in the literature examining the question of high school dropouts, a great deal of attention has been given to the personal attributes of students that are correlates of dropping out, such as low SES status, membership in single parent families or families in which one or both parents dropped out (Ekstrom, Goertz, Pollack and Rock, 1986; Rumberger, 1983); low self-esteem (Sewell, Palmo and Manni, 1981); a sense of helplessness (Hill, 1979); an external locus of control (Ekstrom *et al.*, 1986); and poor attendance and disciplinary problems (Peng, 1983). Indeed, it is very likely that individual and family-related factors are crucial aspects of diminished achievement for Chicano students. As an example, there is some evidence that Chicano students who remain in school receive a qualitatively richer social, emotional, and familial support from their parents to help them deal with school rules and conflicts (Delgado-Gaitan, 1988).

In contrast to approaches that examine the question of school failure from a preventative perspective and at the level of individual student attributes, the present chapter will focus on school failure *after* it is officially recognized and labeled by the educational system. In addition, the educational system itself, as opposed to the students, will be the major concern. More specifically, this chapter will explore the role of the special education system, as an institution, in dealing with low academic achievement of Chicano students once they are judged to be beyond the scope of normal educational interventions by the regular classroom teacher. Embedded within this topic are major policy and research issues that have significant implications related to attempts to study and alleviate Chicano school failure.

The major questions to be addressed in this chapter are as follows: What is the historical relationship between Chicano students and the special education system? How do Chicano students enter the special education system, and what happens to them once they do? What are the emerging issues and changes which have occurred in special education, and what potential and actual impact do these have with respect to the low achievement of Chicano students? Specifically, what does past and current research suggest about the effectiveness of the special education system (referral, assessment, and intervention)? How has this body of research influenced policy and practice? Given this body of research, what is the appropriate role of special education in addressing lowered academic achievement? What are the policy implications of a closer correspondence between research, policy, and practice? Should the special education system (and the theoretical paradigms upon which it is structured) be improved or eliminated? Using these questions as a basis, this chapter will explore the function of the special education system in dealing with diminished academic achievement with particular attention to Chicano students. Included in this review and analysis will be a discussion of suggestions for laying the foundation for closer correspondence between research, theory, policy, and practice in the 1990s and beyond in addressing this long-standing problem.

Before beginning consideration of the above issues, a brief introduction and sketch of certain pertinent features of the special education system with relevance to the present discussion will be provided.

A Brief Look at Special Education: Past and Present

There are many misconceptions among the public, and even among many educators, with respect to the nature and clientele of the special education system. For example, many equate 'handicap' with debilitating physical anomalies such as blindness, deafness, or the need for wheelchairs or other prosthetic devices. In addition, many tend to think of 'handicap' as denoting severe and profound impairments that require intensive services on a permanent, lifelong basis, with diminished access to normal life activities. Although special education began with a concern for students such as those described above, there have been radical changes as special education has passed through its relatively short period of development.

Although educational services for students with learning problems have existed for some time, it is only relatively recently that these have become mandatory and not discretionary on the part of public schools. In California, for example, students with health problems, contagious diseases, physical handicaps, mental illness, or mental retardation were excluded from public school education as a matter of policy in the 1874 revision of the school code, and this remained essentially unmodified for the next fifty years (Mercer and Rueda, unpublished manuscript). When special education was finally funded by the state, in the 1920s and the 1930s, only medically-based biological disabilities were included. The earliest special education services, then, were primarily directed at students with sensory and physical handicaps. It was not until much later, with the advent and popularization of intelligence testing, growth of the field of school psychology, and more permissive legislation, that special education services were provided to students without recognizable biologically-based learning problems.

The most pronounced development of special education was triggered by the 1975 implementation of Public Law 94-142, the Education for All Handicapped Children Act (*Federal Register*, 1977). This law, which represents the current legislative basis for special education at the federal level, was the equivalent of a civil rights law for handicapped students, with the most important provision being the guarantee of a free, appropriate public education for all handicapped students. In essence, this law formalized the right to educational services without regard to the degree of impairment. There were, however, other far-reaching provisions, including the right to due process, the right to nondiscriminatory assessment, the right to an individual education program, and an emphasis on providing services within the least restrictive environment that have played a particularly important role with respect to language minority students.

One of the major changes in special education as a result of this legislation has been in the types and numbers of students served by the system. Currently, there are nearly 4.4 million children with handicaps receiving services, representing slightly less than 11 per cent of the school-age population nationwide (US Department of Education, 1987). Yet, contrary to what many believe, mildly handicapped students make up the largest part of the special education population. These are students who fall in the categories of learning disabilities, mental retardation, serious emotional disturbance, and sometimes language impaired (MacMillan, Keogh and Jones, 1986). In a recent tabulation of national prevalence figures, Forness and Kavale (1989) document that the four categories just mentioned account for over 90 per cent of all children served in special education, while all other types of handicaps (e.g., hearing impaired) account for less than 10 per cent. Moreover, these authors indicate that the category of learning disabled now accounts for 4.7 per cent of the total school enrollment, having experienced a 135 per cent gain in the period from 1976 to 1986. In some areas such as California, the growth is even more pronounced: in this same ten-year period, the numbers of learning disabled students grew by 185 per cent, and represent 5.1 per cent of the school population (Forness and Kavale, 1989). What this means in practical terms is that the majority of students served by the special education system are primarily characterized by low academic achievement and do not fit the traditional stereotype of the more impaired student.[1] This important change has resulted in a great deal of discussion about the development and current role of special education, and will be discussed later — particularly in relation to Chicano students. As the later section exploring the relationship between Chicano students and the special education system points out, this change has profound implications for conceptualizing and dealing with the issue of diminished achievement.

In addition to the fact that most special education students are mildly handicapped, another important change is reflected in the ways that services are provided. Special education has traditionally been structured around a categorical framework. That is, in order to be served, a given student must be diagnosed as qualifying under the eligibility criteria for a specific category such as mental retardation, learning disabilities, serious emotional disturbances, blindness, deafness, etc. Once qualified for services, students are then provided educational services in a variety of settings. More severely impaired students, for example, are often instructed in special education schools, which serve this group of students exclusively. Less impaired students are usually served in self-contained classrooms, which comprise special education students but within a regular school. Finally, most mildly handicapped students are mainstreamed while receiving services on a pull-out basis. That is, they spend a variable portion of the day in the regular classroom, with the remainder of the time spent in a special education setting.

Although Mercer (1973) and others have documented the rather restrictive classroom settings into which many special education students were placed in the past, it is much more usual for most special education students to be mainstreamed for some part of the day. As an example, Forness and Kavale (1989) present data indicating that for learning disabled and speech impaired students, 77 per cent and 91 per cent respectively are in mainstream (regular classroom) settings. In addition, 34 per cent of mentally retarded students and 46 per cent of seriously emotionally disturbed students spend at least a portion of the school day in regular classrooms. It should be recalled that these four categories represent by far the largest portion of the special education population.

In sum, the numbers of students being served by the special education system is increasing. By far the largest part of this group comprise mildly handicapped students. For most of these students, there is no readily apparent biological, neurological, or other physical basis that can be directly related to impaired learning. Rather, they are characterized primarily by low academic achievement and the prospect of continued failure without special educational assistance. As will be seen, these rather significant developments with respect to the special education system are important in understanding both past and present interactions of Chicano students with this system.

Chicano Students and the Special Education System: A Brief Historical Perspective

The focus on Chicano and other minority students in special education is a relatively recent phenomenon. A significant force in bringing about increased concern with both disabilities in general — as well as on minority students within special education — was the Civil Rights Movement during the period of the 1960s. Even as early as 1968, for example, Dunn criticized the practice of placing mildly mentally retarded students in self-contained classrooms. It was not, however, until presentation of empirical data by Mercer (1973) documenting ethnic and racial overrepresentation in certain special education categories such as mental retardation that widespread attention was directed to these issues. For example, Mercer found three times more Mexican American students in self-contained classes for mildly mentally retarded students than would be expected based on their numbers in the general population of the community studied.

In addition to documenting ethnic imbalances in placement distributions, Mercer went a step further and argued that prevailing assessment practices were largely responsible for the overrepresentation that existed. Then, as now, the initial entry point for special education placement is based on teacher referral due to lowered academic achievement, or other factors that might interfere with learning such as behavioral problems or speech and language difficulties. However, placement is not formalized until individual psychological assessment is completed, most often by a school psychologist in conjunction with other ancillary personnel. Mercer's data (and subsequent research by other investigators) suggested that students were often inappropriately tested in English in spite of limited-English proficiency, administered poorly translated or spontaneously translated tests, compared to inappropriate norm groups, etc. In short, the initial entry gate into special education placement was (and continues to be) through the use of standardized tests in individual psychological assessment.

As a result of Mercer's investigation, intensified scrutiny was given to existing testing and placement practices for Chicano and other minority students. One consequence of this work — namely a series of court suits and other legal initiatives challenging public school policies, in particular those related to assessment and placement — has been perhaps the most visible and publicized aspect of Chicano students' participation within special education.

Two of the most far-reaching cases dealing specifically with the evaluation and placement of Chicano and other minority students were *Diana v. California State Board of Education* (1970) and *Larry P. v. Riles* (1979). The prime issue in the *Diana* case was the appropriateness of assessment conducted in a student's native language, while the content of intelligence tests with respect to cultural bias was a major issue in the *Larry P.* case. Although a more extensive discussion of these cases is beyond the scope of this chapter, examination of these and a myriad of other significant court suits on behalf of Chicano (as well as American Indian, Asian and Black) students suggests that both prevailing assessment procedures as well as the assessment instruments themselves (specifically the intelligence test) have been justifiably singled out as largely responsible for unrepresentative special education placement patterns, particularly in classes for the mildly mentally retarded. (More extensive discussion of these and related cases, as well as analysis of their impact on educational practice is found in Cummins, 1984; and Valencia and Aburto, this volume.)

One of the more widely disputed issues has been overrepresentation of minority students in EMR (educable mentally retarded) classes. An early impetus for this concern was publication of data by Mercer (1973) which demonstrated that while Chicano students made up 9.5 per cent of the population in the small California community which she studied, they comprised 32 per cent of those labeled and placed in classes for the mentally retarded. Significantly, because there was little of the due process and procedural protections that currently exist, oftentimes parents and community members were unaware that a given student had been tested, labeled, and placed. Moreover, 62 per cent of those labeled mentally retarded exhibited no 'symptoms' of deficiency except the low IQ score.

Although Mercer's (1973) study focused a great deal of attention on this problem, later studies suggested that in spite of increased awareness of possible abuses, problems continued to exist. For example, Finn (1982) conducted a study using the 1978 OCR (Office of Civil Rights) data, and examined various indices of disproportion. In addition, data were examined across and within geographical location, by size of school district, size of the Hispanic population, and availability of bilingual educational options. The results of this analysis suggested that minority students were overrepresented in classes for the mentally retarded (EMR and TMR), as well as in classes for the emotionally disturbed. Importantly, there were effects due to district size and size of minority enrollment. Moreover, the highest EMR disproportions for Hispanic students occurred where there were small or nonexistent bilingual programs.

Forness and Kavale (1989) point out that nationally, the EMR category has experienced a 29 per cent loss from 1976–77 to 1985–86, and accounts currently for only approximately 1.7 per cent of the school population. However, recent data suggests that overrepresentation in this category continues to be a problem for Chicano and other Hispanic students, although there is wide variation among individual states and school districts (Finn, 1982; Heller, Holtzman and Messick, 1982; Twomey, Gallegos, Andersen, Williamson and Williamson, 1980).

Interestingly, while overrepresentation of minority students in EMR placements may have decreased, there is some evidence that the numbers of minority learning disabled students is increasing (Ortiz and Yates, 1983; Tucker, 1980). For example, Ortiz and Yates (1983, 1984) have reported data from Texas suggesting that Chicano students are dramatically overrepresented in programs for the learning disabled. The 2 per cent estimated incidence figure turned out in actuality to be 6.3 per cent exceeding the expected incidence by 2.15 per cent. In California, Rueda, Cardoza, Mercer and Carpenter (1984) reported data from several school districts of a sample of approximately 1,300 Hispanic students referred for special education placement over the 1984 school year. It was found that the most frequent diagnostic classifications were learning disabilities (63 per cent of the sample) and language impairments (20 per cent of the sample). Although the purpose of the study was not to examine overrepresentation *per se*, it did reveal marked changes in placement patterns in the direction of dramatic increases in learning disabilities and a concomitant decrease in EMR placements.

Although the question of overrepresentation of Chicano students has been among the most widely publicized issues, the participation of minority students in special education has raised a host of other controversies as well. One of the major areas of contention is focused on the conceptualization, measurement, and interpretation of IQ and differences in IQ as a function of SES, race, ethnicity, or language background. It is clear that the notion of IQ is central in the conceptualization and definition of the categories that have been the most problematic with respect to overrepresentation of Chicano students, specifically learning disabilities and mental retardation. Moreover, this is almost exclusively operationalized in the form of an individual IQ test.

In spite of the relatively major role played by IQ in special education practice, a great deal of criticism has been leveled at the viability of IQ as a measurement concept (Mercer, 1988). For example, there exists a great deal of controversy regarding the appropriate interpretation and use of IQ tests with various ethnic and linguistic minority groups. Some have argued that the predictability of IQ scores with respect to school achievement may be a function of bias both in the predictor (IQ score) and the criterion (most often standardized academic achievement tests or even school itself). In addition, Mercer and Lewis (1979) and others have argued that some of the major assumptions of IQ tests, for instance that students from different groups have had equal exposure to the knowledge and experiences reflected in the test, are invalid, and further, the real issues are sociopolitical rather than psychological.

Perhaps the debate over the IQ issue would not be so spirited were it not for the fact that there are important social and educational consequences that result from the use of IQ and other standardized assessment measures (see Valencia and Aburto, this volume). For Chicano students, the most obvious concern from a historical perspective has been the stigmatizing or restrictive nature of some special education placements (Heller, Holtzman and Messick, 1982), leading many researchers and practitioners to address the problem of differentiating language and culture from handicap (Polyzoi, Holtzman and Ortiz, 1987) through the use of more comprehensive, culturally sensitive procedures.

Understandably, these problems have generated a wide variety of proposed solutions, from closer monitoring of schools in complying with current law, to banning, adapting, or modifying assessment instruments, to the adaptation of more culturally and linguistically sensitive practices. As one illustration, for example, Ortiz and Maldonado-Colon (1986) and Ortiz and Garcia (1988) have described a comprehensive prereferral process aimed at reducing inappropriate referrals of Hispanic and other minority students. These authors distinguish between three types of learning problems. These include problems that occur when students are in classroom environments that do not accommodate their individual differences or learning styles, problems due to mild to moderate achievement difficulties which are not the result of handicapping conditions, and problems due to major disorders which interfere with the teaching-learning process. These authors argue that only the last group of students fall into the appropriate realm of special education education, while students in the first two groups more likely represent the results of faulty or inappropriate instructional histories. The model presented by these authors is reflected in a sequential set of questions that must be addressed before a referral to special education can be appropriate, and can be seen as a representative example of attempts to reduce inappropriate referrals and separate linguistic and cultural factors from handicapping conditions.

More recently, others have begun to focus on instructional variables such as the use of native language instruction (Ortiz, 1984), and the use of appropriate instructional models to account for language and cultural differences (Cummins, 1984). For example, Cummins has discussed the notion of students who represent 'curriculum casualties', that is, those students whose apparent learning handicaps are 'pedagogically induced'. The low level, remedial, decontextualized skill-oriented approaches often provided to special education students characterize a 'transmission' oriented approach, in which knowledge is seen as a commodity to be transferred from the teacher to the student. In contrast, 'reciprocal interaction' approaches see knowledge as something to be personally constructed by each student based on interactions with persons and materials (Cummins, 1984; Tharp and Gallimore, 1988).

In summary, it can be argued that linguistic and cultural diversity have not been well tolerated within the special education system. The relationship between Chicano students and the special education system has often been adversarial and plagued at times by inappropriate assessment practices, stigmatizing and restrictive placements, English-only instructional practices, and resulting legal controversy. Perhaps because these issues have been the center of legal controversy, much of the work on Chicano students in special education has focused on assessment — specifically claims of bias in IQ tests — and resulting restrictive and stigmatizing placements. There appear, however, to be problems not only in the area of assessment, but in referral, diagnostic, and instructional practices as well. In spite of these problems, a great deal of change has taken place through litigation and legal mandate. For example, the data presented by Forness and Kavale (1989) shows that most mildly handicapped students now spend a significant amount of time in the regular classroom as opposed to self-contained settings. However, most efforts directed at reform have been externally imposed on the educational system. Moreover, in a recent critical analysis, Rueda (1989) has argued that to date, almost all reform efforts have focused on proposing 'fixes' for elements of the current system which are perceived as problematic, while basically leaving intact the institutional structure and model upon which these are based. The implications of this for Chicano students will be explored in the following sections.

The Role of Special Education in Addressing Lowered Academic Achievement

What is the proper role of the special education system in addressing poor academic achievement among Chicano and other minority students? Certainly special education cannot be said to be a causal factor, in that academic problems do not reach the special education system until they are severe enough such that they cannot be handled through 'normal' educational channels. Yet, although it is not preventative, in the sense that Head Start and other early intervention programs are, and was not initially developed with a primary concern with minority students, it does represent one of the major educational structures set up to deal with diminished achievement. That is, it has become a major institutional response to lowered minority academic achievement once it is formally declared to be beyond 'normal' intervention channels in the regular classroom. Theoretically, one of the major goals is to provide assistance in order to facilitate re-entry and successful future outcomes in the regular classroom, and therefore special education could play a potentially critical role in addressing low achievement. Examination of the current status of the special education system, however, suggests that there are major problems regarding the delivery of services even when linguistic and cultural diversity are not factors. The literature suggests that currently, there are many questions relating to the efficacy of special education as currently structured (Gerber and Semmel, 1984; Ysseldyke, 1983; Will, 1986), especially for students who are mildly handicapped. As will be argued later in the chapter, the participation of Chicano students in the special education system cannot be considered apart from issues and problems which affect the field as a whole. Moreover, these issues have the potential for significantly impacting future research, policy, and practice agendas with respect to Chicano students.

What are these issues and problems, and what are the reasons for dissatisfaction with the current system? It appears that there are significant problems in the referral, assessment, and instructional areas. Rueda (1989) has provided an extensive review and summary of this literature, and these areas will be briefly discussed in the following sections.

The Referral Process

One of the first steps in a child's contact with the special education often begins with a referral by the regular classroom teacher. There is some evidence that teachers may sometimes evaluate a student's competence on the basis of a variety of factors other than ability, such as race, sex, socioeconomic status, or language and cultural characteristics (Jackson and Cosca, 1974; Rist, 1970, 1982; Ysseldyke, Algozzine, Richey and Graden, 1982). These considerations would tend to place Chicano students particularly at risk for inappropriate referrals.

In addition, there is literature which suggests that the decision to refer a particular child for special education is heavily influenced by situational and contextual factors as much as by within-child characteristics, and is characterized by a great deal of 'social negotiation' (Mehan, Hertweck and Miehls, 1986). Finally, even recent developments such as the use of prereferral intervention systems, although promising with respect to reducing inappropriate referrals, still accept the basic notion of 'pure' or 'true' disability independent of the context or means of assessment, in spite of convincing arguments to the contrary (LCHC, 1982).

Assessment

As pointed out earlier, problems related to assessment have been particularly troublesome given the cultural and linguistic characteristics of Chicano students. However, it is increasingly clear that there are rather severe limitations in the ability to reliably and validly differentially diagnose mildly handicapped students who are mainly characterized by poor academic achievement (Ysseldyke *et al.*, 1982), even where cultural and linguistic factors are not involved. At least part of this is due to technical inadequacy of current assessment tools (Coles, 1978; Forness and Kavale, 1989; Shepard and Smith, 1981). In addition, the cost of assessment and the lack of immediate applicability of psychometric, norm-referenced test results to classroom instruction have been criticized as well (Shepard and Smith, 1981).

Instruction

Perhaps because of its medically-based roots, special education traditionally has not aligned itself closely with other school programs — such as bilingual education — that serve language minority students. There has been little if any reciprocal interaction between the bilingual and special education systems. Moreover, there has been little if any concern for language and cultural factors in special education instructional approaches. Although special education placements may have become less stigmatizing and less restrictive than in the past, the dominant instructional approach continues to be based on a 'bottom up' conceptualization of the learning process, which is most often operationalized in English only, drill and practice repetitive workbook activities of a remedial nature (Cummins, 1984, 1986; Flores, Rueda and Porter, 1986). Put simply, a 'bottom-up' approach suggests that complex domains of learning can be hierarchically ordered, and that 'lower' skills need to be mastered as prerequisites to more complex or advanced skills. In reading, for example, such an approach might lead to an emphasis on mastery of sounds and letters of the alphabet before engaging in 'real' reading or writing. Cummins (1986) has termed this instructional approach as 'transmission oriented' as opposed to 'reciprocal interaction oriented'.

One of the primary problems with this system as currently structured, it is proposed here, is the theoretical model upon which it is based. In reality, the model that most often guides contemporary policy and therefore practice in special education is a combination of the medical–diagnostic model adapted from medical roots, and the statistical psychometric model developed in psychology. Rather than one replacing the other, however, the statistical psychometric model has been superimposed on the medical diagnostic model, resulting in a psycho-medical model with elements of both (Mercer, 1988). This psychomedical model is characterized by an emphasis on eligibility criteria, diagnostic psychometric assessment, classification, and intelligence testing (Mercer, 1973, 1988; Mercer and Lewis, 1979). Moreover, this model is so entrenched, for example, that given current definitions, the categories of learning disabilities and mental retardation could not exist without the conceptual notion of intelligence as distinct from achievement.

The rigidity which is inherent in this framework has particularly negative consequences in instances where diminished achievement cannot be fit into one of the predefined disability areas. Under the current system, for example, unless a student is certified as eligible for a given diagnostic category within state, federal, or local criteria, then no services can be provided, even where academic difficulties are well documented and where academic assistance would be beneficial. Perhaps this would not be so problematic in the absence of the problems related to referral, assessment, and placement alluded to earlier. Yet, as currently implemented, schools sometimes find themselves in the position of having to refer a child for special education and a possible label as the only means of securing additional resources for assistance.

Conclusions and Summary

When the entire context of special education is taken into account, many of the problems that have normally been associated with Chicano students in special education exist even when ethnic and language differences are not at issue. The preceding problems with the special education system referred to can be traced, at least in part, to the continued use of a psychomedical model, because past as well as current practice is still heavily influenced by this well-entrenched paradigm (Mercer, 1988; Rueda, 1989). The conclusion from these observations is that the influence of this model is a primary factor in limiting the usefulness of special education not only for Chicano students but for all students as well. At the policy level, this suggests two things. First, efforts to address the inadequacies of the special education system for Chicano students independently of the inadequacies of the special education system itself may be misguided. As a prime example, developing a better intelligence test for Chicano students without examining the meaning and uses of intelligence testing in the first place would likely do little in terms of long-term solutions. Secondly, the role of special education in dealing with lowered levels of achievement is sorely in need of reconceptualization, beginning with the basic model that guides it. If the system is flawed, what should replace it?

Policy Issues and Implications

As this volume and other authors document (e.g., Arias, 1986; McCarty and Carrera, 1988), the issue of low academic achievement by Chicano and other minority students is a serious educational concern. As these data on academic achievement demonstrate, it would be ludicrous to suggest that Chicano students do not exhibit academic problems, or that the problems that do exist are solely the result of the inappropriate use of the psychomedical model. Moreover, given that diminished academic achievement will not disappear any time soon, and *preventative* efforts have not been entirely successful up to this point in time, what is the best educational response that schools can provide?

As suggested earlier, there are many indications that the current special education system has provided less than optimal means of addressing the educational needs of Chicano students who truly demonstrate learning problems in public schools. Although part of this negative perception can be traced to stigma and to the range of factors discussed earlier, the more fundametal problem can be traced to the continued use of an inappropriate paradigm to guide practice and research. In essence, the current model could be likened to the following analogy. It is as if a sinner who wanted to be forgiven had to first go through a long, complicated, and expensive pre-confessional ritual with a highly trained church official other than a priest in order to be declared a sinner. Then and only then could this sinner be allowed to see a priest to be forgiven. The label of sinner would do little to inform the sinner of his own status, in that he/she knew of the sinful behavior from the beginning. Moreover, the label of sinner would do little to inform the priest of the nature of the sinful behavior, the level of penance to recommend, or the nature of the counseling to provide to the individual sinner. If it later came to light that the long and complex process by which one is declared a sinner was largely inaccurate and highly variable, the question would be raised regarding the necessity of keeping this intermediate step between the sinful behavior and the confessional.

In a like fashion, the current eligibility determination procedures embedded in special education policy and legislation, including the long and expensive assessment process conducted by school psychologists, are equivalent to the 'pre-confessional' ritual described above. Moreover, the resulting special education eligibility determination and diagnostic categorization tend to confirm what was already known earlier by the teacher, parents, and the student him/herself at the point of referral, namely that low achievement exists and is a problem. Yet, the determination of eligibility does little in terms of informing the teacher about specific instructional interventions. As a final point of comparison in the analogy, the definitional and measurement problems associated with the special education eligibility determination process should lead to a critical review of current policy and practice especially in light of current research.

Although the current model may have been appropriate to special education during its early development, when severe handicaps were the exclusive or primary domain, by far the largest consumers of special education services at the present time are mildly handicapped students, who are chiefly distinguished by low academic achievement and not organic or biological problems. Moreover, not only are mild handicaps now the major focus of special education practice, but culture and linguistic variety are the norm and not the exception in many public school settings and thus must be directly addressed.

Given these observations, the extension and continued use of the current model is increasingly problematic. Dissatisfaction both from within and without the system has led to a growing movement for reform (Reynolds, Wang and Walberg, 1987). Some efforts at reform, however, such as the use of school-level, informal prereferral teams or consultation models of special education service delivery have not gained wide acceptance (Herron and Harris, 1987; Idol, Paolucci-Whitcomb and Nevin, 1986). A likely reason for this is that the attempt has been made to superimpose these potentially valuable reforms onto the existing system on an extension rather than a replacement basis. As a result, these discretionary practices are rarely allocated resources (Gerber, 1984).

What is the nature of other possibly more extensive reforms, and what are policy implications of these reforms for Chicano students? One widely discussed alternative is the proposed merger between special and regualr education (Stainback and Stainback, 1984; Will, 1986). Although this move to integrate special and regular education has largely been developed outside the context of cultural and linguistic diversity, presumably it could be extended to include a merger of special, regular, and bilingual education as well. Clearly, from a policy perspective, a move to eliminate or reconfigure some aspects of the structure or of specific activities (but not the function) of special education would not be acceptable in the absence of a redistribution of at least an equivalent amount of resources to deal with poor achievement in new and innovative ways. For example, there presently exists a rather formidable arsenal of educational tools from behavioral technology (Howell and Morehead, 1987; White, 1986), to cognitive psychology (Gelzheiser and Shepherd, 1986), to more holistic and contextually sensitive instructional models (Cummins, 1989; Diaz, Moll and Mehan, 1986; Poplin, 1988b; Tharp and Gallimore, 1988). Although low achievement should not be conceptualized entirely as a within-child phenomenon, independent of social and institutional factors (Ogbu and Matute-Bianchi, 1986), the coupling of existing technology with innovative service delivery models offers a great deal of promise.

As one example, Cummins (1989) has reviewed various instructional models and projects that have been especially successful with bilingual students. In the Descubrimiento/Finding Out Program, students are assisted in the acquisition of math and science concepts (as well as in the development of language proficiency) through the active use of oral and written language within the context of small group cooperative activities and critical inquiry (DeAvila, Cohen and Intilli, 1981). In the Pajaro Valley Family Literacy project, rural, poorly educated Spanish-speaking parents have been provided the opportunity to meet and have dialogue on a regular basis about children's literature and to read stories and poems written both by their children and, eventually themselves. The results of participation in this project have included not only increased literacy development on the part of the parents, but have also included turning parents into effective sources of literacy development and experiences for their children (Ada, 1988a, b). Finally, The 'Orillas' project is an example of an effective vehicle for the promotion of English and Spanish literacy through the sharing of elementary school children's writings in both languages across widely scattered geographical regions such as Puerto Rico, Connecticut, San Diego, and Mexico (Sayers, 1986a, 1986b, 1988). In each case, there is evidence that these enriching educational environments have had positive benefits with Chicano students who are likely to experience school failure. Conversely, there is little in the literature to suggest that these types of enriching environments would be any less effective with most special education students who have already been placed.

As previously noted, the current system is dependent on the use of eligibility criteria and categorical labels for the distribution of resources. Given a reconfiguration of the system, how would resources be distributed in an equitable fashion? Specifically, one argument against the elimination of the burdensome eligibility and classification process as it currently exists is that it provides an orderly and systematic way of distributing financial and other resources, for example, the allocation of special education supplementary funds to local school districts based on the number of eligible students identified. This question entails major policy considerations, given that the distribution of educational resources across ethnic, social class, and gender lines has been a significant problem in the United States for some time. If the number of students formally certified as eligible for special education services were not used to distribute supplementary resources to school districts, what would replace it?

One possible alternative would be to eliminate the concept of eligibility in the formal sense as currently existing. In such a system, any time a student experienced difficulty in a given classroom, this would constitute a 'call for assistance' or need for service (Gerber and Semmel, 1984). This would entail reconceptualizing the concepts of low achievement and learning handicaps from within-child, stable characteristics to variable attributes that need to be evaluated from the perspective of an individual child with a specific teacher in a specific classroom. In addition, it might also necessitate massive shifting of resources from the current emphasis on testing for eligibility to short-term interventions with continuous monitoring of academic outcomes. For Chicano students, this would mean greater integration between bilingual and special education specialists, as opposed to the current situation where services in one specialty effectively remove the student from consideration for services in the other. One consequence of such changes, of course, would be the social changes which could be expected as a result of redefining or even eliminating the roles of the myriad of specialists who have developed around various disability categories, and the ways in which they interact with bilingual specialists. (For further discussion of the economic considerations associated with special education funding practices, refer to Hartmam, 1980, and Magnetti, 1982.)

At a more fundamental level, a major policy issue concerns the question of what should replace the predominant psychomedical model as a basis for educational policy and classroom practice. One answer might be found in current discussions about new paradigms upon which to reconceptualize special education. Several authors have argued for a paradigmatic shift (Mercer, 1988; Poplin, 1988a; Skrtic, 1988), suggesting that it has not been profitable to view diminished achievement from under a psychometric lens. These authors have criticized traditional approaches for, among other things, being reductionistic and obsessively focused on low achievement as primarily an individual failure. In special education, this has translated into a focus on quantifying discrete learner characteristics through standardized test batteries, with particularly negative consequences for Chicano students (see Valencia and Aburto, this volume).

As an example of an alternative, Poplin (1988b), for instance, has presented the rudiments of a holistic/constructivist paradigm of teaching and learning that emphasizes learning as the construction of meaning in authentic activities. One likely benefit of such a model is that it is much better able to take into account cultural and linguistic diversity on the part of individual students, given the focus on the personalization of knowledge acquisition. In a similar vein, other theorists have begun to call for more comprehensive perspectives on learning and development (Tharp and Gallimore, 1988) and learning problems in particular (Coles, 1987). That is, given a biomedical handicap such as neurological dysfunction or individual differences in learning, how did these develop over time? What has been the impact of the 'ecocultural niche' in mediating these differences (for example, family interactional patterns, language characteristics, etc.)? How are the child's abilities mediated by institutional arrangements? In terms of a research agenda, little is known about how learning difficulties are created by or mediated by out-of-school factors, and how in-school and out-of-school experiences can be coordinated to provide the most effective learning environments.

Although there is current debate about the exact role of cultural and linguistic 'mismatch' in achievement (Jacob and Jordan, 1987), there is evidence that when culture and language are taken into account, achievement can be raised. Some of the research results with bilingual students that support this notion are noted in Merino's chapter (this volume) on effective instructional programs. Interestingly, these findings do not appear to be confined to Chicano students. By way of example, one successful model that accommodates cultural differences, although outside of special education, is the Hawaiian-based KEEP work on reading comprehension (Tharp and Gallimore, 1988) with Native Hawaiian students.[2] Using the notion of 'assisted performance', the focus on higher-order cognitive abilities is integrated with culturally sensitive instruction, and impressive gains in academic achievement have been demonstrated. In contrast, special education has been dominated by a paradigm that concentrates on within-child dysfunction to the exclusion of cultural and linguistic factors. In attempting to directly translate the findings of these studies for Chicano students, however, it must be cautioned that in the case of the KEEP program and the other studies mentioned, a great deal of time and effort was spent on out-of-school observations before classroom modifications of culturally relevant instruction were attempted. What is missing in the case of Chicano students are data on how teaching and learning are organized in everyday settings as the basis for designing culturally relevant programs, and how learning handicaps may or may not interact with teaching and learning in these same settings. Currently, virtually all that is known about cognitive development and functioning for mildly handicapped students, Hispanic or otherwise, is derived from laboratory tasks or standardized tests (Rueda, Ruiz and Figueroa, 1989). A major research agenda, therefore, with respect to the school failure of Chicano students, would consist of attempting to examine teaching and learning activities in real world settings, linking in-school and out-of-school learning and knowledge in a closer fashion, and exploring the effectiveness of alternative theoretical and paradigmatic models in conceptualizing and designing interventions for learning handicaps.

Summary

In the preceding pages, it has been suggested that although the special education system has become one of the central institutional mechanisms for addressing school failure and low achievement, it is a system unresponsive to the needs of Chicano students. Further, in spite of the severity of the problems of school failure and lowered achievement levels for Chicano students, interactions with the special education system have largely been characterized by adversity and apprehension. Lastly, it was argued that the potential of the special education system for addressing this issue is hindered by continued reliance on a particular paradigmatic model. This model, which has its roots in the medical treatment of severe and often organic disabilities, continues to exert its influence in spite of the fact that the population served now consists of mainly children with mild learning problems without a medical basis, and increasingly children with diverse cultural and linguistic backgrounds. This prevailing model tends to view culture as a minor factor in learning, low achievement as strictly a child-centered phenomenon, and emphasizes the classificatory uses of assessment of discrete individual abilities with only minimal applicability to meaningful classroom practice. Although these factors have become problematic for all students served by the special education system, it has had particularly negative effects on Chicano students — sadly in the face of increasing school failure.

Although the research reviewed here suggests that there are problems with the current system, there are a number of research areas that could be fruitfully explored in addressing this problem. For example, although paradigmatic shifts such as those alluded to earlier appear promising, they do not have sufficient empirical backing to warrant wholesale adoption. What are the instructional implications of conceptualizing low achievement from a broader perspective — that is, to take into account out-of-school knowledge, present and past teaching and learning practices, and familial and cultural interactional features? How can alternative paradigms contribute to the development of more useful assessment practices? What are the effects, at the institutional level, of reconfiguring special education to coordinate with other facets of the educational system that deal with the diminished achievement and school failure of Chicano students? If categorical labeling were to be eliminated as a feature of the current system, how would funding resources be fairly and appropriately distributed, especially given the unequal distribution of academic success across ethnic, SES, and geographic boundaries?

It is clear that special education has not lived up to its potential to deal with lowered levels of Chicano academic achievement. In essence, current policy in this area is not aligned with available research. The system has operated as an isolated system, often negatively perceived, and only recently has it begun to deal with issues of language and cultural diversity. Because of dissatisfaction with the current system and in light of the students currently being served, there is increased movement toward reconceptualizing the guiding assumptions, structure, and even the function of special education. The eventual resolution of the policy questions raised as a result of these developments will play a significant part in the role that public schools play with respect to Chicano academic outcomes. Moreover, these developments have the potential to transform special education from a negatively perceived, stigmatizing, and reactive system to one that is proactive, easily accessible, and successful in impacting the long term academic success of Chicano students in public schools.

Notes

1 There is still a great deal of controversy regarding the role of neurological and other biological factors in mildly handicapping conditions. This is especially true in the case of learning disabilities. See Coles, (1987), for a review of the evidence and controversy related to neurological factors in learning disabilities.

2 An important part of this program has been the conceptualization of instruction and assessment as intricately linked. Consistent with recent developments in cognitive psychology, this work suggests that assessment should be 'on-line', or 'dynamic' (Palinscar and Brown, 1984), contrasting with the state of current practice, that tends to focus on quantification of discrete skills and abilities on static tests.

References

ADA, A.F. (1988a) 'Creative reading: A relevant methodology for language minority children', in L.M. MALAVE (Ed.) *NABE '87, Theory, Research and Application: Selected Papers*, Buffalo, NY, State University of New York Press, pp. 223–38.

ADA, A.F. (1988b) 'The Pajaro Valley experience: Working with Spanish-speaking parents to develop children's reading and writing skills in the home through the use of children's literature', in T. SKUTNABB-KANGAS and J. CUMMINS (Eds) *Minority Education: From Shame to Struggle*, Clevedon, UK, Multilingual Matters, pp. 223–38.

ARIAS, M.B. (1986) 'The context of education for Hispanic students: An overview', *American Journal of Education*, **95**, pp. 26–57.

COLES, G.S. (1978) 'The learning-disabilities test battery: Empirical and social issues', *Harvard Educational Review*, **48**, pp. 313–40.

COLES, G.S. (1987) *The Learning Mystique: A Critical Look at 'Learning Disabilities'*, New York, Pantheon Books.

CUMMINS, J. (1984) *Bilingualism and Special Education: Issues in Assessment and Pedagogy*, San Diego, CA, College Hill Press.

CUMMINS, J. (1986) 'Empowering minority students: A framework for intervention', *Harvard Educational Review*, **56**, pp. 18–36.

CUMMINS, J. (1989) *Empowering Minority Students*, Sacramento, CA, California Association for Bilingual Education.

DEAVILA, E., COHEN, E.G. and INTILI, J.A. (1981) *Multicultural Improvement of Cognitive Abilities*, final report to California State Department of Education.

DELGADO-GAITAN, C. (1988) 'The value of conformity: Learning to stay in school', *Anthropology and Education Quarterly*, **19**, pp. 354–81.

DIANA V. STATE BOARD OF EDUCATION (1970) Civil action no. C-70-37 (ND Cal).

DIAZ, S., MOLL, L.C. and MEHAN, H. (1986) 'Sociocultural resources in instruction: A context-specific approach', in *Beyond Language: Social and Cultural Factors in Schooling Language Minority Students*, Los Angeles, CA, Evaluation, Dissemination and Assessment Center, California State University, Los Angeles, pp. 187–230.

DUNN, L.L. (1968) 'Special education for the mildly retarded — Is much of it justified?' *Exceptional Children*, **35**, pp. 5–22.

EKSTROM, R.B., GOERTZ, M.E., POLLACK, J.M. and ROCK, D.A. (1986) 'Who drops out of high school and why? Findings from a national study', *Teachers College Record*, **87**, pp. 356–73.

FEDERAL REGISTER (1977) 'Education of Handicapped Children', Regulations Implementing Education for all Handicapped Children Act of 1975, August, pp. 42474–518.

FINN, J.D. (1982) 'Patterns in special education placement as revealed by the OCR surveys', in K.A. HELLER, W.H. HOLTZMAN, and S. MESSICK, (Eds) *Placing Children in Special Education: A Strategy for Equity*, Washington, DC, National Academy Press, pp. 322–81.

FLORES, B., RUEDA, R. and PORTER, B. (1986) 'Examining Assumptions and instructional practices related to the acquisition of literacy with bilingual special education students', in A.C. WILLIG and H.F. GREENBERG (Eds) *Bilingualism and Learning Disabilities: Policy and Practice for Teachers and Administrators*, New York, American Library Publishing Co., pp. 149–68.

FORNESS, S.R. and KAVALE, K.A. (1989) 'Identification and diagnostic issues in special education: A status report for child psychiatrists', *Child Psychiatry and Human Development*, 19, pp. 279–301.

GELZHEISER, L.M. and SHEPHERD, M.J. (Eds) (1986) 'Competence and instruction: Contributions from cognitive psychology' (Special Issue) *Exceptional Children*, 53.

GERBER, M.M. (1984) *Problem Solving Teams in California: Appropriate Responses by School Site Staff to Students Who are Difficult to Teach and Manage* (Project Final Report) Santa Barbara, CA, University of California, Special Education Program.

GERBER, M.M. and SEMMEL, M.I. (1984) Teacher as imperfect test: Reconceptualizing the referral process', *Educational Psychologist*, 19, pp. 137–48.

HARRIS, K. and HERRON, T. (1987) *The Educational Consultant: Helping Professionals, Parents, and Mainstreamed Students*, Austin, TX, Pro-Ed.

HARTMAM, W.T. (1980) *Policy Effects of Special Education Funding Formulas* (Policy Report No. 80-B1) Stanford, CA, Institute for Research on Educational Finance and Governance.

HELLER, K.A., HOLTZMAN, W.H. and MESSICK, S. (Eds) (1982) *Placing Children in Special Education: A Strategy for Equity*, Washington, DC, National Academy Press.

HERRON, T. and HARRIS, K. (1987) *The Educational Consultant: Helping Professionals, Parents, and Mainstreamed Students* 2nd ed., Austin, TX, Pro-Ed.

HILL, C.R. (1979) 'Capacities, opportunities, and educational investments: The case of the high school dropout', *The Review of Economics and Statistics*, 61, pp. 9–20.

HOWELL, K. and MOREHEAD, M. (1987) *Curriculum-based Evaluation for Special and Remedial Education*, Columbus, OH, Merrill.

IDOL, L, PAOLUCCI-WHITCOMB, P. and NEVIN, A (1986) *Collaborative Consultation*, Rockville, MD, Aspen.

JACKSON, G. and COSCA, C. (1974) 'The inequality of educational opportunity in the Southwest: An observational study of ethnically mixed classrooms', *American Educational Research Journal*, 11, pp. 219–29.

JACOB, E. and JORDAN, C. (Eds) (1987) 'Explaining the school performance of minority students' (Theme Issue) *Anthropology and Education Quarterly*, 18.

LABORATORY OF COMPARATIVE HUMAN COGNITION (LCHC) (1982) 'Culture and cognitive development', in W. KESSEN (Ed.) *Mussen Handbook of Child Development (Vol. I)* New York, Wiley.

LARRY P. V. RILES (1979) 495 F. Supp. 96 (N.D. Cal.) Aff'r (9th Cir. 1984), 1983–84 EHLR DEC. 555:304.

MACMILLAN, D.L., KEOGH, B.K. and JONES, R.L. (1986) 'Special educational research on mildly handicapped learners' in M. WITTROCK (Ed.) *Handbook of Research on Teaching*, pp. 686–724 NY, McMillan.

MAGNETTI, S.S. (1982) 'Some potential incentives of special education funding practices', in K.A. HELLER, W.H. HOLTZMAN, and S. MESSICK, (Eds) *Placing Children in Special Education: A Strategy for Equity*, Washington, DC, National Academy Press, pp. 300–21.

McCarty, J. and Carrera, J.W. (1988) *New Voices: Immigrant Students in US Public Schools*, Boston, MA, National Coalition of Advocates for Students.

Mehan, H., Hertweck, A. and Miehls, J.L. (1986) *Handicapping the Handicapped: Decision Making in Students' Educational Careers*, Palo Alto, CA, Standford University Press.

Mercer, J. (1973) *Labeling the Mentally Retarded: Clinical and Social Systems Perspectives on Mental Retardation*, Berkeley, CA, University of California Press.

Mercer, J.R. (1988) 'Death of the IQ paradigm: Where do we go from here? in W.J. Lonner and V.O. Tyler (Eds) *Cultural and Ethnic Factors in Learning and Motivation: Implications for Education*, Twelfth Western Symposium on Learning, Bellingham, WA, Western Washington University, pp. 1–21.

Mercer, J.R. and Lewis, J. (1979) *SOMPA: Conceptual and Technical Manual*, New York, The Psychological Corporation.

Mercer, J. and Rueda, R. 'Changing Paradigms in Special Education: Roots of the Current Scientific Revolution', unpublished manuscript.

Ogbu, J.U. and Matute-Bianchi, M.E. (1986) 'Understanding sociocultural factors: Knowledge, identity, and school adjustment', in *Beyond Language: Social and Cultural Factors in Schooling Language Minority Students*, Los Angeles, CA, Evaluation, Dissemination and Assessment Center, California State University, Los Angeles, pp. 73–142.

Ortiz, A. (1984) 'Choosing the language of instruction for exceptional bilingual children', *Teaching Exceptional Children*, **16**, pp. 208–12.

Ortiz, A. and Garcia, S.B. (1988) 'A prereferral process for preventing inappropriate referrals of Hispanic students to special education', in A. Ortiz and B.A. Ramirez (Eds) *Schools and the Culturally Diverse Exceptional Student: Promising Practices and Future Directions*, Reston, VA, CEC, pp. 6–18.

Ortiz, A. and Maldonado-Colon, E. (1986) 'Reducing inappropriate referrals of language minority students in special education', in A. Willig and H. Greenberg (Eds) *Bilingualism and Learning Disabilities: Policy and Practice for Teachers and Administrators*, New York, American Library Publishing Co., pp. 37–52.

Ortiz, A. and Yates, J.R. (1983) 'Incidence of exceptionality among Hispanics: Implications of manpower planning', *NABE Journal*, **7**, pp. 41–53.

Ortiz, A. and Yates, J.R. (1984) 'Linguistically and culturally diverse handicapped students', in R. Podemski, B. Price and G. Marsh (Eds) *Comprehensive Administration of Special Education*, Rockville, MD, Aspen Systems, pp. 114–41.

Palinscar, A.S. and Brown, A.L. (1984) 'Reciprocal teaching of comprehension-fostering and comprehension-monitoring activities', *Cognition and Instruction*, **1**, pp. 117–75.

Peng, S. (1983) *High School Dropouts: Descriptive Information from High School and Beyond*, Washington, DC, National Center for Education Statistics.

Polyzoi, E., Holtzman, W.H. and Ortiz, A. (1987) 'Language Assessment of Speech and Language Disordered Limited English Proficient Hispanic Students: The Use of Pragmatics for Distinguishing a 'True' Handicapping Condition from a Language Difference', paper presented at the meeting of the American Educational Research Association, Washington, DC.

Poplin, M. (1988a) 'The reductionist fallacy in learning disabilities: Replicating the past by reducing the present', *Journal of Learning Disabilities*, **21**, pp. 389–400.

Poplin, M. (1988b) 'Holistic/constructivist principles of the teaching/learning process: Implications for the field of learning disabilities', *Journal of Learning Disabilities*, **21**, pp. 401–16.

Reynolds, M.C., Wang, M.C. and Walberg, H.J. (1987) 'The necessary restructuring of special and regular education', *Exceptional Children*, **53**, pp. 391–8.

Rist, R. (1970) 'Student social class and teacher expectations: The self-fulfilling prophecy in ghetto education', *Harvard Educational Review*, **40**, pp. 411–50.

Rist, R. (1982) 'Labeling the learning disabled child: The social ecology of educational practice', *American Journal of Orthopsychiatry*, **52**, pp. 146–60.

RUEDA, R. (1989) 'Defining mild disabilities with language-minority students', *Exceptional Children*, **56**, pp. 121–9.

RUEDA, R., CARDOZA, D., MERCER, J. and CARPENTER, L. (1984) *An Examination of Special Education Decision-making with Hispanic First-time Referrals in Large Urban School Districts*, (First Report) Los Alamitos, CA, Handicapped Minority Research Institute, Southwest Regional Laboratory.

RUEDA, R., RUIZ, N. and FIGUEROA, R. (1989) 'Home Language and Learning Practices among Mexican-American Children: Review of the Literature', paper presented at the American Education Research Association Annual Meeting, San Francisco, March.

RUMBERGER, R.W. (1983) 'Dropping out of high school: The influence of race, sex, and family background', *American Educational Research Journal*, **29**, pp. 199–220.

SAYERS, D. (1986a) 'From journal to journalism: ESL writers', *Puerto Rico TESOL-Gram*, **13**, pp. 7–8.

SAYERS, D. (1986b) 'Sending messages across the classroom and around the world: Computer-assisted language learning', *Special Supplement No. 3 of TESOL Newsletter*, **20**, pp. 7–8.

SAYERS, D. (1988) ' "We are no longer alone": Sixty-four years of sister classes in Celestin Freinet's Modern School Movement', *Bilingual Literacy Correspondent*, **5**, pp. 2–3.

SEWELL, T.E., PALMO, A.J. and MANNI, J.L. (1981) 'High school dropout: Psychological, academic, and vocational factors', *Urban Education*, **16**, pp. 65–76.

SHEPARD, L. and SMITH, M.L. (1981) *Evaluation of the Identification of Perceptual-communicative Disorders in Colorado* (Final Report) Boulder, CO, University of Colorado, Laboratory of Educational Research.

SKRTIC, T.M. (1988) 'The crisis in special education knowledge', in E.L. MEYEN and T.M. SKRTIC (Eds) *Exceptional Children and Youth: An Introduction*, 3rd ed., Denver, CO, Love Publishing Co.

STAINBACK, W. and STAINBACK, S. (1984) 'A rationale for the merger of special and regular education', *Exceptional Children*, **51**, pp. 102–11.

THARP, R. and GALLIMORE, R. (1988) *Teaching Mind Through Society: A Vygotskian Approach to Educational Theory and Practice*, Cambridge, UK, Cambridge University Press.

TUCKER, J.A. (1980) 'Ethnic proportions in classes for the learning disabled: Issues in nonbiased assessment', *Journal of Special Education*, **14**, pp. 93–105.

TUCKER, J.A. (1985) 'Curriculum-based assessment' (Special Issue) *Exceptional Children*, **52**.

TWOMEY, S.C., GALLEGOS, C., ANDERSEN, L., WILLIAMSON, B. and WILLIAMSON, J. (1980) *A Study of the Effectiveness of Various Nondiscriminatory and Linguistically and Culturally Appropriate Assessment Criteria for Placement of Minority Students in Special Education Programs*, Merced, CA, Planning Associates.

US DEPARTMENT OF EDUCATION (1987) *Ninth Annual Report to Congress on Implementation of Public Law 94-142: The Education for All Handicapped Children Act*, Washington, DC, US Government Printing Office.

WHITE, O.R. (1986) 'Precision teaching — precision learning', *Exceptional Children*, **52**, pp. 510–21.

WILL, M.C. (1986) 'Educating children with learning problems: A shared responsibility', *Exceptional Children*, **52**, pp. 411–6.

YSSELDYKE, J.E. (1983) 'Current practices in making psychoeducational decisions about learning disabled students', *Journal of Learning Disabilities*, **16**, pp. 226–33.

YSSELDYKE, J., ALGOZZINE, B., RICHEY, L. and GRADEN, J. (1982) 'Declaring students eligible for learning disability services: Why bother with the data?' *Learning Disability Quarterly*, **5**, pp. 37–44.

Part V

The Big Picture and Chicano School Failure

There are two chapters in this final part. In chapter 10, 'Systemic and Institutional Factors in Chicano School Failure', Arthur Pearl commences his discussion by arguing that Chicano school failure can only be understood when examined in the broadest political, economic, and cultural contexts. In a lengthy treatise, Pearl analyzes a number of structural aspects and policies that help shape school failure among Chicano students. His macrolevel examination covers such variables and conditions as the general and political economy, a critique of those strategies that have been advanced to reduce Chicano school failure, and what he sees as the most viable approach to promote Chicano school success — 'Democratic Schooling'.

Chapter 11, the final chapter, is by Richard Valencia. Titled, 'Toward Chicano School Success', this brief chapter provides a synthesis of major points and conclusions drawn by the book's contributors. Valencia places the following points of discussion in the context of promoting Chicano school success: keeping Chicanos in school; the social context of schooling; bilingual education; Chicano parental involvement; the assessment context of schooling; Democratic Schooling.

Chapter 10

Systemic and Institutional Factors in Chicano School Failure

Arthur Pearl

Chicano school failure can be fully understood only when analyzed in the broadest political, economic, and cultural contexts. Macropolicies establish the boundaries of possibilities. During periods of economic and political expansion success tends to be non zero–sum. However, when a society is constricting, every success of an individual or a group must be balanced by an equal or greater number of failures. Trying to get a macroperspective on Chicano school failure is no simple task, as information is extremely limited. What exists is uneven, and to make matters more difficult, economic and political systems are undergoing considerable but difficult to understand changes. And yet, for all these problems, there is a need to place the issue we study on a large canvas. This, like any broad-based analysis must be perceived as tentative and provocative rather than conclusive. Particularly important in this analysis is a critique of the impact of policies that influence the configuration of work and promote equal opportunity and the extent to which these policies have hindered or helped Chicano school success. Macropolicies do not exist in a vacuum. Cultural considerations add complexity to the analysis as do accidental events, unpredictable individual relationships and individual efforts by teachers and students.

To make the matter even more confusing is the difficulty of keeping the analysis focused on Chicanos. Most of the available information groups Chicanos with all other Hispanic populations and disaggregation is almost impossible. The history of the experiences (in the United States) of Mexicans, of Cubans, Puerto Ricans, and other immigrants from Latin America are distinctly different and these differences are reflected in schooling success (e.g., Moore and Pachon, 1985; Rumberger, this volume; Velez, 1989). Moreover, even if data were available for solely those with Mexican heritage, problems would remain. Within such a population there are many different considerations. There are profound differences in outlook and behavior of those recently arrived and those who have been in the United States for many generations. There are important political and social differences. The term Chicano came into existence as a political statement; it signified the call for a perspective different than immigrants who wished to assimilate into the existing political economy — Mexican Americans — and different also from those who continued to perceive themselves as strongly connected to the motherland — Mexicanos. Chicano stood for liberation from perceived political, economic and cultural oppression within the United States. Some of the original meaning has been lost in the last quarter-century but the problems for analysis remain. Just whom are we talking about? At best we can operate with rough approximations. Part of the definition is imposed from outside by institutional processes, some from individual perceptions, and some from collective movements. Trying to impose order on situations and definitions that are in flux is fraught with danger, but much more dangerous is to be overwhelmed by chaos.

There are some fairly solid places to begin. There are bits and pieces of evidence, when combined, powerfully suggest that Chicanos do not fare well in school, are increasingly poor, and have high incidences of involvement with crime. The evidence is not powerful enough to lead to a firm conclusion of why this is so. Neither of the two divergent principle theses — 'deficit' explanations, that place the cause of these problems on the individual family or culture, and the structural explanations that postulate etiology in the institutions and societal structure — are firmly established. If cause has not been determined to anyone's satisfaction, proposals for change are on an extremely rocky foundation. Nevertheless, the argument made here posits the cause of Chicanos to be in societal structure and, thus, the proposals for remedy are also largely structural. First, however a brief summary of the factors considered in the analysis.

The Relationship of Economic Conditions and Chicano Educational Success

Many different variables and conditions must be considered before the relation between the economic conditions and educational success of Chicanos in school can be fully understood. One aspect of the relation is the condition of the economy. During periods of rapid growth, opportunities are created to the benefit of those normally excluded from rewarding economic lives. A drop in unemployment does not necessarily lead to an increase in schooling performance among Chicanos and others who have been consigned to marginal economic existences. For Chicanos, a surging economy can lead to better schooling performance as optimism influences daily family activities and expectations for the future, but economic advance could conceivably have the opposite effect — students could leave school to take advantage of new job offerings. A depressed economy can lead to a general state of depression influencing youngsters in school. More importantly, when poverty gets concentrated in a particular area, neighborhood, ghetto or barrio, the inevitable result is a marked increase in criminal activity. Criminal activity is inimical to successful schooling. The effect is not only on individuals, it translates into an ethos, a way at looking at the world.

Political direction has an important bearing on school performance. When the emphasis is in providing political support for Chicanos — categorical aid, affirmative action, financial aid, etc. — school performance changes. The change is not universal and sometimes the incentives tend to be counterproductive. There has been a general tendency to lump all 'categorical aid' and anti-poverty measures together and thereby dismiss them. In fact, some programs were very successful while others may have been destructive. Only with a careful analysis of particular programs — something that was rarely done — can the impact of government-sponsored programs be accurately assessed. When the emphasis is on political direction, the issue is not whether a program is good or bad but whether there is political will to support any program — good *or* bad. Later, some brief comments will be made about the qualities of good and bad 'government' programs. The crucial consideration today is the prevailing negative attitude among political leaders for such programs. Tied to the issue of political direction of a country is Chicano influence on that direction. Chicano political power has not been nearly proportionate to its potential voter base (Moore and Pachon, 1985). The relation between political powerlessness in the broadest sense and school failure is part of the equation that has not been sufficiently explored.

One application of political power is influence over school policy and practice. School policy and practices in turn are crucial determinants of school performance. It is conceivable that Chicano power or powerlessness could be irrelevant because for over twenty-five years there has been a declared national commitment to improving the educational performance of the economically disadvantaged. These efforts can take one of two forms: repairing alleged deficits, or changing school structures. Political power is important in determining which direction schools take. If the powerlessness results in an ineffective approach then powerlessness becomes a crucial issue in school failure. The effectiveness of repairing deficit and altering structures is considered in this essay.

School is an increasingly important intervening institution in the political economy. In many ways school has become the dominant status flow institution. In a society that claims to be one that provides everyone equal opportunity, schools direct students to different walks of life. Desirable employment has educational prerequisites and students without these prerequisites cannot be considered for such employment. For most of the twentieth century the United States has been rapidly progressing into a credential society. Increasingly economic status correlates highly with the degree attained from schooling. The trend has been, until very recently, for the number of college degrees awarded to be in rough equivalence to the available positions requiring such degrees. A person graduating from college had a reasonable assurance that a decent career was there for the asking. The higher one went in school, the better paying occupation one had available to him or her. Actually, this situation was more true when higher education in the US was a White male province. Two very important changes have taken place over the past few decades. The number of university students has increased significantly. The shape of the work world has also changed enormously.

The increase in college enrollments has been dramatic. Almost 9 million more students were enrolled in colleges and universities in 1985 than were enrolled in 1960. This increase represents a dramatic change in the life activities of young people. Over the past twenty-five years, college went from a privilege for élite youth to something the majority of youth experienced. The demography of higher education has also changed — what was once a male preserve has become increasingly female — in 1960, 64 per cent of college students were male; in 1985, more than half were female. In some ways the changes may indicate the success an anti-sexism campaign in education has had (see Table 10.1).

Table 10.1: Postsecondary student enrollments (1960–1985): United States (in millions)

	Year					
	1960	1965	1970	1975	1980	1985
Total	3.6	5.7	7.4	10.9	11.4	12.5
Male	2.3	3.5	4.4	5.9	5.4	5.9
Female	1.2	2.2	3.0	5.0	6.0	6.6
% male	63.9%	61.4%	59.5%	54.1%	47.4%	47.2%
Rate 100,000[1]	375	na	387	443	651	791

Note: 1 ages 18–21; na = not available
Source: US Statistical Abstract — 1987.

Table 10.2: Median years school completed by race/ethnicity, 1970–1985

	Year		
	1970	1980	1985
Race/Ethnicity			
White	12.1	12.5	12.7
Black	9.8	12.0	12.3
Hispanic	9.1	10.8	11.5

Source: US Statistical Abstract — 1987.

When only a small percentage of students went to college, those that did attend were somewhat buffered from the vicissitudes of the economy. Because the numbers of college students were relatively small and the employment opportunities were large, only cataclysmic events, such as major depressions, negatively impacted college graduates. Those with limited education, however, were most vulnerable during economic slowdowns. What has not been determined is the nature of the relation. Is the relation between college education and economic success caused by the college experience, or is the opportunity to go to college largely given to those who have certain economic advantages? Is the primary purpose of school the reproduction of the existing social system (Apple, 1979; Bowles and Gintis, 1976)? Or, are schools to become the 'great equalizer' that Horace Mann (1848) insisted that they could be? In a general sense this chapter attempts not only to answer those questions but also suggests policies and practices consistent with the answer. Whatever the primary purpose of education, there is no disputing that at the present time, Hispanics *in toto*, and Chicanos in particular, have limited schooling success and limited economic success and there is some kind of relation between these two conditions.

Hispanics as an aggregate group — Chicanos, Cubans, Puerto Ricans, Central Americans, South Americans — have lower school grade attainment than either Anglos or Blacks and while the gap has narrowed over the last fifteen years, the differences remain large. When compared with Blacks and Anglos, only the Hispanic (median) has less than a high school education (see Table 10.2).

Not surprisingly, Hispanic high school dropout statistics are consistent with years of school completed. Different studies, using different definitions of dropout and different populations, nonetheless come to the same conclusions. As

Table 10.3:   Studies by race and ethnicity (per cent dropout)

	Anglo	Black	Hispanic
Study			
High School and Beyond[1]	14.4	18.0	25.4
Los Angeles Schools[2]	7.6	9.9	9.9 (1 yr)
High School Dropouts[3]	12.0	17.0	18.0
California/Department Education[4]	15.3	27.7	28.8

Sources:
[1] National Center for Educational Statistics, 1983
[2] Research and Evaluation Branch, Los Angeles School District, 1986
[3] US Department of Education, Center for Education Statistics, 1985
[4] California State Department of Education, 1980

Table 10.4:   Income of households by educational achievement by race and ethnicity, 1984

Education	Annual Mean Income		
	White	Black	Hispanic*
less than 8 years	$14,501	$11,321	$15,219
8 years	$17,002	$12,164	$16,288
1–3 years high school	$19,894	$14,041	$17,061
4 years high school	$26,541	$18,427	$23,429
1–3 years college	$30,215	$21,700	$27,261
4 or more years college	$43,642	$32,057	$37,339

* Hispanic refers to all persons where Spanish surname predominates — includes those of
  Mexican, Puerto Rican, Cuban, etc., descent.
Source: United States Statistical Abstract — 1987.

shown in Table 10.3, Hispanics, more than Blacks or Anglos will leave school prior to high school graduation (see also Rumberger, in this volume).

School attainment correlates with income for all ethnic groups. Families whose breadwinners have the most education earn the most money. This relation is not as strong for Hispanics as it is for other racial/ethnic groups (see Table 10.4). Hispanics with less than an eighth grade education tend to earn more than either Anglos and Blacks. And while education beyond a college degree brings more economic return for Hispanics than it does for Blacks, that amount of education earns considerably less for them than it does for Whites. If decisions about life are made on the basis of collected aggregated statistics, Hispanics would have good reason to believe that they have less to gain from continuation in school than do Anglos. The statistics indicate that school is less important for them than it is for Blacks. And while it is highly unlikely that medium family income is a conscious consideration of students in their dedication to schooling, the relation nonetheless is sufficiently consistent that it must be adequately explained.

If Hispanics drop out of school far more often than do Blacks and Anglos, it would follow that they would be underrepresented in higher education and that certainly is the case. In 1986, more than 27 per cent of public school enrollments in California were Hispanic (the vast majority of these are of Mexican heritage), but Hispanics constituted only 8.4 per cent of University of California enrollees,

Table 10.5: *University of California admissions: underrepresentation and overrepresentation by race and ethnicity, 1986*

	American Indian	Black	Hispanic	Pilipino	Asian	White
Public school enrollments	.9%	9.7%	27.9%	1.8%	6.7%	53.1%
UC enrollments	.6%	4.7%	8.4%	3.0%	14.4%	68.9%
UC BA degrees	.4%	2.5%	4.9%	1.2%	13.1%	75.0%
UC doctorate degrees	—	2.4%	4.1%	—	8.4%	85.1%

Source: *University of California, Santa Cruz, EOP.*

Table 10.6: *Unemployment rates of high school graduates and dropouts: Anglos v. Hispanics, persons aged 16 and over, 1975, 1980 and 1986*

	1975		1980		1986	
	Graduate	Dropout	Graduate	Dropout	Graduate	Dropout
Unemployment rates						
White	8.4	14.0	5.9	11.6	7.0	13.5
Hispanic	10.5	18.4	7.1	14.3	8.9	17.1

Source: *US Statistical Abstract — 1987.*

and less than 5 per cent of bachelor degrees were awarded to Hispanics. Hispanics received an even smaller percentage of doctoral degrees. At every step of the educational process Hispanics lose ground (see Table 10.5).

There are few positive signs in this picture, but the few should not be overlooked. The number of Hispanics receiving doctorate degrees from the University of California increased from sixteen in 1976 to fifty-nine to 1986 (from 1.2 per cent to 4.1 per cent).

Hispanics not only trail Anglos in educational accomplishment and family income, they are also more likely to be unemployed. Hispanic unemployment is high for Hispanic graduates; it is much higher for Hispanics whose schooling was terminated before high school graduation (Table 10.6).

As previously mentioned, being Hispanic obscures some significant relations. Some groups within this classification do much better than others. Persons of Cuban extraction have lower unemployment rates than persons who trace their origins to Mexico. Cuban Americans also are more likely to work in higher paid occupations than Mexican Americans. Unemployment of those with Mexican heritage parallels somewhat the unemployment of those with Puerto Rican heritage, although Mexican extraction males have a slightly higher unemployment rate than Puerto Ricans. The unemployment of Puerto Rican females is considerably higher than Mexican American women (Table 10.7). There are some similarities in experiences that all Hispanics share but there are considerable differences as well. Chicanos (broadly defined) are by far the largest group and the fastest growing in the United States (see Valencia, chapter 1, this volume). Chicanos are more concentrated in the West, Puerto Ricans in the East. Econom-

Table 10.7: Unemployment rates, professional employment: Hispanics, 1984

Unemployment	Mexican	Puerto Rican	Cuban	Other Hispanic
Males	12.6%	11.8%	8.6%	8.9%
Females	11.9%	15.6%	4.8%	11.5%
Employed in Managerial Professional Positions	9.4%	13.1%	20.0%	16.7%

Source: US Statistical Abstract — 1987

ic and political conditions differ greatly in these areas, and yet all are part of an economy that is increasingly global.

The dearth of Hispanic (Chicano) college graduates has a direct effect on Hispanic school experiences. As the Hispanic population grows, the number of Hispanics available to teach them declines. A large Hispanic student population with few or no Hispanic teachers is generally recognized as a negative condition (Valencia and Aburto, in press). Some theorists lament the lack of role models, others the lack of cultural understanding, others unfamiliarity with the language spoken by students, and still others the lack of visible examples of achieved success in lawful activities. Yet others focus on the the reproduction of those conditions that led to the limited school success of generations that preceded those now in school. Whatever the cause, it should be apparent that significant improvement in Chicano school experiences will be more difficult without a significant increase of Chicanos as teachers and administrators (Valencia and Aburto, in press). But where will these teachers come from? This is an especially difficult question to answer since the Chicano college population increases by only a trickle and the demand for them by different employer groups grows rapidly.

There is a source of potential Chicano teachers that is largely untapped — the non-professionals who work for the school districts. In the twenty-five largest districts in California that serve 30 per cent of California's 4.4 million K-12 students, almost 40 per cent of the students are Hispanic; less than 10 per cent of the teachers are Hispanic; and almost 25 per cent of the classified staff are Hispanic. In every one of these districts, more Hispanics work for the district as non-professionals than work as professionals. In fact, there are almost three times as many non-professional Hispanics than professional Hispanics employed by California's twenty-five largest school districts (Table 10.8). A strategy to increase Chicano teachers and administrators by resurrecting a different approach to credentialling is described and critiqued in the New Careers section of this chapter. Elevating non-professionals to professionals in addition to directly reducing Chicano poverty has, as an additional value, the potential of changing the dynamics of politics within a school district and, if organized, having an impact in the local community, the state, and the nation.

The official government position is that, contrary to all of the information depicting the economic decline of Hispanics (including Chicanos, presumably), they have benefitted from recent economic expansion. 'The 1983–86 civilian employment of Hispanic workers has risen 2.3 million since the expansion began'

Table 10.8: Hispanics in California's twenty-five largest school districts, 1987–88

	Students			Teachers			Classified Employees		
	Total	Hispanic	%	Total	Hispanic	%	Total	Hispanic	%
Los Angeles	589,311	334,954	56.8	25,071	2,564	10.2	26,606	7,565	28.4
San Diego	116,557	25,357	21.8	5,168	438	8.5	5,688	956	16.8
Long Beach	66,253	17,072	25.8	2,836	128	4.5	4,007	467	11.6
San Francisco	63,881	11,773	18.4	3,108	232	7.5	3,413	508	14.9
Fresno	61,539	20,245	32.9	2,233	280	10.2	1,804	770	25.5
Oakland	51,298	6,631	12.9	2,283	119	5.2	2,850	300	10.5
San Juan	46,710	2,172	4.6	2,183	66	3.0	1,996	79	4.0
Sacramento	46,064	8,098	17.6	1,941	131	6.8	2,298	415	18.1
Santa Ana	38,184	28,792	75.4	1,601	224	14.0	1,504	787	52.3
Garden Grove	36,289	10,031	27.6	1,494	35	2.3	1,743	178	10.2
San Bernardino	35,033	11,940	33.8	1,442	180	12.5	1,861	536	28.8
Mount Diablo	31,763	2,308	7.3	1,445	37	2.6	1,108	73	6.6
Montebello	31,154	25,986	83.4	1,167	401	34.4	970	970	72.6
Stockton	31,050	9,879	31.8	1,315	135	10.3	1,438	440	30.6
San Jose	29,333	10,320	35.2	1,508	150	10.0	2,958	995	33.6
Richmond	28,222	3,509	12.4	1,307	70	5.4	1,480	169	11.4
Riverside	27,474	6,542	23.8	1,117	73	6.5	1,035	314	30.3
Sweetwater	26,285	13,650	51.9	1,049	161	15.4	874	361	41.3
Compton	26,205	10,976	41.9	1,134	28	2.5	1,459	214	14.7
Fremont	25,974	2,821	10.9	1,138	32	2.8	963	88	9.1
Orange	24,618	4,332	17.6	1,066	62	5.9	1,291	248	19.2
Pomona	23,852	11,764	49.3	1,007	149	14.8	978	365	37.3
Hacienda	22,762	12,262	53.9	994	104	10.5	1,053	450	42.7
East Side/San Jose	22,507	7,071	31.4	968	165	17.0	683	229	33.5
Saddleback	22,294	1,393	6.2	927	23	2.5	912	71	7.8
TOTAL	1,524,612	599,878	39.3	65,502	5,987	9.1	70,972	17,548	24.7

Source: California Basic Educational Data System (CBEDS)

Table 10.9:   Hispanic poverty in the United States, 1985

Total Hispanic Population in poverty	5.2 million
Median Family Income	$19,027
Hispanics in Poverty	29.0%
Number of Children under age 18 in poverty	2.6 million
Children in Poverty	40.0%
Hispanic Elderly in Poverty	23.9%
Married couples in poverty	12.2% Black
	6.1% White
	17.0% Hispanic
Female-headed families in poverty	50.5% Black
	53.1% Hispanic
Children in poverty in female-headed families	66.9% Black
	72.4% Hispanic
Men in poverty	27.4% Black
	27.4% Hispanic
Hispanic poverty in the US South	27.7%
in the US West	26.0%
Full-time employees in poverty	1 in 15 Hispanic Workers*

* Higher than Black or White
Source: Center on Budget and Policy Priorities (1985)

(*Economic Report of the President*, 1988, p. 59). It is further claimed that the growth is in good jobs, '. . . nearly two-thirds of the new employment growth has been in managerial, professional, technical, sales or precision production occupations' (*ibid.*, pp. 60–1). However, another branch of the Government, the US Labor Department, provides statistics that are not that glowing — projecting far more growth in janitor, nurse, and truck driver jobs in the next decade than growth in computer programers or other jobs that demand advanced educational requirements (*US Statistical Abstract*, 1987).

Also contradicting the positive description of Chicano employment is the prevalence of Hispanic poverty. Hispanics are deeply mired in poverty and the condition is worsening. The Center on Budget and Policy Priorities reports Hispanic poverty has risen during the past decade and if the trend continues, Hispanics soon will be more impoverished than the more dramatically emphasized American underclass — Blacks. In 1985, nearly 3 in 10 Hispanics were poor. Forty per cent of Hispanics under the age of 18 were poor. More than half of Hispanic female-headed families were poor; almost three-quarters of children in these families were poor (Table 10.9).

The US Census Bureau provides evidence of the increase in Hispanic poverty reporting a decline in median family income of Spanish origin families (the catch-all category used by the Census Bureau) from a high of $21,097 (1985 dollars) in 1973 to $19,027 (1985 dollars) in 1985 (*US Statistical Abstract*, 1987). (See Valencia, chapter 1, for more Vecent data.)

In a sense, the *Economic Report of the President* and its claim for a rapid increase in 'good' jobs and the Labor Department projections of large growth in low-paying, no educational prerequisites, dead-ended positions are both correct. A very peculiar change is occurring in the configuration of work in the United States — the middle is disappearing while the top and the bottom are growing.

The numbers of executives, professionals and 'high-tech' occupations are increasing rapidly, but so too are low-level service, clerical, semi-skilled and unskilled positions. The work world is simultaneously calling for more education and for a 'dumbing down'. The bridge jobs that enable people to move up the ladder are being eliminated (Hodgkinson, 1988). The change has many implications for education. The alternatives of either security or poverty and nothing in between will intensify the competition for desirable jobs and for which leads to those occupations. The present is foretelling the future; in 1986, 20 per cent of college graduates were hired in jobs that required no college education (Hodgkinson, 1988). The competition for what appears to be a growing scarcity of higher education admissions and professional careers after graduation almost certainly will be divisive and threaten the limited gains that have been made by Chicanos and other minorities. Without an organized political strategy to recreate the middle and generate more openings at the top, the most likely consequence will be more intense and destructive rivalry between minority groups and within them.

Adding to the already complicated internal dynamics of the United States is the crush of those who want to enter it. Two-thirds of all emigrants in the world come to the United States; one-third of these settle in California. The immigrants come to the US to escape poverty, oppression, and the devastation of war. They are from all areas of the world, and are culturally, linguistically, and ethnically varied. They add significantly to the challenges of schooling and the political economy. California, the largest of the union's states, more than any other augurs its future.

California's population increased by 5 million in the past decade, and it is projected to grow by 5 million a decade for the foreseeable future. California is the nation's most wealthy state with the most diverse economy. Its $14 billion annual agricultural industry is somewhat troubled, but the decline suffered in this area is more than balanced by a yearly infusion of $28 billion in defense contracts. A substantial cutback in the defense, budget however, would wreak havoc with California's economy. California is important in 'high tech' but not as important as the Northeastern US, where 35 per cent of the major corporations are located. The annual income per workers covered by Workman Compensation in California is high ($23,100 in 1987). Only workers in Washington, DC ($28,477), Alaska ($28,008), New York ($24,634), Connecticut ($24,322) and New Jersey ($23,842) had higher average wages that year (US Labor Department, 1988). For all of its wealth, California does not invest much in elementary and secondary school education. In the school year of 1986–87, $3,751 was spent on every student in California, which was $219 less than the national average, $2,548 less than New York's expenditure, and over $1,000 less than Pennsylvania's investment in students (Guthrie et al., 1988). The differences in per student expenditures are not reflected in large interstate discrepancies in teacher salaries; they show up in class sizes. California pupil-teacher ratios (23:1) are five students larger than the national average and over seven more students per teacher than is found in New York. If the investment in education in California was the same as it was in New York the result would not necessarily be higher paid teachers. It would, however, produce more teachers. Increasing the number of teachers in California by roughly one-fourth would bring 50,000 more people into the profession, would significantly increase the number of jobs in the middle-income range of occupations, and would create opportunities for Chicanos and other underrepresented minorities in teaching. A much larger number of Chicanos could take advantage of these opportunities if a means (such as New Careers) were created to allow non-professional employees of schools to become professionals.

California's niggardly investment in education is the logical consequence of two initiatives passed by the voters. One restricted the ability of local districts to raise money ('Proposition 13', or the 'Jarvis Amendment' enacted June 6, 1978); the other limited the State Government tax increases to population growth and inflation ('Proposition 4' or the 'Gann Amendment' enacted in 1979). The limitations are particularly severe on minority populations who are younger and more likely to have children, with Chicanos being the most hard hit. California ranks forty-third in the nation's states in per cent of population under age 18 and thirty-fourth in per cent over 65. 'The average US white is 31 years old, the average black is 25, the average Hispanic is 22. . . . Add to this the current Chicano fertility rate of 2.9 children per female and the white birth rate of 1.7 children per female' (Hodgkinson, 1986, p. 2) and the implications of the 'read my lips' (George Bush) no tax increase refrain of the leading politicians in both parties is clear: for Chicanos to succeed in school, they will have to do more with less. Even if the resistance to increasing taxes was overcome, schools would not necessarily benefit. Those generated funds would go to education only if a successful coalition for that purpose was organized. Such a coalition would have to include those without children, a goodly number of whom are over the age of 65 with growing unmet needs of their own. If this kind of political alliance is not difficult enough, adding another degree of complication is the element of race — those without children tend to be White, while those with school-age children are increasingly racial/ethnic minorities. In the present political climate, these interest groups find themselves in adversarial relationships; finding ways to establish a common ground with a common vision is not given sufficient consideration in the current effort to reduce Chicano school failure.

Not too long ago race was a Black-White issue. That oversimplification contributed to a failure to reduce inequality. Latinos rightfully objected to the lack of attention given them in the early days of the anti-poverty program. Race and ethnicity are much more entangled today. In 1979, 83 per cent of all immigrants to the United States came from Asia and Latin America and were equally divided between the two (Hodgkinson, 1986). In the absence of a unifying vision, the more diverse the population the more difficult it is to build effective political coalitions. Alliances between minorities have always been difficult to maintain. Part of the history of the United States has been conscious efforts at divide and conquer. With policies that drive wedges between minorities, establishing and sustaining inter-minority coalitions becomes even more difficult. Hispanics are not necessarily unified or unifiable. The Chicano population is by far the largest contingent, representing 60 per cent of all Hispanics in the United States in 1980 (US Bureau of the Census 1980). By 1990 Chicanos are projected to constitute 69 per cent of all Hispanics in the United States (US Bureau of the Census, 1980). (The current figure is closer to 63 per cent; see Valencia, chapter 1.) In 1980, 40 per cent of US Hispanics drew their heritage from seventeen countries other than Mexico — the largest single proportion from

Table 10.10: *California median family income, 1983*

Race/Ethnicity	Income
Japanese	$27,388
Chinese	24,409
Asian Indians	23,722
Pilipino	23,586
White	22,784
Korean	20,713
Hispanics (all)	16,087
Black	14,887
Vietnamese	11,852

Source: Hodgkinson, (1986)

Puerto Rico (14 per cent in 1989, projected to decline to 12 per cent in 1990; US Bureau of the Census, 1980). For the various Hispanic immigrant groups, there is no assurance that they will automatically come together now that the US is their home.

One-third of the 5 million US Asian-Americans live in California. Asian-Americans, like Hispanics, have a wide range of different backgrounds and cultures. Most numerous are immigrants whose roots are China, Japan and the Philippines; growing rapidly, however, are Asian-Indians, Koreans, and Vietnamese. Chinese and Vietnamese hostility has a long history and there is nothing in the current political framework that will transform that hostility into an alliance. There is an enormous discrepancy in Asian-American income. Median Asian-American income is both California's highest and lowest (Table 10.10).

The new mix may be politically destabilizing. Black power that has been a factor in promoting issues of equality may be effectively undermined by the new and soon-to-be-larger groups that do not have a similar history of effective political action. As Blacks decline, who will replace them? And how will this emerging group come together to be a force for a coherent political program? Unless a new political thrust comes into prominence, a more ethnically diverse United States, even one whose majority is 'minority', may be more easily controlled by a White minority than it is now. That control may also result in very high levels of crime, poverty, and social unrest.

The detailing of the economic and educational condition of Hispanics — and by inference Chicanos — sets the stage for the analysis that follows. This is especially important because the thrust of the paper is that objective economic and political conditions are the important variables that dynamically interrelate with schooling experiences influencing incidences of school success and failure. Any serious effort to reduce Chicano school failure must address the convoluted path to success in a credential society, and the failure that results when one is denied access to those credentials. In such an analysis, logistics — for example, being where the jobs are — as well as the effectiveness of interventions at critical stages in the lengthy stochastic process of schooling must be given serious and thorough treatment. The analysis is particularly difficult because it requires both an ongoing assessment of the opportunity structure and the individuals and groups striving for success within the constraints of that system. The more restricted the opportunities, the greater the number of failures.

Over the course of the past two decades, two strategies have emerged to reduce Chicano school failure. The first was a compensatory effort designed to eliminate attributed deficiencies that Chicanos (and other disadvantaged groups) brought into the schools; the second — which developed as a response to the compensatory strategy — the Effective School, was designed to provide Chicanos with the identical school program the advantaged received. Both of these efforts are conservative in the sense that neither demands change in the existing political economy. Both, by accepting a social system that tolerates enormous inequality, have as the ultimate goal — the equalizing of inequality.

In a political economy that has built into its structure unemployment, poverty and insufficient good jobs for all who aspire to them the best possible result is an equalization of inequality. Equal opportunity in such circumstances would require every group — ethnic minority, gender, etc. — to have the identical proportion in good jobs and in institutions that are prerequisite for good jobs. The feasibility of such a strategy will be critiqued, as are proposals that aim at restructuring aspects of the political economy.

Strategies to Reduce Chicano School Failure

The Compensatory Education Strategy

The Compensatory Approach has been the primary response to the conditions briefly reviewed above. This strategy consists of a number of activities designed to remediate certain specified problems of educability. The logic of the strategy is that our society has overcome its historical injustices and has reached a point where all its citizens are treated fairly and equally. The strategy is a school-centered one, with this reasoning: given the existence of a credential society, a school that provides everyone with an equal chance to obtain a credential will successfully fulfill its function as a great equalizer. Thus, the strategy focus is on eliminating the scars that remain from past injustices. Once it is assumed that an equal society exists there is no need to be concerned with institutional change. The strategy, because it is not involved in systemic change, acts as a gyroscope for the status quo. Moreover, the approach is extremely circumscribed. Larger issues of unemployment and the configuration of work are ignored. And with the exception of self-serving activity of a special interest group brought into existence by the strategy — e.g., paraprofessionals, compensatory educators, and administrators — the strategy is apolitical. As originally formulated, it was almost exclusively an early intervention strategy. The dominant theoretical explanation for disproportionate school failure of the poor and the minority was 'accumulated environmental deficit' — that is, students entered school with a build-up of handicaps incurred in early formative years that would be irreversible unless significant action was taken when children were very young (Deutsch, 1967; Hunt, 1961). If, however, intervention begins early enough the child can recover from the lack of intellectual stimulation at home and the dearth of language (Bernstein, 1970; Engelmann, 1970). The compensation for the deficits that are hypothesized to have occurred before a child enters school results in the leveling of the playing field giving everyone an equal chance at a desirable future. From a game's tree

Figure 10.1: *Early intervention strategy*

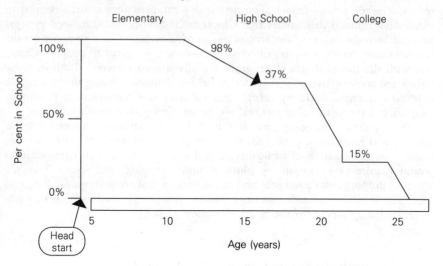

Table 10.11: *Head Start results, autumn 1984: A comparison between Head Start and control cohort at age of 19*

	Head Start	Control
Employed	59%	32%
High School Graduate	67%	49%
Enrolled in College	38%	21%
Been Arrested	31%	51%
On Welfare	18%	32%

Source: Hodgkinson (1988) derived from High/Scope Foundation, Michigan, September 1984

perspective the logic of the intervention is to get the student as quickly as possible into the mainstream (Figure 10.1).

The key element in the early intervention strategy was Operation Head Start. Initiated in 1965, as the show-case case element in President Johnson's fledgling anti-poverty program, it, unlike many other 'Great Society' projects, survived and even prospered. In 1985, an average of 452,000 children were enrolled every month in Head Start programs at a total annual cost of 1.3 billion dollars (*US Statistical Abstract*, 1987). There is some evidence that Head Start has been effective. When a cohort consisting of 19-year-olds with Head Start experience is compared with a same age control (fifteen years after beginning involvement with Head Start) there are some impressive findings. Those with Head Start experience are more likely to be employed, graduate from high school, go on to college, and are less likely to have been arrested or be on welfare (Hodgkinson, 1988) (Table 10.11). The impressive findings for Head Start are not necessarily a vindication for the strategy. The Head Start cohort has, for all its accomplishments, a large percentage not graduating from high school, a substantial arrest record, and a large percentage unemployed. The percentage of Head Start cohort

Figure 10.2: *Total compensatory strategy for equal education*

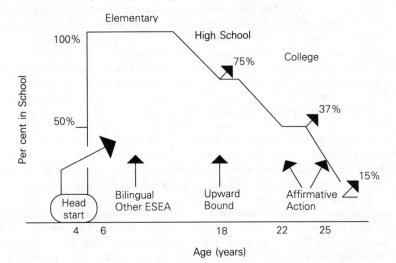

college enrollees is much lower than the percentage of college admissions from advantaged backgrounds. The most favorable reading of Head Start is that while it did not eliminate disadvantagement, poverty may have been worse without it.

In reality, for all of the theoretical emphasis on the importance of early intervention, the compensatory strategy did not put all of its emphasis on a single action. From its beginning and throughout the quarter century of its existence, bits and pieces were added to the compensatory strategy at every stage of a student's schooling career. Over the years the approach has become increasingly protean. By adding components at every level of schooling — whatever it may have gained in additional weaponry against disadvantagement — it lost in theoretical clarity. Not included in the range of compensatory tactics was a serious consideration of possible institutionally imposed unequal treatments, nor was there any effort to bring into the approach activities that would take into account the rapid changes occurring outside of the school that could conceivably impact student performance. The emphasis has been on repairing damaged goods and the collection of thrusts ranged from remedial programs for elementary and secondary students — including bilingual education for limited- and non-English-speaking students, migrant education (Elementary and Secondary Education Act — ESEA) and affirmative action to create opportunites for the underrepresented (Upward Bound and other special admissions to college and inclusion of the underrepresented in hiring practices; see Figure 10.2).

Depending on its focus, bilingual education can fit into any strategy. From a compensatory perspective, anything other than English is considered to be a handicap and thus, bilingual education is instituted as a means to facilitate students into the mainstream and is discontinued as soon as the student gains facility in English. This perspective on bilingual education has engendered considerable opposition and has been used as a focal point for mobilizing political action against 'special treatment' for the disadvantaged and for reasserting the common core of 'Americanism' (e.g., Epstein, 1977). If educational funds continue to be tight, the attack against special treatment will intensify. For example, US English, a group that has emerged as an opponent of bilingual education has been able to coalesce a range of support with highly emotional and sometimes disingenuous campaigns. Whether a compensatory version of bilingual education is politically winnable, or whether compensatory bilingual education is where the stand on bilingualism should be taken, are issues that need to be fully debated.

Affirmative action is another highly controversial aspect of compensatory education (see Figure 10.2). Hiring and admitting underrepresented populations into employment or higher education makes good sense from a compensatory perspective if the intervention is perceived to be a temporary adjustment to be employed only until the other compensatory catchup efforts have been given time to be effective. An early intervention strategy would take two decades to reach a favorable conclusion. Until Head Start students (and ESEA, bilingual, etc.) are able to graduate from school, a tactic of admitting persons with 'less qualifications' is intellectually and politically defensible. If affirmative action continues beyond that reasonable time, however, the compensatory justification for it is weakened and the political opposition to it grows. The cries of 'reverse discrimination' are becoming increasingly shrill and the responses to that cry, using a compensatory logic, are increasingly unpersuasive. The mismatch between ethnicity of teachers and students has not been significantly altered by affirmative action. The strategy has not resulted in equal representation of minorities into the professions or into institutions leading to professional careers or anything near that, but that has not silenced an adamant opposition far more vociferous than the limited impact would seem to have warranted.

The compensatory strategy is a top-down strategy. It was designed by an intellectual élite for persons deemed to be inferior to it. As a consequence, the approach never developed a substantial constituency. 'Deficits of the world unite, you have no brains to lose' is not a very inspirational rallying cry. Compensatory education was not designed as a political movement. To the contrary, it was an effort to employ science for the benefit of the species. Thus, it has tried to defend itself on the basis of accomplishment rather than constituency. As lofty as such a conception might be, the system does not work that way. Education interventions are political. Compensatory education came into being because the political times were right for it, and the administration in power built it into its program. At the present time, compensatory education suffers from both a lack of strong scientific support and from a dwindling of political support; it continues primarily because of inertia.

In that compensatory education is not a system change strategy, its goal is for a fairer representation of Chicanos and other minorities in the political economy. It is doubtful that even the most fervent supporters of the compensatory strategy foresaw a time of complete equalization of inequality. The programs were initiated at a time of rising expectations for the economy and the belief was expressed by many economists that in the not too distant future (less than a quarter century) poverty in the United States would be completely eliminated. Therefore, even if inequality would remain, no one would be poor. Times have changed; economists no longer project a poverty-free future, and therefore, expectations of a compensatory strategy have to be scaled down accordingly. At best, it would now be argued that effective compensatory programs would enable people to gain employment in growth industries. The strategy may not

achieve equality, but it should improve employability. The difficulty with determining the validity of that thesis is the time gap between the reception of
compensatory education and entrance into the job market. The longer the period
between the educational intervention and the beginning of an adult work life, the
more slippage there is in the system. Without immediate tangible rewards as
students — and without a clear indication of a gratifying future — many Chicanos become willing accessories to a process that shunts them out of education as
dropouts or as juvenile delinquents years before they could enter into an economically advantageous life career. The effort to increase Chicano participation in
desirable facets of the political economy through cumulative compensatory
efforts is contrasted with 'New Career' strategies discussed later in this chapter.
In 'New Careers', the work world is changed to accommodate the characteristics
of the applicants. The job comes first and education and training are offered afterwards. In the former instance, the Chicano (or other underrepresented person)
has to climb a ladder fraught with pitfalls before entering the work world. In the
latter case, climbing the ladder occurs after entrance into an occupation. The
compensatory strategy seemingly has made little or no progress in stimulating
Chicanos to become teachers, nor has it prevented Chicanos to continue to slide
further into poverty.

The long time lapse between the interventions and the terminal condition
makes evaluation of any particular compensatory program exceedingly difficult,
if not impossible. The programs conceivably could have worked at cross purposes and the whole may be less effective than some of the component parts.
Future research should try to establish how much improvement, if any, can be
attributed to a particular intervention. Perhaps of greater importance is the
possible serendipitous gain from parent empowerment, minority paraprofessional
employment and positive teacher expectation (possibly compromised and over-
balanced by an increase in negative expectations of performance by 'intellectually
handicapped students'), that has accompanied compensatory programs. Head
Start, for example, did much more than bring preschool educational enrichment
to ghettos and barrios; it also infused poor communities with buying power,
provided some limited opportunity for parents of the children to receive higher
education and become politically mobilized. These programs also provided nutri-
tion and health services and advice to parents. The possible political and economic stimulation has been inadequately considered in Head Start analysis, and, as a
consequence, its most significant impacts may be overlooked.

When concern is focused on Chicano school failure, it must be remembered
that Chicanos were an afterthought in the compensatory education movement.
Thus, the activities were not specifically designed for Chicanos. The research on
which the movement was based was not on Chicanos; the political support did
not come from Chicanos, and the political benefits, as little as they were, were
not directed to Chicanos. Whatever its other merits, compensatory education was
not an 'of the Chicanos, by the Chicanos, and for the Chicanos' program.

In sum, allowing for the paucity of relevant data and the recognition that the
final effects of the compensatory strategy may not have been fully realized, it is
still possible to say with certainty that, if the goal of the approach was to
overcome poverty and to substantially reduce inequality in educational achievement, the strategy has failed. The inability to make substantial progress toward
equality led Arthur Jensen to state in the now famous introduction to his highly

influential article that, 'compensatory education has been tried and it apparently has failed' (Jensen, 1969, p. 2). Jensen — without any consideration of other possibilities — decided that a disproportionately large number of Blacks and Chicanos were genetically incapable of learning much of anything that was complicated. We look now to a possibility that Jensen never gave credence — minority failure to learn is caused by existing unequal encouragement in the school.

The Effective School Movement

The Effective School movement rejects the deficit argument and looks for remedy in some form of system change. The changes sought are encapsulated in the schooling process and those resources directly tied to education. The Effective School movement coincided with the general mood of reform that has informed public consciousness in the 1980s. The 'reforms' have been a conservative claim on education. The primary targets have been teachers and the 'educational establishment'. The current process began with a commission appointed by Ronald Reagan's then Secretary of Education, Terrel H. Bell. The report issued by this commission, *A Nation at Risk*, is highly inflammatory, reminiscent in many ways of McCarthyite claims of subversion by foreign agents. The inferences are there: 'If an unfriendly foreign power had attempted to impose on America the mediocre educational performance that exists today, we might well have viewed it as an act of war' (National Commission, 1983, p. 1). As the cold war against communism lost steam it was replaced with a not so cold war against the '... rising tide of mediocrity' (*ibid.*, p. 1). The risk was not subversion but an educational complicity in the failure to keep pace with Asians and West Europeans in the fight for dominance in the global economy. To overcome the risks of functional illiteracy, falling performance in scholastic achievement, the lack of 'higher order' intellectual skills, the need for more and more remedial classes (for everybody, not just the disadvantaged), and the general business and military unhappiness with the quality of performance of public school graduates, the Commission recommended more and better education. The salvation of America required: 1) more rigorous traditional curriculum combining the old basics with the new basics of computer literacy; 2) measurable standards and higher expectations — e.g., frequent standardized testing, grades based on performance, and upgraded textbooks; 3) more time on task — longer school years and school days, and mandatory homework; 4) better teaching — higher standards for admission to the profession, professionally competitive salaries, and recognition and rewards for the best in the business; and finally, 5) more demands on educators and elected officials responsible to meet these proposed goals. The Commission had more stick than carrot to its Report.

The Effective School movement latched on to some of the reform thinking. The thrust was that if advantaged youth go to bad schools, the poor — and especially the minority poor — go to much worse ones. And further, the compensatory approach not only failed to help the minority poor, it likely made matters worse for them. The late Ronald Edmonds was an acknowledged leader in the Effective Schools movement. He disputed the importance of outside-of-school factors on student performance and pointed to research that clearly indicated, '*School response to family background* [emphasis his] is the cause of depressed achievement for low-income and minority students' (Edmonds, 1984, p. 37). Edmonds' synthesis of the research findings led him to define the following as characteristics of an Effective School for disadvantaged minorities: 1) strong administrative leadership; 2) high expectations from students; 3) a safe and orderly environment; 4) an emphasis on basic skills; and 5) frequent monitoring of pupil progress using measurable curriculum-based criterion-referenced evaluation (Edmonds, 1979, 1984). The thrust of the Effective School is to provide the minority with what has been proposed and provided for the advantaged. It is directed at improving the delivery of services; it is not directed at changing the nature of schooling.

The Achievement Council is a California-based organization promoting Effective School principles. One of the distinctive features of the Achievement Council is its strong Chicano leadership which distinguishes it from efforts that had focused almost exclusively on Blacks. The distinction may not signify a difference because the program emphasis closely parallels Effective School activities. The Achievement Council responds to the data that have been presented above. Chicano and other minority students are far behind advantaged populations in school achievement and twenty-five years of compensatory education has not enabled them to catch up. The Council identifies the following points as 'roots of underachievement': an unchallenging curriculum with tracking for 'low ability' students, fewer able and experienced teachers, ill-prepared and often culturally unaware administrators, inadequate services, and low teacher expectations (Haycock and Navarro, 1988). The Achievement Council's prescription for success follows logically from the diagnosis of the problem — a determined principal, demanding teachers, a rich and rigorous core curriculum, parents as partners of teachers, support services for students and teamwork between administrators, teachers, students, and parents (Haycock and Navarro, 1988).

The Achievement Council points to some significant changes among some of California's 'worst' high schools once the proposed principles were transformed into action. Sweetwater High School and Claremont Middle School are two that have been 'turned around'. Sweetwater High School is located in San Diego County and is predominantly Latino (Chicano). Under the leadership of a strong principal it has gone from a compensatory-oriented school to one where educational excellence is promoted. The school now emphasizes academics and its college preparatory courses are jammed. 'A key to Sweetwater's move up has been the elimination of remedial math courses, as well as auto shop and home economics, and a goal of at least 50 per cent Latino enrollment in Advanced Math and Science courses' (Haycock and Navarro, 1988, p. 26). Also featured is an independent study, work-at-your-own pace computer program for potential dropouts. The positive changes include: more Sweetwater students took Scholastic Achievement Tests (SATs) than any other school in the district, many of the graduating class won scholarships and grants, and for the first time in its history more than half of the graduating class went on to college. These changes are attributed to the implementation of Effective School principles (Haycock and Navarro, 1988).

Claremont Middle School in California was once a dumping ground for troublesome low achievers. It was given a new principal. Six years later that school has also been transformed. Using Achievement Council principles, label-

Table 10.12: A comparison of CTBS results — eighth grade, Clearmont Middle School, 1983–86 (in percentiles)

	Reading	Language	Math	Science	Social Science
1983	36	38	37	39	46
1986	70	65	65	62	65

Source: Haycock and Navarro (1988).

ing students as inadequate learners has been discontinued and with that low expectations from students. Remedial courses have been eliminated. In place of a compensatory approach an orientation toward achievement has led to the following accomplishments: institution of a core academic course, individualization of instruction, participation of parents in school and in their children's education, and teamwork among teachers. Test scores at Claremont have risen sharply. In 1983, in the five basic academic subjects tested in the California Test of Basic Skills the highest percentile score for Claremont's eighth graders was 46. Three years later, the lowest eighth grade score was at the 62nd percentile (see Table 10.12).

The Effective School's orientation to bilingual education departs markedly from the compensatory approach. A non- English-speaking and limited-English-speaking student is not perceived to have a handicap, even though the goal is to integrate the non- and limited-English-speaker into the educational mainstream by moving them systematically to a mastery of English. For that to happen, the principles applied to Effective Schools in general, are applied specifically to bilingual instruction. When those principles are scrupulously followed the results have been quite positive.

> A close examination of one particular effective school [not Claremont], serving more than 50 per cent Mexican American students with limited English proficiency and low socioeconomic status indicated that goals and objectives along with grade-level expectations were clear. In most curricular areas, rich Spanish-language materials were utilized on a continuum of Spanish-to-English instruction. The school was in the lowest quartile of district schools in SES but in the top quartile in achievement as measured by district proficiency tests ... the school staff worked together ... to improve instruction ... The emphasis [was] on ... continual instructional improvement. (Garcia, 1988, p. 390)

In this school, bilingual and monolingual teachers collaborated for total school ownership of the program. 'In addition one-third of student participants were non-Hispanic furthering an adoption of program ownership by non-Hispanic parents' (Garcia, 1988, pp. 390–1). By enriching the curriculum and elevating the standards, an Effective School bilingual program simultaneously led to higher academic performance as measured by standardized proficiency tests and built a constituency among monolingual non-Hispanic parents. Reducing divisiveness is an attribute of the Effective School that is not to be found in compensatory programs.

Although affirmative action is not an articulated component in the Effective Schools strategy, there is more than implicit commitment to increasing minority leadership in schools. Because of the emphasis on standards however, there is also an insistence on high quality of performance. The internal logical problem for the Effective School is its strict adherence to existing standards. With that approach, equal representation in teaching and administration would have to be postponed until the Effective School is universal and in operation long enough for all students to have profited from its cumulative benefits. There is a contradiction between an insistence on traditional standards and the desire to have more minority teachers that is largely left unattended by the Effective School.

The elimination of tracking and the instilling of high teacher expectations for students are crucial elements in the Effective School thinking. Tracking (and ability grouping) are processes used to provide students an education commensurate with alleged level of current functioning and a decreed potential for growth. The level of assignment is highly correlated with background factors, and students in different tracks get different educations. The differences in curriculum and nature of instruction are extensive. Their extent have been carefully chronicled in recent years (Oakes, 1985). Compensatory education is consistent with tracking, but the Effective School advocate sees tracking as a major structural impediment to minority school success.

Throughout the Effective School's limited history the concern has been with the treatment students receive in the classroom. The strong leadership, the rich curriculum, the collaboration between teachers, and teacher with parents, are all designed to bring about better instruction (see Figure 10.3). A vital component is the expectations that teachers have of students. Although often reduced to a slogan — expect more, get more; expect less, get less — there is much more to teacher expectations than that. A considerable body of knowledge has been developed on which programs can be based. The importance of teacher expectations has been both hailed and ridiculed. The most celebrated experiment that claimed strong student effects from raised teacher expectations (Rosenthal and Jacobson, 1968) was highly controversial (Elashoff and Snow, 1971). But as the dust settled and data were accumulated, a consensus has been reached — teachers beliefs about student abilities do influence student performance. The influences are not allpowerful — teachers expectations do not affect all students nor is the effect found in all situations, but differing expectations lead to very different classroom practices. That is, students who are expected to achieve do more meaningful things, have more autonomy, are more often challenged to think, are encouraged to self-evaluation, receive honest feedback, and get more respect. Students expected to perform poorly are the Rodney Dangerfields of education. They get no respect (Cooper and Good, 1983; Good and Brophy, 1986).

The Effective School is for change, but for a very restricted change. The change advocated is extension, not reformation. The Effective School aspires for the disadvantaged the same curriculum, support, and expectations of success the advantaged have always had. The criticism of education or other institutions by the Effective School proponents are directed neither at the size of the pie nor the baker. The objections are to the servings. The Effective School is an argument for a larger slice of the pie. The focus has been on getting a fair share of university admissions (based on merit) and let things go from there. The inescapable inference is that if more Chicanos graduate from the university and from

Figure 10.3: Chicano school performance: Existing v. Effective School

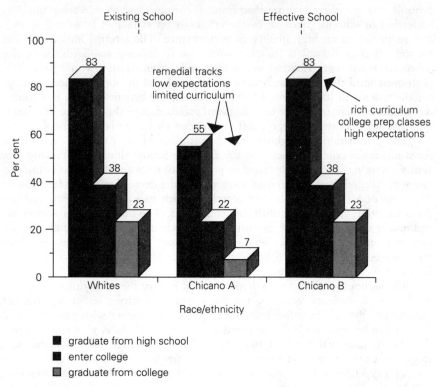

college, the entire community will also benefit. The income base of the community will be raised, its poverty reduced, hope will replace hopelessness, and even crime will somehow be reduced. The knowledge and the resources that knowledge brings will ineluctably extend to the entire community. It would be hard to dispute that if successful in its mission, the Effective School approach will reduce the incidence of poverty in the Chicano community.

There are dangers inherent in the strategy that have been ignored. William Pink summarizes criticisms of the Effective School movement. He faults it for:

1) not developing a single definition of an effective school; 2) using different selection criteria to identify schools for study (e.g., random vs. purposeful selection) and for not comparing 'effective' with 'average' schools; 3) using different instrumentation, and in some cases different methodological paradigms, to generate and analyze data; 4) using only correlational data where causality was specified; 5) failing to detail a definition for each of the effective schools' components such as 'strong leadership' and 'high expectations', and how each of these components is related to each other and in turn to school effectiveness; 6) failing to specify which instructional strategies are effective for which students; 7) failing to explore how the effective school components were originally

developed in those schools in which they were observed; and finally 8) failing to explore how the effective schools' components can be successfully transported to another building (1988, p. 201).

There is no assurance that the Effective School can be generalized or that it can sustain its gains. The successful Effective School experiments have had outstanding leadership. Whether there are enough such leaders for all schools is certainly unknown, nor can it be determined with any certainty whether that leadership can continue over a long haul or get the support it needs once education is no longer in the limelight. At the present time we do not know whether the gains cited for the Effective School are treatment effects — caused by the intervention — or selection effects of two kinds: non-representative leadership and a non-random selection of minority students.

The selection effect of students can be an important vitiating variable. Careful culling of students would make transportation from site to site exceedingly difficult. As an Effective School gets a good reputation it becomes a magnet and upwardly mobile families strive to enroll their children in it; conversely, to sustain a safe and orderly environment, undesirable students (and sometimes teachers) are sent to some less effective school. It is also possible that the gains, whatever they may be, are transient. Education reform has seen a great many breakthroughs and turnarounds that did not last very long. These cautions should not detract from what has been a very encouraging beginning. One result should never be allowed to be lost. Regardless of the ultimate fate of the Effective School, it demonstrated to a considerable degree that students — officially consigned with scientific approval to uneducability-demonstrated that they could master subjects normally only offered to the best and the brightest.

The Effective School may have some difficulties in demonstrating that it can sustain gains for minorities, but that is not where its greatest difficulties lie. The greatest problem for the Effective School is its fit in the political economy. Those who advocate the approach persistently refuse to consider the relationship of school to the work world and to dominant government policy. Although the thrust is to get *everyone* to succeed in a rigorous academic curriculum, unfortunately the world is not organized for that much academic success. The more success, the more unhappiness there will be if the work world continues in its current pattern and is unable to increase good jobs at the same rate that credentials and degrees are earned. A mismatch between too few available jobs and too many qualified applicants can be explosive. In such a situation, every good job gained by a Chicano means that an Anglo or Black or Asian comes up empty. It is because there is a willingness to accommodate a system that demands unemployment, underemployment and poverty; the Effective School is characterized here as an equal inequality strategy. Unless there is substantial growth in good jobs or improvement in transfer payments, the lowering of poverty for Chicanos must mean a rise in poverty for some other group. In fairness to proponents of the Effective School, they appear to accept the *Nation at Risk* vision of a rapidly increasing demand for a highly educated work force. At the present time that vision is not supported by either a compelling logic or by data.

The Effective School, like the the Compensatory Approach model, is top down and élitist. It has not come into existence as a response to a populist demand, although it can rightfully claim that there is increasing community support for its activities. This support, however, is not organized nor recognized in places where key political decisions are made. Many advocates of the Effective School wistfully believe that as the ethnic/racial makeup of the country and the state changes so too will its political power structure. Undoubtedly changes will accompany demographic change but not necessarily in the direction of an equally educated society. Unless there is a substantial reorientation of priorities and political thinking, the extent of education provided children will reflect more fiscal policy than educational policy. A nation that is not willing to spend much money on education will not get an equal education society, regardless of the value systems of its educational leadership. Providing a quality education for all becomes an even greater challenge when tight budgets are confronted with a rapidly growing, largely non- and limited-English-speaking student population. These are the crucial policy issues for California's education that most directly impact Chicanos that tend to be ignored by the Effective School movement (Guthrie *et al.*, 1988). The huge immigration to California does mean California will soon be a minority state, but this may be more destabilizing than it will be constructive. As Blacks decline in numbers their leadership for equality will be diluted and there is no indication that any other ethnic group is ready to assume the historic role Blacks have played in generating political support for equality. As different minority groups vie for power and try to get a larger piece of a shrinking pie, one very distinct possibility is increased squabbling. Without more vision than the Effective School, the most likely political response to increased eligibility for a too small credential society is unhealthy division. As the middle of the economy disappears and the choices are either affluence or poverty, the most likely consequence is more abrasive division within an ethnic group as well as between ethnic groups.

The Effective School is necessarily authoritarian. A major emphasis is on strong leadership, and students succeed to the extent they follow the leader. Because so much of the program is prescribed, development is also prescribed. Today, when democratic considerations are at a low ebb, authoritarianism in the school may not be regarded as a serious deficiency. Underestimating the importance of democratic schooling could be, however, a serious mistake.

The Effective School is not only authoritarian, it is also conservative. Like all conservative strategies, its goal is to facilitate assimilation into the society. Such assimilation requires an unexamined acceptance of existing curriculum and standardized evaluation. The mad rush to erase everything real and imaginary attributed to the permissive 1960s and the deleterious effects these heady times supposedly had on schooling has led to a general acceptance of a challenging 'core' curriculum. That was the central thrust of *A Nation at Risk*. Designing a rich core curriculum is a bandwagon on which many have jumped. Mortimer Adler and some of his friends dreamed up a core curriculum, *The Paideia Proposal*, that they think would enable all individuals to develop into well-rounded 'culture carriers' who with that knowledge could work cooperatively to solve the world's most pressing problems (Adler, 1982). Allan Bloom wants an élite curriculum to exclude women and minorities, believing their inclusion has ruined the academy. His *Closing of the American Mind*, not coincidentally, has been a runaway best seller (Bloom, 1987). E.D. Hirsch believes only when heretofore excluded populations, Blacks and other minorities, become 'culturally literate' (i.e., share a common understanding), will they be able to escape poverty and ascend to first-class citizenship. He has generated a list of what he insists is culturally necessary knowledge (Hirsch, 1988).

The need for a shared understanding is not the significant issue. An interconnected shared understanding is an essential ingredient in a quality education. At issue is the nature of that knowledge and how decisions are made regarding it. Effective School advocates believe that the curriculum served up to the affluent contributed to their affluence. Perhaps, but it is just as likely that the curriculum was organized to entertain affluence not to edify them. Furthermore, a curriculum that organizes persons to positions of superiority may not be the curriculum needed to overcome conditions of oppression. The anthropologist Jules Henry, after examining the textbooks in the 1960s concluded that students went to school to learn to be 'stupid' about: race, labor, economics, poverty, communism, and war (Henry, 1968). Frances Fitzgerald makes a similar point in *America Revised* (Fitzgerald, 1979). The Effective School 'rich' curriculum may be just that, a curriculum for the rich. It too, may be an updated education for stupidity. Because there is an unwillingness to truly examine the very hard problems the world faces, the core curriculum is likely to be a sugar-coated placebo. It is organized only for school. Textbooks,

> ... portray the world as a utopia of the eternal present — a place without conflicts, without malice or stupidity ... these bland fictions propagated for the purpose of creating good citizens, may actually achieve the opposite; they give young people no warning of the real dangers ahead. (Fitzgerald, 1979, p. 218)

Fitzgerald refers specifically to history books, but the Effective School core curriculum suffers — as do all other projected core curriculums — from a lack of reality in all subject areas.

It is difficult to get an accurate perception of reality when all the important evaluation measures are so closely linked to the classroom. Because there is no external validation — applying school-obtained knowledge to important out-of-school problems — the amount of bias in measures is difficult to determine. The Effective School strives for achievement on standardized tests that may underrate what Chicanos really know. The bias may exist in the psychometric structure of the test. It is also likely to be in reactions to the testing procedures (e.g., test anxiety).

Jaime Escalante, an outstanding Effective School educator depicted in the film, *Stand and Deliver*, organized his calculus teaching to help his Chicano and Chicana students succeed in a subject normally monopolized by Anglo students who attend high status schools. His students scored very high on the standardized test developed by the Educational Testing Service (ETS), causing the ETS to investigate and ultimately require those students to submit to brutal nonstandardized retesting. Escalante did not object to the test, but to the differential treatment his students received in the testing, which he clearly believed was prejudicial along ethnic and social-class lines. Thus, Escalante, like all good Effective School educators, accepted the system's parameters, he just wanted his students to be treated no differently than advantaged students who attended highly regarded high schools. As Valencia and Aburto (this volume) underscore, he wanted to demonstrate conclusively, and he did, that Chicanos were not only educable, but as educable as students reputed to be intellectually superior. While indeed Escalante's students appear to be as educable as youth from the most advantaged backgrounds, what he demonstrated may not be either enough or the most desirable path to take.

In sum, the Effective School movement is a promising development. Some aspects of it — high expectations and a quality curriculum — appear to be vital to any successful effort to reduce Chicano school failure. Its strength is its clarity of purpose. Its weaknesses are too narrow a focus and too imprecise actions. The strategy operates without consideration of broader political and economic issues. Because it is totally a school-centered strategy it may have even less impact on the political economy than the compensatory strategy it has moved to displace. The attack on the compensatory strategy could lead to a dismantling of categorical aid (e.g., ESEA) and the loss of revenues that those programs have brought through the hiring of community residents. Such a possibility could also lead to an even greater disparity between Chicano adults in the classroom (e.g., teacher aides) and Chicano students than currently is the case. The lack of consideration of broader issues is reflected in curriculum and evaluation. The Effective School accepts existing curriculum and evaluation and wants only an equal share of the existing world for minorities. According to current law, a fair share of admissions to the University of California would be the top 12.5 per cent of Chicanos graduating annually from California's high schools. That would require a threefold increase in the current eligibility rate for University admission. Tripling the Chicano admission rate to the University would be a remarkable achievement, but would still leave 87.5 per cent unaccounted for. What would happen to them?

The prospects for the 12.5 per cent who conceivably get to the University because the Effective School succeeds is also in doubt. Effective School proponents are exceedingly optimistic about future opportunities for academically successful minority students. The optimism ignores important realities. The Effective School approach rose to prominence during a very conservative decade in American history and seems to have absorbed much of the orientation of that period. A very strong element in the Effective School is collaboration with business leaders, and while it is important for education to be symbiotically related to business, it is also important to have a measure of critical independence. Business leader pronouncements are not gospel; they reflect a particular slant not necessarily supportive of the political and economic health of minority communities. In planning for the future, consideration should be given to the 'sustained prosperity' during the decade the Effective School has been in existence. This prosperity not only failed to help Hispanics (and presumably Chicanos) — they got poorer (see Valencia, Chapter 1). Imagine what would have happened to Hispanics if, instead of prosperity, there had been a depression? One very distinct possibility would be a demand for greater change than is found in the Effective School. Effective School supporters claim that if Hispanics had not been assigned to unchallenging tracks and taught by teachers that expected little from them, they would have been able to benefit from the economic conditions. But the economic conditions, as good as they were, were not good enough to provide all college graduates with good jobs — as previously reported. In 1986, 20 per cent of college graduates were in jobs that required no college education. If in this period Chicanos had greater representation in the college graduate group it is very likely that their representation in less than college requirement jobs would in all probability have been even greater since Chicanos have lower incomes for years of education than Anglos. Moreover if Chicanos were more represented in the ranks of the college graduates, Anglos would have had less representation in this advantaged group with very difficult to predict results. It is not at all clear that increased education would in itself overcome the other political advantages and sponsorships into employment that Anglos presently enjoy. Attempting to gain advantage within a political economy without a clearly defined vision and a political strategy to reach that vision is a risky proposition, at best. It is much too early to conclude that the Effective School approach will either help or hinder Chicano advancement in the political economy.

A Democratic Education and its Implications for Chicano School Success

There is no unanimity about democratic education. Dewey's, 'what the best and wisest parent wants for his own child, that must the community want for all of its children' (1900, p. 7), is an attempt to enlarge the concern of democracy beyond the individual. That is certainly a part of a democratic education. The foundation on which the Effective School rests is the idea that the disadvantaged minority child deserves the same education 'the best and wisest want for their children'. To that extent the Effective School is democratic. But the best and the brightest may be very wrong (see Halberstam, 1972). Amy Gutmann goes far beyond Dewey in her definition of democratic education and warns about abuses in the name of democracy.

> Citizens and public officials can use democratic processes to destroy democracy. They can undermine the intellectual foundations of future democratic deliberations by implementing educational policies that either repress unpopular (but rational) ways of thinking or exclude some future citizens from an education adequate for participating in democratic politics. A democratic society must not be constrained to legislate what the wisest parents want for their child, yet it must be constrained not to legislate policies that render democracy repressive or discriminatory. A democratic theory of education recognizes the importance of empowering citizens to make educational policy and also constraining their choices among policies in accordance with those principles — of non-repression and nondiscrimination — that preserve the intellectual and social foundations of democratic deliberations. A society that empowers citizens to make educational policy, moderated by these two principled constraints, realizes the democratic ideal of democracy. (Gutmann, 1987, p. 14)

Democratic education is persuasion rather than coercion. It is not 'kinder and gentler' authoritarianism, or even authoritarianism that can be established to be in the interest of those being led. It is not any kind of persuasion; it is universal and significant discussion about significant issues. Democratic education is neither subordinating the individual to the interest of any group, nor is it the elevation of the individual over the group. It is most certainly not everyone doing his or her thing. Dewey's idea of voluntary association is a critical element that works only if there is persuasiveness to the association. Democratic education is both a means and an end. The means is informed debate leading to reflective action; the ends are a society 1) where decisions are made on the basis of universal participation in informed action; 2) where the majority rules only to the extent that specified rights of minorities are respected; and 3) where the decisions made equally encourage all members of the society to full participation in every facet of the society.

Shirley Engle and Anna Ochoa identify five tenets of democracy: 1) respect for the dignity of the individual accompanied by respect for differences of feelings and opinion; 2) the right of individuals and groups to participate in decisions within the society as a whole; 3) the right of all individuals to be informed — '... the widest and freest distribution of information to all of the people is a democratic necessity, and therefore the education of the masses is a central concern of a democracy' (Engle and Ochoa, 1988, p. 10); 4) the assumption of an open society where change and improvement are taken for granted; and 5) an independence of the individual from the group.

Presented here is a particular version of a Democratic School that embraces many of the practices of the Effective School, but not all of them. Elimination of tracking and expecting high levels of competence are indispensable to a democratic education, but these are not deemed to be sufficient for the elimination of Chicano school failure. The fundamental difference between the two strategies is in the assessment of the nature of the problem facing education. A Democratic School advocate does not believe that the problems to be solved rest solely within the school nor does he/she believe equality can be attained by extending the schooling to minorities that affluent populations presently receive. The long-term goals of change are far more ambitious in a Democratic School than in either the Compensatory or Effective School models. The day-to-day practices are no more ambitious. The problem posed in this book — Chicano school failure — is perceived to be the consequence of the failure to institute democratic schooling practices. A truly democratic school is not only an equal opportunity school, it is also one that takes into consideration poverty and other pressing world problems. One important difference between the Effective School and a Democratic School is that the latter strives for more than a redistribution of the pie; it critically examines the ingredients of the pie.

Democratic Schooling involves an articulated challenge to everyone to participate in the development of an understanding of the requirements of a democratic educational process. A Democratic School is one in which there is a conscious striving to organize all school activities toward compliance with mutually agreed-upon requirements. A Democratic School can be conceived to have four components: knowledge; participation; rights; and equal encouragement (Pearl, 1988). These components are similar to the tenets identified by Engle and Ochoa (1988).

When knowledge is addressed from a democratic perspective, a crucial question is raised: knowledge for what? And that question is an invitation to a debate. What the Effective School considers closed is wide open in the Democratic School. In a Democratic School every student is provided with sufficient knowledge to permit each to be an informed participant in debates about policies directed toward: establishing world peace, overcoming poverty, preserving the livability of the environment, and defining and achieving racial, ethnic, and gender equality. The Effective School asks adult authorities to solve the problem of inequality; in the Democratic School students are expected to play a significant role in studying the problem, proposing solutions, and acting on those proposals. The difference is active participation in the development of knowledge versus passive absorption of authority defined knowledge.

A Democratic School is not only concerned with big issues, there is also concern for individual quality of life. In a Democratic School every student is provided with the knowledge and experience to have *equal* choice in work, politics, culture, leisure and personal development (Pearl, 1972). With work, the Democratic School and the Effective School differ in that, in the latter, students are asked to help shape the configuration of work.

Equality from the Democratic School perspective moves from solely an evaluative judgment to a curricular concern. Chicano school success, for example, becomes a subject to be taught, and subsumed under it are the artificially abstracted subjects — English, social studies, math, science, foreign languages, and the arts. These same 'subjects' provide the intellectual foundation for solving other problems, but in each instance, the knowledge is developed with the problem in mind, not the other way around. Unless *all* students are taught that they are responsible for solving both their own and the world's problems and the school has the responsibility for providing them with the opportunity to develop the knowledge necessary for solving important issues, the resolution of pressing problems must be delegated to some unspecified 'others'. Unfortunately, in important areas the 'others' do not agree and they are forced to turn to the uninformed to adjudicate the differences. Ignorance does not relieve any citizen in a society that aspires to be democratic from responsibility, but merely guarantees that the final decision will not be based on knowledge or logic. Even if a group of 'super knowers' could come to a consensus on a particular matter there is no assurance that the people not involved in the decision-making would permit effective action to be taken. An uninformed electorate may not be able to solve any problems, but that ignorance does not prevent the sabotaging of solutions imposed on the ignorant by some élite. In many instances the élite-inspired solutions were wrong. The errors made by élites and sabotaged by ignorance do not constitute a defense of ignorance. The inability of élites to be right on all or even most important issues only makes the case for a Democratic School more powerful.

Chicano school failure is both a big picture and an individual concern. The knowledge developed and organized for solving the problem is presented at both levels. At one level, the student is prepared to be a citizen with responsibility for determining school policies and other policies that impinge on the issue of Chicano school failure. At the other level, all students are encouraged to succeed in all of society's legal activities and in all of society's sanctioned activities and to derive fully the benefits of citizen in a democratic school. The two levels are interrelated and are taught with the interrelationship in mind.

The issue of knowledge is a critical one for education. Two separate issues require more illumination. One, is the knowledge sufficient to meet the goal of informed citizen? The other, does the curriculum fairly treat all groups and individuals? It is hard to dispute the low level of knowledge requirement in today's schools. Almost every observer of the school finds it a stupid place

(Cusick, 1983; Goodlad 1984; Jackson, 1986; Welsh, 1986). Reform has not made schools more intellectually stimulating; if anything, they are more vapid and deadly. Ask any high school student, 'how was school today?' and the vast majority will answer, 'borrrrring'. That response stimulates school authorities to lower intellectual demands. The Effective School seems bound and determined to make schools as deadly for the minorities as it has been for the affluent. The issue is not only that school knowledge is unengaging. It may also be off the mark. What is taught is not what people really need to know to be creative influences in the emerging world (Sirotnik, 1983). What is taught about peace, poverty, labor, race, gender, class and ethicality is both superficial and often distorted.

Peace is not an important curriculum area in US education. Most textbooks on education give it no more than a line, including it as an elective topic in social studies (Gutek, 1983; Hessong and Weeks, 1987; Johanningmeier, 1985; Johnson, Collins, Dupuis and Johansen, 1988; Levine and Havighurst, 1989; Ornstein and Levine, 1984; Provenzo, 1986; Selakovich, 1984; Smith, 1987; Walker, Kozma and Green, 1989; Wynn and Wynn, 1988). The *History-Social Science Curriculum Framework* issued by the State Department of California makes passing references to issues of war and peace but these are only incidental and tend to reinforce existing US foreign policy. The course descriptions included in the framework are designed to provide 'an integrated and sequential development' (State Department of California, 1988, p. 29). The course descriptions are intended to be merely 'illustrative' (*ibid.*, p. 29) rather than prescriptive, but these guides clearly indicate an absence of concern for preparing students to be leaders in foreign policy development. It is not until students reach the tenth grade that they begin to deal with peace issues. In this year students learn about World Wars I and II and the rise of totalitarianism under Hitler and Stalin. They are expected to discover how '... Western leaders abandoned the Polish government-in-exile and acquiesced to Stalin's demands for Poland ...', and learn about, '... the Vietnam War and its aftermath, particularly the genocide committed in Cambodia by the Pol Pot regime' (*ibid.*, p. 89). In the eleventh grade students are introduced to foreign policy. They learn about Theodore Roosevelt's '"big stick" policies ... President Wilson's Fourteen Points and the League of Nation', and from World War II they learn, '... this war taught Americans to think in global terms ... [and to] grasp the geopolitical implications of the war and its importance for postwar international relations' (*ibid.*, pp. 96–7). A major concern in the eleventh grade is on the Cold War and on the actions based on cold war thinking. In this year students are made aware of 'President Eisenhower's warning about a "military-industrial complex"' (*ibid.*, p. 98) and the impact that increased military demands have on the ability to meet civilian needs. It is at this time in a student's career that she or he learns about policy toward Latin America, '... and the spread of Cuban influence, indigenous revolution, and counterrevolution in Nicaragua and El Salvador in 1908' (*ibid.*, p. 98). Students are asked to consider foreign policy from different political party perspectives. Recommended for the concluding element of a one semester twelfth-grade 'Principles of American Democracy [course is] ... an activity in which students analyze a major social issue.... Among the topics that might be addressed are: ... nuclear arms proliferation and arms control ...' (*ibid.*, p. 107). Nowhere in this panoramic sweep of events and concepts is there a specific call for a systematic analysis of four competing approaches to foreign policy: peace through strength (current policy), peace through multinational actions (United Nations or some extension of that approach), bi-lateral agreements (SALT and extensions of that approach), and unilateral disarmament initiatives (large-scale reduction in military expenditures).

While all students should know more about different approaches to foreign policy, Chicanos have a particular concern with peace issues. The East Los Angeles Chicano Moratorium, at which the demand for an end to the Vietnam War was made, signaled in may ways the consolidation of a Chicano conscious-ness (Munoz, 1989). A foreign policy dictated by overwhelming military strength could also impact heavily on Chicanos. Any unnecessary dollars spent on defense could have adverse effects on the quality of Chicano life because those expenditures could preclude funding activities that could reduce poverty and as previously cited Chicanos are disproportionately involved in poverty.

Poverty receives an interesting treatment in education. It is a part of the curriculum but only as an historical oddity, and it is also presented as a justifica-tion for compensatory education. In the course descriptions provided in the *History-Social Science Curriculum Framework* (State Department of California, 1988), poverty crops intermittently. In the eighth grade students are expected to learn that the early years of the Republic were characterized by boom and bust that 'created both progress and poverty' (p. 71) and later, during the rise of industrialism after the Civil War, students are to be told there was a dark side to America — sweat shops, grinding impoverishment, and prejudice directed against Hispanics, Blacks, Jews and others. Toward the end of the year students learn that great strides have been made in the twentieth century to overcome poverty 'while a significant minority ...' (p. 75) continue to be left behind.

During high school students are expected to become more analytical. Social studies in these years are designed 'to deepen and extend their understanding of the more demanding civic learnings' (p. 76). The deepening of understanding of poverty begins in the eleventh grade with an 'in-depth study ... the Progressive Era' (p. 94) and the efforts of muckrakers, for example, Lincoln Steffens, and novelists, Upton Sinclair for instance, to awaken concern for the downtrodden and poor. Poverty again becomes a topic for discussion in connection with the Great Depression of the 1930s (also in the eleventh grade). Since World War II, poverty is treated as a minority problem, and as a minority problem it is neither accurately described nor seriously analyzed. The Poverty Program of the 1960s is given at most a quick once-over with particular interventions, such as Affirma-tive Action, illuminated neither by a logic nor sufficient supportive evidence for students to make sense of the efforts to reduce poverty in populations where it is concentrated. Of much greater importance is the dearth of consideration of different possible strategies for the elimination of poverty. This is particularly true today when there is virtually no political debate of alternative approaches to any social problem. Not too long ago progressive taxation or other governmen-tal interventions were given some consideration as measures to improve the lot of those at the bottom of the economic heap. Now, no idea is floated until there is substantial evidence of an already existing large-scale support. Notions and visions that stimulated debate twenty years ago — guaranteed annual income, stimulation of the economy, government-generated full employment and com-munity action (Lampman, Theobold, Pearl and Alinsky, 1966) — simply are not part of the current intellectual scene.

Education textbooks are organized to produce one of two effects; poverty is either an important cause of school failure or schools are organized to keep the poor at the bottom of the social ladder (e.g., Ornstein and Levine, 1984; Smith, 1987). In one instance the inference is that compensatory education is the desired response and in the other there is the implicit conclusion that nothing can be done. And while some textbooks are critical of current school practices there are virtually no practical suggestions for improving schooling. Receiving no mention is the idea that poverty should be part of the curriculum and students should be challenged to review and evaluate alternative solutions as they struggle to develop solutions of their own.

The environment has become increasingly a topic of class discussion. As early as the fourth grade the *History-Social Science Curriculum Framework* (State Department of California, 1988) calls for children in California schools 'to explore the relationship between California's economic and population growth in the twentieth century and its geographical location and environmental factors' (p. 50). Textbooks on social studies in the elementary school subsume the environment under the study of geography. Human alteration of the environment for good and bad are briefly and superficially considered in elementary school. Energy is a topic to be considered. The proposed curriculum does not do what Schunke insists is needed.

> The world is facing a number of energy problems such as dwindling fossil fuels, increasing energy costs, the nuclear controversy, energy-related environmental problems, and the unequal distribution of energy resources throughout the world. These and other problems require confrontation and resolution. (Schunke, 1988, p. 73)

Consideration of energy or any other environmental problem is not likely to improve the lot of Chicanos. When the environmental movement caught the imagination of Americans, it displaced concern for the plight of minorities. And while Chicanos and other minorities tend to suffer the most from environmental devastation — working in unsafe conditions, living in and about toxic waste, suffering the most during periods when energy costs rise, etc., it is also true that Chicanos can be the victims of environmental action. A recommendation in the *History-Social Science Curriculum Framework*, calls for an examination of 'the conflict between increased economic growth and environmental priorities' (State Department of California, 1988, p. 78). This conflict often translates into livelihood (jobs) versus livability (the environment). Chicanos have difficulty getting jobs when unemployment is low. When the economy is restricted because of environmental considerations those who have the greatest difficulty securing employment suffer the most. Asking students to invent a full-employment, non-poverty economy that sustains a healthy environment is never a consideration in current curriculum frameworks.

The argument of ideological bias in the curriculum designed to reproduce class, gender and racial inequality is substantive. It is not merely that issues of justice are inadequately treated in the curriculum, school practices reinforce unequal treatment (Apple, 1979; Friere, 1985; Giroux, 1981). The argument goes like this: 'Schools are not insulated from racism, sexism, classism, and handicapped in society. They mirror these forms of social stratification, and in several ways contribute to their reproduction' (Grant and Sleeter, 1985, p. 142). Research tends to support lack of equality in curriculum. Subtly, and not so subtly, students learn that the 'most important things are done by white, wealthy men; that students have little power to shape the conditions of institutions within which they live; and that injustices ... are in the past tense and are no longer issues' (Grant and Sleeter, 1985, p. 144). Grant and Sleeter examine how the most celebrated reports on educational reform have dealt with these inequalities and find them timid and superficial. For example, Mortimer Adler in *The Paideia Proposal* (1982) allows that many students grow up immersed in poverty but he does not recommend 'that schools help them critically examine this problem, its roots, and possible avenues for change' (Grant and Sleeter, 1985, p. 150).

Probably the most dramatic evidence of exclusion of Chicanos from the curriculum is found in E.D. Hirsch's *Cultural Literacy* (1988). Hirsch, like Adler, calls for a common core of knowledge that all in the society must know if they are to be 'culturally literate'. He and a few colleagues develop a listing of critical knowledge consisting of approximately 5,000 names, dates, quotations, events, etc. In that enormous inventory the word Chicano is included but, apart from Joan Baez, no Chicanos or Chicanas. John Wayne is on the list, as is Shirley Temple and Babe Ruth and Superman. Not to be found in this compendium of *What Every American Needs to Know* (the subtitle of Hirsch's book) are the likes of Ernesto Galarza, Tomás Rivera, Luisa Moreno, Josefina Fierro, the Sleepy Lagoon Defense Committee, or Caesar Chavez. It is not only Chicanos that are excluded from this list but virtually all Latinos. Laurel and Hardy and W.C. Fields are there, but not Cantinflas — the Mexican Charlie Chaplin. Of course, the non-Mexican Charlie Chaplin made it. Benito Juarez receives no mention, while Davy Crockett, Bing Crosby, Al Capone, and John Dillinger and even Archie Bunker get included — some might conclude that is because he helped create the list. In this instance, Chicanos receive very much worse treatment than do Blacks. Hirsch includes a number of distinguished Black writers — Maya Angelou, Countee Cullen, Paul Laurence Dunbar, Gwendolyn Brooks, Langston Hughes; some Black musicians are in the list — Louis Armstrong, Scott Joplin, Ella Fitzgerald, Chuck Berry (curiously Duke Ellington and Count Basie are out); a sprinkling of Black scientists — Benjamin Banneker and George Washington Carver; and assorted social activists — Nat Turner, Sojourner Truth, Harriet Tubman, Frederick Douglass, Booker T. Washington, W.E.B. Du Bois, Marcus Garvey, Martin Luther King, Jr. and Paul Robeson (who could have been listed as an athlete and artist as well). Making Hirsch's list is a distinguished Black educator, Mary McLeod Bethune, a community leader, Ralph Bunche, and a sampling of athletes — Joe Louis, Jesse Owens, Jackie Robinson, Hank Aaron, Muhammad Ali. Nowhere to be found are such Hispanics as Carlos Fuentes or Gabriel Garcia Marquez and countless other artists, scholars, political leaders, even athletes. The only Latin Americans that Hirsch feels are worthy learning about are Diego Rivera and Fidel Castro.

The absence of a Chicano body of knowledge in the curriculum is a contributing factor to Chicano school failure but how much the addition of a number of names sporadically thrown about in unconnected bits and pieces would help is not at all clear. Many of the Blacks Hirsch recognizes are included in the curriculum and their inclusion has not materially improved school performance of Blacks. The arbitrary and somewhat capricious identification of vital knowledge is a problem no matter who or what is included. Knowledge, like everything in education, becomes universally appreciated when that knowledge is used to solve important individual and social problems. Hirsch makes claims for the utility of his definition of 'cultural literacy'. But the claims ring hollow, there are no specific problems that he shows will be solved with his notions of common knowledge. How does knowing of the existence of Jimmy Stewart (included by Hirsh) aid us in anything other than trivia? Why should Jimmy Stewart be on the list and Gary Cooper and Henry and Jane Fonda excluded? That the Hirsch book could have received some critical acclaim is an indication of the inadequacy of the debate over necessary knowledge. That debate will not be improved by experts writing better books. That debate will be improved by involving a much wider range of people in the discussions about necessary knowledge. The decisions made about curriculum must be far more democratic than is currently the case. In Democratic Schooling the debate about necessary knowledge is ongoing and unending. Inequality becomes a major part of the curriculum, and the nature of its existence is examined in depth as are all plausible solutions. The debate is democratic when everyone participates with equal power and access to knowledge.

Democratic participation is equal involvement in decisions that affect one's life. In Democratic Schooling, students and parents are deeply involved in decisions about curriculum, discipline, budgets, co-curricular activities, school organization, and selection of staff and administrators. Their opinions are taken seriously. While both Democratic Schooling and the Effective School require strong teacher and administrative leaders, the leadership is very different. The Democratic Schooling leader is a leader to the extent that she or he is able to persuade with logic and evidence. One standard against which a democratic leader is judged is acceptance of his or her authority. If no one voluntarily follows, she or he is no leader. Winning a following is not sufficient; that following has to be won on the basis of the quality of the argument. Such leadership generates an atmosphere of reasonability and mutual responsibility. The Effective School leader sets the tone and commands. There is little in that system that is negotiable. The curriculum and the standards are fixed. Leadership in such instances is efficiency. There is shared decision-making, but only on the means to non-negotiable goals.

The two approaches differ in their understanding of accountability. The authoritarian Effective School is accountable upwards — students to the teacher, teacher to the principal, principal to the school superintendent, and ultimately to national interest. In Democratic Schooling, accountability goes downward — the ultimate determination is made by the student. Being accountable downward is defending with logic and evidence all requests made of students, to students. The strength of the school is the quality of the arguments. In both types of schools, effort is made to generate loyalty and student ownership of the process. In the Effective School, the loyalty is won with immediate payoffs in improved performance on standardized achievement tests and the long-term return is promise of economic success. In Democratic Schooling, the immediate pay-off is political influence in classroom activities (although academic performance would be an important consideration in the decision-making); the long-term pay-off is an extension of this gratification. Participation is intended to bring about a change in definition of self, from a less self-centered to a more citizen-centered individual.

In this sense, participation is a logical extension of cooperative learning that is featured in some Effective Schools.

Student rights are important in a Democratic School. Included in these rights are: 1) freedom of expression — the right to express unpopular political sentiments and disagree with the teacher and other school authorities; 2) privacy — protection from prying and intrusion into personal space; 3) a due process system of presumption of innocence, the right not to testify against oneself, the right to counsel, the right to trial before an independent tribunal, and protection against cruel and unusual punishments; and 4) the right not to be a captive audience. Neither the Effective School nor the Compensatory Approach gives much attention to student rights, which are often sacrificed in the interests of efficiency. Even when fully understood and appreciated rights are not easily practiced; there are strains between different democratic requirements. Universal education and the right not to be a captive audience do not fit neatly together, and such strains test the leadership of the teacher and administrator. In democracy, the test is whether the authority can persuade rather than coerce. It is the lack of serious effort to be persuasive on student rights that makes the Effective School an authoritarian school. For rights to be a reality, they must be prominent in the curriculum. It is inconceivable that anyone educated about democracy and rights would elevate, for example, Oliver North to a hero status.

Equal encouragement in all legitimate activities of a society is a democratic requirement that addresses both the distribution of benefits in the society and the limitations in the opportunity structure. In Democratic Schooling there would be considerable discussion and experimentation with three different understandings of equality: equal treatment, equal result, and equal encouragement. The first of these is espoused by the Effective School whose approach calls for treating all students in an identical manner. Equal results require some form of redistribution, either voluntary or confiscatory, whereby some assets, wealth or special services, of the advantaged are transferred to the disadvantaged. The Compensatory Approach is a very modest and quite flawed form of redistribution. The third would offer such treatment to encourage all to maximum competence. Each of these requires thorough examination of a range of policies including: wage policies, tax policies, the role of government in the creation of services, or in the redistribution of wealth and income, university admission policies, and credentialing policies. Currently there is precious little discussion about equality of any kind anywhere in our society and most of it is acrimonious attacks on limited efforts to ameliorate underrepresentation of women and minorities.

The requirements of democracy enter into every phase of education — school structure, curriculum, classroom management, discipline, and governance. Democratic Schooling is organized on the premise that Chicano students fail in school because Chicanos are victims of undemocratic practices in and out of school. The lack of democracy extends far beyond a denial of schooling affluent students receive. More important, by far, is the exclusion from the decision-making that determines the education a person receives. In Democratic Schooling situations are created that enable the powerless to become powerful — powerful in the sense that they can understand the systems that act on them sufficiently well to change them in a defensible and predictable direction. If the goal of the Effective School is to master academics, the goal of Democratic schooling is to put knowledge to work.

Democracy is never an all-or-nothing affair. In Democratic Schooling, democracy is conceived of as a more-or-less proposition. The intent is not to arrive at a perfect democracy, but rather to develop one that is more equitable and better. Today, some populations in the society get closer to the benefits of democracy than do others, and when they do they build barriers that make it more difficult for the others to enjoy that which an imperfect democracy provides. Such a distortion is discussed in Democratic Schooling as a prologue to developing in students the need to consider large systems, because only when democracy is considered as a total system will it be possible for the excluded to be included. When those in power create policies that deny access to the excluded, they undermine the foundations of democracy on which they stand. A Democratic School thus is one that makes the world a better place for all, but not without struggle or sacrifice. Part of Democratic Schooling curriculum is learning how to produce change democratically. In Democratic Schooling students learn not only what should be changed but how to participate in Democratic Social Change.

The basic assumption of a Democratic Social Change is that inequality is deeply imbedded in all of society's structures and only a total political strategy will lead to a significant and sustained reduction in Chicano school failure. The strategy is informed by the belief that all change is political and that only democratic political change can reduce inequality because it is only in democracy that there is an interest in equality. Turning to democracy at this time may appear to be a futile endeavor in that commitment to democratic understanding is crumbling almost everywhere. Not only is there little concern for the democratic concept but there is little interest in democratic activities. Fewer and fewer people vote with each succeeding election. It is possible to extrapolate to a time when an election will be called and nobody will come. Democracy is a meaningless irrelevant term to school children; it never has had a footing in US education. And yet, unless there is a turn to democracy, the conditions of inequality that introduced this essay (and the other conditions that are related to it: a deteriorating environment, a non-responsive government, an inability to achieve non-violent resolution to international dispute, runaway growth in crime and substance abuse, etc.) can only get worse. If democracy does not inform education, some action distinctly undemocratic will.

Democracy is important to education because education can never be understood on its own terms (as much as the Effective School and Compensatory Approach educators would like that to happen). Education always is, and always should be subsumed under national purposes. Joel Spring generates a list of national purposes that education has been required to serve (Spring, 1985). In the 1950s a right-wing initiative directed schools to win the war in space. In the 1960s a liberal Democratic administration appealed to schools to overcome racism and poverty. In the 1970s the Nixon-Ford administrations called on education to overcome unemployability (as distinct from unemployment) with expanded vocational education. And in the 1980s education was reformed so that the United States can regain its rightful position in the world economy. 'In none of these eras did the public schools win the military arms race, end poverty, or cure unemployment ... Education has been a political football and has been made to serve special interests' (Spring, 1985, pp. 86–7). Education as a subservient institution must continue until a democratic education itself is raised to the level of 'national interest'. Anything less will be a repetition of failed efforts.

The case for a Democratic Social Change stems from two historical sources: social reproduction theorists and social reconstruction theorists. The social reproduction theorists (Apple, 1979; Bowles and Gintis, 1976; Giroux, 1981) present both logic and considerable evidence that schools reproduce the economic structure and ideological foundations of a society. Schools are structured to direct students to appropriate stations in life and thereby preserve race, class, and gender inequality. According to this line of thinking students are taught to accept conditions of inequality as necessary and fair. In practice, ideological reproduction has changed over time. Once patriotism was a major emphasis of the curriculum and the teaching. Frances Fitzgerald traces the changes in history textbooks.

> Ideologically speaking, the histories of the fifties were implacable, seamless. Inside their covers, America was perfect: the greatest nation in the world, and the embodiment of democracy, freedom, and technological progress.... Who, after all, would dispute the wonders of technology or the superiority of the English colonists over the Spanish? Who would find fault with the pastorale of the West or the Old South? Who would question the anti-Communist crusade? (Fitzgerald, 1979, p. 10)

Today, social production is less acts of commission — the active teaching of mindless loyalty — and more acts of omission — the not teaching enough of anything, and thereby discouraging students from becoming intellectually involved with important issues. Students are taught just enough to be intellectually paralyzed.

> ... texts have changed and with them the country that American children are growing up into. The society that was once uniform is now a patchwork of rich and poor, old and young, men and women, blacks, whites, Hispanics and Indians. The system that ran so smoothly by means of the Constitution under the guidance of benevolent conductor Presidents is now a rattletrap affair. The past is no highway to the present; it is a collection of issues and events that do not fit together and that lead in no single direction. (Fitzgerald, 1979, pp. 10–11)

Social reproduction analysts make a strong case for what schools do, whether by omission or commission, however, they leave us with very few specific practical suggestions for change. No coherent program of action stems from their analysis.

The social reconstructionists believe schools can be active initiators of social change. Although he never formally identified with the classification, the most celebrated social reconstructionist was George Counts (1932). His *Dare the Schools Build a New Social Order?* made the case in the extreme. The argument is less outrageous when put in the context of its time. A great economic depression was sweeping the world and confidence in traditional leadership was low. Counts took the position that since some group of adults would necessarily impose themselves on the child why should it not be teachers,

> ... if [teachers] could increase sufficiently their stock of courage, intelligence and vision [they] might become a social force of some magnitude ... To the extent that they ... fashion the curriculum and the procedures of the school they will definitely and positively influence the social attitudes, ideals, and behavior of the coming generation. (Counts, 1932, p. 26)

Counts believed teachers could not be greater bunglers than the financiers, politicians and businessmen who he would have them replace. He did not advocate that teachers indoctrinate students with a particular point of view, but rather offer to them 'visions'against which all 'our social institutions and practices ... should be critically examined' (Counts, 1932, p. 27). In those dismal days, Counts consigned capitalism to history's junk heap and looked to some form of democratic collectivism for salvation. He was not particularly optimistic. His reading of history informed him that brutal oppression and injustice were the ways the American privileged responded to challenge. But he accepted Justice Oliver Wendell Holmes' reading of Natural Law, 'We are all fighting to make the kind of world that we should like'. He believed that teachers were obliged to present students with a

> ... finer and more authentic vision [if they were critical of] ... so-called patriotic societies [which] ... though narrow and unenlightened, ... nonetheless represent an honest attempt to meet a profound social and educational need.... Only [when we as teachers offer] a legacy of spiritual values will our children be enabled to find their place in the world, be lifted out the present morass of moral indifference, be liberated from the senseless struggle for material success, and be challenged to high endeavor and achievement. (Counts, 1932, p. 52)

Counts' call for democracy is neither convincing nor operational. A more modest and defensible democratic change strategy, couched in a current context, would be a paraphrase of Counts, something like, *Dare the School Prepare Students for Democratic Citizenship?* Such a call is consistent with the State Department of California's *History-Social Science Curriculum Framework* (1988). The guidelines recommend that for the twelfth-grade course on 'Contemporary Issues', students prepare research on current social problems and present their positions at a school-wide consortium (State Department of California, 1988). A Democratic Social Change strategy would be more adventurous than that, but not much more adventurous. In a democratic strategy, more debate would be encouraged as well as action consistent with the position taken.

An education that prepares students for democratic change asks them to accept responsibility for governance in the classroom, and the issues of race, gender and ethnic equality faced by students on a daily basis. Students not only formulate tactics to deal with inequality, they also evaluate the effectiveness of their efforts. It is not expected that all students would be for equality. It is expected that in a fair and complete debate, most people will be for equality and that the will of the majority will prevail, while the rights of the minority are protected. If that is not true, we are in very serious trouble.

One basic difference between the Effective School and Democratic Schooling is the responsibility given students to define and solve the problem of inequality. Democratic Schooling takes the Effective School notion of 'everyone can learn' and carries it one step further. If every student can learn, then every student can act independently on that learning. That additional step transcends the student from being a pawn in someone else's game to being an independent agent in the creation of the future. The next step would be to allow those students to find ways for voluntary association with others in collective action. Democracy goes an additional step: democratic citizens not only act, they also evaluate the effectiveness of that action and make the appropriate adjustments. The strategy consists of ongoing intellectual action and reflection (Freire, 1968).

A democratic education may sound too theoretical or abstract to be useful. Is there any evidence to indicate desirability and feasibility with particular relevance to minority school failure? Not surprisingly, Democratic Schooling has had far too few rigorous tests. What little there is, however, is encouraging. In the 1960s, the Upward Bound Program at the University of Oregon was an experiment in Democratic Schooling. Special admission students (i.e., poor white and minority low achievers) were challenged to be involved in the governance of the program and to participate in other school reform activities at the University. At the same time, they were encouraged to be excellent university students. Four years later most of those 'inadmissible students' graduated from the University. One who did not graduate on time was Mary Groda. She was recruited to the University from a training school for delinquent girls. She was beset with many learning difficulties and personal problems, but that did not prevent her from becoming a medical doctor. Her story is presented in the 1986 CBS film, *Love Mary*. The democratic nature of the education she received did not get much attention, nor did the fact that others in that program with equally undistinguished pre-college academic records graduated and went on to successful postgraduate careers.

What distinguished the project was that it combined a rigorous traditional curriculum with a curriculum that challenged students to create the future. The workings of the University were demystified so that students would understand the logic and functioning of the institution that they first had to survive if they were ever to change it. The project only had a few elements of Democratic Schooling and yet it succeeded beyond all expectations.

New Careers is perhaps a more spectacular example that not only assisted minorities to graduate from the University but at the same time effectively recruited underrepresented minorities into teaching and other professions. In New Careers, rather than having the applicant meet the requirements of the job, a career ladder was created — e.g., teacher aide, teacher assistant, teacher associate, teacher. The entry position required no prior skill or experience. New Careerists worked their way each step of the ladder through a combination of work experience, university courses delivered at the work site and liberal art courses at the university (Pearl and Riessman, 1965). The largest of the New Career programs was the Career Opportunity Program (COP) of the Educational Professional Development Act (EPDA) of 1967.

> The centerpiece of COP was the paraprofessional aide who was usually minority (54 per cent Black, 14.2 per cent Hispanic-American, 3.7 per cent Native American).... Nearly nine-tenths of those enrolled were members of low-income families (88 per cent were female) ... The

program embraced 132 separate sites, roughly 18,000 participants ...
(Carter, 1977, pp. 183–4)

The goals of the Career Opportunity Program were diverse, broad and
ambitious. In retrospect, probably too broad, too diverse and too ambitious. The
COP was designed to: increase underrepresented minority teachers, demonstrate
that inadmissible students can succeed in higher education, lift people mired in
poverty out of poverty, better meet the needs of low-income children, improve
staffing in schools, and 'respond to the growing belief that the then-present
designs of teacher education were inadequate, particularly in preparing teachers
for the children of the poor' (Carter, 1977, p. 184).

New Careers apparently made progress on all fronts. How much progress is
difficult to gauge since the program was short-lived, inconsistent within and
between sites and only superficially evaluated. Despite these considerable difficulties there is powerful evidence to suggest that many minorities were recruited
into teaching.

COP was designed to serve low-income and minority adults. Nearly
nine-tenths of those enrolled were members of low-income families and
some seven-tenths were non-white. The continuing shortage of teachers
with such backgrounds is seen, for example, in Alaska where 95 per cent
of the children in the State Operated Schools were Native (Aleut,
Eskimo, or Indian), while 99 per cent of the teachers at the start of the
COP project were non-Native. On the Crow and Northern Cheyenne
Reservations in Montana only five of the 210 certified teachers in 1970
were Indians. At their conclusion, the Alaska Career Opportunity Program (run in conjunction with Teacher Corps) will have quadrupled the
number of Native teachers, while the project serving the Crow and
Northern Cheyenne will have increased the number of Indian teachers
tenfold.

Throughout the Hispanic-American and Indian communities there
was still a woeful underrepresentation of 'indigenous' teachers. In Texas
and the Southwest, for example COP projects emphasized bilingual and
bicultural (Hispanic) education, and in New York City, a significant
focus was placed in meeting the needs of part of that city's Puerto Rican
children.

Of the 142 degree-earning COP participants in the Chicago project,
118 became teachers in 'target area schools', that is, in schools populated
by children of low-income, minority (Black and Hispanic) background.
(Carter, 1977, pp. 187, 204)

Students in the COP project did extremely well in higher education. An
evaluation of four COP projects in Pennsylvania found among those

... people who normally would have been rejected in a standard (college) admissions review ... less than four per cent of all COP participants were dropped from the program for academic problems ... in
Philadelphia 85 per cent had a C average or better and 46 per cent had an
average of B or higher ... (in Philadelphia 27 students had graduated

with grade point average 3.5 or higher and been named Presidential Scholars). (Carter, 1977, p. 188)

Did COP better meet the needs of low-income children and improve staffing in schools? Again the evidence, though uneven and necessarily inconclusive, is generally positive. In the four Pennsylvania projects the Educational Research Associates of Bowie, Maryland — an independent evaluator — concluded

> the schools were affected in a positive way. [Noted were] ... the greatly increased use of teacher aides, a significant change in the way they were used, the beneficial impact of aides on the environment (specifically in the case of Eire with a history of racial tension and violence, the reduction and ultimate disappearance of the disturbances that plagued one location), an increased leadership role for teachers, increased opportunities for minority administrators, greater dependence on local neighborhoods as a source of new teachers, and a general acknowledgment that the COP-trained teachers would be more effective than others who had entered the various systems. (Carter, 1977, pp. 196–7)

Other research also supported the notion that COP was a good way to recruit teachers.

> The COP program based at the University of North Dakota, with participants from four Indian reservation communities, provided college degrees and teacher certification for 51 new teachers of American Indian origin, Virtually all returned to their communities as full-fledged teachers, thereby creating or improving those conditions: Better relations between children and their schools, a probable slowdown in the rate of teacher turnover, teachers thoroughly attuned to children and their problems, community pride in Indian-related attitudes, and, far from least, proof that schools with Indian children could thrive with significantly larger percentages of Indian teachers. (Carter, 1977, p. 204)

Similar results were found in other communities where the racial/ethnic composition of the student body was much different than the teachers. COP teachers did more than bring a sense of the community to the schools. They were, in many other ways, excellent additions to the teaching profession. When compared with a comparable cohort of non-COP first-year teachers the COP teacher appeared to be a better teacher. On tests designed to measure teacher attitude, the COP had more positive attitudes. They performed '... in a more desirable manner ... there was more interchange between student and teacher and students' talk was more responsive and extended ... [and] more highly correlated with positive student performance' (Carter, 1977, p. 207).

The success of COP teachers did not appear to fade the longer teachers were employed. If anything the differences between COP and non-COP teachers increased in the second year of teaching,

> COP-trained second year teachers were more aware than their peers of the 'ethos' of the schools ... and the gap [between them and the

non-COP group] was widening ... COP teachers tended to be more accepting of individual differences among pupils and felt a greater sense of responsibility and accountability for the pupil's progress. (Carter, 1977, pp. 209–10)

In a follow-up assessment of two bilingual programs (Crystal City and Port Isabel, Texas) the differences between the COP and non-COP teachers were even more marked, 'notably in the areas of two-way exchanges between pupils and teachers.... These higher standards were attributed to the unique qualities of bilingual education' (Carter, 1977, p. 210).

The impact of a New Career program can be seen after two decades. The University of Minnesota, in conjunction with many social agencies, had a New Career program, which included the COP, and twenty years after its inception efforts were made to evaluate its success. Like most other such efforts, the program participants had been poor, predominantly Black single women (welfare recipients with children). Virtually none had completed high school. Twenty years later, of the 207 persons who had been in the program, at least one had earned a doctorate, dozens had masters degrees and about half, on whom information was found, had graduated from the University. New Careerists reported that the program had changed their lives around from existences hopelessly mired in poverty to well-established ways of life (Amram, Flax, Hamermesh and Marty, 1988).

New Careers programs met some of the requirements of democratic education. The efforts to extend knowledge were not very extensive, but much of the knowledge obtained by the New Careerist and from them to those they taught, was organized in ways to be more understandable. The learning was much more active and as a consequence the participation in decisions in matters that affected the students' lives was considerable (both for the New Careerists and those they taught). Rights may have been a consideration in some New Career projects but they were not a quality emphasized in the authorizing legislation nor were they noted in any evaluative report. The most notable democratic achievement was in the area of equal encouragement. When New Careerists were given the opportunity to succeed in both higher education and in professions, they not only performed far better than expected, but they equaled or exceeded the performances of those from advantaged backgrounds.

The New Career strategy meets affirmative action objectives on the basis of merit. New Careerists earn their way up the ladder without special treatment. Moreover, the record of New Careerists raises doubts about the fairness of existing academic systems. Despite its successes, New Careers was dismantled. Recently (1988), a Task Force on Minority Teachers appointed by Secretary of Education Cavazos has recommended that 20 million dollars be appropriated every year to reinstitute a New Career strategy to facilitate the recruitment of minorities into teaching. Federal legislation and legislation in California authorizing New Career approaches are currently wending their way through the machinery. Without more democratic input such legislation is likely to suffer the fate of earlier New Career projects.

While it is undeniable that New Careers had important democratic qualities, it also is true that the programs as conceived and implemented had serious flaws. The most serious problem was an unwillingness to critically examine the fundamental purposes of education. New Careers burst onto the scene when the credibility of education was at its lowest ebb, simultaneously attacked from the left that called for the end of schooling, not its reform, while the right crusaded against permissiveness which was blamed for everything from the war in Vietnam to the beginnings of a drug epidemic. A serious examination of education was not undertaken then, just as today's reforms are derived from a superficial examination and analysis. New Careers, like the Compensatory Approach and the Effective School was a top-down program. It rose when an élite supported it and it fell when that élite lost interest or power. A revitalization of education, particularly an education devoted to true equal encouragement and the full realization of the potential of Chicanos, among others, requires a political constituency powerful enough to produce such an education. Anything less is not only undemocratic, it is also impossible. Whatever else is to be learned from the New Career experience that is one very important lesson. The potential political constituency for a truly democratic education comes from an alliance of professionals, paraprofessionals, students and their parents and others in the community who recognize the critical need for a democratic education.

The democratic influence of New Careers, while noteworthy, was transient and limited. Many individual teachers have come closer to the ideal. Those experiences need to be accumulated and contrasted with the experiences of the other models. One dimension of New Careers is very important: it evaluates performance in real life situations which standardized evaluation techniques simply cannot do. The New Career experience raises questions about the validity of standardized measures. In real life situations New Careerists performed much better than they did in the confines of the classroom on very similar challenges (Carter, 1977).

A Democratic Schooling strategy requires the same dedication that is found in the Effective School. It would, however, be no more difficult to institutionalize. Unless a strong political force can be mobilized, both models will meet a great deal of resistance. The Effective School can count on more help from the business community than will be available to Democratic Schooling, but whether business support is an important ingredient in a campaign to reduce Chicano school failure is yet another unknown.

In one vital capacity the true test of Democratic Schooling has not been made. Democratic Schooling is brought into existence by democratic means. For that to happen a political constituency for Democratic Schooling must be mobilized. At present, a democratic-initiated education is a largely unexamined alternative to authoritarian education. The constituency organized to implement Democratic Schooling also would have to promote companion policies that would change among other things the priorities of a society, the configuration of work, and the admission standards to the university.

Increasing university admissions present a peculiar political problem for Chicano success. That problem underscores the rethinking required for a political revival on which Chicano school success rests. At the present time, university growth places Chicano aspiration in opposition to those who oppose such growth because of difficulties brought to local communities, thus rupturing what had been a 'progressive' coalition. A New Career strategy would be uniquely helpful here because it would allow far more people to be admitted to the university without overburdening existing physical plants. Bringing a university education to the place where people work increases the likelihood for enlarging the education in support of equality in education. Presently that coalition is weak and not gathering strength.

While much less is known about Democratic Schooling than the other models, the inherent problems with the others recommend that more study be given to a democratic alternative. One aspect of Democratic Schooling deserves emphasis: it, far more than either of the two other models, rejects cumulative deficit as the cause of Chicano school failure. Because this position posits inequality in institutions, its actions can be introduced at any time and for any age student. The argument advanced is that if the institutional impediments to success are removed, Chicanos — or any other victim of unfair treatment — will be able to keep up with those who have not been unjustly treated. That orientation not only led to the invention of New Careers and Upward Bound at the University of Oregon, it also was instrumental in the success of those programs.

In conclusion, when the problem of Chicano school failure is cast in the broadest social context, we are left with much that is not yet known. Some recent attempts at an Effective School provide powerful evidence that Chicano students can master college preparation academic subjects, if given a reasonable opportunity to learn. What is not as yet known is whether: (a) the material they are taught is important or even useful, (b) the existing political economy has the capacity to absorb a rapid increase in college educated persons, or, if that is not the case, (c) there is the political will and know-how to create a work world that is consistent with a learned society. There is a great need to broaden the range of experiments and directly connect these experiments to public policy.

The relationship between the educational research findings and school policy is in itself a research question that needs to be explored much more completely and intensively than it has been. The relationship is confounded by two distinctly different research problems. One deals with the nature of educational research and its lack of connection to policy considerations. The other is research into the political factors that surround policy decisions. Educational research, by and large, is remotely if at all connected to educational policy. The research suffers from a number of serious deficiencies, among the most glaring being: (1) a lack of synchronization between what is most important in schools and what is most important for researchers — the schools and the researcher are often not on the same page; the concern of the academic researcher is very largely determined by what referee journals accept for publication, while schools are most concerned with meeting very specific educational goals; (2) even when generally aligned on a particular issue, differences in understanding of the nuances of the issues and differences in basic loyalties between school personnel and researchers generate difficulties in design and interpretation of findings; (3) academic research is too limited in scope — a necessary condition of 'good' research is either statistical or experimental control over variables, but the school is an extraordinary complex place and control represents distortion of reality and that in turn makes translation of the research findings into policy exceedingly difficult; (4) most educational research is organized into rather short time frames, the results obtained are often transient, and when implemented as school practice fade away, thus contributing to the suspicion that practitioners have of researchers; (5) research findings are often ungeneralizable as policy — results may be obtained under impossible to duplicate conditions, e.g., the teachers and administrators used in research may be far superior to staff that would have to translate the results into regulariz-ed practice, or the excitement and fanfare generated by research cannot be maintained once incorporated into the ordinary day to day work schedule.

What makes the relationship between research and educational policy even more difficult is the political acceptability of research findings. As Galileo learned in 1633, findings obtained from careful research can get the researcher in trouble if the findings conflict with the belief structure of established authority. Edu-cation, being a political entity responds to political pressures; research findings that are not supported politically will not be considered. Rarely is the offending researcher tried, as Galileo was, by an inquisitional body; more often the findings are ignored until the time they become politically acceptable, that is, until a large enough political constituency has been mobilized to force a reconsideration. The New Career program illustrates the relationship between research and social policy quite vividly. In every possible way the research supported New Careers. Not only was it demonstrated that New Careers met its intended goals, but it was further shown that the gains from the project could be sustained for long periods of time. It was also shown that the New Career approach could be carried out successfully in many places with a wide range of populations, how-ever, that success had little long term impact on educational policy.

> *Nothing Fails Like Success.* Success is meaningless if the game has been changed. It makes no difference how good a Mahjong player you are if no one plays Mahjong anymore, and that is what happened to New Careers and other paraprofessional programs. (Pearl, 1981, p. 38)

When researching the political implications of research findings on educa-tional policy, two very different problems arise. One involves the sustaining interest in a society that is increasingly titillated by new fads; such a society is without memory and without vision. It knows neither where it has been, nor where it is going, and woe unto anyone who raises questions about either the past or the future. The research impact on educational policy under such condi-tions is not likely to be significant or long lasting. Perhaps of even greater importance is the ability of the society to tolerate the implications of the research findings. Research findings that if utilized would increase educational attainment in a society that cannot integrate more educational success into its economic structure is not going very far. A society that aspires to policy based on know-ledge must build knowledge into its decision-making systems. Of the three approaches discussed in this chapter — the Compensatory, the Effective School and the Democratic Schooling approaches — only the last makes that a conscious part of its program. Similarly, a society gets an education it is willing to pay for, and research findings that in effect call for policies more expensive than a society wishes to spend are not going to get implemented. In that sense it should be quite clear that from a political-economic perspective, changes in education in California and elsewhere are likely to depend much more on the ability to develop a large enough constituency to overturn the constitutional restrictions on taxation than it will on any specific educational practice based on research findings. The relationship between calls for educational change and an effective political constituency is perhaps the single most important unknown. Connecting education and political action is a characteristic that only a Democratic Schooling for Democratic Social Change model has.

Chicano school failure and Chicano school success are inextricably linked to larger complexly interrelated social issues — the shape of the political economy, the condition of the environment, the lingering and at times festering conditions of race and ethnic hatred and sexual domination, the ever-changing face of international relations, the use and misuse of technology — and unless these issues are an integral part of the education Chicanos and all others receive, educational progress for Chicanos will be slow, uneven, and most likely illusory.

References

ADLER, M. (1982) *The Paideia Proposal*, New York, Macmillan.

AMRAM, F., FLAX, S., HAMERMESH, M. and MARTY, G. (1988) *New Careers: The Dream That Worked*, Minneapolis, MN, University of Minnesota.

APPLE, M. (1979) *Ideology and Curriculum*, London, UK, Routledge and Kegan Paul.

BERNSTEIN, B. (1970) 'A sociolinguistic approach to socialization with some reference to educability', in F. WILLIAMS (Ed.) *Language and Poverty* Chicago, Markham Press, pp. 25–61.

BLOOM, A. (1987) *The Closing of the American Mind*, New York, Simon and Schuster.

BOWLES, S. and GINTIS, H. (1976) *Schooling in Capitalist America*, New York, Basic Books.

CALIFORNIA STATE DEPARTMENT OF EDUCATION (1980) data reported in D. STERN, J. CATTERALL, C. ALHADEFF and M. ASH, *Reducing the High School Dropout Rate in California: Why We Should and How We May*, Berkeley, CA, California Policy Seminar, University of California.

CARTER, W.T. (1977) 'The Career Opportunities Program: A summing up', in A. GARTNER, F. RIESSMAN, V. CARTER-JACKSON (Eds) *Paraprofessionals Today*, New York, Human Services Press, pp. 183–221.

CENTER ON BUDGET AND POLICY PRIORITIES (1985) *Hispanic Poverty in the United States*, Washington, DC, Author.

COOPER, H.M. and GOOD, T.L. (1983) *Pygmalion Grows Up: Studies in the Expectation Communication Process*, New York, Longman.

COUNTS, G.S. (1932) *Dare the School Build a New Social Order?* New York, John Day Co.

CUSICK, P.A. (1983) *The Egalitarian Ideal and the American High School*, New York, Longman.

DEUTSCH, M. (1967) *The Disadvantaged Child*, New York, Basic Books.

DEWEY, J. (1900) 'The school and society', in *The Child and the Curriculum and the School and Society*, Chicago, University of Chicago Press (1956).

ECONOMIC REPORT OF THE PRESIDENT (1988) Washington, DC, US Government Printing Office.

EDMONDS, R. (1979) 'Effective schools for the urban poor', *Educational Leadership*, **37**, pp. 57–62.

EDMONDS, R. (1984) 'School effects and teacher effects', *Social Policy*, **15**, pp. 37–40.

ELASHOFF, J. and SNOW, R.E. (Eds) (1971) *Pygmalion Revisited*, Worthington, OH, C.A. Jones.

ENGELMANN, S. (1970) 'How to construct effective language programs for the poverty child', in F. WILLIAMS (Ed.) *Language and Poverty*, Chicago, IL, Markham Press.

ENGLE, S.H. and OCHOA, A.S. (1988) *Education for Democratic Citizenship*, New York, Teachers College Press.

EPSTEIN, N. (1977) *Language, Ethnicity and the Schools: Policy Alternatives for Bilingual-Bicultural Education*, Washington, DC, Institute for Educational Leadership.

FITZGERALD, F. (1979) *America Revised*, Boston, MA, Atlantic-Little, Brown.

FREIRE, P. (1968) *Pedagogy of the Oppressed*, New York, Seabury Press.

FREIRE, P. (1985) *The Politics of Education: Culture, Power and Liberation*, South Hadley, MA, Bergin and Garvey.

GARCIA, E.E. (1988) 'Attributes of effective schools for language minority students', *Education and Urban Society*, **20**, pp. 387–98.

GIROUX, H. (1981) *Ideology, Culture and the Process of Schooling*, Philadelphia, PA, Temple University Press.

GOOD, T.L. and BROPHY, J.E. (1986) *Educational Psychology: A realistic Approach*, New York, Holt, Rinehart and Winston.

GOODLAD, J.L. (1984) *A Place Called School*, New York, McGraw-Hill.

GRANT, C.A. and SLEETER, C.E. (1985) 'Equality, equity and excellence: A critique', in P.G. ALTBACH, G.P. KELLY and L. WEIS (Eds) *Excellence in Education: Perspectives on Policy and Practice*, Buffalo, NY, Prometheus Books, pp. 139–59.

GUTEK, G.L. (1983) *Education and Schooling in America*, Englewood Cliffs, NJ, Prentice-Hall.

GUTHRIE, J.W., KIRST, M.W., HAYWARD, G.C., ODDEN, A.R., ADAMS, J.E. JR., CAGAMPANG, H.H., EMMETT, T.S., EVANS, J.W., GERRANIOS, J., KOPPICH, J.E. and MERCHANT, B.M. (1988) *Conditions of Education in California 1988*, Berkeley, CA, Policy Analysis for California Education.

GUTMANN, A. (1987) *Democratic Education*, Princeton, NJ, Princeton University Press.

HALBERSTAM, D. (1972) *The Best and the Brightest*, New York, Random House.

HAYCOCK, K. and NAVARRO, S.M. (1988) *Unfinished Business: Fulfilling Our Children's Promise*, Oakland, CA, The Achievement Council.

HENRY, J. (1968) 'Education for stupidity', *Reason and Change in Elementary Education*, 2nd National Conference, US Office of Education, Tri-University Poject in Elementary Education, pp. 117–34.

HESSONG, R.F. and WEEKS, T.H. (1987) *Introduction to Education*, New York, Macmillan.

HIRSCH, E.D. JR. (1988) *Cultural Literacy: What Every American Needs to Know*, New York, Vintage Books.

HODGKINSON, H.L. (1986) *California: The State and Its Educational System*, Washington, DC, The Institute for Educational Leadership.

HODGKINSON, H.L. (1989) 'Institute for Educational Leadership', Presentation to Danforth Foundation Seminar, Washington, DC.

HUNT, J. McV. (1961) *Intelligence and Experience*, New York, Ronald Press.

JACKSON, P.W. (1986) *Life in Classrooms*, New York, Holt, Rinehart and Winston.

JENSEN, A.R. (1969) 'How much can we boost IQ and scholastic achievement?' *Harvard Educational Review*, **37**, pp. 1–123.

JOHANNINGMEIER, E.V. (1985) *Americans and Their Schools*, Prospect Heights, IL, Waveland Press, Inc.

JOHNSON, J.A., COLLINS, H.W., DUPUIS, V.L. and JOHANSEN, J.H. (1988) *Introduction to the Foundations of American Education*, 7th ed., Boston, MA, Allyn and Bacon.

LAMPMAN, R., THEOBALD, R., PEARL, A., ALINSKY, S. (1966) *Poverty: Four Views, Four Solutions*, Eugene, OR, University of Oregon.

LEVINE, D.U. and HAVIGHURST, R.J. (1989) *Society and Education*, 7th ed., Boston, MA, Allyn and Bacon.

MANN, H. (1848) 'Twelfth annual report to the Massachusetts Board of Education', in L.A. CREMIN (Ed.) *The Republic and the School: Horace Mann and the Education of Free Men*, New York, Teacher's College Press.

MOORE, J. and PACHON, H. (1985) *Hispanics in the United States*, Englewood Cliffs; NJ, Prentice-Hall.

MUNOZ, C. (1989) *Youth, Identity, Power: The Chicano Movement*, New York, Verso.

NATIONAL CENTER FOR EDUCATIONAL STATISTICS (1983) *High School Dropouts: Descriptive Information from High School and Beyond*, Washington, DC, US Department of Education.

NATIONAL COMMISSION ON EXCELLENCE IN EDUCATION (1983) *A Nation at Risk: The Imperative for Educational Reform*, Washington, DC, Government Printing Office.

OAKES, J. (1985) *Keeping Track: How Schools Structure Inequality*, New Haven, CT, Yale University Press.

ORNSTEIN, A.C. and LEVINE, D.U. (1984) *An Introduction to the Foundations of Education*, 3rd ed., Boston, MA, Houghton Mifflin Co.

PEARL, A. (1972) *The Atrocity of Education*, New York, Dutton.

PEARL, A. (1981) 'The paraprofessional in human service', in S.S. ROBIN and M.O. WAGENFELD (Eds) *Paraprofessionals in the Human Services*, New York, Human Services Press, pp. 23–53.

PEARL, A. (1988) 'The requirements of a democratic education', in R. SLEE (Ed.) *Discipline and Schools*, Melbourne, Australia, Macmillian of Australia, pp. 225–43.

PEARL, A. and RIESSMAN, F. (1965) *New Careers for the Poor*, New York, Macmillan.

PINK, W. (1988) 'School climate and effective school programmes in American education', in R. SLEE (Ed.) *Discipline and Schools*, Melbourne, Australia, Macmillian of Australia, pp. 199–224.

PROVENZO, E.F. JR. (1986) *An Introduction to Education in American Society*, Columbus, OH, Charles E. Merrill.

RESEARCH AND EVALUATION BRANCH (1986) *Early School Leavers: High School Students Who Left School Before Graduating, 1983–84* (Publication No. 459), Los Angeles, CA, Los Angeles School District.

ROSENTHAL, R. and JACOBSON, L. (1968) *Pygmalion in the Classroom: Teacher Expectation and Pupils' Intellectual Development*, New York, Holt, Rinehart and Winston.

SCHUNKE, G.M. (1988) *Elementary Social Studies: Knowing, Doing, Caring*, New York, Macmillan.

SELAKOVICH, D. (1984) *Schooling in America*, New York, Longman.

SIROTNIK, K.A. (1983) 'What you see is what you get', *Harvard Educational Review*, **53**, 16–31.

SMITH, T.E C. (1987) *Introduction to Education*, St. Paul, MN, West Publishing Co.

SPRING, J. (1985) 'Political and economic analysis', in P.G. ALTBACH, G.P. KELLY and L. WEIS (Eds) *Excellence in Education: Perspectives on Policy and Practice*, Buffalo, NY, Prometheus Books, pp. 75–89.

STATE DEPARTMENT OF CALIFORNIA (1988) *History-Social Science Curriculum Framework*, Sacramento, CA, State Department of Education.

UNIVERSITY OF CALIFORNIA, SANTA CRUZ (1986) data from Educational Opportunity Program.

US BUREAU OF THE CENSUS (1980) *Supplementary Report: Persons of Spanish Origin by State*, PC80-S-7, Washington, DC, US Government Printing Office.

US DEPARTMENT OF EDUCATION, CENTER FOR EDUCATION STATISTICS (1985) *In Dealing with Dropouts: The Urban Superintendent's Call to Action*, Washington, DC, Author.

US LABOR DEPARTMENT, BUREAU OF STATISTICS (1988) *Employment and Wages, Annual Wages 1987*, Washington, DC, Author.

US *Statistical Abstract* (1987) US Department of Commerce, Bureau of the Census, Washington, DC, US Government Printing Office.

VALENCIA, R.R. and ABURTO, S. (in press) 'Competency testing and Latino student access to the teaching profession: An overview of issues', in J. DENEEN, G.D. KELLER and R. MAGALLÁN (Eds) *Assessment and Access: Hispanics in Higher Education*, Albany, NY, State University of New York Press.

VELEZ, W. (1989) 'High school attrition among Hispanic and non-Hispanic white youths', *Sociology of Education*, **62**, 119–33.

WALKER, J.H., KOZMA, E.J. and GREEN, R.P. JR. (1989) *American Education: Foundations and Policy*, St. Paul, MN, West Publishing Co.

WELSH, P. (1986) *Tales out of School*, New York, Viking Penguin.

WYNN, R. and WYNN, J.L. (1988) *American Education*, 9th ed., New York, Harper and Row.

Chapter 11

Conclusions: Towards Chicano School Success

Richard R. Valencia

In this concluding chapter, I will offer some final thoughts on the promotion of school success for Chicano students. Particular focus will be on a synthesis of ideas presented by the various contributors of this volume. Based on our discussion thus far, the task here is to address how might Chicano school success be realized. We tackle this inquiry by zeroing in on the following specific areas: (a) keeping Chicanos in school, (b) the social context of schooling, (c) bilingual education, (d) Chicano parental involvement in schooling, (e) the assessment context of schooling, and (f) 'Democratic Schooling'.

Keeping Chicanos in School

Clearly, one of the major challenges of improving schooling for Chicano students is to keep them in school. As Rumberger (chapter 3) has underscored, the dropout problem among Chicanos is so acute that the social and economic welfare of the general Chicano population is not likely to improve until its educational status improves. In part, the 'quality of life' for the next generation of Chicanos hinges on solving the scandalous dropout rate. Although there are effective programs that are combatting the dropout issue among Chicanos (see Rumberger; see also Trueba, chapter 6), a growing number of educational reformers are calling for deep-rooted systemic reform — necessitating changes in the fundamental nature of broad economic, political, cultural, and school curricular contexts (see Pearl, chapter 10). In short, the Chicano dropout issue is not just an educational problem. Those Chicano students who drop out of secondary schooling compared to their Chicano peers who remain in school, tend to be of lower socioeconomic status, are of immigrant background, and are more likely to be proficient in Spanish than English. Thus, one can readily identify a host of correlates of dropping out. As such, there needs to be a broad-based dropout reform agenda encompassing principles of Democratic Schooling, counseling, desegregation/integration, economic restructuring of schools and society, and so much more.

The Social Context of Schooling

Chapter 2 by Donato, Menchaca and Valencia provides an overview of the problems associated with Chicano students attending segregated schools. There is no doubt that segregation of the 1920s has cast a rigid mold for future generations of Chicanos. Furthermore, as Donato *et al.* emphasize, the current segregation of Chicanos is proliferating. Sadly so, it is predicted that Chicano students of the 1990s and those of the early twenty-first century will attend schools of even greater segregation than their contemporary peers. In the most pessimistic sense, the deleterious consequences of attending ethnically isolated schools — particularly the adverse outcomes of low achievement and high dropout rates — are likely to intensify.

The move towards Chicano school success must have school desegregation and integration as part of its agenda. The current era in which ethnically different students attend separate schools has to end. In a nation that often boasts of its culturally diverse population, it is shameful for children and youth of such diverse backgrounds not to share the same schools and classrooms in an equitable fashion. As our society becomes more and more ethnically diverse in the decades ahead, we have a grand opportunity to see that students from different cultural backgrounds attend the same schools in an integrated manner. It is essential that the social context of school reform for Chicanos embraces desegregation and integration (see Donato *et al.* for further discussion on how desegregation/integration might be promoted).

Bilingual Education

In light of the linguistic variation among Chicano students, it is not surprising that the schooling of Chicano language minority students is a dominant theme of this book. Discussions by Garcia (chapter 4), Merino (chapter 5), and Donato *et al.* (chapter 2) speak to the educational needs of Chicanos as second language learners. Coverage of pertinent research and issues by these authors points to several major conclusions. First, Chicano language minority students are quite capable of dual language learning, and there is increasing evidence that bilingualism leads to cognitive advantages. Second, the attainment of school success for Chicano students in bilingual classrooms can be empirically demonstrated. Third, the vast percentage of limited-English proficient (LEP) Chicano students who are in need of bilingual education are not receiving it. Fourth, for those Chicano LEP students who do receive bilingual education, there is an increasing trend for them to have such schooling in linguistically segregated settings.

In spite of the mounting evidence that bilingual education helps to promote Chicano school success, there is a growing anti-bilingual intolerance making its cowardly way through the nation. Proponents of bilingual education, especially policymakers, must assert their continued advocacy for such programs on behalf of Chicano second language learners, because there is no doubt that the future need for bilingual education will increase. As Pallas, Natriello and McDill (1988) predict, the national number of LEP children (of which will be mostly of Mexican origin) will triple from 2 million in 1982 to 6 million in the year 2020 (also see Donato *et al.*, chapter 2). In sum, given what we know about the values of bilingual education — especially how it can help promote enhanced schooling outcomes for Chicano students — it makes so much sense to include bilingual education as a major element in the goal of Chicano school success. As Merino (chapter 5) reminds us, the available research shows that bilingual education helps to promote school success among Chicano students. The point is that researchers, practitioners, and policymakers need to combine forces and work together *now* to make these successes occur on a much larger scale for Chicano second language learners.

Chicano Parental Involvement

At the broadest level, 'the evidence is clear. When parents are involved in their youth's schooling, children do better in school ...' (Marburger, 1990, p. 82). Given the connection between parental involvement and children's improved academic performance, it is vital that schools act assertively getting Chicano parents involved in their children's schooling (see Marburger for a clarification of the roles parents can play).

But, the question is sometimes asked, do Chicano parents truly value education? Indeed, they do. The brief legal history of Chicano-initiated desegregation court cases covered by Donato *et al.* (chapter 2) and special education litigation described by Valencia and Aburto (chapter 8) informs us that Chicano parents care deeply about their children's schooling, especially in the struggle for equal educational opportunities. As well, Laosa and Henderson (chapter 7) provide empirical vidence that many Chicano parents play important roles in fostering their children's academic motivation and in providing enriching home intellectual environments.

Although there is considerable evidence that Chicano parents get involved in many ways in their children's education, negative stereotypes persist about the lack of such involvement. In a recent major incident, a misconception about Chicano parental involvement came from the mouth of our nation's top-ranked education official. In early 1990 in San Antonio, Texas, US Education Secretary Lauro Cavazos commented to the effect that education was once highly valued by Latino parents, yet '... somewhere along the line we lost that' (Editorial, 1990). It is clear that Secretary Cavazos has little knowledge and comprehension of the many problems Chicano parents face in attaining equitable schooling for their offspring. To blame the Chicano parent is to blame the victim. Cavazos should look for solutions — not scapegoats. *Increasing* the existing degree of Chicano parental involvement should be a vital part of current school reform because the role of Chicano parents is a key in realizing their children's school success.

The Assessment Context of Schooling

A major reality of the schooling experience is that all students must undergo academic assessment for various purposes. Valencia and Aburto (chapter 8) provide ample discussion that many Chicano students suffer from serious problems in the assessment context of schooling, particularly stemming from the abuses of intelligence and competency tests. As Valencia and Aburto comment, the two primary issues of test abuse involve (a) the administration of psychometrically questionable instruments, and (b) the 'high-stakes' nature of some forms of testing (i.e., the heavy reliance of single test scores in some instances of educational decision-making). When these two explosive abusive practices combine, a test can have potent consequences in helping to shape school failure among Chicanos.

The problems associated with the assessment of Chicano students (especially testing) are so severe that some scholars are discussing the need for paradigmatic shifts (e.g., Mercer, 1989; Rueda, chapter 9; Valencia and Aburto, chapter 8). There are increasing calls for sociocultural norming, curricular-based testing (i.e., all testing should be tightly and functionally linked to instruction), use of multiple data sources, and so forth. Suffice it to say that the promotion of Chicano school success will necessitate many challenges to the status quo of current assessment and testing practices. Abusive practices can be remedied or eliminated in the years ahead if appropriate attention is paid to the integration of sound science and ethics.

Democratic Schooling

Since the beginning of public education in our nation, there has never been agreement that schools promote school success for all students. Hence, there has been an ongoing debate of what constitutes workable school reform. Pearl's analysis (chapter 10) points rather clearly to those strategies that have not shown to be successful. On the other hand, his ideas about 'Democratic Schooling' offer us a vision of what it will take to achieve Chicano school success. I believe that his notions of students' rights, equal encouragement, useful knowledge, and so forth, can serve as beacons for structuring and implementing school success for Chicanos. As Pearl notes, the bottom line of workable school reform is to connect education with political action. In the years ahead, failure to pay attention to the linkages of schooling with a number of social issues, macro policies, and the features of Democratic Schooling will very likely result in the continuation of Chicano schooling problems.

Before concluding this final chapter, I wish to return to a point I discussed in the introductory chapter — that is, the subject of the 'changing demography'. One of the most remarkable projections we previously discussed was that in the next thirty years, Chicanos and other Latinos will account for *nearly all* of the growth in the national youth population. With respect to long-range projections, in sixty to seventy years from now the United States will witness a very significant demographic shift. It is predicted that in the middle of the twenty-first century, the Chicano and other Latino populations (both the general and school-age segments) will surpass Blacks in numerical status to become the nation's single largest ethnic minority group. In light of the steady and predictable growth of Chicano students, attention to their many schooling problems must be addressed in a timely fashion. Without workable school reform beginning now the individual and social costs of Chicanos dropping out of high school will only rise as time goes by. Not investing in appropriate classroom instruction now for Chicano second language learners will exacerbate their schooling problems. Not dismantling the system of segregated schools now will only aggravate the problems Chicanos face attending ethnically/racially isolated schools. Without reform in testing now, the problems of test abuse *vis-à-vis* Chicano students will escalate, and so on. Suffice it to say that current Chicano students and their families cannot — and should not — wait for our nation's next generation to get on with the business of making school success a realization. The message is simple; either our society pays now or pays an enormous amount in the future.

In the final analysis, although the plight of Chicano students continues to exist there must be optimism as we travel the road to Chicano school success. It is important to continue with a 'language of critique', but also to make room for a 'language of possibility'. *¡ Sí se puede!* It is also critical to embrace the Chicano community in order to share its views on how to attain school success for Chicano youth. Community participation in school reform, if designed right, can be an emancipating democratic activity. Then there is the curriculum. It is important to develop a perspective that curricular practices for Chicanos — in both products and processes — should incorporate aspects of equity, shared ownership, and empowerment. We also need to keep in mind that Chicano school success is intricately tied to macrolevel realities and thus any ultimate reform needs to be viewed in the context of counter-hegemonic potential. And finally, there is Chicano youth. We should adopt a view that the educability of Chicano students is without limits. We also need to value and guide Chicano youth, as well as learn from them. Most importantly, Chicano youth and adults need to discuss together their visions and plans of a better world.

References

EDITORIAL (1990) 'Cavazos hardly being a friend to Latino community', *Austin American-Statesman*, April 17, p. A8.

MARBURGER, C.L. (1990) 'The school site level: Involving parents in reform', in S.B. BACHARACH (Ed.) *Education Reform: Making Sense of it All*, Boston, MA, Allyn and Bacon, pp. 82–91.

MERCER, J.R. (1989) 'Alternative paradigms for assessment in a pluralistic society', in J.A. BANKS and C.A. McGEE-BANKS (Eds) *Multicultural Education: Issues and Perspectives* Boston, MA: Allyn and Bacon, pp. 289–304.

PALLAS, A.M., NATRIELLO, G. and McDILL, E.L. (1988) 'Who Falls Behind: Defining The 'At Risk' Population — Current Dimensions and Future Trends', paper presented at the meeting of the American Educational Research Association, New Orleans, LA, April.

Notes on Contributors

SOFIA ABURTO is Education Specialist, Art, Research and Curriculum Associates, Inc. Her research and writing interests are in applying measurement theory to the development of teaching examinations. She is particularly interested in addressing equity issues that arise when assessing bilingual/bicultural or other non-mainstream examinees. Ms Aburto is the co-author, with Richard Valencia, of two book chapters dealing with Latinos and teacher competency testing.

RUBEN DONATO is Assistant Professor of Educational Curriculum and Instruction, Texas A & M University. His scholarly interests are in the areas of history of American education and issues related to educational equity. He has recently published articles in the *Harvard Educational Review* and *Equity and Excellence Quarterly*.

EUGENE E. GARCIA is Dean of the Social Sciences Division, University of Californiia, SSSanta Cruz. He has publishesed extensivvvely in the areas of language teaching and bilingual development. Dr Garcia's most recent publications include articles in the *Handbook of Research on Teacher Education* (1990), *The Journal of Early Childhood Development* (1990), and the edited research volume, *Children at Risk* (1990), for the National Association of School Psychologists.

RONALD W. HENDERSON is Professor of Education and Psychology and Provost of Crown College, University of California, Santa Cruz. His research includes the study of intellectual socialization in minority communities (Mexican American and Native American), the application of cognitive theory to the development and validation of technology-based instructional materials in mathematics, and the investigation of academic motivation and its effects on self-regulated learning in school settings. Professor Henderson is the co-author, with J.R. Bergan, of *The Cultural Context of Childhood* and *Child Development* (both from C.E. Merrill), the editor of *Parent-Child Relationships: Theory, Research and Prospects* (Academic Press) and has produced numerous research articles.

LUIS M. LAOSA is Principal Research Scientist with the Educational Testing Service, Princeton, New Jersey. Dr Laosa is best known for his research on the factors associated with children's cognitive development and academic performance and for his writings on social policy and cultural and ethnic diversity. He has served as member of the Committee on Child Development Research and Public Policy of the National Academy of Sciences and also as chairman of the Committee on Child Development and Social Policy of the Society for Research in Child Development.

MARTHA MENCHACA is Assistant Professor of Anthropology at the University of Texas, Austin. Her research explores issues of race and ethnicity in the United States, with a specific focus on the reconstruction of local minority group histories. Dr Menchaca has recently published on topics dealing with the ideological base of Chicano school segregation, Chicano-Mexican group conflict in response to acculturation pressures, and the use of legal records and oral sources to reconstruct the history of US minority groups.

BARBARA JEAN MERINO is Associate Professor, Division of Education and Committee on Linguistics, University of California, Davis. Her principal research interests are language acquisition in bilingual children, language assessment and classroom discourse. Dr Merino's most recent publications include: 'classroom talk in English immersion, early-exit and late-exit transitional bilingual education programs' (co-authored with D. Ramirez) and 'Interaction at the computer by language minority boys and girls paired with fluent English proficient peers' (*Computers in the Schools*).

ARTHUR PEARL is Professor of Education and Acting Provost of College Eight, University of California, Santa Cruz. He has published widely in the areas of the political economy of education and school reform. Dr Pearl's most recent publications include 'Theoretical trends in youth research' in *International Social Science Journal* (1985) and 'Characteristics of a democratic school' in *Disruptive Behavior and Effective Schooling* (1988), edited by R. Slee.

ROBERT RUEDA is Associate Professor in the School of Education, University of Southern California, Los Angeles. He has published numerous articles and chapters on issues related to the education of language minority students, especially those impacted by the special education system. A major focus of his research has been on processes of learning and cognition, especially as they impact instruction and assessment. Dr Rueda's most recent work has been primarily concerned with the social and cognitive processes related to students' acquisition of literacy.

RUSSELL W. RUMBERGER is Associate Professor of Education in the Graduate School of Education, University of California, Santa Barbara. His research specializations include the economics of education and education policy. Recent research has focused on school dropouts, the educational requirements of work and the economic returns to college major and college quality. Among Dr Rumberger's publications is *The Future Impact of Technology on Work and Education*, co-edited with Gerald Burke (1987) Falmer Press

HENRY T. TRUEBA is Associate Dean of Letters and Science and Director of the Division of Education, University of California, Davis. He has published extensively on the topic of language minority children, particularly in the context of meshing anthropology and education. Dr Trueba's recent publications include *Cultural Conflict and Adaptation: The Case of Hmong Children in American Society* written with Lila Jacobs and Elizabeth Kirton (1990) and *Crossing Cultural Borders: Education for Immigrant Families in America* written with Concha Delgado–Gaitan (1991) both from Falmer Press.

RICHARD R. VALENCIA is Associate Professor of Educational Psychology and Speech Communication at the University of Texas at Austin. His research and scholarly interests include the intellectual and academic development of racial/ethnic minority children, test validity/bias, social and psychological foundations of minority schooling, and teacher competency testing. He has published widely in his research areas, particularly on testing issues and Chicanos. From 1987 to 1990 he served as Associate Editor for the *Journal of Educational Psychology*. In 1983, Dr Valencia was awarded a National Research Council/Ford Foundation Postdoctoral Fellowship for Minorities.

Author Index

Politzer, R., 134
  (1980), 121, 122, 125
Polyzoi, E., Holtzman, W.H. and Ortiz,
  A.A. (1987), 258
Poplin, M. (1988a), 264
  (1988b), 263, 265
Population Reference Bureau (1985), 17
Prior, D.R. (1974), 182
Provenzo, E.F. (1986), 302
Purkey, S.C. and Smith, M.S. (1983), 109

Rafferty, J.R. (1988), 242n6
Ramirez, A. (1985), 98
  and Stromquist, N. (1978), 135, 136
  (1979), 121, 122, 125, 126, 132, 133,
    134, 136, 140
Ramirez, D.
  and Del Refugio Robledo, M. (1987), 85
  and Merino, B. (1986), 122
    (in press), 131
Ramirez, J.D.
  and Merino, B. (in press) 124, 125, 126,
    128, 129, 138
  et al (1984), 121
  et al (1986), 122, 124, 125, 126, 127
Ramist, L. and Arbeiter, S. (1986), 173,
  187, 188
Rangel, S.C. and Alcala, C.M. (1972), 35,
  37
Rankin, R.J., Gaite, A.J.H. and Heiry, T.
  (1979), 172
Regional Policy Committee on Minorities
  in Higher Education (1987), 165
Reschly, D.J. (1978), 212
  (1979), 212, 214, 220, 221
  (1980), 209
  and Reschly, J.E. (1979), 213
  and Sabers, D. (1979), 213, 243n14
Resnick, D.P. (1979), 204, 205, 206
  (1981), 205
Resnick, L.B. (1979), 242n4&5
Reynolds, A. (1933), 4
Reynolds, C.R. (1982), 212, 213, 216
  (1983), 212
  and Brown, R.T. (1984), 212
  and Gutkin, T.B. (1980), 213
Reynolds, M.C., Wang, M.C. and
  Walberg, H.J. (1987), 263
Richards, J. (1987), 153
  and Rogers, T.S. (1986), 100
Rist, R.C. (1970), 47, 260
  (1979), 39
  (1982), 260
Roos, P.D. (1978), 42–3

Rosenthal, R. and Jacobson, L. (1968), 293
Rossell, C.H.
  and Hawley, W.D. (1983), 54
  and Ross, J.M. (1986), 106
Rueda, R., 14, 201, 204, 252–70, 324
  (1989), 259, 261
  (in press), 259
  Ruiz, N. and Figueroa, R. (1989), 265
  et al (1984), 257
Rumberger, R.W., 9, 64–89, 273, 277, 321
  (1983), 70, 72, 73, 74, 76, 252
  (1987), 77, 78, 82
  (1990), 77, 79, 80, 83, 85
  (in press), 64
  et al (1990), 74
  et al (in press), 73
Rutter, M. (1979), 178

Sagar, H.A. and Schofield, J.W. (1984), 55,
  56
Salvia, J. and Ysseldyke, J.E. (1988), 204,
  218, 138, 241n3
Sameroff, A.J. (1983), 167
Sanchez, G.I. (1966), 4
Sandoval, J. (1979), 212, 213
San Miguel, D. (1987), 39
San Miguel, G. (1986), 7, 36
  (1987), 7, 36, 38
Santrock, J.W. and Warshak, R.A. (1979),
  178
  and Elliott, G.L. (1982), 178
Sapiens, A. (1982), 124
Sato, C. (1982), 131
Sawyer, R.L. (1985), 187
  (1987), 173, 187, 188
Sayers, D. (1986a,b) (1988), 264
Scheunemann, J.D. (1984), 237
Schinke-Llano, L. (1983), 122, 128
Schneider, S.G. (1976), 111
Schulz, J. (1975), 121, 123, 124
Schumann, J.H. (1976), 104
Scot-Jones, D. (1984), 176
Schwartz, R. and Hargroves, J. (1986–7),
  84
Selakovich, D. (1984), 302
Seliger, H.W. (1977), 105
Serow, R.C. (1984), 224, 225, 226, 228
Sewell, T.E., Palmo, A.J. and Manni, J.L.
  (1981), 252
Shantz, C. (1977), 98
Shepard, L. and Smith, M.L. (1981), 260
Shepard, L.A. (1982), 219–20
  and Kreitzer, A.E. (1987), 222
Shulman, L. (1987), 129, 142

Subject Index